ADDITIONAL ADVANCE PRAISE FOR *SPY SITES OF WASHINGTON, DC*

"This delightfully informative book is a *Who's Who* of spy vs. spy skullduggery in the world's most powerful city. Spy experts Robert Wallace and H. Keith Melton take us on a mesmerizing tour of traitors and tradecraft revealing the wheres and whys of Washington's second-oldest profession. It's a must read for both curious and serious researchers."

—**PETE EARLEY,** author of *Family of Spies: Inside the John Walker Spy Ring* and *Confessions of a Spy: The Real Story of Aldrich Ames*

"*Spy Sites of Washington, DC* is admirably detailed and thoroughly enjoyable. If you loved their book *Spycraft* on the intricate world of espionage tradecraft, you will find *Spy Sites* an essential guide to the intelligence landmarks in and around Washington."

—**David E. Hoffman,** author of *The Billion Dollar Spy: A True Story of Cold War Espionage and Betrayal*

"The authors' incredibly well-researched *Spy Sites* explores every nook and cranny of the nation's capital where a vast number of American spies and their foreign collaborators lived, worked, and secretly betrayed the country's secrets for over two centuries. This is not just a guidebook of those landmarks but a must-read, comprehensive history of espionage in America."

—**Michael J. Sulick,** retired director of the CIA's National Clandestine Service and author of *Spying in America: Espionage from the Revolutionary War to the Dawn of the Cold War*

SPY SITES

OF WASHINGTON, DC

SPY SITES

OF WASHINGTON, DC

A GUIDE TO THE CAPITAL REGION'S SECRET HISTORY

ROBERT WALLACE AND H. KEITH MELTON

WITH HENRY R. SCHLESINGER

FOREWORD BY
PETER EARNEST

GEORGETOWN UNIVERSITY PRESS
WASHINGTON, DC

All statements of fact, opinion, or analysis expressed are those of the authors and do not reflect the official positions or views of the CIA or any other U.S. Government agency. Nothing in the contents should be construed as asserting or implying U.S. Government authentication of information or Agency endorsement of the authors' views. This material has been reviewed by the CIA to prevent the disclosure of classified information.

Library of Congress Cataloging-in-Publication Data

Names: Wallace, Robert, author | Melton, H. Keith (Harold Keith), author. Schlesinger, Henry R., author.
Title: Spy Sites of Washington, DC : A Guide to the Capital Region's Secret History / Robert Wallace and H. Keith Melton ; with Henry R. Schlesinger ; foreword by Peter Earnest.
Description: Washington, DC : Georgetown University Press, 2017. | Includes index.
Identifiers: LCCN 2016010529 | ISBN 9781626163768 (pb : alk. paper)
Subjects: LCSH: Espionage—Washington (D.C.)—Guidebooks. | Espionage—Maryland—Guidebooks. | Espionage—Virginia—Guidebooks. | Spies—Washington (D.C.) | Spies—Maryland. | Spies—Virginia.
Classification: LCC UB271.U5 W35 2017 | DDC 327.1209753—dc23
LC record available at https://lccn.loc.gov/2016010529

∞ This book is printed on acid-free paper meeting the requirements of the American National Standard for Permanence in Paper for Printed Library Materials.

18 17 16 9 8 7 6 5 4 3 2 First printing

Printed in the United States of America

Project manager, Glenn Saltzman, Georgetown University Press.
Cover designer, Tim Green, Faceout Studio.
Text designer, Paul Nielsen, Faceout Studio.
Cartographer, Chris Robinson.
Cover images courtesy of Getty Images (Moody sky over silhouette of trees by Cris Figueroa/EyeEm) and Stocksy (Looking through blinds by Tatjana Ristanic).

CONTENTS

FOREWORD

Do you remember the snow globe? Turn it upside down, and thick "snow" blanketed the inside. Now think of a globe with a scene of Washington, DC, with a tiny White House, US Capitol, and Washington Monument. Turn it upside down. See the swirling snow. Each tiny "flake" could easily stand for one of the hundreds of spies, men and women, who have walked the streets of our capital since the city was founded in 1790.

At the International Spy Museum, we say, "Today there are more spies in Washington than in any other city in the world." Why have spies been drawn to this city for over two hundred years? Because Washington is the capital of the United States, the city where the president and our other national leaders make decisions. Making decisions to form policy depends on having the latest and best information, what today we call "intelligence."

Leaders throughout history demand timely, accurate information to know everything possible about hostile countries or other threats they face. In the United States, this material is classified with distribution limited to the president, his close advisers, and other authorized users, whether it is derived from overhead satellites, electronic eavesdropping, or our own spies in foreign lands.

As the center of our national leadership, the Washington metropolitan area is where America's intelligence agencies are headquartered and where intelligence flows in seven days a week. That's why foreign countries and hostile groups such as terrorist organizations send their spies here—to steal our secrets and influence American policy.

Wars and the lead-up to wars always bring spies to the capital. In the years after the American Revolution, there was the British burning of the city in 1814, the Civil War (with spies from the North and the South), two world wars, the Korean War, the Vietnam War, and today's continuing military involvements in the Middle East, Africa, and South Asia. There was also the most intelligence-driven and spy-ridden conflict of all, the Cold War. Each conflict brought new generations of spies to the city who used the latest espionage tradecraft and devices.

The spies in our midst may be Americans or others recruited or dispatched by foreign agents. Think of Benedict Arnold, who volunteered to spy for the British, as well as Central Intelligence Agency (CIA) officer Aldrich Ames and Federal Bureau of Investigation (FBI) special agent Robert Hanssen, who both offered to spy for the Soviet Union. Even Cuba and China successfully recruited a number of Americans to spy for them in Washington.

In *Spy Sites of Washington, DC*, you will learn the names of many of these spies, where they lived and worked, who they spied for, and about the secrets they stole. You'll discover where the spy agencies are located, the places spies are known to frequent, and many of the sites used for secret caches or "dead drops" for passing intelligence, cash, jewelry, and even gold. Now you'll have the street addresses and sometimes even a high-resolution photo to pursue your interest. With *Spy Sites* in hand, you might even stumble upon a secret agent meeting or uncover a hidden cache of gold.

Peter Earnest
Executive Director
International Spy Museum
Washington, DC

PREFACE

Spies are successful when their espionage is never suspected. Not surprisingly then, spies usually spy where they normally work, play, and live. Effective spies blend into their environment using the camouflage of normality to avoid suspicion. In researching locations in the Washington area with ties to intelligence operations, we found spy sites in homes, hotels, restaurants, parks, monuments, brothels, bars, and governmental offices. We found them at street corners, under bridges, and on telephone poles. Some of these historic sites remain; others have been demolished in redevelopment. Addresses change over centuries, and buildings are rebranded or repurposed. Private homes where spies once lived are sold to new owners who may be unaware their residence occupies a place in America's clandestine history. As you visit any nonpublic place we describe, please respect the property rights and personal privacy of present-day owners.

We recognize that no book about spy sites can be complete, as many operations remain unknown except to the few who participated or those authorized to read their secret files. Some major spies—John Walker, Aldrich Ames, Robert Hanssen, and Ana Montes—used dozens of operational sites for their espionage. Therefore, numbers themselves present a limiting factor for any book that has the good fortune to draw upon such a richness of material. Not every interesting site for every case can be included. For this volume, we chose 220 spy stories, selected more than 350 images, and provided over 400 site location addresses depicting intelligence and clandestine operations from our master index of 1,000 locations in the Washington metropolitan area. Today, with perhaps more spies operating in Washington than at any time in recent history, the need for clandestine signal sites, meeting sites, and dead-drop locations continues to grow.

This guidebook covers sites throughout Washington *and* suburban Virginia and Maryland. There are even a few entries that are slightly farther afield. Each entry pairs a primary site that the reader can visit along with the spy story. When only a street address is given, this means that the location is in the District of Columbia. Sites in Maryland and Virginia include the town/city and state as well as the street address. The entries proceed chronologically and cover many of the most important, astounding, and either glorious or notorious episodes in the nation's intelligence history. Most entries also list secondary sites for those readers with a desire to visit even more places where spies lived or operated. Appendix A offers a different way for readers to approach the book, by listing sites by neighborhood, city, or county. Also in appendix A, maps with pinpointed numbers that correspond to entries in the text allow the reader to create his or her own spy tour itinerary.

Accounts of hundreds of other secret operations in Washington remain undiscovered and untold. If you know of a story and a site not included in this book, we would love to have you send us information about ones we missed. Thank you for your interest in our work.

ACKNOWLEDGMENTS

Four years ago we published *Spy Sites of New York City*, followed by a complementary work, *Spy Sites of Philadelphia*. Our research into America's espionage history of those two cities inevitably pointed us south—to Washington, DC, whose importance as an espionage target increased as the United States grew. Our interest in capturing Washington's spy history was shared by Don Jacobs, senior acquisitions editor at Georgetown University Press, and we have benefited greatly from his involvement and professional guidance in preparing the manuscript. Glenn Lisa Saltzman and the Georgetown University production team skillfully guided the book's final design. We thank Burton Gerber for recommending Don to us for this project. Daniel Mandel, of Sanford J. Greenburger Associates, skillfully managed contract and business elements of the publication. We were inspired by and indebted to Pamela Kessler for her groundbreaking book on Washington area spy locations, *Undercover Washington: Touring the Sites where Famous Spies Lived, Worked, and Loved*. First published in 1992, it remains a fascinating read 25 years later.

Due to the sheer number of intelligence organizations, spy cases, and operational sites that originate in Washington, we recognized the need for assistance from historians and photographers, government as well as private. Hayden Peake read early drafts of the manuscript and offered knowledgeable commentary on historical cases. Darryl Garrett and Mark Bellemah provided valuable historical perspectives on the National Geospatial-Intelligence Agency and the Foreign Broadcast Information Service, respectively. Bill Kline, Alan Kohler, John Fox, Keith Clark, Paul Cook, David Robarge, and Jerry Richards each contributed significant insights into specific operations. We thank freelance copy editor Don McKeon for his meticulous work and helpful suggestions on style and substance.

Except when otherwise credited, the images in the book are courtesy of the Melton Archives. We are indebted to Mr. T and Ms. S for their detective work in locating and photographing many obscure but historically important sites. Mark Reges at the Old Angler's Inn in Potomac, Maryland, and Billy Martin Jr. at Martin's Tavern in Georgetown graciously offered images and anecdotes from their businesses. One-of-a kind photos were provided by Edward J. Wolfrum, PhD, of Audio Graphics Services and by Scott Gower and Dachun Bao at the National Defense University library. Melissa Walker-Schlesinger and Mary Margaret Wallace read many drafts and properly insisted that government acronyms be explained, spy jargon exiled, and wordiness eliminated.

We extend our personal appreciation and thanks to each.

INTRODUCTION

Washington, DC, stands apart from the world's great capital cities. It rose neither out of a center of commerce nor a seat of monarchy, and, as envisioned by the Founding Fathers, America's capital is not part of any state in the union. Created by legislation known as the Residence Act of 1790 (officially titled An Act for Establishing the Temporary and Permanent Seat of the Government of the United States), the location itself was a compromise between seemingly implacable political adversaries, Alexander Hamilton and Thomas Jefferson. In exchange for adopting Hamilton's plan for the federal government to pay the states' war debts, Jefferson saw his wish fulfilled that the nation's capital be located in the South.

"I proposed to him [Hamilton] however to dine with me the next day, and I would invite another friend or two, bring them into conference together," Jefferson later wrote, "and I thought it impossible that reasonable men, consulting together coolly, could fail, by some mutual sacrifices of opinion, to form a compromise which was to save the union."

In this sense, locating Washington on the Potomac resolved one of America's first political budget battles.

The three commissioners appointed to oversee the creation of the capital, Thomas Johnson and Daniel Carroll of Maryland and David Stuart of Virginia, proposed that the city be named Washington. The name honored Gen. George Washington, who selected the specific site fifteen miles north of his Mount Vernon estate and, as president, signed the enabling legislation.

History best remembers Washington as a brilliant commanding officer and savvy politician. Less known is his skill in managing intelligence operations. Washington's meticulous planning and execution of covert operations were as inspired as his military tactics and played a crucial role in America's eventual victory. As intelligence commander, he recruited agents, ran double agents, spread disinformation, conducted counterintelligence operations, and adopted available technology for covert communications, such as new formulations of invisible ink. Spying in the late 18th century encompassed, as it does today, a wide range of clandestine actions undertaken by a government to advance its interests and often to the detriment of an adversary.

Washington would marvel at the modern city that bears his name. The Capitol—sitting atop what he knew as Jenkins Hill—was not yet completed when the first president died in 1799. The great dome of the building, now a universally recognizable landmark, was not expanded to its current size until more than half a century later.

Today Washington would marvel at a nation that, when only "four score and seven" years old, sacrificed the lives of hundreds of thousands of its young men in a civil war that could have destroyed the states he left united.

Washington would marvel at the transportation and manufacturing industries enabling worldwide wars and capable of delivering destructive powers that reduce cities to rubble in minutes.

Washington would marvel at satellites and sensors that spy from afar on the military capabilities and movements of would-be adversaries.

Washington would marvel at the international cyber battlefield and the army of digital warriors with expertise and weapons that the nation requires for its security.

However, what the father of our country would still find familiar is the silent, continuing work of spies in times of peace as well as war. After all, before he was president, Washington was the fledgling nation's spymaster-in-chief.

ABBREVIATIONS

AFSA	Armed Forces Security Agency
AIPAC	American Israel Public Affairs Committee
AMTORG	Amerikanskoe Torgovlye (Soviet trade representation)
ANC	African National Congress
APL	American Protective League
BOI	US Bureau of Investigation
BSC	British Security Coordination
CAT	Civil Air Transport
CIA	Central Intelligence Agency
CM	Communications Machine
CNC	Counternarcotics Center
COG	Continuity of Government
COI	Coordinator of Information
COMINT	communications intelligence
CPUSA	Communist Party USA
DARPA	Defense Advanced Projects Research Agency
DCI	Director of Central Intelligence
DIA	Defense Intelligence Agency
DINA	Dirección de Inteligencia Nacional (Chilean intelligence agency)
DNC	Democratic National Committee

DNI	Director of National Intelligence
DOD	Department of Defense
ELINT	electronic intelligence
FBI	Federal Bureau of Investigation
FBIS	Foreign Broadcast Information Service
FBMS	Foreign Broadcast Monitoring Service
FCC	Federal Communications Commission
FEMA	Federal Emergency Management Agency
FISA	Foreign Intelligence Surveillance Act
FISINT	foreign instrumentation signals intelligence
GEOINT	geospatial intelligence
GRU	Glavnoye Razvedyvatel'noye Upravleniye (Soviet, and later, Russian Millitary Intelligence Service)
G-2	military intelligence staff (US Army)
HUAC	House Un-American Activities Committee
HVA	Hauptverwaltung Aufklärung (East German external intelligence service)
IC	US Intelligence Community
INR	Bureau of Intelligence and Research
INS	Immigration and Naturalization Service
JIB	jack-in-the-box evasion device
KGB	Komitet Gosudarstvennoy Bezopasnosti (Soviet intelligence and counterintelligence service)
MASINT	measurement and signature intelligence
MfS	Ministerium für Staatssicherheit (East German intelligence and counterintelligence service, aka the Stasi)
MID	Military Information Division
MI-8	Military Intelligence Division, Section No. 8
MIS-X	Military Intelligence Service-X
MIS-Y	Military Intelligence Service-Y
NASA	National Aeronautics and Space Administration
NATO	North Atlantic Treaty Organization
NGA	National Geospatial-Intelligence Agency
NIMA	National Imagery and Mapping Agency
NIS	Naval Investigative Service
NISC	Naval Intelligence Support Center

NKVD	Narodnyy Komissariat Vnutrennikh Del (Soviet intelligence and counterintelligence service, 1930's–1940's)
NPIC	National Photographic Interpretation Center
NRO	National Reconnaissance Office
NSA	National Security Agency
ONI	Office of Naval Intelligence
OPC	Office of Policy Coordination
OSC	Open Source Center
OSO	Office of Special Operations
OSRD	Office of Scientific Research and Development
OSS	Office of Strategic Services
PFIAB	President's Foreign Intelligence Advisory Board
POW	prisoner of war
PRC	People's Republic of China
RAF	Royal Air Force
RID	Radio Intelligence Division
SAS	Special Air Service
SD	Sicherheitsdienst des Reichsführers-SS (Nazi party intelligence agency)
SDECE	Service de Documentation Extérieure et de Contre-Espionnage (French external intelligence service)
SIGINT	signals intelligence
SI	Secret Intelligence
SIS	Secret Intelligence Service or Signal Intelligence Service
SOE	Special Operations, Executive
SS	Schutzstaffel (armed wing of Nazi Party)
SSG	Special Surveillance Group
StB	Státní Bezpečnost (Czechoslovakian intelligence and counterintelligence service)
SVR	Sluzhba Vneshney Razvedki (Russian external intelligence service)
TASS	Telegrafnoye Agentstvo Sovyetskogo Soyuza (Soviet news agency)
UN	United Nations
U-1	Bureau of Secret Intelligence (US Department of State)
USSR	Union of Soviet Socialist Republics
WFO	Washington Metropolitan Field Office of FBI

1

A NEW CAPITAL FOR ESPIONAGE

(1790–1860)

Well-known stories about the courage of Nathan Hale and duplicity of Benedict Arnold only hint at the role espionage played in America's Revolutionary War. Founding Fathers such as George Washington, Alexander Hamilton, John Jay, and Benjamin Franklin all involved themselves with clandestine operations to advance the cause of independence. These 18th century American patriots employed secret agents, couriers, spy rings, and propagandists to advance their cause. Code names, aliases, secret writing, disguises, and ciphers were just as essential to 19th century tradecraft as they are to contemporary intelligence operations.

Intelligence from American spies traveling by foot, carriage, horse, and sailing ship informed General Washington's combat strategy. As an intelligence commander and military leader, Washington funded and directed intelligence networks that reached from the taverns and inns of colonial cities into the royal courts and palaces of European capitals. Although Washington's spies had none of the "advanced technology" such as photography, telegraphy, or steamships that would appear in the 19th century, their clandestine efforts were critical to the birth of the United States and led to the foundation of a new capital city.

Mount Vernon, George Washington's estate on the banks of the Potomac River, is also the grave site of America's first spymaster.

■ 1. SPYMASTER GEORGE WASHINGTON

MAP 8 ➤ Mount Vernon: 3200 Mount Vernon Memorial Highway, Mount Vernon, Virginia

George Washington is remembered as the father of our country—America's great commanding general during the Revolutionary War and the nation's first president. Henry "Light Horse Harry" Lee, father of Confederate general Robert E. Lee, in his December 1799 eulogy remembered Washington as "first in war, first in peace, and first in the hearts of his countrymen."

Washington was also America's first spymaster, overseeing operations extending from colonial battlefields to European capitals. He had learned the consequences of faulty intelligence early in his career. Serving as a young officer under British general Edward Braddock during the French and Indian War, Washington experienced the disastrous 1755 battle near Fort Duquesne (on the site of what is now Pittsburgh) and is reported to have carried the mortally wounded general off the battlefield. The battle's outcome, according to some historians, was largely decided by lack of reliable intelligence.

"Everything, in a manner, depends upon obtaining intelligence," Washington wrote in a letter to Massachusetts major general William Heath at the start of the Revolutionary War. Indeed, for Americans fighting the British, intelligence would come to play a major role in their eventual victory.

Washington placed a high value on intelligence gathered by trusted individuals as well as networks of citizen spies and scouts. Just weeks after assuming command of the Continental Army in 1775, he authorized the first major payment for intelligence, $333.33 (more than $100,000 in today's dollars), to a still unidentified source in Boston to establish a spy network. From Trenton, New Jersey, on December 3, 1776, at a low point in the war and with funds growing perilously short, he wrote to Revolutionary War financier Robert Morris, requesting funds to "pay a certain set of people who are of particular use to us." Morris hurriedly scraped together what he could, sending Washington two bags filled with Spanish dollars, English crowns and shillings, and a French half crown.

No detail seemed too small to escape Washington's attention when it came to espionage. Writing to an operative in the invaluable Culper Spy Ring in New York City, he described the proper use of invisible ink, called "sympathetic stain." Instructing the agent to write information on the blank leaves of a pamphlet, he then cautioned that attention must be paid to the quality of the paper to ensure legibility.

Washington also planted disinformation as a means to gain advantage. In one instance, after learning of a British spy in his ranks, he arranged for the traitor to see documents that greatly inflated his troop strength, causing the British to underestimate their military advantage over a weakened revolutionary army. When the loss of Philadelphia to the British seemed inevitable, Washington established stay-behind spy networks in anticipation of his strategic pullback to Valley Forge. The spies would remain in Philadelphia under a "mask of friendship" with other citizens who supported the British.

Today, fifteen miles south of Washington, DC, the spymaster's Mount Vernon home and grave site are open to the public. The 50-acre estate along the Potomac River features more than a dozen original structures.

FORT WASHINGTON

In 1794, President Washington urged that a fort to protect the capital be built at Digges Point, a small section on the Potomac where the river briefly narrows. Construction did not begin until 1805 and was not completed until 1809. Initially called Fort Warburton, the name of the Digges estate, it was later changed to Fort Washington (now Fort Washington National Park, 13551 Fort Washington Road, Fort Washington, Maryland). Its own garrison destroyed the fort in 1814 to prevent it from falling into British hands during the War of 1812. The fort was later rebuilt, modernized several times, and remained in active service until 1939.

2. THE HANDSOME AMERICAN

MAP 13 ➤ **Warburton Estate:** Fort Washington Park, 13551 Fort Washington Road, Fort Washington, Maryland

Thomas Attwood Digges remains problematic for historians. Was he a rogue and scoundrel or Revolutionary War hero? History has yielded no conclusive answers. Digges, born a son of privilege in 1742, grew up on the family estate, Warburton Manor. Located on the banks of the Potomac River in Maryland, the stately home stood nearly directly across the river from George Washington's Mount Vernon estate. Its grounds included what is today Fort Washington National Park.

Located within the Fort Washington National Park, Warburton Manor was the home of Thomas Attwood Digges, who spied in Europe at the behest of Benjamin Franklin.

Arriving in England around 1774, Digges became known as the "handsome American" and quickly set about making a splash in London's lively social scene. Covertly he was given several sensitive missions by Benjamin Franklin. Operating under a series of cover names, including Pierre J. DuVall and Pierre J. Bertrand, Digges began a clandestine campaign of assisting American ships' imprisoned crews, while also acting as a courier between Franklin and British officials. He also provided a safe house for prisoners who escaped the dreaded Mill and Forton Prisons and then smuggled them out of the country.

Digges, careful not to keep incriminating papers, also did a poor job of tracking expenses. His financial records were either lost or destroyed. Money became an issue with the scrupulous Franklin. Digges's inability or unwillingness to provide a full accounting of funds prompted Franklin to turn against him with withering censure, in writing to London merchant William Hodgson on April 1, 1781:

> He who robs the Rich even of a single Guinea is a Villain; but what is he who can break his sacred Trust by robbing a poor Man and a Prisoner of eighteen Pence given charitably for his Relief, and repeat that Crime as often as there are Weeks in a Winter, and multiply it by robbing as many poor Men every Week as make up the Number of near 600? We have no name in our Language for such atrocious Wickedness. If such a Fellow is not damn'd it is not worth while to keep a Devil.

Digges would never live down the attack, and a full explanation was never offered. When he was later imprisoned in Ireland under mysterious circumstances, some say he had been trying to ship equipment and skilled laborers to America, though his incarceration seemed to bolster Franklin's claims that Digges had cheated many.

However, by Digges's own dubious accounting, he aided more than a hundred American men stranded in England, some of them hunted as fugitives by British authorities. At one point he was forced to leave London one step ahead of arrest and live undercover.

Digges remained in Europe for years following the Revolution before returning to his family home and renewing the tradition of being rowed across the Potomac to dine at Mount Vernon. He also kept up friendly relations with Thomas Jefferson and James Madison, yet, if remembered at all, it was less as a spy and more as a swindler and a target of Franklin's wrath.

ARCHITECT AND MONEY

Pierre Charles L'Enfant, the primary city planner of Washington, clashed with the commission assigned to oversee his work. L'Enfant claimed he answered only to Washington but was mistaken. Dismissed first by the commissioners and then later from a job rebuilding Fort Washington following its destruction in the War of 1812, L'Enfant fell into dire financial circumstances. Thomas Digges came to his rescue, offering the famed architect and Revolutionary War hero a place to stay at Warburton Manor.

3. DOLLEY MADISON AND GEORGE WASHINGTON'S PORTRAIT

MAP 2 ➤ **White House:** 1600 Pennsylvania Avenue NW

While every schoolchild knows the story of First Lady Dolley Madison saving the White House portrait of George Washington from marauding British troops, her role as lookout has gone largely ignored. With President Madison in the field attempting to rally his forces, she went to the White House roof with a spyglass to survey the distant battles and received situation reports from the field by courier. She maintained her observation post even after the 100-man contingent assigned to guard the White House scattered, with British troops only a few miles away.

The White House after being burned by the British during the War of 1812.

Eventually Dolley gathered every official document she could find into a waiting carriage along with red silk velvet draperies from the Oval Room, a silver service, and the blue and gold Lowestoft china purchased for the state dining room.

After the wagon was dispatched to the Bank of Maryland in Baltimore, the first lady was about to leave when she remembered Gilbert Stuart's portrait of Washington known as the Lansdowne portrait. Unable to unscrew it from the wall, she ordered it broken from its ornate gilt frame, then handed it off to Jacob Barker, a wealthy ship owner, and Robert G. L. De Peyster from New York to guard. Grabbing a copy of the US Constitution from its display case, she hurriedly stuffed it into a suitcase and made her escape. The British troops would arrive not long after to ransack and burn the White House.

Saving the unwieldy eight-by-five portrait was a daunting task for the two New Yorkers. After leaving the White House, they deposited the painting with a farmer on the banks of Tiber Creek (sometimes called Goose Creek), which ran from Florida Avenue NE to the Potomac. The humble farmer's barn became a safe house for Washington's portrait during the remainder of the war.

4. DANIEL WEBSTER'S CLANDESTINE OPERATION

MAP 2 ➤ **Daniel Webster residence:** H Street and Connecticut Avenue NW (now site of the US Chamber of Commerce Building, 1615 H Street NW)

Daniel Webster, distinguished US senator for Massachusetts, statesman, lawyer, and orator, may also have orchestrated a 19th century covert influence operation. While serving as President John Tyler's secretary of state in the early 1840s, Webster helped resolve a simmering border dispute with Britain that had inflamed the passions of the citizens of Maine. Activists seemed on the brink of creating an international conflict with Britain over a modest patch of land on the border of Maine and the British colony of New Brunswick. The militia was called out for what became known as the Aroostook War or, more colorfully, the Pork and Beans War. No shots were fired, but tensions continued rising.

Daniel Webster

Webster sought to defuse the conflict without seeming to appease the British. Using money from the State Department's contingency fund intended for diplomatic foreign espionage, he paid former Maine congressman O.J. Smith to launch a covert campaign to sway public opinion in the Pine Tree State in favor of a compromise. Smith planted stories in local papers, spoke to politicians across the state, and lobbied vigorously. More money, some $14,500, would eventually come from a representative of the British Crown, Alexander Baring, 1st Baron Ashburton, sent to the United States to negotiate a settlement.

One of the operatives employed by Webster and Smith, Jared Sparks, a respected Harvard College professor of history, presented maps of questionable origin that made the case for the British. For the governor of Maine and other local politicians, Sparks's argument was clear: If the British should ever find out about the maps, then they might demand even more land. Better to compromise while the maps were still secret.

The dispute ended with the Webster-Ashburton Treaty of 1842. However, with details of the operation coming to light in 1846, Webster's efforts caused a scandal. The chairman of the House Foreign Affairs Committee sought to impeach Webster retroactively, accusing him of using secret funds to corrupt

The Painting's Secret Code

Gilbert Stuart made several copies of the painting depicting Washington refusing a third term as president. To differentiate the copies from the original, Stuart hid clues within the paintings. In the White House version, one of the books in the lower left-hand corner has the intentional misspelling of United States as "United Sates" on its binding.

The Webster Law Building was located at 6th Street and Louisiana Avenue, NW. While serving as secretary of state, Webster launched a covert-influence campaign that averted a war over the US-Canadian border.

When opened in the 1800s, St. Elizabeths Hospital was a model for humane treatment of the mentally ill. Today its campus is the home of the Department of Homeland Security.

the press in Maine. Webster was eventually cleared of all charges, and Sparks became president of Harvard College in 1849.

A statue of Daniel Webster stands at the intersection of ***Massachusetts and Rhode Island Avenues NW*** in Washington. The historic Ashburton House, site of the treaty negotiations, is located near ***Lafayette Park at 1525 H Street NW***.

■ 5. LANDMARK FOR HOMELAND SECURITY

MAP 6 ➤ **St. Elizabeths Hospital:** East Campus, 1100 Alabama Avenue SE; West Campus, 2700 Martin Luther King Jr. Avenue SE

Today the west campus of the St. Elizabeths Hospital complex, at ***2700 Martin Luther King Jr. Avenue SE***, is the headquarters of the US Department of Homeland Security. However, few are aware of the facility's colorful history.

Dorothea Dix, the superintendent of US Army nurses during the Civil War and longtime advocate for the indigent and mentally ill, first conceived of a humane treatment center and successfully lobbied Congress to create the facility in the 1850s. The multibuilding complex, now encompassing more than 350 acres, began as the Government Hospital for the Insane before given a less culturally offensive name, St. Elizabeths Hospital, in 1916. Its expansion eventually included an east and west campus.

Over the years the hospital was home to a number of well-known residents. Ezra Pound, the poet, was committed to the facility following World War II under a plea bargain arising from prosecution for the pro-fascist broadcasts he made during the war. John Hinckley, President Ronald Reagan's would-be assassin, and silent film star Mary Fuller were among those confined to the facility.

During World War II, the facility served as a laboratory for the Office of Strategic Services (OSS), which was in search of a truth drug. Marijuana was among the drugs tested. The Central Intelligence Agency (CIA) also used St. Elizabeths for research and experiments on mind-altering drugs in the 1950s. Existence of the CIA program, known as MKULTRA, was revealed by the 1975 Rockefeller Commission Report, officially titled *Report to the President by the Commission on CIA Activities within the United States*. Although the CIA had closed down MKULTRA more than a decade earlier, revelations of experiments with LSD and other substances on human subjects were sensational and remain controversial. Awareness of the program fueled elaborate conspiracy theories about classified government programs and provided plots for novels, including Stephen King's 1980 best seller, *Firestarter*.

CIVIL WAR SPIES

(1861–1865)

The American Civil War presented both sides with the motivation and operational environment for espionage. Spies and spy hunters shared common language, family ties, and a porous 2,000-mile border between the two belligerents. All of this created seemingly unlimited opportunities and challenges. Neither side had an official intelligence organization at the start of the war, though both quickly assembled ad hoc cadres of spies and spymasters.

Adding to the traditional tradecraft George Washington practiced during the Revolutionary War, 19th century advances in technology in the forms of telegraphic communication and, to a lesser extent, photography and aerial surveillance began emerging as intelligence tools.

In the North, Allan Pinkerton and Lafayette C. Baker were the best-known heads of intelligence efforts. The South also claimed its share of notable citizen and military spies, such as the Washington hostess Rose O'Neal Greenhow and the scout Benjamin Franklin Stringfellow.

The Union's counterintelligence problem with Confederate spies was particularly acute in Washington, although many men favoring the South's cause left the city to join the Confederate army. Of those sympathizers who chose to remain, some worked clandestinely while others were defiantly open about their opinions and made willing spies. Included were prominent personalities in Washington society as well as obscure government employees.

Nobody seemed above suspicion. Even President Abraham Lincoln's wife, Southerner Mary Todd Lincoln, became the target of gossips. They viciously labeled her "Lady Davis" in a damning reference to Confederate president Jefferson Davis and accused her of communicating secrets to the rebels. These claims arose from her family's deep roots in the South and the fact that her brother, along with three of her stepbrothers, served in the Confederate military.

When the war ended, the celebrity spy emerged. Memoirs published by those who engaged in intelligence operations, such as Isabella Maria "Belle" Boyd, Lafayette C. Baker, Allan Pinkerton, and Benjamin Franklin Stringfellow, found a public eager to learn of their wartime exploits. With loose adherence to facts, the authors often portrayed themselves as daring, resourceful, and courageous in a manner that foreshadowed the heroics of the fictional James Bond nearly a century later.

Allan Pinkerton's arrest of Confederate spy Rose O'Neal Greenhow was a counterintelligence success.

6. THE PINKERTON WAY

MAP 2 ➤ **Pinkerton office:** 288 I Street NW (structure no longer stands)

Best known for his namesake detective agency, Allan Pinkerton headed the Union's secret service during the first year of the Civil War. Although harshly criticized by some historians for his strike-breaking activities in later years on the part of industrial "robber barons," the Scottish-born detective was also a staunch abolitionist and early participant in the Underground Railroad. As a strong supporter of the Union, he provided security for President-elect Lincoln on part of the journey to Washington for inauguration in 1861. In the first year of the Civil War, Union general George B. McClellan employed Pinkerton to provide battlefield intelligence, in part because McClellan, who previously worked for the railroads, knew Pinkerton personally.

Pinkerton organized his intelligence-gathering efforts from an office on I Street NW. He assigned himself the alias Maj. E. J. Allen but remained a civilian.

According to his own account, Pinkerton made a reconnaissance tour through several Southern states, but whatever intelligence he collected from those clandestine surveys has been lost.

Despite his enthusiasm for the task, Pinkerton's lack of experience in military intelligence soon became apparent. During the 1862 Peninsula (sometimes referred to as the Peninsular) Campaign, Pinkerton inflated figures of Confederate troop strength. The exaggerated estimates, combined with the Confederate deception of "Quaker guns"—logs disguised to look like artillery—may have caused McClellan to delay his attack despite possessing superior forces.

7. PRESIDENT LINCOLN'S PRIVATE SPY

MAP 2 ➤ **White House: 1600 Pennsylvania Avenue NW**

Security at the 19th century White House during the Civil War was remarkably lax. Lincoln observed an "open door" policy for visitors.

In the summer of 1861, President Lincoln hired William A. Lloyd as his personal spy. When the publisher of railroad and steamship guides asked the new president for a passport to travel to the Confederate States for business, Lincoln recognized an opportunity. He approved the passport and recruited Lloyd to spy with the promise of expenses plus $200 a month. Lincoln wanted reporting on the location of Confederate troops and military infrastructure but stipulated that Lloyd report directly to him and nobody else.

Lloyd, accompanied by an employee, dutifully sent reports to his brother in Washington for hand delivery to the White House. According to historians, the president did not share the intelligence with even his closest advisers. Rather, he used Lloyd's reports to check the accuracy of intelligence from his field generals.

Virtually nothing is known about the content or value of Lloyd's reports, but he served the president throughout the war. Detained and incarcerated on four different occasions, Lloyd was forced at one point to destroy his written contract with Lincoln. This would lead to the 1875 Supreme Court case *Totten v. United States*, when Lloyd's estate unsuccessfully sued the government for the uncollected $200-a-month stipend. The claim was ruled unenforceable, as courts cannot hear cases involving espionage contracts because public disclosure of the details may harm national security.

The original F Street NW site of the Signal Corps headquarters is now part of the Georgetown University Law Center.

An ideal location for the Signal Corps to send messages to Union camps around the capital was from a cupola on the roof of the city's tallest building, the Winder Building.

8. SIGNALING WASHINGTON: CAN YOU SEE ME NOW?

MAP 1 ➤ **Signal Corps headquarters:** 158 F Street NW (now part of the Georgetown University Law Center campus)

Army doctor Albert J. Myer understood communications. He put himself through medical school working as a telegrapher in that nascent industry. By the late 1850s, while assigned to a regiment in the Southwest, he developed a system for coded signaling that used flags (torches replacing flags at night). Nicknamed Wig-wag, Myer's single-flag, line-of-sight system was not new in concept but innovative in its simplicity.

When appointed chief signal officer of the Signal Corps in 1860, Myer created an organization filled with enormous potential but not fully integrated into the army until 1863. He set up shop at ***158 F Street NW***. A training site named the Signal Camp of Instruction for the Signal Corps was established in 1861 in Georgetown on Red Hill or Pole Hill, today known as Mount Alto or Glover Park.

However, by 1863 Myer had

Still a Signals Site

General Myer chose the Mount Alto section of Georgetown for his Signal Corps training camp with care. At 350 feet above sea level, it is one of the highest points in Washington and provided the capability for long-range line-of-sight communications. More than a century later, the Soviet Union selected the nearly identical site for its new embassy. The KGB recognized that the elevated Mount Alto location was ideal for intercepting transmissions from the region's microwave towers.

Field-Testing Signals

A marker commemorates the spot where signaling turned the tide in the First Battle of Bull Run. The Confederates successfully used the Wig-wag flag system to warn of a Union Army flanking maneuver.

The initial battlefield test of Myer's wigwag signaling during the First Battle of Bull Run (also called First Manassas) was an unqualified success—for the Confederates. While Union officials were cautious about implementing the new system, Confederate commanders immediately saw its value. Implementation was not a problem. Southern officers already knew all they needed about Wig-wag signaling because Confederate captain Edward Porter Alexander had worked with Myer on early tests of the system. Lt. Col. Robert E. Lee had been a member of the 1859 board that approved testing and evaluation of the system, while Confederate president Davis had chaired the US Senate Military Affairs Committee prior to the war. The Manassas National Battle Park is located at ***6511 Sudley Road, Manassas, Virginia***.

crossed bureaucratic swords with Secretary of War Edwin M. Stanton in a dispute over control of telegraphy. Relinquishing his command of the Signal Corps, Myer continued to work in communications, developing a cipher disc and formalizing methods for interrogation. Following the war, he was reinstated as head of the Signal Corps and moved the operation across the Potomac to Fort Whipple (later known as Fort Myer and today called Joint Base Myer–Henderson Hall). Leaving the corps, he launched the Division of Telegrams and Reports for the Benefit of Commerce in 1869, forerunner of the National Weather Service.

■ 9. REBEL SPY NETWORK IN WASHINGTON

MAP 2 ➤ **War Department:** Winder Building, 600 17th Street NW

Confederate spy networks were operating in Washington months before the first shots of the Civil War were fired. Among those spies was John "Honest John" Letcher, a former member of Congress and governor of Virginia, as well as Capt. Thomas Jordan, an assistant quartermaster stationed at the War Department's Winder Building at ***600 17th Street NW***.

Jordan, a Virginia native, a graduate of West Point (where his roommate

Constructed in 1848, the Winder Building was Washington's first structure with central heating. Housing government offices and portions of the War Department, it became a target for Confederate spies.

was William Tecumseh Sherman), and a veteran of the Seminole Indian and Mexican Wars, may have started a spy network as early as 1860. His best-known recruit, Rose O'Neal Greenhow, was taught the basics of espionage, including a simple cipher.

Jordan later crossed lines to become a Confederate colonel and head of intelligence, operating under the alias Thomas J. Rayford for Gen. Pierre Gustave Toutant-Beauregard (also known as P. G. T. Beauregard). Although little is known of his Confederate intelligence work, it must have been effective: Jordan had been promoted to the rank of general by the end of the war. Afterward, he eventually settled in New York City.

■ 10. WASHINGTON ROYALTY AND CONFEDERATE SPY

MAP 2 ➤ **Rose O'Neal Greenhow residence:** Civil War address of 398 16th Street NW is today in the area of the St. Regis Hotel courtyard, 16th and K Streets NW

Confederate spy Rose O'Neal Greenhow was accompanied by her daughter, "Little Rose," to prison. The prison grounds included a former boarding house once run by Greenhow's aunt.

The widow Rose O'Neal Greenhow was a fixture in Washington society when the Civil War began. She was likely recruited in the spring of 1861 by Thomas Jordan. During her time as a Confederate operative, she aided a ring of spies in the nation's capital that included bankers, Union soldiers, government workers, and prominent society women. These informants entrusted their intelligence tidbits to Greenhow to relay to couriers heading south. Through this network, she passed information to the Confederacy that proved valuable for their victory at the First Battle of Bull Run.

Greenhow did not hide her advocacy for the Confederacy. A friend of former president James Buchanan, she also dined at the White House with President Lincoln. Her niece, the granddaughter of Dolley Madison, was married to Stephen A. Douglas, Lincoln's Democratic Party opponent. She lived in grand style, hosting congressmen, diplomats, and other notables in her parlor. Once she fell under suspicion for spying, Greenhow became the target of surveillance by Allan Pinkerton. According to legend, Pinkerton removed his boots and stood on the shoulders of two subordinates to peek into the windows of the Greenhow home at what was then numbered 398 16th Street NW (the house no longer exists), in order to gather evidence against her.

Greenhow's arrest included much drama. Apprehended outside her home, she was able to signal nearby agents to warn them away while her nine-year-old daughter, "Little Rose," climbed a tree and began shouting to passersby that her mother had been arrested. Escorted back inside, Greenhow was unwisely given permission to go with a friend to her room where they attempted to hide evidence of her spying. After she was placed under house arrest, her home became known as "Fort Greenhow," and she continued to smuggle messages to Confederate cohorts. However, the brazen plan backfired when Pinkerton followed the couriers.

Greenhow was eventually moved to the ***Old Capitol Prison, First and East Capitol Streets NE***, a portion of which had previously been a boarding house run by her aunt. Even imprisoned, the indomitable Greenhow continued to spy, wrapping messages around rubber balls and tossing them through a window to waiting agents. Finally exchanged for Union prisoners of war, she was greeted by Jefferson Davis on her arrival in the Confederate capital of Richmond, Virginia, and dispatched to Europe to drum up support for the Confederacy.

Although Jordan and others downplayed the quality of her spying, Greenhow relished her clandestine role. She penned a best-selling book (with the help of a ghostwriter) titled *My Imprisonment and the First Year of Abolition Rule at Washington*, which made her a small fortune on a European tour. The profits from the book were converted to gold and sewn into her dress for her return to the United States. However, in August 1864, Greenhow fell overboard from a small boat while attempting to get ashore in North Carolina. Weighted down by the gold in her clothing, she drowned. Her grave is in the Oakdale Cemetery, New Hanover County, North Carolina.

■ 11. THE UNION'S SPY HUNTER

MAP 1 ➤ **Provost Marshal headquarters:** 217 Pennsylvania Avenue NW (now redeveloped)

According to his own claims, Lafayette C. Baker was one of the Civil War's most effective counterintelligence operatives. Unquestionably, he was relentless in self-promotion, as well as the pursuit of suspected spies and criminals.

Lafayette C. Baker

Lafayette C. Baker's Secret Service headquarters at 217 Pennsylvania Avenue NW seen years later in 1917 during the funeral procession of Adm. George Dewey.

First hired by Gen. Winfield Scott, Baker traveled behind enemy lines to Richmond posing as an itinerant photographer. He carried a broken camera without any glass plates for exposures, which apparently was sufficient to establish legitimacy for his cover story.

Brought into the War Department by Secretary Stanton, Baker assumed the title of special agent, then special provost marshal. He established headquarters at 217 Pennsylvania Avenue NW, which, according to some historians, was a building situated between a house of ill repute and a gambling den. Today the western steps of the Capitol look down on the site, a parking area.

As an admirer of France's Eugène François Vidocq, the father of modern criminology, Baker instituted lasting practices in American law enforcement. He was among the first to compile organized files on Confederate troops and sympathizers, developed what would become an early system of mug shots, and created a number of innovative interrogation techniques.

Baker ran afoul of Stanton when he tapped the secretary's telegraph line, and he was summarily fired. However, the spy catcher was reemployed following President Lincoln's assassination to track down John Wilkes Booth and his coconspirators. In doing so, he eventually received a portion of the reward money. Briefly hired by President Andrew Johnson to establish the first US Secret Service detail to protect the president, Baker soon antagonized Johnson and was again fired.

Leaving government service permanently, Baker retired to his Philadelphia home to write his memoirs, *A History of the Secret Service*, published in 1867. Like many Civil War memoirs, Baker's account is an exciting, if not a wholly factual, reminiscence of his wartime exploits. He died the following year.

Walt Whitman

■ 12. ALWAYS A POET, NEVER A SPY

MAP 3 ➤ **Carver Barracks:** 16th and Euclid Streets NW (now the site of Meridian Hill Park)

Rebel spies were suspected everywhere in Washington during the Civil War. In an often-told tale of the times, the poet Walt Whitman was questioned by police while walking home one night from Carver Barracks Hospital on Meridian Hill, at 16th and Euclid Streets NW. Whitman, who had come to Washington after his brother was wounded at Fredericksburg, Virginia, stayed on to work as a nurse. As recounted in a 1907 ***Atlantic Monthly*** article, Whitman was approached by a policeman on the darkened street and ordered to remove his "false face." The poet, who often wore his beard at an eccentric length, explained patiently that he wasn't wearing a disguise. Then, unable to resist his poetic nature, added, "Do we not all wear false faces?"

Walt Whitman's work at the Carver Barracks Hospital as a nurse during the Civil War was said to have inspired his poem "The Wound-Dresser."

The account may have been propagated by Whitman himself. The great man of exuberant American poetry was not above burnishing his own image. In at least one documented instance, he wrote, under a pseudonym, a glowing review for his own book, *Leaves of Grass*.

Thaddeus S. C. Lowe's hydrogen gas balloons pioneered military aerial reconnaissance during the Civil War.

■ 13. TAKING THE HIGH GROUND WITH BALLOON RECONNAISSANCE

MAP 10 ➤ **Fort Taylor Park:** North Roosevelt Street and Ridge Place, Falls Church, Virginia

Recognizing the potential value of emerging technology, President Lincoln supported the development of new

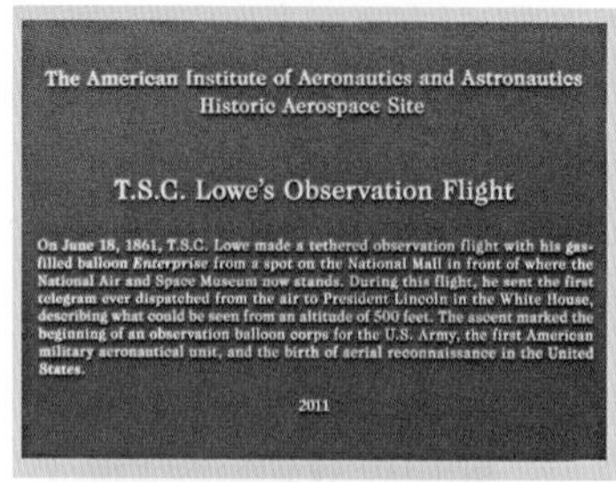

This plaque commemorates the birth of aerial reconnaissance in America.

methods of aerial reconnaissance and clandestine communications capabilities for his Union army. The president authorized the modest sum of $250 for Professor Thaddeus S. C. Lowe to carry out an experiment combining two nascent technologies. In mid-June 1861, Lowe and a telegraph operator ascended to 500 feet above the National Mall in front of the Washington Armory. From this site at ***Sixth Street and Independence Avenue SW***, now occupied by the National Air and Space Museum, Lowe's balloon, Enterprise, trailed a telegraph wire directly into the White House.

The telegraph operator keyed, "This point of observation commands an area nearly 50 miles in diameter. The city, with its girdle of encampments, presents a superb scene. I have the pleasure of sending you the first dispatch ever telegraphed from an aerial station and in acknowledging indebtedness to your encouragement for the opportunity of demonstrating the availability of the science of aeronautics in the military service of the country. T. S. C. Lowe."

Several days later, on June 24, Professor Lowe observed Confederate cavalry from a tethered balloon platform near Taylor's Tavern in Falls Church, Virginia, conducting the first aerial combat reconnaissance in our nation's history. The tavern sat near a major crossroads between Union and Confederate lines. A few months later, a hill by the tavern was fortified as the Union's Fort Taylor. Today two historical markers at the tiny Fort Taylor Park commemorate the ascent. The park sits alongside Koons Ford and Oakwood Cemetery, by the intersection of North Roosevelt and Broad Streets, with its entrance at North Roosevelt and Ridge Place.

■ 14. LADIES WHO PLOT

MAP 9 ➤ **Fort Corcoran:** Intersection of Key Boulevard and North Ode Street, Arlington, Virginia

At the beginning of the Civil War, Rose O'Neal Greenhow's network of spies included Confederate sympathizers from every walk of life and level of government. Some were well placed for espionage, such as F. M. Ellis, a member of General McClellan's staff. Greenhow also concocted one of the most ambitious schemes of the Civil War when she envisioned cutting the telegraph wires into the War Department, kidnapping McClellan, and disabling the defensive guns at two forts.

Greenhow's plot was more than fantasy. First she obtained detailed plans for Fort Corcoran, today identified by a marker at the intersection of ***Key Boulevard and North Ode Street, Arlington, Virginia***, and Fort Ellsworth, now the site of the ***George Washington Masonic National Memorial, 101 Callahan Drive, Alexandria,***

Virginia. As cover for reconnaissance missions, Greenhow took lady friends and coconspirators on pleasant carriage rides. However, the group was already under suspicion and surveilled by Allan Pinkerton's agents. Greenhow was arrested before she could follow through on her ambitious plot.

The George Washington Masonic National Memorial occupies the former site of the Union's Fort Ellsworth. Rose O'Neal Greenhow surveilled this key defensive position for a possible Confederate attack on the capital.

A second female spy played a crucial role during Greenhow's arrest. Shortly after Pinkerton's men apprehended Greenhow, Ann Lillie Mackall arrived at the house. The two women, who were friends and neighbors, feigned illness and were allowed to retreat privately to a bedroom. Behind closed doors, MacKall secreted in her silk stockings and shoes evidence that could have been used against Greenhow.

Another of Greenhow's notable operations involved her friend Betty Duvall (sometimes spelled Duval). In one operation, Greenhow placed an encrypted message in a small silk purse and hid it in Duvall's long black hair. Duvall, disguised as a "country girl," then rode out of Washington on Chain Bridge Road and crossed the heavily guarded Chain Bridge to the Fairfax County Courthouse. There she delivered intelligence on Union troop strength and marching routes to General Milledge Luke Bonham.

Responding to spying charges in March 1862, Greenhow remained slyly unrepentant. "If I gave the information you say I have," she said, "I must have got it from sources that were in the confidence of the government. . . . If Mr. Lincoln's friends will pour into my ear such important information, am I to be held responsible for all that?"

Betty Duvall and Ann Lillie Mackall are buried at ***Oak Hill Cemetery, 3001 R Street NW***. The inscription on MacKall's stone reads: "IN MEMORY OF ANN LILLIE MACKALL, FRIEND OF ROSE O'NEAL GREENHOW AND BRAVE-HEARTED CONFEDERATE COURIER, WHO DIED DECEMBER 12, 1861, AGED 22 YEARS."

The Washington Arsenal (today Fort Lesley J. McNair) was the target of Confederate spies and saboteurs.

15. CONGRESSIONAL SPY HUNTERS

MAP 6 ➤ **Washington Arsenal:** 103 Third Avenue (now Fort Lesley J. McNair)

Shortly after the first shots of the Civil War were fired at Fort Sumter on April 12, 1861, the US House of

Representatives formed a committee to investigate federal government employees disloyal to the Union. Chaired by John F. Potter, a Wisconsin Republican, the intent of the committee was to weed out those known to entertain sentiments of hostility to the government. Potter soon proclaimed he was "astonished" by the number of disloyal federal employees. The Washington press, even then eager for scandal, echoed his sentiments, calling the number of potential spies "startling." The committee met in secret, interviewed some 450 witnesses, and investigated more than 500 charges. Testimony was largely based on slim evidence and hearsay, while those accused were not given the opportunity to defend themselves.

Nevertheless, Confederate saboteurs were at work in Washington. A dozen workers at the Washington Arsenal (today Fort Lesley J. McNair, located at the tip of Greenleaf Point in Southwest) were found filling artillery shells with sawdust and sand. However, the Potter Committee's methods and lack of due process rankled many, including Treasury Secretary Salmon P. Chase, as well as Secretary of State William H. Seward. Eventually Seward would launch his own investigations into allegations of disloyalty among government employees.

It did not take much evidence to fall under suspicion of possessing Confederate sympathies or worse. In one example, Lt. John Watt, whose White House duties included gardening, was accused of disloyalty because he mocked the Union's defeat at Bull Run, calling Union troops "rubbish" and "cowards," as well as leaking one of the president's speeches to the press. Watt's commission was revoked, and he was relieved of horticultural and all other White House responsibilities.

John Mosby

16. PROTECTING THE "GRAY GHOST"

MAP 11 ➤ Laura Ratcliffe residence: 2346 Centreville Road, Herndon, Virginia

Laura Ratcliffe was 20 years old when she became involved in espionage quite by accident. Living in what was then called Frying Pan, Virginia, her family members were Confederate sympathizers but did business with Union troops out of economic necessity. On February 7, 1863, a Union officer taunted the young woman about a trap set for cavalry commander John Singleton Mosby, who was known as the "Gray Ghost."

This country home, named Merrybrook, once belonged to the family of Laura Ratcliffe. As a young woman, Laura's spying assisted Confederate officers John Mosby and J. E. B. Stuart. She lived in this house after the Civil War.

"I know you would give Mosby any information in your possession," a Union soldier is reputed to have taunted Ratcliffe. "But, as you have no horses and the mud is too deep for women folks to walk, you can't tell him; so the next you hear of your 'pet' he will be either dead or our prisoner."

According to legend, Ratcliffe set off on foot to warn Mosby of the Union trap and then continued providing intelligence to him and Confederate cavalry officer J. E. B. Stuart while also acting as a banker for rebel soldiers. Ratcliffe and Mosby held secret meetings to exchange intelligence and money at an outcropping later called Mosby's Rock, which has a historical marker and is accessible through the parking lot of the ***Mount Pleasant Baptist Church, 2516 Squirrel Hill Road, Herndon, Virginia***.

Although Ratcliffe's original house in Frying Pan no longer exists, Merrybrook, the home she lived in after the war with her husband, Milton Hanna, a Union army veteran, still stands at ***2346 Centreville Road in Herndon*** and is on the National Register of Historic Places. She died in 1923 at age 90 and is buried in a family cemetery on what are now the grounds of the ***Washington Dulles Marriott Suites, 13101 Worldgate Drive, Herndon***.

Rebel Tech

In late 1864, the Confederate House of Representatives in Richmond introduced secret legislation to create a Bureau of Special and Secret Service. The law also established an organization to focus on new technologies that could be applied to espionage and sabotage. Unfortunately for the Confederate cause, the forward-thinking piece of legislation aimed at applying the latest technology to intelligence collection and clandestine operations was not enacted until March 1865, one month before Gen. Robert E. Lee's surrender at Appomattox, and was never implemented.

Although primitive by today's standards, this Confederate cipher device provided cryptographic security during the Civil War.

Col. John Mosby captured 30 Union soldiers billeted at the Fairfax County Courthouse.

Confederate spy Antonia Ford erred by keeping incriminating evidence in her family home, shown here today. Her cherished commission as honorary aide-de-camp from Confederate general J. E. B. Stuart sent the Southern belle to prison.

■ 17. CONFEDERATE SPY AND UNION OFFICER

MAP 11 ➤ Old Fairfax County Courthouse: 4000 Chain Bridge Road, Fairfax, Virginia

On the night of March 3, 1863, a daring Confederate raid captured Union general Edwin H. Stoughton along with more than 30 men billeted at the Fairfax County Courthouse in Fairfax, Virginia. Secretary of War Stanton, suspecting the Col. John Mosby–led attack was based on intelligence from a local spy, put Lafayette C. Baker on the case. Baker's investigation focused on Antonia Ford, a young woman who lived near the courthouse in what is now called the Ford Building.

A search of Ford's home turned up incriminating evidence, including an honorary aide-de-camp commission from Gen. J. E. B. Stuart. Ford was arrested and imprisoned in the ***Old Capitol Prison, First and East Capitol Streets NE***. However, her confinement was shortened by Union major Joseph Willard, a former provost marshal at the Fairfax Courthouse, who gained her release after she signed a loyalty oath. The couple later married and moved into a large home at ***14th and G Streets NW***.

Antonia, now Mrs. Willard, died shortly after the end of the war and is buried in the ***Oak Hill Cemetery in Georgetown, 3001 R Street NW***. Joseph Willard, who resigned his commission after marrying, operated the ***Willard Hotel (today the Willard InterContinental Hotel), at 1401 Pennsylvania Avenue NW***. The original Willard was demolished, and the current structure was built in 1901–4.

The family's connection to espionage would continue decades later. A descendant, Belle Willard, was the wife of army intelligence officer Kermit Roosevelt Sr. and mother of Kermit "Kim" Roosevelt Jr., an officer of the OSS and later of the CIA.

18. MISTRESS OF DISGUISE

MAP 8 ➤ **Carlyle House Historic Park and Mansion House Hotel:** 121 North Fairfax Street, Alexandria, Virginia

Sarah Emma Edmonds ran away from her home in Canada to Michigan while still a teenager. There being limited business prospects for women, she disguised herself as a man, assumed the name Franklin Thompson, and began selling Bibles door-to-door. When the Civil War broke out, she enlisted in the Second Michigan Infantry. For two years she served undetected as a male field nurse, regimental mail orderly, postmaster, and spy.

Following the war, she wrote a best-selling memoir, *Nurse and Spy in the Union Army: Comprising the Adventures and Experiences of a Woman in Hospitals, Camps, and Battle-Fields*. According to her own telling, Edmonds became an expert at disguise when working undercover behind enemy lines. She once used silver nitrate to darken her skin and posed as an African American laundress, then later as an African American man named Cuff. In another instance, she disguised herself as an Irish peddler, assuming the name Bridget O'Shea, and then as a courtly Southern gentleman named Charles Mayberry.

Fearful of being discovered after she contracted malaria, Edmonds

The Mansion House Hotel (now demolished) was once located in front of the Carlyle House in the 100 block of North Fairfax Street and served as a Union hospital during the Civil War. There Union spy Sarah Emma Edmonds worked as a nurse.

Sarah Emma Edmonds

The Carlyle House

deserted and recuperated in a private hospital, then returned to nursing under her real name at the Mansion House Hotel in Alexandria, Virginia, which had been converted into a Union hospital. Reputed to be one of the finest hotels in the area before the war, only a portion of the building, now occupied by the ***Bank of Alexandria, exists at 133 North Fairfax***. The hotel/hospital was on the same lot as the Carlyle House mansion, the present-day ***Carlyle House Historic Park, 121 North Fairfax Street***. A PBS television drama, *Mercy Street*, that aired in 2016 was inspired by the people and events surrounding the Mansion House Hospital.

Edmunds later worked as a nurse at a hospital in Harpers Ferry, West Virginia, and, as with many memoirs following the war, just how much of her tale is true is debatable. However, her military service was recognized by a congressional act in 1884 that granted her a pension of $12 a month, and in 1886 the charge of desertion was belatedly removed from her record.

19. THE CONFEDERATE JAMES BOND

MAP 2 ➤ **Kirkwood House Hotel:** 12th Street and Pennsylvania Avenue NW

Benjamin Franklin Stringfellow

Benjamin Franklin Stringfellow was a Virginian by birth and a spy by profession. At five feet, eight inches tall and weighing no more than 100 pounds, "Frank," as he liked to be called, made several attempts to enlist before he was finally accepted in Company E, Fourth Virginia Cavalry. He was a scout for Gen. J. E. B. Stuart and, according to legend, an emissary for Jefferson Davis. In one early clandestine mission in Alexandria, Virginia, he assumed the cover of a dental student along with the alias Edward Delcher. He scanned local papers for news of troop movements and other intelligence and ran a spy ring in Washington. His agents, posing as patients of a Dr. Richard Sykes, dropped off their intelligence at the dental office.

One of Stringfellow's more dramatic successes as a scout occurred in 1862 when he traveled to Warrenton, Virginia, to locate Union general John Pope's field headquarters and supply station depot at Catlett's Station. An historical marker at ***Elk Run Road (County Route 806) and Fernridge Road*** notes the site of Stuart's subsequent raid on the depot.

Returning to Alexandria, Stringfellow worked in a retail store for cover. For at least part of his stay in Alexandria, he lived at the Mansion House Hotel,

Confederate spy Benjamin Franklin Stringfellow and George Atzerodt, a coconspirator of John Wilkes Booth, stayed at the Kirkwood House Hotel at different times. Incriminating evidence left by Atzerodt in his Kirkwood House room led to his capture.

later turned into the Union's Mansion House Hospital.

Stringfellow eventually married Emma Green, the daughter of the hotel's owner. He was believed to have also stayed at the ***Kirkwood House hotel in Washington, 12th Street and Pennsylvania Avenue NW***, which was the Washington home of Vice President Andrew Johnson and is now the site of a multistory office building.

Following a brief self-imposed exile in Canada after the war, Stringfellow returned to study for the clergy. He served as rector of the Episcopal Christ Church in Martinsville, Virginia, from 1891 to 1894, then as the first chaplain of the ***Woodberry Forest School, 898 Woodberry Forest Road, Woodberry Forest, Virginia***, a boys boarding school.

Much of what is known about Stringfellow's exploits is attributed to newspaper reportage of his postwar lectures and is unverified. In one report, Stringfellow is said to have attended a Washington ball in honor of George Washington's birthday, dressed as a woman. In another adventure, he claimed to have hidden beneath the petticoats of a proper Southern lady while Yankee soldiers searched her home. In a letter dated April 4, 1915, to Judge Tom Duke Jr., Col. John Mosby commented, "Most of Frank's tales would have been equally true if told of the Argonauts. . . . He was a brave soldier, but a great liar." Stringfellow, who died in 1913, is buried at ***Ivy Hill Cemetery, 2823 King Street, Alexandria, Virginia***.

■ 20. DECEIVING THE CONFEDERACY

MAP 2 ➤ **US Patent Office:** Eighth and F Streets NW (now site of the Smithsonian National Portrait Gallery, Donald W. Reynolds Center for American Art and Portraiture)

Dr. Mary Walker was a physician in an age when most women in medicine were nurses. Eccentric in dress for the time, she insisted on wearing male clothing and was once even arrested for impersonating a man. After volunteering for the war effort, she was consigned to nursing duties at the makeshift hospital in the US Patent Office Building, today the Smithsonian Institution's National Portrait Gallery, Donald W. Reynolds Center for American Art and Portraiture, Eighth and F Streets NW.

Although officially a nurse, Walker performed many of the duties of a surgeon. Her repeated letters petitioning officials for certification as a doctor went

Mary Walker

unanswered, though they caught the attention of the media. As the press and government officials debated whether she should be given official recognition, she became a celebrity.

"Dressed in male habiliments . . . she carries herself amid the camp with a jaunty air of dignity well calculated to receive the sincere respect of the soldiers," Horace Greeley's *New-York Tribune* reported in December 1862. "She can amputate a limb with the skill of an old surgeon, and administer medicine equally as well. Strange to say that, although she has frequently applied for a permanent position in the medical corps, she has never been formally assigned to any particular duty."

Eventually Walker was appointed field surgeon for the 52nd Ohio Infantry, serving during battles at Warrenton, Fredericksburg, Chickamauga, Chattanooga, and Atlanta. In addition to her surgical duties, she reportedly often crossed enemy lines alone on scouting expeditions. A letter to Secretary Stanton in 1862 made her intentions clear. "I refer to my being sent to Richmond under a 'flag of truce' for the relief of our sick soldiers and then use the style (of double communication in writing their necessities) that I invented, to give you information as to their forces and plans and any important information. No one knows what the style of writing is, except Hon. Mssrs. Cameron Seward and Mr. Allan of the Secret Service."

Riding alone with two pistols concealed in her saddle, Walker apparently was successful in her clandestine missions. The army's judge advocate general later wrote in 1865 that "at one time [she] gained information that led General Sherman to so modify his strategic operations as to save himself from a serious reverse and obtain success where defeat before seemed to be inevitable."

Walker was captured by Confederate troops in April 1864 and sent to Richmond's notorious Castle Thunder prison, then released four months later as part of a prisoner exchange for a male doctor. She returned to Washington and following the war started a medical practice in her home at ***374 Ninth Street NW*** (now the site of a modern office building) and became a vocal advocate for woman's suffrage and prohibition. President Johnson, seeking to recognize Walker's contribution to the war effort, directed Judge Advocate General Joseph Holt to look into the matter of her wartime service. In 1865, Holt found Walker's service commendable yet noted in his report that "her sex is to be deemed an insuperable obstacle to her receiving the official recognition."

Nevertheless, Johnson awarded her the Medal of Honor. It was said she wore it every day, but in 1917, two years prior to her death, the honor was rescinded when more than 900 names were stricken from the honor roll as undeserving. In 1977, President Jimmy Carter reinstated her name as a rightful recipient, and she remains the only female to receive the honor.

■ 21. PHOTOGRAPHY: A NEW SPY TECHNOLOGY

MAP 2 ➤ **Alexander Gardner's Gallery:** 511 Seventh Street NW (now redeveloped)

Alexander Gardner was managing famed photographer ***Mathew Brady's Washington studio, 625–633 Pennsylvania Avenue NW***, when the Civil War erupted. Joining Allan Pinkerton's organization, which provided intelligence to General McClellan, Gardner began photographing terrain in Confederate and Union territories. The topographic images were then turned into maps used to inform battle strategy. Gardner also began photographing Union regiments so the images could be studied to identify suspected Southern spies who might have infiltrated the ranks. His after-battle photographs, used for intelligence at the time, today provide a remarkable photographic record of the war.

"It was during the winter of '61–'62 that Gardner became attached to the Secret Service Corps, then under my father," William A. Pinkerton was quoted in *The Photographic History of the Civil War*. "I used to travel around with Gardner a good deal while he was taking these views and saw many of them made."

Alexander Gardner's gallery, 1863. His photographs assisted in the creation of topographic maps for the Union Army and endure as a visual record of the Civil War.

The Secret of the Buttons

The Confederacy was every bit as innovative with photography as the Union. Southerners adopted the new technology of microphotography from the 1852 work of the British scientific instrument maker John Dancer and French inventor René Patrice Dagron. The result was an early microdot technique that created tiny collodion images approximately 2 mm square that could be hidden in the carved or metallic buttons of military uniforms. One of Dagron's novelties for viewing microdots incorporated a Stanhope lens to magnify the image. This would be used by the CIA a century later and become known as the "bullet lens."

So successful was Gardner's use of images for intelligence that General Sherman, during his March to the Sea, employed photographers who used portable darkrooms called Dark Wagons, which the troops nicknamed "What-Is-It Wagons." The wagons were necessary since early glass photographic plates required rapid processing following exposure.

After Lincoln's assassination, Gardner, at the request of Provost Marshal Lafayette C. Baker, photographed the crime scene as well as the conspirators at their execution, making him, arguably, the first crime scene investigator. In the years after the Civil War, Gardner opened his own studio and gallery at 511 Seventh Street NW, now a restaurant and commercial area. In photographing convicted criminals for the Washington police force, he also created one of the first collections of mug shots for law enforcement.

Decades later Gardner became a controversial figure when observant historians identified the same battlefield fatalities in multiple images. Apparently Gardner had arranged the corpses for dramatic effect. In one instance he moved a body 40 yards from one photo to the site of another photo. Gardner, who died in 1882, is buried in ***Glenwood Cemetery, 2219 Lincoln Road NE***.

Confederate agents surveilled the movements of President Lincoln from Lafayette Park as part of a kidnapping plot.

■ 22. A PRESIDENTIAL KIDNAPPING PLOT

MAP 2 ➤ **Lafayette Square Park:** 16th Street and Pennsylvania Avenue NW

When Pierre Charles L'Enfant, who had served with Washington at Valley Forge, was commissioned to design the new capital city, he placed a park directly north of the White House. This was to be the President's Park and part of the White House grounds. Thomas Jefferson and others protested the design. A front lawn of over 18 acres was judged too royal, too extravagant, and much too European. The solution was to extend Pennsylvania Avenue, originally intended to terminate at the White House grounds, thereby dividing the park from the White House lawn.

The President's Park (the name change would come later) was open to the public, though President Andrew Jackson commandeered the space for riotous parties following his election, and President Ulysses S. Grant started up a small zoo on the grounds.

During the Civil War, the park served as an observation post for rebel scout Thomas Nelson Conrad. Disguised as a chaplain, Conrad positioned himself in the park to watch President Lincoln's daily comings and goings. The plan was both simple and ambitious: kidnap the president and exchange him for Confederate prisoners of war.

Conrad later described his surveillance in his memoir, *A Confederate Spy*. "I had to ascertain Mr. Lincoln's customary movements first; then plan accordingly afterwards. Lafayette Square, only a stone's throw North of the White House entrance, was the very place I needed as vantage ground," he wrote. "Partially concealed by the large trees of the park, I found no difficulty in observing the official's ingress and egress; noting about what hours of the day he might venture forth; size of the accompanying escort, if any; and all other details, to be thoroughly informed about which, would have no stone unturned, to possibly foil our attempt."

Conrad's plot was foiled when Lincoln suddenly began taking his daily rides with an armed cavalry escort. Certain none of his trusted men betrayed the conspiracy, Conrad later learned that Col. John S. Mosby was plotting a very similar action. When Mosby's activity was discovered by Lafayette C. Baker and the Government Detective Bureau, Lincoln increased his security detail. Unbeknownst to Baker, the additional security would discourage not one but two plots to kidnap the president.

Following the war, Conrad became the third president of the Virginia Agricultural and Mechanical College (today known as the Virginia Polytechnic Institute and State University, or simply Virginia Tech).

23. FROM CAPITOL TO PRISON TO SUPREME COURT

MAP 1 ➤ **Old Capitol Prison:** First and East Capitol Streets NE

Several Civil War spies, including Belle Boyd and Rose O'Neal Greenhow, were incarcerated in the Old Capitol Prison at First and East Capitol Streets NE.

During the Civil War, inmates of the Old Capitol Prison at First and East Capitol Streets NE, the present-day site of the US Supreme Court, included infamous Confederate spies Belle Boyd, Rose O'Neal Greenhow, and her daughter, "Little Rose." The prison consisted of a muddled collection of structures. At its center was a three-story brick building along with several wooden homes annexed to the facility, which was sometimes called Carroll Prison (or Place). Although the prison housed an estimated 30,000 prisoners over the course of the Civil War, fewer than 100 deaths were recorded.

Overseeing the Old Capitol Prison was Superintendent William P. Wood, who occupied room 19 of the brick headquarters. Wood was a no-nonsense lawman who later served as first chief of the US Secret Service. He is remembered at the time by Gen. William E. Doster, provost marshal of the District of Columbia, as "short, ugly, and slovenly but crafty."

Wood often interrogated prisoners with the head of the Secret Service, Lafayette C. Baker, employing the proven good cop / bad cop strategy. Wood played the role of the good cop and, according to his own account, would not approach subjects until after a long confinement when they were anxious to talk. He also used jailhouse informers to gather intelligence and through one informant learned of Belle Boyd's fear of the ghost of a Union soldier said to haunt the prison.

Wood also claimed to have operated outside the prison, running a secret mail interception operation on behalf of the Union. In a rare interview two decades after the war, he recounted the operation. "My agents secured charge of the underground mail service between Richmond and Washington, and inspected and distributed contraband mail matter up to the year 1864," he told the Washington's *Sunday Gazette* in 1884. "I had in my employ the most reliable male and female assistants, and by these means I was enabled to furnish Secretary Stanton with reliable information as to the contemplated action of Confederate authorities and the movements of the Confederate troops."

Before becoming a prison, the building was known as the Old Brick Capitol because it was the temporary home for Congress during the rebuilding of the Capitol following the War of 1812. The structure then served a variety of functions, including boardinghouse, school, and, after the Civil War, headquarters for the National Woman's Party. The government acquired the property in 1929 and razed the Old Brick Capitol to construct the Supreme Court Building on the site.

■ 24. BELLE REBELLE

MAP 1 ➤ Carroll Prison: Southeastern corner, First and A Streets SE

Belle Boyd

According to some Civil War accounts, Isabella Maria Boyd, while only a teenager and waving her bonnet, sprinted across the battlefield at Front Royal, Virginia, to deliver vital intelligence to Confederate general Thomas J. "Stonewall" Jackson. The courageous young woman became known as Belle Boyd, though other less flattering names, such as "Belle Rebelle," "Pet of the Confederacy," "Siren of the Shenandoah," and "Secesh Cleopatra" were also applied ("secesh" being slang for "secessionist"). Acquiring intelligence through charm and eavesdropping, she was captured multiple times by Union forces but each time was sent back to Confederate territory. With every arrest Boyd's legend as a wily spy grew. A hero to the Confederacy, she was pilloried in the Northern press. "She passes, indeed, if not for a village courtesan, at least for something not far removed from that relation," editorialized the *Washington Evening Star* on August 4, 1862. Breaking the basic tenets of espionage, Boyd brazenly bragged about her escapades to reporters, openly reveling in her Confederate sympathies and celebrity.

The now demolished Carroll Prison (in the foreground), formerly a boarding house, was a part of the Old Capitol Prison.

Boyd claimed she held the rank of lieutenant colonel in the Fifth Virginia Regiment and that Stonewall Jackson himself had appointed her honorary aide-de-camp. In addition to spying and serving as a courier, she also is reported to have stolen weaponry, weaving handguns into the steel coils of her hoop skirt, and smuggled fever-fighting quinine to Confederate troops. Boyd may have also acted for a profit. According to some historians, she charged soldiers $3 for carrying personal letters and $2 for liquor.

When Boyd was captured in 1862, she was held for a month in the ***Old Capitol Prison, on the southeastern corner of First and East Capitol Streets NE***. Belle was imprisoned twice in Washington, the second time in 1863 at Carroll Prison, which was later demolished to make way for the Library of Congress's Jefferson Building.

Released in a prisoner exchange, she boarded a ship for England, but when the blockade runner was stopped by a Union vessel, she was again arrested and sentenced to death. A Union officer, whom Boyd later married, helped gain her freedom.

Boyd's multiple arrests, interviews with the press, and flamboyant style likely hampered her work as a spy but boosted her later career as a celebrity. Following the war, she (and a ghostwriter) produced a book, *Belle Boyd in Camp and in Prison*, and recounted often embellished adventures on the lecture circuit. "I have lied, sworn, killed (I guess) and I have stolen," she said in one of her last interviews. "But . . . I thank God that I can say on my death bed that I am a virtuous woman."

■ 25. THE SMITHSONIAN'S SUSPICIOUS SIGNALS

MAP 6 ➤ Smithsonian Castle: 1000 Jefferson Drive SW

Joseph Henry's new signaling technology produced a mysterious light that emanated from the roof of the Smithsonian Institution Building and alarmed some citizens.

Joseph Henry, one of America's most esteemed scientists, joined the Union's war effort despite his long-time friendship with Jefferson Davis. As secretary of the Smithsonian

Institution, Henry was appointed to the Permanent Commission to the Navy Department. Charged with evaluating proposals for warship designs, communication systems, and state-of-the-art ordnance, members of the commission brought science to warfare.

However, the work undertaken by Henry and other members of the Permanent Commission also included some lighter moments. According to one story, Henry climbed the tower of the Smithsonian Institution Building, known as the Castle, 1000 Jefferson Drive SW, to experiment sending signals with a powerful "lime-light" lantern. The idea was to signal between the tower and the ***Soldiers' Home, 140 Rock Creek Church Road NW***, approximately four miles distant.

In his biography of Lincoln, Carl Sandburg described Henry being marched in front of the president by an army officer who presented the scientist as a traitor. "'Mr. President,' said the officer, 'I told you a month ago Professor Henry is a rebel. Last night at midnight he flashed red lights from the top of his building, signaling to the secesh,'" Sandburg wrote. "'I saw them myself.' Lincoln turned. 'Now you're caught! What have you to say, Professor Henry, why sentence of death should not immediately be pronounced upon you?' Then, turning to the army officer, Lincoln explained that on the previous evening he and others had accompanied Henry to the Smithsonian tower and experimented with new army signals."

26. INTERNATIONAL WOMAN OF MYSTERY

MAP 2 ➤ **US Treasury Building:** 1500 Pennsylvania Avenue NW

Historians still debate the case of Loreta Janeta Velázquez. The Cuban-born adventuress fought as a Confederate soldier during the Civil War, seeing action in the battles of Bull Run, Fort Donelson, Shiloh, and Ball's Bluff.

Loreta Janeta Velázquez, a Cuban-born adventuress and Confederate spy, made grandiose assertions about her Civil War exploits in a 600-page memoir, *The Woman in Battle*. For instance, she claimed she disguised herself as a male Confederate officer named Lt. Harry T. Buford to pass between the lines.

Adopting the name of Harry T. Buford, her specially fitted clothing with extra padding or wires presented a male physique. Sometimes dressed as a man and sometimes as a woman, she crossed and recrossed the lines between North and South, moving between Richmond, Washington, Philadelphia, and New York. However, her greatest accomplishment may have been fooling Lafayette C. Baker, the savvy head of the US Secret Service.

Meeting Baker at the Willard Hotel (today the Willard InterContinental), 1401 Pennsylvania Avenue NW, Velázquez agreed to become a double agent. However, her loyalties remained with the Confederacy, and her acquiescence to spy for Baker was a sham. Instead, Velázquez continued to take orders from Gen. John Henry Winder, head of the Confederate Secret Service Bureau, infiltrating the US Treasury, 1500 Pennsylvania Avenue NW, and other government offices. An international woman of intrigue, Velázquez traveled on a blockade runner, making numerous trips to Europe, and instigated an elaborate plan to devalue US currency on the international market.

Following the war, she led an expedition to resettle Confederate loyalists in Venezuela, though her compatriots soon found the multicultural makeup of that country not to their liking. In need of money, Velázquez wrote a book, *The Woman in Battle: A Narrative of the Exploits, Adventures, and Travels of Madame Loreta Janeta Velázquez, Otherwise Known as Lieutenant Harry T. Buford, Confederate States Army*. The hefty 600-page tome was immediately controversial, denounced and hailed simultaneously. Reading more like an adventure story than history, its pages are packed with romance, feats of daring heroism, and clever betrayal. How much of her book is true remains in dispute.

■ 27. BIOLOGICAL WARFARE ON PENNSYLVANIA AVENUE

MAP 2 ➤ **National Hotel:** Pennsylvania Avenue at Sixth Street NW (demolished)

With the Confederacy on the verge of defeat, its intelligence operations became increasingly desperate. In the summer of 1864, Confederate intelligence officers based in Canada resorted to an attempt at biological warfare. The plan, according to one participant, was to distribute clothing contaminated with yellow fever, smallpox, and other contagious diseases among Union troops and even to President Lincoln. Godfrey Hyams, a British citizen living in Canada, was recruited with the promise of $60,000 and glory to

The National Hotel, founded by John Gadsby, was John Wilkes Booth's residence prior to the assassination of President Lincoln.

deliver trunks of clothing to military centers. Checking into the ***National Hotel, Pennsylvania Avenue and Sixth Street NW***, under the name J. W. Harris, Hyams delivered the five trunks filled with dozens of shirts and coats to W. L. Wall, an auction house then located at the corner of Ninth Street and Pennsylvania Avenue NW, to be placed on sale for a commission. Another trunk was delivered to the Union military base of operations near New Bern, North Carolina.

It is doubtful the Confederate plan would have worked. Decades later, scientists discovered that yellow fever, also known as the "American plague," is a viral disease transmitted by mosquitoes. There was a small chance the smallpox-contaminated clothing could have spread that disease, since there have been verified instances of fabric-borne transmission among people who worked in smallpox hospitals. According to Hyams's later testimony, he refused to deliver a valise containing clothing intended for President Lincoln, athough another operative later made the drop-off. In the end, Hyams received just $100 for his troubles.

Hyams's full role in Civil War espionage operations remains somewhat murky. By the fall of 1864, he may have begun playing the role of double agent. Some historians credit him with informing Union officials of a planned arson attack on New York City.

The National Hotel, which was also home to the War Department official news censor during the Civil War, was razed during the 1940s. The Newseum now stands on its site at 555 Pennsylvania Avenue NW.

28. LINCOLN'S FOREIGN SPYMASTER

MAP 2 ➤ William H. Seward Residence: 717 Madison Place NW (originally 17 Madison Place and now the Howard T. Markey National Courts Building)

William H. Seward

Secretary of state under President Lincoln, William H. Seward is best remembered for surviving an attack on the night of Lincoln's assassination and negotiating America's 1867 purchase of Alaska for 2¢ an acre. Less well known is his role as spymaster.

During the Civil War, Seward oversaw the Union's foreign spy operations. Among his European spies was Henry Sanford, whose family had made its fortune manufacturing brass tacks. Officially Sanford was ambassador to Belgium. Unofficially he ran European espionage operations for Seward.

William H. Seward's home. As secretary of state, Seward authorized intelligence operations against the Confederates within the United States and abroad. From *Frank Leslie's Illustrated Newspaper*, May 20, 1865.

The site of Seward's home is now the Howard T. Markey National Courts Building. A plaque in the building's courtyard commemorates the historic location.

With a $1 million budget (about $15 million today) for "special activities," Sanford built informant networks throughout Europe. Mail carriers in England were paid £1 a week to provide information, while employees of telegraph offices were similarly recruited to report on Confederate dealings. Intelligence gathered through his networks sometimes allowed Sanford to outbid Confederate purchasing agents for armaments.

In Belgium, Sanford paid the editor of the leading newspaper *L'Indépendance Belge* 6,000 francs to tilt coverage to favor the Union. In a letter to Seward, Sanford wrote, "We now have a pulpit to preach from which reaches a large audience and I consider it a very important gain." Comparable efforts were undertaken in England and France where journalists and editors were put on the payroll to write pro-Union stories.

The Confederate operations in Europe were run by James Dunwoody Bulloch, a former naval officer and Theodore Roosevelt's uncle. Bulloch, grudgingly and obliquely, acknowledged the success of Sanford's clandestine efforts when he wrote in 1863 to the secretary of the Navy of the Confederate States of America, "The extent to which the system of bribery and spying has been and continues to be practiced by agents of the United States is scarcely credible." Bulloch did not receive amnesty following the war and settled in Liverpool as a cotton broker. He occasionally managed to visit his family and nephew, the future president, in the United States.

■ 29. THE ASSASSINATION OF PRESIDENT LINCOLN

MAP 2 ➤ **Ford's Theatre:** 511 10th Street NW

The assassination of President Lincoln at Ford's Theatre, 511 10th Street NW, by 26-year-old actor and former Confederate courier John Wilkes Booth represented both a national tragedy and an intelligence operation gone

John Wilkes Booth

badly awry. In early 1865, Booth and his coconspirators conceived of an operation to kidnap Lincoln and hold him hostage in exchange for a mass release of Confederate prisoners of war.

However, Booth's network delivered poor intelligence at every phase of the operation. In mid-March, Lincoln was scheduled to attend a play at the ***Campbell US General Hospital, Florida Avenue and Seventh Street NW***. Along with his coconspirators, Booth waited in vain on the route for the president, who changed plans at the last minute in favor of a military ceremony at the ***National Hotel, Pennsylvania Avenue and Sixth Street NW***. For Booth this must have been a particularly frustrating development, since he was living at the hotel at the time.

Throughout March, the situation continued to deteriorate for the Confederacy. Then, in the first week of April, Richmond was taken by Union troops. A week later, on April 9, Lee surrendered near the Appomattox Courthouse. Jefferson Davis became a fugitive.

With the war lost, Booth changed plans from kidnapping to murder. Now he plotted the simultaneous assassinations of President Lincoln, Vice President Johnson, and Secretary of State Seward. The three dramatic killings would, in Booth's fevered mind, rekindle the Confederate cause. Using ***Mary Surratt's boardinghouse, 604 H Street NW*** (now the Wok and Roll Restaurant) for a base

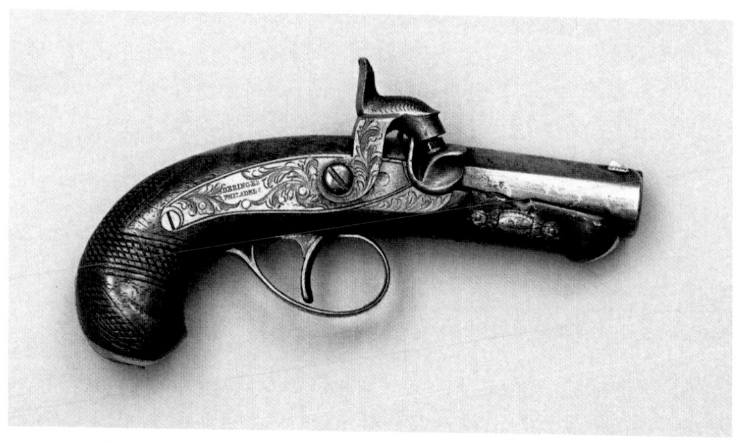
A bullet from this single-shot Deringer killed President Lincoln.

Following President Lincoln's assassination, the government purchased Ford's Theatre and assigned ownership to the National Park Service in 1932.

Mary Surratt's boardinghouse was the site of meetings by conspirators in plots to kidnap and subsequently assassinate President Lincoln.

In a courtroom on the third floor of Building 20 of the Washington Arsenal (now Grant Hall at Fort Lesley J. McNair), a military tribunal found the Lincoln assassination conspirators guilty.

of operations, Booth, along with Lewis Powell, David Herold, and George Atzerodt, formed a plan.

On the evening of April 14, Booth shot the president at Ford's Theatre. The fatally wounded Lincoln was carried across the street to ***William Petersen's boardinghouse, 516 10th Street NW***, where he died the next morning.

At Seward's home, now the site of the ***Howard T. Markey National Courts Building, 717 Madison Place NW*** (originally 17 Madison Place), the plot fell apart. Powell broke into the house of the secretary of state, who was recovering in his bedroom from a carriage accident, but his gun misfired when he encountered Seward's oldest son, Frederick. A scuffle followed, leaving Frederick severely injured. Running into the bedroom, Powell attacked Seward's younger son, Augustus, and a soldier nurse with a dagger, then stabbed Seward several times in the face and neck as he lay in bed. Convinced he had killed Seward, Powell ran downstairs, confronted a messenger, and stabbed him. Miraculously, none of those attacked by Powell died.

Outside the house, Herold, who was minding the getaway horses, heard the screams, panicked, and fled. Powell, being unfamiliar with Washington, hid for three days before making his way back to Surratt's boardinghouse, where, despite attempting to disguise himself as a laborer, he was captured.

Atzerodt was assigned to kill Vice President Johnson, who lived at the ***Kirkwood House Hotel, 12th Street and Pennsylvania Avenue NW***. Atzerodt took a room in the hotel but lost his nerve, began drinking heavily at the hotel bar,

Lincoln assassination conspirators Surratt, Powell, Herold, and Atzerodt were hanged on July 7, 1865, in the courtyard of the Old Arsenal Penitentiary, near the present location of the Fort Lesley J. McNair tennis courts.

and eventually wandered off to the ***Pennsylvania House hotel (also known as Kimmel House), 357–359 C Street NW***, before fleeing the city the next morning. Evidence found in Atzerodt's room at the Kirkwood House linked him to Booth.

A massive manhunt began immediately. Booth was found and shot on April 26 at a farm near Bowling Green in Caroline County, Virginia.

Eight defendants were eventually apprehended and tried before a military tribunal. More than 300 witnesses were called during the seven-week trial

Where They're Buried

GEORGE ATZERODT
Old St. Paul's Cemetery
West Redwood Street and Martin Luther King Jr. Boulevard, Baltimore, Maryland

JOHN WILKES BOOTH
Initially beneath the floor of the cell block at Fort McNair, later disinterred and moved to Green Mount Cemetery, 1501 Greenmount Avenue, Baltimore, Maryland

DAVID HEROLD
Congressional Cemetery
1801 E Street SE
Washington, DC

LEWIS POWELL
Geneva Cemetery
240 First Street, Geneva, Florida

MARY SURRATT
Mount Olivet Cemetery
1300 Bladensburg Road NE, Washington, DC

at the ***Washington Arsenal's building 20 (now Grant Hall on Fort Lesley J. McNair)***. All defendants were found guilty on June 30, and Powell, Atzerodt, Surratt, and Herold were sentenced to death by hanging. Samuel Mudd, a doctor who had treated Booth for a broken leg during his attempted escape, was sentenced to life in prison, as were Samuel Bland Arnold and Michael O'Laughlen, early coconspirators who later dropped out of the plot. Edmund Spangler, a stagehand at Ford's Theatre who held Booth's horse for him, received a six-year sentence.

Twelve weeks after Lincoln's assassination, on July 7, 1865, Surratt, Powell, Herold, and Atzerodt were hanged in the courtyard of the Old Arsenal Penitentiary (now part of Fort Lesley J. McNair). Their bodies were buried in shallow graves near the gallows, then moved to other grave sites. Surratt was the first woman executed by the US government. O'Laughlen died in prison of yellow fever in 1867. Mudd, Arnold, and Spangler were pardoned in February 1869 by President Johnson. Spangler maintained his innocence until his death in 1875, insisting he had no connection to the plot beyond holding the horse for Booth.

30. INNKEEPERS FOR SPIES

MAP 13 ➤ **Surratt's Tavern:** 9110 Brandywine Road, Clinton, Maryland

Surratt's Tavern in Clinton, Maryland, functioned as a tavern, post office, and inn. Lincoln assassin John Wilkes Booth and coconspirator David Herold stopped there on their flight from Washington to retrieve weapons and ammunition.

Mary Surratt ran the family tavern at ***9110 Brandywine Road, Clinton, Maryland*** (today the Surratt House Museum) before opening a boardinghouse at ***604 H Street NW*** (then numbered 541 H Street) in 1864. The popular tavern functioned as the Surratt home as well as an inn and post office. After Lincoln's assassination, the tavern gained dubious fame as the site of a brief stop by John Wilkes Booth and David Herold during their panicked flight from Washington to retrieve Spencer carbines, ammunition, and other supplies cached there.

The tavern's owners were well known for their long-standing Southern sympathies. Before his death in 1862, John Harrison Surratt, Mary's husband, sided with the Confederate cause. The tavern served as a safe house as well as an accommodation address (mail drop) for Confederate spies. The couple's son, John Surratt Jr., who acted as a courier for Confederate intelligence, was an early coconspirator in the initial plan to kidnap President Lincoln. Following Lincoln's murder, he fled to Canada, then Europe. Eventually returning to America, he stood trial but was found not guilty of having a role in the assassination.

Predating the better-known Washington Monument in the District of Columbia by six decades, the 34-foot-high Washington Monument in Maryland's Washington Monument State Park was used as a Civil War signal tower.

■ 31. THE OTHER WASHINGTON MONUMENT

MAP 14 ➤ **Washington Monument State Park:** 6620 Zittlestown Road, Boonsboro, Maryland

The first Washington Monument did not dominate the Washington skyline. Rather, the 34-foot high, stone structure built to honor George Washington in Boonsboro, Maryland, was erected in 1827, nearly six decades before its larger and more famous namesake was completed in 1885. While not as grand as the stately marble obelisk in the nation's capital, the Boonsboro monument has a special Civil War history as a signal tower for Union sentries on the lookout for Confederate troop movements. Located in the Washington Monument State Park, part of the Appalachian National Scenic Trail, the tower is best accessed through the park's main entrance.

■ 32. TWO CENTURIES OF SECRETS

MAP 2 ➤ **The Willard:** 1401 Pennsylvania Avenue NW (rebuilt in 1901)

A Washington landmark, the Willard InterContinental Washington, 1401 Pennsylvania Avenue NW, has seen multiple transformations during its 200-year history. Popularly known as "the Willard," the renowned hotel has a history that began with a Supreme Court decision. In the mid-1800s, the Willard brothers, Henry and Edwin, wanted to unite several buildings to create a single structure and were enabled to do so by a Supreme Court ruling that allowed payment for the land in paper money, rather than gold or silver.

During the Civil War, the Willard was a hotbed of intrigue as well as literary creativity. Abolitionist Julia Ward Howe was inspired to compose "The Battle Hymn of the Republic" in one of its rooms after a meeting with Abraham Lincoln at the White House. "This hotel, in fact, may be more justly called the center of Washington and the Union than the Capitol, the White House or the State Department," Nathaniel Hawthorne wrote while covering the war for the *Atlantic Monthly.* A century later, after the hotel was rebuilt, Martin Luther King Jr. composed the majority of his historic "I Have a Dream Speech" there.

Some have associated the term lobbyist with the Willard to describe those

The Willard Hotel as it appeared in the 1850s during President Franklin Pierce's administration.

who loitered in its ornate lobby hoping to catch the ear of passing political figures. Etymologists have sought to correct the history, placing the origins of the somewhat pejorative label in Great Britain before the hotel was built, but the mythology has stubbornly stuck.

Lafayette C. Baker, the Union spymaster of the Civil War, was said to have agreed to become the intelligence chief in April 1861 in the Willard suite of Gen. Winfield Scott. The Willard was also a favorite residence for detective Allan Pinkerton, who checked in under the cover name E. J. Allen, and was where he first learned of a plot to assassinate Lincoln prior to the 1861 inauguration.

In the 20th century, the Willard provided temporary housing for British spy and future author Roald Dahl when he was first assigned to Washington. During the 1962 Cuban Missile Crisis, the Willard's Occidental Grill served as a lunchtime meeting place for back-channel diplomacy between the White House and the KGB. A commemorative plaque hangs at the approximate location where the historic lunch occurred.

WESTERN UNION
TELEGRAM
GERMAN LEGATION
MEXICO CITY
via Galveston
JAN 19 1917

3

WORLDWIDE INTELLIGENCE AND WORLD WAR

(1866–1932)

Fifty years after Civil War cannons fell silent, new weaponry produced unprecedented carnage on European battlefields while innovative technologies were transforming espionage. America, reluctant to engage in a distant European war, was drawn into World War I by the relatively new discipline of signals intelligence (SIGINT) and the ancient craft of decryption. In 1917, an encrypted telegram sent by the German foreign secretary was intercepted and decrypted by British intelligence. Its incendiary contents promised Mexico large tracts of the United States if it joined the German cause—a revelation that stoked America's passion to fight.

Following "the war to end all wars," the United States attracted spies and intelligence officers from around the globe. Anarchists resorted to violence in efforts to overthrow the government, and the newly formed Soviet Union dispatched spies as diplomats and trade officials, while the British and Germans both attempted to influence post–World War I American policy.

Housed in an unpretentious downtown building, the Alibi Club limits membership to 50 of Washington's most influential leaders.

■ 33. WASHINGTON'S ELITE CLUBHOUSE

MAP 2 ➤ **Alibi Club:** 1806 I Street NW

The publicity-shy Alibi Club has occupied the same modest three-story building for all but two years of its long history. Founded in 1884 by seven members of the larger Metropolitan Club, the organization was initially known as "the Little Club." According to legend, the name change occurred when a member showed up one night in need of a viable alibi to explain to his wife his absence from home. The name, apparently, was just mischievous enough to stick. Members also affectionately call it "the Joint."

The outward appearance of genteel disrepair at 1806 I Street NW belies its deserved reputation as one of Washington's most exclusive clubs: New members must be voted in unanimously.

The interior walls festooned with eclectic memorabilia and bric-a-brac are jammed with caricatures of past members, which have included Supreme Court justices, high-ranking military officers, congressmen, and, in the 20th century, an assortment of spies. Among the club's former members with ties to the intelligence community are David K. E. Bruce, OSS commander of covert operations in Europe during World War II; Robert Lovett, secretary of defense and a leading figure in creation of the CIA; Director of Central Intelligence (DCI) Allen Welsh Dulles; DCI Richard Helms; DCI William H. Webster; and DCI and US president George H. W. Bush.

According to one legend, the club eschewed installation of a telephone for years, making members intentionally difficult to reach. When a phone was finally installed, a sign with a price list for alibis—such as "Just Left," "On His Way," and "Who?"—was posted jokingly nearby.

■ 34. THE FIRST HOME OF US MILITARY INTELLIGENCE

MAP 2 ➤ **State, War, and Navy Department Building (now called the Dwight D. Eisenhower Executive Office Building):** 639 17th Street NW (Pennsylvania Avenue and 17th Street NW)

The US Army's first peacetime intelligence component was established in 1885. Embedded in the Adjutant General's Office, it was headquartered in the State, War, and Navy Department Building, today known as the Dwight D.

Leland Harrison

Maj. Ralph Van Deman

Eisenhower Executive Office Building. Created under Brig. Gen. Richard C. Drum, the Military Information Division (MID) had by 1889 begun to analyze reports from a newly formed military attaché element. The attachés stationed in capital cities throughout Europe provided firsthand perspectives and intelligence to Washington officials.

The headquarters of Maj. Ralph Van Deman's Military Intelligence Section were in the Old Executive Office Building, now the Dwight D. Eisenhower Executive Office Building.

The value of the MID's intelligence was proven during the Spanish-American War of 1898, but by 1915 the intelligence function had moved to the War College Division of the army's General Staff at Fort Leslie J. McNair. Productivity of the division languished, with one account asserting that reports piled high on a table went unread.

One army officer, Maj. Ralph Van Deman, with intelligence experience from his posting in the Philippines, recognized the need to create a modern intelligence function. However, his efforts to influence the chain of command proved fruitless and frustrating. Van Deman acknowledged that the chief of staff was a fine officer but one who appeared to know nothing about the vital importance of an intelligence service. Believing it was impossible to carry on a war without an effective intelligence and counterintelligence organization, Van Deman was determined to build a suitable structure for intelligence work.

The major engaged acquaintances who could perhaps offer some influence, including British intelligence officer Claude Dansey and the Washington chief of police, who frequently dined with Newton Baker, the secretary of war. Whether it was the British with the contacts in President Woodrow Wilson's administration, the police chief, or a private party, someone arranged a meeting with Baker. On May 3, 1917, the Military Intelligence Section, War College Division, War Department General Staff, was created with Van Deman as its head.

Those Thirsty, Thirsty British

In 1921, US operatives picked up some disturbing intelligence about British diplomats in Washington. At the height of Prohibition, members of the British diplomatic legation were importing liquor in quantity. Intelligence reports based on intercepted correspondence revealed that 18 embassy employees had pooled their resources to import 83 cases of liquor through the London-based shipping company Joseph Travers & Sons. Technically, diplomats could legally consume liquor at formal embassy functions, but these illicit shipments seemed destined for personal consumption and were illegal under the 1919 Volstead Act, which prohibited the production, sale, and transport of intoxicating liquors. Rather than move to legal action, US authorities allowed the matter to be quietly hushed up.

The Military Intelligence Section began modestly with a staff of two officers and two civilian clerks. Van Deman divided intelligence into two categories: "positive" for intelligence collection and "negative" for those efforts aimed at denying the enemy intelligence, what is now called counterintelligence. Van Deman's subcategories or components were "administration," "information," "military attachés," "translation," "maps and photographs," "codes and ciphers," and "combat intelligence instruction." Under the category of negative intelligence, Van Deman's office oversaw counterespionage, foreign influence and counterespionage within the civilian community, news censorship, travel, passport fraud, and port control.

By the war's end, Van Deman's organization, structured along the lines of the British security service and now headed by Brig. Gen. Marlborough Churchill, had expanded to 282 officers and more than 1,100 civilians. Van Deman's ambitious vision led to an organization that foreshadowed the areas of responsibility now shared among today's sixteen US Intelligence Community (IC) organizations.

Van Deman's was not America's only World War I intelligence operation. Secretary of State Robert Lansing sensed the need for a national intelligence clearinghouse and, on April 4, 1916, quietly created the Bureau of Secret Intelligence (sometimes referred to as U-1), which was tucked into the Office of the Counselor in the same building as Van Deman's Military Intelligence Section.

U-1 was headed by Leland Harrison, whose job was the collection and examination of all secret information. Harrison's agents, operating primarily in Washington and New York City, conducted investigations, put the German embassy and consulates under surveillance, and tapped phone and telegraph lines. He coordinated information from War Department and naval intelligence offices, the Secret Service, and other US government entities. Daily reports were

Edith Wharton and the Father of Military Intelligence

Ralph Van Deman, the acknowledged father of American Military Intelligence, faced a roadblock early in his career. Assigned to the Army War College in 1915, the young major recognized the value of effective military intelligence but was unable to convince his commanding officers of the decisive role intelligence could play in warfare.

Not only was Van Deman's advocacy for an intelligence component ignored as America prepared to enter World War I—he was forbidden from pleading his case to the higher-ups. Then an opportunity presented itself by way of a chance meeting. Assigned to give a "lady authoress" with connections to "the highest levels" a tour of Washington military facilities, Van Deman made his case to the influential writer. Within weeks of acting as tour guide, he was summoned to the office of Secretary of War Baker and directed to establish the Military Intelligence Section.

Edith Wharton

Who was the mysterious writer? Van Deman never named her. The most likely candidate, according to historians, is Edith Wharton. A New York socialite and Pulitzer Prize winner, Wharton is best known for her novels *The House of Mirth*, *Ethan Frome*, and *The Age of Innocence*, as well as a large body of poetry and nonfiction. She was also a tireless advocate of the United States joining the war in Europe.

submitted to Lansing, who reported directly to the president. Just how much attention President Wilson paid to Lansing's intelligence is unclear.

35. Gentlemen Reading Each Other's Mail

MAP 2 ➤ **Hooe Iron Building:** 1330 F Street NW (building now demolished)

Herbert O. Yardley

Shortly after the United States entered World War I, code breaker Herbert O. Yardley, as a second lieutenant in the Signal Corps, set up a cryptographic program in modest offices of the Hooe Iron Building, 1330 F Street NW (current site of the National Press Club Building). The office, officially designated Military Intelligence Division, Code and

The Hooe Iron Building on F Street, today the site of the National Press Club Building, was home to the US Army's Code and Ciphers Section (MI-8), which had responsibilities for code breaking, code creation, and secret-ink formulas.

Ciphers Section No. 8 (MI-8), included code breaking and code creation among its functions and had a secret-ink laboratory. After the war, when Yardley's budget was cut, the State Department stepped in to provide funding. However, due to regulations restricting the use of State Department funds in Washington, the code breakers were moved to New York City.

The cryptographic effort again faced problems in 1929 when Secretary of State Henry L. Stimson defunded the program with the reputed admonition "Gentlemen do not read each other's mail." Yardley then wrote an unauthorized book on US cryptographic efforts called *The American Black Chamber* (1931). The ominous title was actually a reference to *cabinet noir*, the term for where the spies of the French king Henry IV examined mail. The work earned Yardley the ire of government officials.

Unable to secure another cryptology post with the government, Yardley set about earning a living by writing. Another book, *The Blonde Countess*, promoted by an ad that revealed a secret message when dipped in water, was made into the 1935 movie *Rendezvous*, starring Rosalind Russell and William Powell. There was also a stint in China from 1938 to 1940, where Yardley—operating under the cover name Herbert Osborn—decrypted Japanese codes for the Chinese government. Following his return from China, he briefly worked for the Canadian government on ciphers.

When America entered World War II, Stimson, then secretary of war, reversed his stance on code breaking and mail reading. However, Yardley, the gifted code breaker, remained unable to reenter the field because of his past disclosures. The still out-of-government cryptographer purchased the ***Goodacre White Coffee Pot Restaurant, 1306 H Street NW***, renamed it the Rideau Restaurant, and ran it for nearly a year. Next he took a job with the wartime Office of Price Administration as an enforcement officer. After the war ended, Yardley wrote *All Crows Are Black*, about his work for the Chinese government. He opened an appliance firm, Osborn Sales Company, then worked for the Public Housing Administration. Yardley's last book, *The Education of a Poker Player*, was published in 1957. He died in 1958, still out of favor with his government.

Four decades passed before the significance of his work was officially recognized. In 1999, Herbert O. Yardley was inducted into the Cryptologic Hall of Honor of the National Security Agency (NSA).

36. FORGERY AND THE GREAT WAR

MAP 3 ➤ **German embassy:** 1435–1441 Massachusetts Avenue NW (demolished 1959)

Germany packed its embassy with intelligence officers leading up to World Wars I and II.

From its imposing embassy on Massachusetts Avenue NW near Thomas Circle (now replaced by apartments and office buildings), Germany launched sabotage and intelligence operations during World War I while the United States was still neutral. These included supplying spies with fraudulent passports, conducting propaganda campaigns, blowing up ships at sea, and damaging factories producing war matériel. An international railway bridge at Vanceboro, Maine, was almost destroyed, while a similar plot to disable the Welland Canal linking Lake Erie and Lake Ontario, a lifeline of raw materials, was foiled at the last minute.

Count Johann Von Bernstorff, German ambassador to the United States before World War I.

Heading these operations was military attaché Capt. Franz von Papen and naval attaché Capt. Karl Boy-Ed. Eventually both von Papen and Boy-Ed were ordered out of the country, von Papen in 1915 and Boy-Ed in 1917. Despite these provocations,

President Wilson maintained a firm stance of neutrality that was shared by a large segment of the American public.

This American policy and public opinion were abruptly turned by a brief, inflammatory message known as the Zimmermann Telegram. On January 16, 1917, an encrypted telegram was sent by Germany's foreign minister, Arthur Zimmermann, to Ambassador Johann von Bernstorff in Washington, with instructions that it be forwarded to the German ambassador in Mexico. Intercepted and decoded by British cryptographers, it revealed a proposed deal with Mexico to return parts of the continental United States to Mexico following German-Mexican cooperation in an armed conflict. It read, in part: "Make war together, make peace together, generous financial support, and an understanding on our part that Mexico is to reconquer the lost territory in Texas, New Mexico and Arizona. The settlement in detail is left to you."

The British, unwilling to reveal they had broken the code, arranged for a second source that used a different cipher to come to light. The telegram was turned over to President Wilson, who leaked it to the Associated Press. Seemingly overnight, public attitudes shifted, and America entered World War I in April 1917.

A mystery tunnel under P Street NW was discovered in 1917. Some speculated that it was used by German agents.

37. UNDERGROUND MYSTERIES

MAP 3 ➤ Tunnel area: 2100 block, P Street NW

Suspect tunnels had appeared in Washington decades before the Cold War, prompting speculation about both their origin and purpose. In May 1917, construction crews building an apartment complex at ***2115 P Street NW*** uncovered a tunnel 22 feet in circumference extending hundreds of feet beneath the city and outfitted with electric lights and glazed brick walls. Theories about who dug the tunnel and why ran wild. Was it a nest of German spies? Perhaps Confederate soldiers had operated out of the subterranean stronghold?

Harrison G. Dyar, an entomologist at the Smithsonian Institution, eventually claimed credit and asserted that he had dug the tunnel between 1906 and 1916 "for exercise." Dyar's tunnel returned to the public eye in 1924 when a truck broke through its ceiling. Inside, reporters found German newspapers from 1917 and 1918 with references to German submarine missions. Could it be that German spies were somehow alerted to the existence of the tunnel and used it during the Great War? That mystery remains unsolved.

Neither the number of tunnels Dyar dug nor all of their locations have been conclusively established. In addition to those on P Street, he dug one at his next home at ***804 B Street SW*** (now Independence Avenue). Dyar died in 1929 leaving little information about his motivation for such an uncommon hobby or how he disposed of all that dirt without coming to the attention of the authorities.

38. SCIENTIST SPIES FROM THE COSMOS CLUB

MAP 2 ➤ **Cosmos Club:** 1518 H Street NW (club later relocated to its present location at 2121 Massachusetts Avenue NW)

Charles Sheldon feeding a gray jay, likely in Denali National Park.

In 1917, at the former Lafayette Square location of the Cosmos Club, Office of Naval Intelligence officer Charles Alexander Sheldon recruited archeologist Sylvanus Morley to spy against Germany.

Charles Alexander Sheldon and Sylvanus Morley quietly met in March 1917 at the Cosmos Club, then located at the northeastern corner of ***Lafayette Square at 1518 H Street NW***, now site of a Department of Veterans Affairs building. Both were members of the prestigious club, but the meeting was far from social. Sheldon, a gentleman sportsman who retired from business at age 35 to devote his life to the outdoors and become a noted wildlife conservationist, represented the Office of Naval Intelligence (ONI). America, about to enter World War I, anticipated that German submarines would seek safe harbor in Mexico and Guatemala.

Morley was a Harvard-trained archeologist and expert on Mayan culture. During their meeting, Morley identified four other American archeologists as potential spies for the ONI. Sheldon understood that archeologists using the cover of field research could secretly acquire information on German operations throughout Central America. The scholar-spies would work with the full backing of their sponsoring institutions, including the American Museum of Natural History and the Carnegie Institution.

Morley, code-named AGENT 53, traveled more than 2,000 miles of coastline, surveying southern Mexico, Guatemala, Nicaragua, and Honduras. He eventually recruited an estimated two dozen agents and subagents. Reports to

Sheldon, who was designated AGENT 246, were addressed to cover names Taro Yamamoto or Adolph Schwartz at P.O. Box 139, Boston, Massachusetts. When in Washington, Morley often worked from the Cosmos Club.

39. MULE SABOTAGE PLOT

MAP 7 ➤ Anton Dilger residence: 5503 33rd Street NW (private residence)

The prospect of unconventional warfare reached America during World War I. Although virtually forgotten today, a German agent, Anton Dilger, attempted to infect horses and mules bound for the Allies in Europe with deadly diseases such as glanders. Stevedores in Norfolk and Newport News, Virginia, were recruited to inject the animals, but how many animals actually died as a result remains unknown.

The son of a Civil War Medal of Honor recipient, Dilger had graduated from Johns Hopkins University, but he lived a significant part of his life in Germany where he acquired a loyalty to the Fatherland. His American roots, his US citizenship, and his Washington residence at 5503 33rd Street NW made him an ideal covert agent for German intelligence.

The operation reportedly ended in 1916, a year before America entered the war. Once Dilger came under suspicion, he fled to Mexico and then Spain, before dying in 1918, a victim of the Spanish Flu pandemic.

During World War I, German agent Dr. Anton Dilger lived in this Washington home.

40. CITIZEN SPYBUSTERS

MAP 4 ➤ **American Protective League headquarters:** 1719 H Street NW (now an office complex)

Badge worn by citizen spies of the American Protective League.

Chicago advertising executive A. M. Briggs, who made his fortune in poster advertising, launched a civilian security network in 1917 called the American Protective League (APL). Briggs envisioned an army of volunteer citizen spy hunters to support America's war effort. It is unclear whether Briggs was mainly motivated by profit, patriotism, or self-promotion, but the concept quickly grew into a formidable organization.

After Briggs received official approval and wary cooperation from the military and Department of Justice, the APL reportedly enrolled more than 250,000 members in 600 cities. Those who paid dues received a badge and identification card. The APL became the largest of many similar patriotic organizations that sprang up throughout the country.

With its success, the APL moved its headquarters from Chicago to ***1537 I Street NW in Washington***, then to larger spaces at 1719 H Street NW. However, the growing organization remained controversial. Members broke into offices, searched homes, conducted surveillance operations, opened mail, and reported instances of word-of-mouth-propaganda. To conduct what they called "slacker round-ups," APL members stationed themselves outside office buildings and raided restaurants demanding to see the draft cards of military-age men. Clashes with radical unions, such as the Industrial Workers of the World, were common. Although some members of Congress and local communities advocated that the APL continue to fight the perceived threat of anarchists and communists after the war, the organization eventually disbanded and faded into history.

41. THE BOMBS OF 1919

MAP 3 ➤ **Alexander Mitchell Palmer residence:** 2132 R Street NW (private residence)

At 11:15 p.m. on June 2, 1919, a powerful bomb exploded on the front doorstep of Attorney General A. Mitchell Palmer's stately home at 2132 R Street NW. The blast damaged the lower front portion of the home and shattered windows of houses along the street. It also propelled a portion of the ill-fated bomber's body across the

A powerful bomb, part of several coordinated nationwide attacks, exploded in front of Attorney General A. Mitchell Palmer's stately R Street NW home in 1919.

street to the doorstep of future president Franklin D. Roosevelt, who lived at ***2131 R Street NW***. Another body part crashed through the window of a Norwegian diplomat's house at ***2137 R Street NW***. Roosevelt, giving an interview from the scene, noted that judging from the socks recovered, the bomber appeared poorly dressed.

The bomb was part of a nationwide coordinated plot by anarchists. At approximately the same time, bombs exploded in Philadelphia, New York, Boston, and Cleveland. However, it was the Washington bomb targeting a high-ranking public official that made national headlines.

Among the scattered pieces of the bomber were charred leaflets proclaiming a radical and violent ideology. Dated the same day as the bombing, the leaflets' message read in part, "The time has come when the social question's solution can be delayed no longer. . . . Class war is on, and cannot cease but with a complete victory for the international proletariat."

The US Bureau of Investigation (BOI), predecessor organization to the FBI, launched an investigation, with Palmer, now in the limelight, leading a counterattack on the radicals. He established the General Intelligence Division within the BOI, naming a young J. Edgar Hoover as its head. Government agents infiltrated groups with radical ties and launched a series of 33 "Palmer Raids" in early 1920 in cities across the country. Thousands of radicals and union members were apprehended and questioned. When no significant conspiracies were uncovered, Palmer's methods came under criticism, and what became known as the First Red Scare faded from the headlines.

The bumbling bomber was eventually identified as Carlo Valdinoci, an Italian immigrant in his mid-twenties with a history of publishing leftist literature and ties to the anarchist Luigi Galleani, who advocated terrorism to bring about social change. The relatively small group of radical "Galleanists" eventually faded from sight as well.

The June 1919 bombings and attempt to kill Attorney General Palmer were not isolated acts of terrorism. Two months earlier, 36 prominent Americans, including businessmen and government officials, were sent mail bombs. The intended victims included the postmaster general, members of the Commission on Immigration, and Supreme Court Justice Oliver Wendell Holmes Jr., as well as various congressmen and state politicians. Alerted to the threat, the US Postal Service intercepted the majority of the bombs, although one US senator's housekeeper was injured by a blast after opening the package.

When another anarchist plot was reported for May Day 1920, Palmer moved to protect public officials and physical targets across the country. However, when no attacks occurred, Palmer became the subject of ridicule and harsh criticism in editorial pages. Once viewed as a strong potential presidential candidate, Palmer had his political future brought to an abrupt end.

42. MADAME X: CODE BREAKER EXTRAORDINAIRE

MAP 9 ➤ Agnes Meyer Driscoll grave: Arlington National Cemetery, section 35, site 4808, Arlington, Virginia

Agnes Meyer Driscoll

As one of America's most talented cryptologists, Agnes Meyer Driscoll broke new professional ground for women along with codes. Born in 1889 in Ohio, Driscoll attended Ohio State University where she studied mathematics, physics, music, and foreign languages. She was teaching school in Amarillo, Texas, when World War I began.

Driscoll joined the US Navy in 1918 and held a rank of chief yeoman (F)—the *F* designating female. She served briefly at the Postal and Cable Censorship Office, examining correspondence for signs of espionage, then, following the war, transferred as a civilian to the Code and Signal Section of the Office of the Director of Naval Communications. There her cryptographic talents blossomed, and over the next 30 years Madame X or Miss Aggie, as she was known to colleagues, broke some of the enemy's most complex codes.

Working at the forefront of American cryptography, Driscoll spent a short time at Herbert O. Yardley's MI-8 in New York City before returning to Washington in the early 1920s to collaborate with Lt. Cdr. William Gresham, head of the navy's Code and Signal Section. Together they developed the Communications Machine (CM), which became the Navy's standard cryptographic system. In 1930, Driscoll partnered with Lt. (j.g.) Thomas Dyer to break the Japanese navy's codes manual, known as the Blue Book. She made critical progress in 1940 in deciphering messages from its successor, JN-25, the Japanese fleet's latest operational code. Thanks to her inroads, JN-25 was exploited throughout the remainder of World War II.

The project had commercial as well as technical significance because the new IBM "tabulating machine" was employed to track cipher groups. Following the war, Driscoll worked for the Armed Forces Security Agency (forerunner to the NSA) and then the NSA. She retired from the NSA in 1952, after having served the nation in two world wars and the start of the Cold War. Madame X died in 1971 and is buried in Arlington National Cemetery. In 2000, she was inducted into the NSA's Cryptologic Hall of Honor.

■ 43. THE CODE WARRIORS

MAP 4 ➤ **Munitions Building:** Constitution Avenue and 19th Street NW (demolished in 1970 and now site of the Vietnam Veterans Memorial)

The Army Signal Intelligence Service once occupied the now demolished Munitions Building on Constitution Avenue NW.

A reorganization of the military's code-breaking efforts beginning in 1930 revitalized American cryptologic capabilities. Cryptologists in the Army's Signal Intelligence Service (SIS) based in the Munitions Building were able to break the Japanese diplomatic code in 1940 through a top-secret program known as PURPLE. They then reverse-engineered the Japanese cipher machine using components from telephones and other common electronic

William and Elizebeth Friedman

The World War II–era SIGABA, or ECM (Electrical Enciphering Machine), was a joint project of the US Army and US Navy.

devices. Remarkably, when an actual Japanese encryption machine—the 97-shiki O-bun Injiki (Alphabetical Typewriter 97)—was eventually captured, the American version bore an uncanny resemblance.

The code-breaking team was led by William F. Friedman, a geneticist by training and a cryptologist during World War I. His wife, Elizebeth, also a code breaker, worked for the US Coast Guard during Prohibition solving rum-runner codes. She later made a name for herself by breaking the World War II Japanese "Doll Code," which used postal correspondence describing toy dolls to conceal intelligence about American naval forces.

The SIS relocated to Arlington Hall, a former women's school, in Arlington, Virginia, in 1942. The Munitions Building was razed in the 1970s, and the site is now occupied by the Vietnam Veterans Memorial and Constitution Gardens.

The Unbroken Code

William F. Friedman and his SIS team are best known for breaking Japanese codes. However, they can also be credited with helping to develop one of the best cipher machines ever devised. Called SIGABA (or ECM, for Electrical Enciphering Machine), the electromechanical unit was technically advanced for its time. The result of a joint project by the US Army and US Navy, SIGABA was first put into service in 1938 and used into the 1950s. There is no evidence that its cipher system was ever cracked during its decades of service.

SPIES OF WORLD WAR II

(1933–1945)

Foreign intelligence operations in Washington intensified through the 1930s as the nation's capital increasingly focused on war preparations. Foreign governments maneuvered to influence America's international relations. German, Japanese, Soviet, and British networks all sought secrets from officials at the highest levels of government. Propaganda campaigns, sexual entrapment operations, and disinformation offensives aimed at lawmakers and media moguls alike sought to sway public opinion and legislation.

On December 7, 1941, Japan attacked Pearl Harbor, and America's long-anticipated entrance into World War II became a reality. Now, as the United States mobilized, Washington also needed spies abroad and spy catchers at home. While FBI director J. Edgar Hoover expanded his organization's counterintelligence operations, the Office of Strategic Services (OSS), founded in 1942 under Col. (later Maj. Gen.) William "Wild Bill" Donovan, became America's global intelligence service.

With advice from British intelligence officers, Donovan shaped a daring and innovative service. OSS officers were recruited from all strata of American society and performed heroically behind enemy lines. As America's industrial companies rolled out battleships, tanks, and aircraft for invading armies, other firms quietly became secret developers of spy gear for the intelligence war.

Though short-lived, the OSS planted the seeds of America's peacetime, civilian intelligence community. Among the few thousand individuals who fought the intelligence battles of World War II in the OSS were future heads of the CIA, lawmakers, and a future Supreme Court justice. Tested against the forces of the Axis Powers during war, within less than a decade they would prove themselves against the Soviet Union in a new type of global conflict.

44. HITLER'S PAL PUTZI

MAP 8 ➤ **Bush Hill Estate historical marker:** Eisenhower Avenue, 0.8 mile east of Metro Road, Alexandria, Virginia

A Nazi sympathizer and personal friend of Adolf Hitler, Ernst "Putzi" Hanfstaengl, spent a portion of World War II under house arrest at the Bush Hill Estate outside Alexandria, Virginia.

Ernst Hanfstaengl (left) confers with Hitler and Hermann Göring.

An early follower of Adolf Hitler, Ernst Franz Sedgwick Hanfstaengl claimed a distinguished lineage. His father was a wealthy Munich businessman, while his mother descended from the Sedgwicks, one of New England's most prominent families. Nicknamed Putzi (Little One) by his nanny, Hanfstaengl attended Harvard, then later returned to Germany where he became a close friend of Hitler. Hanfstaengl financially supported the Nazi newspaper, edited *Mein Kampf*, and hid the future Führer in his country house following the failed Beer Hall Putsch of 1923. An accomplished amateur musician, Hanfstaengl played Harvard football fight songs and Wagner for Hitler on a piano to cheer him up and even advised him to change the style of his mustache. The grooming tip was not accepted.

When Hitler rose to power, Hanfstaengl was made foreign press chief. Arrested in 1939 in England as an enemy alien, he was sent to a detention camp in Canada. Although reports differ, he either reached out to President Roosevelt, whom he knew from the Harvard Club, or was tracked down by someone in the administration. Eventually handed over to the Americans, Hanfstaengl was interned briefly at Fort Belvoir, Virginia, then was placed under house arrest at Bush Hill, a historic estate outside Alexandria, Virginia. For the remainder of the war, he monitored Nazi broadcasts, reported on Hitler's inner circle, and even proposed clandestine operations against his fellow Germans. Following the war, he returned to Munich, where he died in 1975.

The Bush Hill Estate has since been turned into a housing subdivision. A marker on Eisenhower Avenue near Metro Road notes its location.

■ 45. HIGH-FLYING GERMAN PROPAGANDIST

MAP 3 ➤ German embassy: 1435–1441 Massachusetts Avenue NW (demolished in 1959 and redeveloped as apartments and offices)

Laura Ingalls, who held numerous flight records as a pilot, became a paid Nazi propagandist in the lead-up to World War II.

Laura Ingalls was one of the "darlings of the skies" in pre–World War II aviation. With a reputation to rival Amelia Earhart's, she held records for loops (344) and barrel rolls (714), as well as the longest solo flight ever made by a woman (17,000 miles). But the New York–born aviator adopted isolationist political views and, in September 1939, flew over Washington, dropping pamphlets across the city, including on the White House grounds. The Civil Aeronautics Authority (forerunner of the Federation Aviation Administration) viewed the stunt as a safety and national security concern. However, Baron Ulrich von Gienanth, a German aristocrat and Gestapo officer stationed at the German embassy in Washington, saw an opportunity.

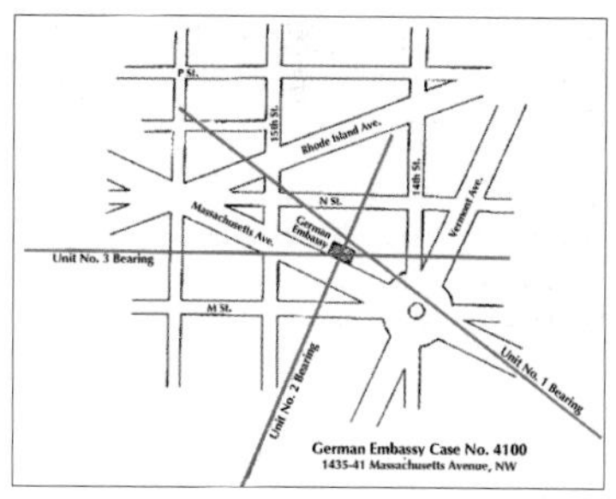

Prior to World War II, the FCC's Radio Intelligence Division used state-of-the-art technology to pinpoint clandestine signals emanating from the German embassy.

Von Gienanth, working undercover as the second secretary of the embassy, then located at 1435–1441 Massachusetts Avenue NW, belied the image of humorless Gestapo officers portrayed in movies. The German diplomat was charming, jovial, and a much sought-after guest on the Washington social circuit. His mission included keeping America out of "a European war" by supporting isolationist groups and dispensing a steady stream of pro-German propaganda.

Agents of the FCC's Radio Intelligence Division operated from mobile, as well as fixed, intercept sites to detect clandestine broadcasts.

Tracking Nazis across the Airwaves

Among the lesser-known organizations of the war, the Radio Intelligence Division (RID) of the Federal Communications Commission (FCC) monitored foreign broadcasts and tracked suspected spies using radio signals. The monitoring activities were identified as the National Defense Operations, then the name was changed to the RID. In addition to monitoring the airwaves around the world, the RID designed equipment for the OSS and helped train the organization's recruits.

On December 9, 1941, two days after Pearl Harbor, an RID monitoring station picked up a strong, unrecognized radio signal with the call sign UA. The RID dispatched three mobile units to identify the signal's source. The searchers tracked the mysterious signal to the German embassy on Massachusetts Avenue NW, where an antenna stretched between two buildings provided nearly decisive evidence.

Concerned that crashing the embassy doors could prompt Nazi reprisals against American diplomats still stationed in Germany, the FCC coordinated a counterbroadcast plan with the Potomac Electric Power Company. The company installed power cutoff switches beneath the streets, while the FCC set up two radio jammers a short distance from the embassy. Although the signal never returned, when the embassy was seized following the declaration of war against Germany, the FCC discovered a fully equipped radio room inside.

In Ingalls, he perceived the perfect spokesperson. Von Gienanth put her on the Third Reich's payroll at $300 a month. She barnstormed the country in her plane giving fiery isolationist speeches. Following the declaration of war against Germany in December 1941, Ingalls was arrested as a nonregistered agent of Germany. Found guilty, she served nearly two years in prison. After her release, repeated attempts to receive a presidential pardon proved unsuccessful. Eventually fading into obscurity, she died in 1967 in Burbank, California, at age 66.

■ 46. MADCAP MERRY AND THE NAZIS

MAP 3 ➤ **Restaurant Pierre, Anchorage Building:** 1555 Connecticut Avenue NW

Mary "Merry" Fahrney's exploits rivaled those of any of today's celebrities or scandals. The heiress to a Midwest patent medicine fortune, she called Washington home in the late 1930s. Born in 1910, she later began spelling her name "Merry" and became known as "Madcap Merry" for her outrageous and frequently shocking antics. After inheriting $6.5 million at age 20, she spent her wealth with a wild flourish that kept both gossip columnists and news reporters busy. She crashed multiple planes in attempts to become a pilot and threw cocktail parties that allegedly cost upward of $50,000 and lasted for days. She was once smuggled out of a hotel in a trunk to avoid

Socialite "Madcap Merry" Fahrney volunteered to spy for the Nazis at the Restaurant Pierre in the Anchorage Building.

a lawsuit and gave an interview in the living room of her New York City apartment while shooting a BB gun at plastic birds. Between her ill-fated adventures, she accumulated several marriages and divorces, including to the young fashion designer Oleg Cassini, and landed a small role in *Cleopatra*, the 1934 Cecil B. DeMille epic starring Claudette Colbert.

She also took a liking to Hitler and the Third Reich. During a reception in January 1938 at the German embassy, then located at ***1435–1441 Massachusetts Avenue NW***, she approached Dr. Herbert Scholz with a clandestine proposition. Rumors swirled that Scholz was a German spy, and indeed he was but not for the well-known Amt Ausland/Abwehr im Oberkommando der Wehrmacht (German military intelligence). Scholz, as it happened, was the resident director in the United States for the Sicherheitsdienst des Reichsführers-SS (SD), the intelligence service of the paramilitary organization Schutzstaffel (SS) and of the Nazi Party.

Within a few days after their first meeting, Fahrney and Scholz dined at the fashionable ***Restaurant Pierre in the Anchorage Building, 1555 Connecticut Avenue at Q Street NW***, just off Dupont Circle. Fahrney was direct: She wanted to spy for Germany.

Scholz, who likely knew Fahrney's reputation for impulsiveness, was also aware she moved in the elite circles of Washington's high society. The German spy accepted the American heiress as a volunteer. Remarkably, she turned out to be an effective spy. Wearing a gold swastika and quoting *Mein Kampf* were seen as mere eccentricities at the time. Although unconventional in lifestyle, Fahrney was socially adept and arranged meetings with prominent Washington

Medicine That Worked

The patent medicine empire that produced the Fahrney fortune was as colorful as Madcap Merry herself. Forni's Alpen Kräuter laxative promised to ease upset stomachs, flatulence, nervousness, and headaches. Its alcohol content of 14 percent made it a popular remedy during Prohibition. Likewise, Dr. Fahrney's Teething Syrup was promoted as the "grandest and safest medicine for babies of all ages." Its secret ingredient was morphine.

The Anchorage's Clandestine History

Ernest Cuneo, a National Football League player, lawyer, confidant of New York City mayor Fiorello La Guardia, journalist, and intelligence officer, served as liaison between the OSS and British Security Coordination (BSC) during World War II. While in Washington, Cuneo made the Anchorage Building, 1555 Connecticut Avenue NW, his home.

Immersed in intrigue, Cuneo befriended British naval intelligence officer Ian Fleming, as the two shared a mutual taste for nightlife in Washington and New York City. Fleming, creator of the world's most famous fictional spy, James Bond, credited Cuneo in his writings. *Thunderball* is dedicated "To Ernest Cuneo, Muse," while *Diamonds Are Forever* includes a Las Vegas cab driver with the similar name Ernie Cureo. Cuneo died in 1988, and his ashes were placed in Arlington National Cemetery's columbarium.

Other OSS tenants of the Anchorage included Arthur Goldberg, later a Supreme Court justice, and George Bowden, OSS assistant director. Besides spies, the Anchorage's notable residents included movie star Tallulah Bankhead, Charles Lindbergh, Robert Kennedy, and House of Representatives speaker Sam Rayburn.

figures for Heribert von Strempel, a propagandist and the first secretary at the German embassy. Reportedly, she also used business cards with the name Susan Wadsworth that identified her as an employee of the Civil Service Commission and visited army bases in the South, asking about armaments.

While Fahrney's fascist antics may have been tolerated or amusing to the upper crust, they also attracted the attention of the FBI. Her German handler at the time, Dr. Hans Thomsen, suggested that she leave the country. When Fahrney learned US authorities had canceled her passport, she quickly married a Swedish waiter in New York, paying him $1,500 to become her fifth husband, thereby gaining Swedish citizenship and a passport. Eventually Fahrney moved to Argentina and, with the Swedish waiter long forgotten, continued to spy and marry. She died in 1974, by then having left her eighth husband.

■ 47. CROOK IN CONGRESS

MAP 1 ➤ **House of Representatives,** Capitol Hill

Elected to the House of Representatives in 1922, Samuel Dickstein (D-NY) was on the payroll of the Soviet intelligence service Narodnyy Komissariat Vnutrennikh Del (NKVD) from 1937 until 1940. Operating under the code name CROOK, he accepted a monthly stipend from the NKVD, which must have viewed him as a prize, at least at first. Unfortunately for the Soviets, the lawmaker would become more trouble than he was worth. The decryptions that became known as VENONA revealed both the lawmaker's involvement with the Soviets and his troubled relationship with his handlers. Dickstein's demands for additional money, combined with providing intelligence of negligible value, caused the NKVD handler in America, Peter Gutzeit, to gripe in a memorandum on May 25, 1937, "CROOK is completely justifying his code name. This is an unscrupulous type, greedy for money, [who] consented to work because of the money, a very cunning swindler."

US congressman Samuel Dickstein

With historical irony, Dickstein cosponsored a failed bill to outlaw Communist Party membership in the United States. He then supported establishment of the House Un-American Activities Committee (HUAC), which eventually became known for its efforts to identify communist sympathizers and Soviet spies. Dickstein served in Congress until 1945 and then as a justice on the New York State Supreme Court. His espionage activities remained unknown until nearly 40 years after his death in 1954.

48. CONGRESSIONAL SPY HUNTERS

MAP 1 ➤ **Old House Office Building (now the Cannon House Office Building):** 200–299 New Jersey Avenue SE

In the Cannon House Office Building caucus room, the House Un-American Activities Committee heard Whittaker Chambers accuse Alger Hiss of being a Soviet agent.

The HUAC has been both lauded and criticized for its work during the 1930s, 1940s, and 1950s. From the Old House Office Building (renamed the Cannon House Office Building in 1962 for former speaker of the House Joseph G. Cannon), it attempted to expose subversives, communist sympathizers, and spies in government, unions, private businesses, the military, and Hollywood. In the Cannon caucus room, the HUAC hearings took testimony from Soviet spies Elizabeth Bentley and Whittaker Chambers, which sparked the Alger Hiss face-off against Chambers in August 1948.

■ 49. BOOKSTORE OR COMMUNIST FRONT?

MAP 2 ➤ Washington Cooperative Bookshop: 916 17th Street NW (site now redeveloped)

The Washington Cooperative Bookshop, 916 17th Street NW, by Farragut Square, opened in 1938. Offering discounted books to its members, it also served as lecture hall and concert venue. Annual dues were a reasonable $1. Decidedly left-leaning, the store featured a selection of works by Karl Marx and Friedrich Engels, as well as the *Daily Worker* newspaper. Some employees had ties to a local communist party.

Was the store a front for the Communist Party USA and, by extension, Soviet intelligence? It became a target of investigation by the FBI and the HUAC and was one of 11 organizations labeled subversive by Attorney General Francis Biddle in 1941, although no hard evidence of espionage was ever developed. Those named, and others added by subsequent attorney generals, became known as the "Biddle List." Biddle later became a judge at the post–World War II Nuremberg trials.

Alban Towers was home to Japanese intelligence officer Tamon Yamaguchi during the tense pre–World War II years.

■ 50. JAPANESE SPYMASTER IN WASHINGTON

MAP 5 ➤ Tamon Yamaguchi residence: Alban Towers, 3700 Massachusetts Avenue NW

Suave, sophisticated, and fluent in English, Tamon Yamaguchi was a Japanese James Bond during the years leading up to World War II. As Japan's naval attaché in Washington, he mixed effortlessly with the city's elite while living in the stylish Alban Towers apartment complex, 3700 Massachusetts Avenue NW, and throwing lavish parties at the Mayflower Hotel.

Less publicly, as Japan's spymaster in Washington, he was also busy recruiting agents. One, John Semer Farnsworth (code name AGENT K), was a disgraced and dishonorably discharged naval officer. Deeply in debt, Farnsworth used his contacts in the military to spy for the Japanese.

By early 1936, the ONI was convinced Yamaguchi was an active intelligence officer and placed his luxury apartment under surveillance. An ONI team then made a surreptitious entry into the apartment in the guise of painters but found nothing of significance. Yamaguchi remained in the United States until recalled to Japan and promoted to rear admiral. He then worked with Cdr. Isoroku Yamamoto to plan the attack on Pearl Harbor. Yamaguchi died in the Battle of Midway when he chose to go down with his ship, the *Hiryū*. Farnsworth, convicted of espionage in the summer of 1936, served 11 years in prison.

51. GOLF COURSE ESPIONAGE

MAP 12 ➤ Burning Tree Club: 8600 Burdette Road, Bethesda, Maryland

Japanese intelligence officer Hidenari Terasaki belonged to the exclusive Burning Tree Country Club prior to World War II.

One of the senior Japanese intelligence officers in Washington prior to World War II was an accredited diplomat from Japan, Hidenari Terasaki. Fluent in English, he had attended the Brown University graduate school. In 1931, he married an American from East Tennessee, Gwendolyn Harold, and joined the private "men only" Burning Tree Club, 8600 Burdette Road, Bethesda, Maryland, where he could socialize and play golf with diplomats and Washington's political elite. From his position as first secretary of the Japanese embassy, Terasaki oversaw information, propaganda, and all intelligence operations in the Western Hemisphere.

When the MAGIC decryptions revealed Terasaki's secret role, the diplomat fell under close scrutiny by the FBI. One bureau document stated that Terasaki "will be the guiding influence in intelligence work and will establish an intelligence unit which will maintain liaison with private and semi-official organizations."

Following the attack on Pearl Harbor, Terasaki was among the diplomats held as virtual hostages inside Japan's Massachusetts Avenue embassy by an angry mob that gathered at the main gate. Eventually detained with other diplomats, he was sent to an internment camp and later returned to Japan in a swap for US diplomatic personnel.

When the war ended, Terasaki acted as translator and adviser to Emperor Hirohito, as well as official liaison between the palace and the supreme Allied commander, Gen. Douglas MacArthur. His wife wrote a memoir, *Bridge to the Sun*, which was made into the 1961 film of the same title, starring Carroll Baker, James Shigeta, James Yagi, and Tetsuro Tamba. Both the film and book offered a sympathetic and somewhat benign view of the role of diplomat-spy.

A few days before the attack on Pearl Harbor, Japanese diplomats were observed burning papers in the garden of their embassy.

52. EAST WIND RAIN

MAP 3 ➤ **Japanese embassy (now the ambassador's residence):** 2516 Massachusetts Avenue NW

Built in 1931, the Japanese embassy in Washington and its personnel were of intense interest for US intelligence as Japan's influence expanded in the Far East. War with Japan seemed increasingly likely, and, from reading incoming and outgoing coded messages, the Roosevelt administration could see that chances for a diplomatic solution were rapidly fading. On December 2, 1941, the embassy received a secret dispatch that ordered codebooks burned and cryptographic machines destroyed. Some of the burning was done in the garden, and the US Navy sent an observer to confirm that the diplomats were indeed burning papers. Inside, cryptographic machines were disassembled to their smallest components and dropped into acid. Similar actions occurred in other Japanese embassies. Once the codes and machines were destroyed, a simple confirmation message was sent to Tokyo.

If commercial communication channels between Tokyo and Washington were disrupted, Japanese diplomats expected to be informed about deteriorating relations between the two countries by a plain text code inserted into a daily shortwave weather forecast broadcast internationally. If the words *higashi no kaze ame* (east wind rain) appeared in the middle of the broadcast, diplomatic relations between Japan and America were being severed. Historians remain divided as to whether the *higashi no kaze ame* message was broadcast prior to Japan's attack on Pearl Harbor.

Six months later, the *Chicago Daily Tribune* inadvertently committed one of the gravest intelligence breaches of World War II. Reporting on the Battle of the Coral Sea, an editor unintentionally turned a vague description of the battle into a vital piece of intelligence for the Japanese. The story, with an inaccurate Washington, DC, dateline, asserted that American commanders had known the Japanese battle plans, attributed the information to reliable sources in Naval Intelligence, and implied that the United States was reading the Japanese military code.

What the editor could not have known was that cryptologists really had broken the Japanese naval code, an invaluable strategic intelligence achievement. By spicing up the story, the unwitting editor potentially exposed one of the most closely held secrets of the war. The paper's owner, Robert McCormick, a staunch isolationist and fierce opponent of President Roosevelt and the New Deal, could have been charged with treason. However, since a trial would have only generated more publicity and further endangered national security, the matter was quietly hushed up. Fortunately for the United States, the Japanese either never saw the story, did not believe it, or did not discern its intelligence value.

53. THE DISTINGUISHED GENTLEMAN FROM "MITZI-GAN"

MAP 7 ➤ Arthur Vandenberg residence: Wardman Park Hotel apartments (now the Marriott Wardman Park Hotel, 2600 Woodley Road NW)

US senator Arthur Vandenberg

As World War II erupted in Europe in 1939, the horrors of World War I were still fresh in the memories of American isolationists who wanted the United States to stay out of European conflicts. One of the most committed of the isolationists was Sen. Arthur Vandenberg, a Michigan Republican. The married Vandenberg's affair with Emelia "Mitzi" Sims, the Danish wife of a Canadian diplomat and neighbor in the upscale Wardman Park Hotel apartments, was an open secret in Washington's elite social circles. Washington's wags labeled him "The Senator from Mitzi-Gan," and British intelligence was reputed to have had a hand in the affair.

Sims's influence was widely cited as a reason for Vandenberg's dramatic change of heart from diehard isolationist to pro-British in 1940, although this account may not be the entire story. Sims left Washington following her husband's death of a stroke in 1940, but another of Vandenberg's Wardman Park

Apartments in the fashionable Wardman Park Hotel were sites for espionage, intrigue, and romantic liaisons during World War II.

neighbors, Amy Elizabeth Thorpe (British code name CYNTHIA), was an American spying for the British and who later worked for the OSS. Thorpe's mother maintained a close friendship with Vandenberg, which provided family access to the senator. Finally, Eveline Paterson, who worked for the British War Relief Society, was allegedly the senator's mistress when he cast his vote for the controversial Lend-Lease program in 1941. According to some accounts, Vandenberg and Paterson remained together until 1948, the year he voted in favor of the North Atlantic Treaty Organization (NATO).

■ 54. MURDER BY SUICIDE

MAP 1 ➤ Bellevue Hotel (now the Hotel George): 15 E Street NW

Walter Krivitsky (also known as Samuel Ginsberg, code name ENEMY by the Soviets following his defection) was the first high-ranking Soviet intelligence officer to defect to the United States. Rather than return to the horrors of Joseph Stalin's purges in 1937, he walked into the French Ministry of the Interior in Paris with his wife and young child and traveled to the United States in 1938. During the next three years, Krivitsky provided a wealth of secret intelligence to US and West European governments while also exposing the Soviet atrocities through interviews and articles in popular publications.

On February 9, 1941, Krivitsky, using the alias Walter Poref, checked into a $2.50-a-night room at the ***Bellevue Hotel (today the Hotel George) at 15 E Street NW***, near Washington's Union Station. The next day the hotel's maid

The Bellevue Hotel, now the Hotel George, was the site of an unsolved 1941 espionage-murder mystery.

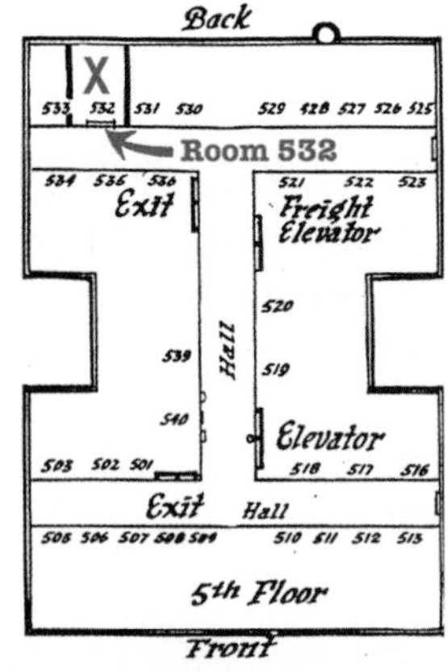

The 1941 floor plan of the Bellevue Hotel shows the location of Walter Krivitsky's room at the time of his death. (Adaption of a diagram that appeared in Gary Kern's book *A Death in Washington: Walter G. Krivitsky and the Stalin Terror* and in the *New York Journal-American*.)

entered locked room 532 and found him dead of a single gunshot wound to the head. Also found were three suicide notes, which the police and FBI accepted as legitimate.

Officially, the case was closed, although few in the press accepted the official finding. "If they ever try to prove that I took my own life, don't believe it," Krivitsky previously told *The New York Times*.

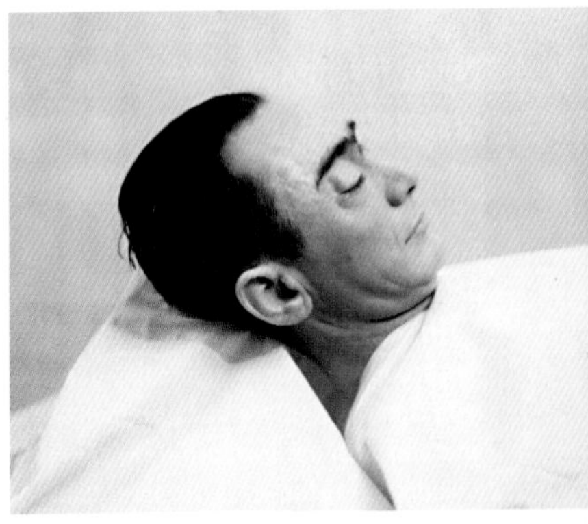

Morgue photo of George Krivitsky's body.

During the ensuing years, room 532 became an object of morbid curiosity. Amateur investigators scoured it for clues, and guests specifically booked it. More recently the Bellevue was transformed into an upscale boutique hotel, and multiple reconfigurations have obscured the location of the room. Krivitsky's death, still classified as a suicide, remains a matter of historical debate.

■ 55. THE SCREWBALL DIVISION

MAP 1 ➤ **Foreign Broadcast Monitoring Service original headquarters:** 316 F Street NE

Arguably the oldest component of the CIA, the Foreign Broadcast Information Service (FBIS) predated the agency by six years when it was established on February 25, 1941, as the Foreign Broadcast Monitoring Service (FBMS) under the FCC. Responsible for monitoring publicly broadcast signals of foreign commercial radio stations as well as shortwave signals, the FBMS had its first headquarters in a converted garage at 316 F Street NE. Staff described the location as "three blocks from Union Station and three miles from a decent place to eat." Other installations were even more far-flung. With sites scattered in California, Florida, Texas, and overseas, the FBMS recorded, translated, and transcribed speeches by foreign leaders such as Hitler and propaganda broadcast by enemy "black stations."

A renovated garage on F Street NE was the first headquarters of the Foreign Broadcast Information Service, then known as the Foreign Broadcast Monitoring Service.

One German propaganda station targeting Americans before the United States entered World War II was Radio Debunk (sometimes spelled D.E.B.U.N.K).

Nazi Propagandist: Axis Sally

Following World War II, American-born Nazi propagandists were arrested and returned to the United States to stand trial for treason based on broadcasts recorded at FBIS monitoring stations. Among them were Jane Anderson, Robert Henry Best, Herbert John Burgman, Donald S. Day, Edward Leo Delaney, Fred W. Kaltenbach, Douglas Chandler, and Constance Drexel.

However, one defendant, Mildred Gillars, known as "Axis Sally," stood out. Her broadcasts were especially despicable. Many included taped interviews with American POWs she obtained while posing as a Red Cross worker, interspersed with her own pro-Nazi commentary. Frequently addressing American women, her rants were virulently anti-Semitic, anti-British, and anti-Roosevelt. "As one American to another—do you love the British? Well of course the answer is no," Gillars asked during one broadcast. "Do the British love us? Of course—I should say not. But we are fighting for them. We are shedding our good, young blood for this kike war, for this British war—oh girls, why don't you wake up. . . . I love America—but I do not love Roosevelt and all of his kike boyfriends who have thrown us into this awful turmoil."

At first the failed actress from Maine seemed to revel in the media attention during her 1949 trial in Washington's District Court on eight counts of treason. The thrill of fame faded when she was convicted and sentenced to 10 to 30 years in prison. Gillars was released after serving 12 years, moved to Columbus, Ohio, and taught music and kindergarten before dying in 1988 at the age of 87.

After America entered World War II, FBIS needed larger quarters for its growing staff of linguists and technicians and moved to this building on K Street NW.

The station, which claimed to be broadcasting from the Midwest, was actually based in Bremen, Germany. The station's programs included patriotic songs and folksy commentary dedicated to "knocking the fit out of profiteers" and combating war "propaganda and hysteria." In fact, the station was aimed at influencing public opinion to keep America out of the war.

By 1942, America was fully mobilizing for war. At the relocated FBIS headquarters, ***1424 K Street, NW***, a sign in the monitoring room proclaimed, "We Have An Axis To Grind." FBIS attracted a disparate and often eccentric staff. Affectionately called the "Screwball Division," FBIS included some 60 linguists, described in a

January 30, 1943, *Collier's* magazine article as "the greatest collection of individualists, international rolling stones, and slightly batty geniuses ever gathered together in one organization."

FBIS became a CIA component in 1947 and may have been best known for publishing translated broadcasts and press reports originating in Iron Curtain countries. After the creation of the Office of the Director of National Intelligence (DNI) in 2004, FBIS was designated an Intelligence Community resource and renamed the Open Source Center (OSC). Today the OSC continues the historic FBIS work, collecting information from all forms of public media, including broadcast, print, and the Internet.

■ 56. "NOTHING DECEIVES LIKE A DOCUMENT"*

MAP 2 ➤ Mayflower Hotel: 1127 Connecticut Avenue NW

A map purported to show Hitler's plan for dividing South America into vassal states was a British forgery intended to stir American emotions and sentiment to enter the war.

President Roosevelt shocked the nation on October 27, 1941, with a revelation of enemy plotting. Speaking at the annual Navy Day dinner in the ballroom of the Mayflower Hotel, the president described a secret plan by the Nazis to establish a fascist presence on America's doorstep: "I have in my possession a secret map made in Germany by Hitler's government, by the planners of the new world order," Roosevelt announced in the speech broadcast nationwide. "It is a map of South America as Hitler proposes to reorganize it."

The claims were explosive. According to the map, South America, plus Panama and the Panama Canal Zone, would be divided into five vassal states under the iron-fisted control of the Third Reich. With Hitler waging war against nearly all of Europe, the plan was audacious enough to seem plausible.

Except it wasn't true. The map was created by British intelligence and given to Col. William Donovan, then Coordinator of Information, America's fledgling intelligence service and predecessor to the OSS. The cover story constructed by British intelligence was that the map had been pilfered from Gottfried Sandstede, a diplomat in Argentina killed soon afterward by the Gestapo. As it turned out, Sandstede was still alive. A variation of the story included a map showing designs for South American shipping and air routes that Sandstede

*Attributed to Sir William Stephenson

hung on the wall of his Buenos Aires headquarters. At some point British intelligence may have obtained a copy of that map and tweaked it.

In another version, and according to his own telling, the creative cartographer was John "Ivar" Bryce, working under the BSC's head, William Stephenson. Bryce claimed to have first sketched the map for the "Nazification of South America" on his desk blotter. "It made me feel the heady power of king-makers, and I drew most carefully a detail extension of the idea, as it would appeal to Hitler, for submission to the powers that be, to wit Bill Stephenson," Bryce wrote in his memoir, *You Only Live Twice*. However, Bryce, who was renowned for his good looks, personal fortune, and friendship with Ian Fleming, may have been practicing a bit of postwar disinformation in claiming credit.

Exactly how the map was surfaced remains in dispute. In one account, the British arranged for the FBI to discover the map during a raid on a Nazi safe house in Cuba. In another version, British officers simply handed it to Donovan, who then passed it along to the president.

Not surprisingly, the German government and American isolationists questioned the map's authenticity. FDR refused to release it to the press, creating even more questions. Despite the challenges, the map was generally accepted as another indication of German intent. A few weeks later, restrictions on the Neutrality Acts were repealed by both the House and the Senate.

Historians dispute whether Roosevelt suspected or knew the map was a forgery. The evidence is inconclusive, although a September 5, 1941, memo by Assistant Secretary of State Adolf Berle warned of potential British forgeries. "I think we have to be a little on our guard against false scares," he cautioned.

57. A WASHINGTON "POWER HOUSE"

MAP 5 ➤ William Donovan residence: 2920 R Street NW (private residence)

A World War I Medal of Honor recipient, staunch Republican, and Wall Street lawyer turned spy, William Donovan lived at 2920 R Street NW while heading America's World War II spy agency, the OSS. As forerunner to the CIA, the OSS conducted clandestine operations in Europe, North Africa, and the Far East while laying the groundwork for America's postwar espionage and covert-action operations.

William J. "Wild Bill" Donovan

William Donovan's Washington home remains as impressive today as when the OSS chief lived there.

Where Did He Live?

There has been confusion as to exactly where William Donovan lived in Washington. Was it at 1647 30th Street NW, as cited in his correspondence, or the stately mansion at 2920 R Street NW, as many historians point out? The answer is both. During Donovan's time in Washington, the home's address was 1647 30th Street NW but was later changed to 2920 R Street NW. In 1938, before becoming head of the OSS, Donovan also acquired a country home at *300 Chapel Hill Lane, Berryville, Virginia*. The site is now on the National Register of Historic Places.

Donovan's Georgetown home offered features that made the residence suitable for its spymaster. Set discreetly back from the street, it could be entered and exited by officials and operatives without attracting unwanted attention. Once owned by Pulitzer Prize–winning journalist Walter Lippmann, the Donovan house was a postwar media bastion and center of Washington society after it became the home of *Washington Post* publisher Katharine Graham.

■ 58. HOME TO AMERICA'S SPIES

MAP 4 ➤ **OSS and original CIA headquarters:** 2430 E Street NW

The OSS, America's World War II spy agency, headed by William Donovan, is the acknowledged predecessor of the CIA. However, for almost a year before creation of the OSS in June 1942, an executive order by President Roosevelt established America's first centralized intelligence organization, the office of Coordinator of Information (COI), with Donovan as its chief. COI was authorized 92 people and Donovan given an office of two and a half rooms in the ornate ***Old Executive Office Building (now the Eisenhower Executive Office Building) at Pennsylvania Avenue and 17th Street NW***.

The East Building on Medicine Hill at E and 23rd Streets NW was part of the headquarters compound for the OSS and later the CIA.

As the organization grew, the staff moved to the ***Apex Building, 600 Pennsylvania Avenue NW***. Growth to more than 600 staffers in less than a year meant another move into the ***National Institutes of Health Building (then***

This sign once marked the CIA's E Street NW headquarters in Washington.

called the Hygienic Laboratory Building] at the corner of 23rd and E Streets NW. Neither the facility nor its inhabitants suggested a spy headquarters. Labs with live animals inoculated with diseases still occupied the top floor of the building. Charles Whiting, author of *The Spymasters*, quoted Nazi propagandist Joseph Goebbels's characterization of America's intelligence service as "fifty professors, twenty monkeys, ten goats, twelve guinea pigs, and a staff of Jewish scribblers."

Donovan's COI organization's colorful beginning was described somewhat more charitably by Col. Edwin L. Sibert after he visited the rapidly expanding headquarters. Sibert is quoted in *The Old Boys: The American Elite and the Origins of the CIA*: "[It] closely resembled a cat house in Laredo on a Saturday night, with rivalries, jealousies, mad schemes, and everyone trying to get the ear of the director. But I felt that a professional organization was in the making, and I am glad to say that I was right."

Six months after Pearl Harbor, the COI became the OSS and again relocated, this time to a fenced compound on a small hill at 2430 E Street NW. This address would be the last home of the OSS and the first for CIA headquarters, from 1947 to 1961. Although no sign identified the agency, the address and the occupants of the compound were an open secret for most of Washington. Nevertheless, in the early 1950s, after a White House driver encountered a problem finding the entrance, President Dwight Eisenhower requested that an identifying sign be placed by the gate. Today that sign, created by presidential order,

Donovan's Loophole

President Roosevelt expressly prohibited the OSS from carrying out espionage operations in the United States. All domestic intelligence and counterintelligence operations were to be the exclusive domain of J. Edgar Hoover's FBI. However, William Donovan was also a lawyer. Years of practicing law on Wall Street taught him to search for loopholes—and he found a good one. Legally, foreign embassies are not on American territory. According to international law, embassies are considered to be "foreign soil" and have many benefits of extraterritoriality. Therefore, Donovan reasoned, foreign embassies were fair game, so he launched multiple wartime operations against them. His actions followed the letter, if not the spirit, of the president's dictum and earned him Hoover's lasting enmity.

Donovan versus the Bureaucrats

The history of Washington bureaucratic intransigence holds a special place of honor for Ruth Shipley. As head of the Passport Division of the Department of State, she ruled her unit by the book and the letter of the law. However, in the OSS's spymaster, William Donovan, Shipley found a worthy opponent. She first insisted that Donovan's officers, despite traveling under cover, have passports stamped "OSS" and refused to issue "cover passports" for foreign agents. Donovan tried every bureaucratic trick, including hiring Shipley's brother for a spot in the spy organization, but to no avail. Eventually, Donovan appealed directly to President Roosevelt. Shipley relented but only under presidential pressure.

The formidable Ruth Shipley, head of the Passport Division of the Department of State, battled OSS chief William Donovan over matters of cover for OSS operatives.

The formidable Shipley was not alone in her questioning of some OSS mission requirements. Interior Secretary Harold Ickes fired off an angry missive to Donovan when a patrol officer pulled over an OSS courier rushing to deliver film to a departing aircraft. The offense of zooming across the Arlington Memorial Bridge at the breakneck speed of nearly 50 mph, Ickes declared, "was reprehensible."

is preserved and displayed at the in-house museum at the CIA's headquarters in McLean, Virginia.

From 1961 to 1989, buildings on the former OSS/CIA headquarters site housed the CIA's Technical Services Division, comprising engineers, scientists, artists, and technical artisans who created the spy gadgets and devices described in *Spycraft: The Secret History of the CIA's Spytechs from Communism to al-Qaeda*. Redevelopment is now threatening preservation of these historical structures.

■ 59. TRAINED TO SPY

MAP 11 ➤ **Prince William Forest Park:** Triangle, Virginia

OSS recruits received intensive, secret training outside Washington under the stern command of Garland H. Williams, a no-nonsense Louisianan with military and law enforcement experience. The program was loosely modeled on the training of officers of the British Special Operations, Executive (SOE) and Secret Intelligence Service (SIS). Williams trained recruits at two New

This OSS mess hall served recruits at Prince William Forest Park, Triangle, Virginia, where training areas "Alpha" and "Charley" had been located.

The infirmary is one of the few remaining OSS buildings at Training Area A in Prince William Forest Park.

Deal–era federal recreation areas: Chopawamsic Recreation Area (today called Prince William Forest Park) in Triangle, Virginia, and Catoctin Mountain Park, near Thurmont, Maryland. Each included some 9,000 forested acres and fit Garland's requirements for isolation, as well as proximity to Washington.

Training for OSS recruits included proficiency in small arms.

The first classes began in April 1942 at Catoctin (Training Area B), with advanced training starting a few weeks later at Prince William Forest Park's western sector (Training Area A). By all accounts, the training was rigorous and sometimes harrowing. One young recruit, William Casey, who later became Director of Central Intelligence, inadvertently triggered a trip wire during a maneuver. The subsequent explosion sent debris flying in all directions, breaking the future DCI's jaw.

Following the war, the newly established CIA unsuccessfully attempted to obtain the Prince William Forest Park facility as its permanent training site. Some of the structures used by the OSS recruits, including the infirmary, still stand. Part of the Catoctin Mountain Park, it later became notable as a presidential retreat named Camp David by President Eisenhower in honor of his grandson.

60. GOLF MAKES WAY FOR ESPIONAGE

MAP 12 ➤ Congressional Country Club: 8500 River Road, Bethesda, Maryland

The Congressional Country Club was leased to the government during World War II for an OSS training site.

The OSS version of the Fairbairn-Sykes fighting knife incorporated a spatula-appearing sheath manufactured by an American housewares company.

When Herbert Hoover, then the secretary of commerce, helped lay the cornerstone to a new country club building in 1923, he could not have imagined that twenty years later the private Congressional Country Club would become a training camp for the OSS. The spacious Mediterranean-style clubhouse and golf course where presidents, cabinet members, and military officers played the same 18 holes that hosted US Open

Country Club Knife Fighting

The Congressional Country Club hosted notable guests during its OSS days. One of those was William Ewart Fairbairn. A former Shanghai police officer, Fairbairn was also a hand-to-hand combat expert and cocreator of the Fairbairn-Sykes stiletto for England's commandos. The OSS commissioned its own version of the deadly knife from the housewares company Landers, Frary & Clark, based in New Britain, Connecticut. The knife, 11.25 inches long and weighing just seven ounces, fit into a scabbard stamped from an existing mold for the Ekco Kitchen Utensils pancake flipper.

Fairbairn also designed the Smatchet, a broad-bladed weapon with a matte finish that was issued to both the OSS and British Special Operations, Executive (SOE). The OSS described it as a cross between a machete and a bolo. Edged-weapons experts have likened the heavy knife to a design used in World War I.

"In close-quarters fighting there is no more deadly weapon than the knife," Fairbairn wrote in his 1942 manual *Get Tough! How to Win in Hand-to-Hand Fighting*. "An entirely unarmed man has no certain defense against it, and, further, merely the sudden flashing of a knife is frequently enough to strike fear into your opponent, causing him to lose confidence and surrender."

Target Practice in the Oval Office

Presidents have traditionally worked closely with the nation's intelligence chiefs. One of the stranger meetings between president and spymaster took place during World War II. While President Roosevelt was dictating a letter, OSS chief William Donovan walked unobserved into the Oval Office, casually placed a small sandbag in one corner of the room, drew a pistol from his shoulder holster, and fired ten nearly silent shots into the sandbag. The weapon, a High Standard HDM .22-caliber semiautomatic pistol equipped with an integral sound suppressor, was later adopted by the OSS.

The episode, described by OSS engineer Stanley Lovell in *Of Spies and Stratagems*, recounted that the president, engrossed in dictation, heard nothing. When Donovan presented him with the gun, its muzzle still hot, FDR reportedly said, "Wild Bill, you're the only . . . Republican I'll ever allow in my office with a weapon like this!"

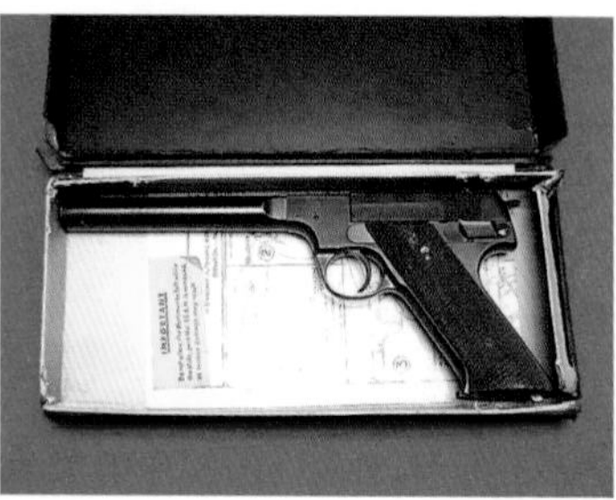

An OSS .22 caliber High Standard HDM semiautomatic pistol equipped with an integral sound suppressor.

championships was leased by the government during World War II and code-named AREA F. More than 2,500 recruits for OSS operational groups were trucked in under cover of night from 1943 through 1945 to AREA F for rigorous spy training. They lived in tents on the club's grounds and prepared for missions behind enemy lines with live ammunition and grenades. The golfers' practice range was converted to a rifle range. Greens and outbuildings became targets for mortar practice. So rigorous was the training, in comparison to the expectations of some, that one recruit dubbed it

Scientists in the Clubhouse Basement

The Office of Scientific Research and Development (OSRD) was a sprawling wartime organization. Under the leadership of the brilliant Vannevar Bush, the OSRD worked on everything from the Manhattan Project and radar to missiles and medicine. Buried deep in the organizational chart was Division 19, charged with creating the tools of sabotage for the OSS. Headed by H. M. Chadwell and his assistant, Dr. W. C. Lothrop, the unit worked in a lab located in the lower level of the Congressional Country Club's clubhouse. While OSS recruits endured harsh training on the club's grounds, the clubhouse scientists created special weapons and devices, ranging from timed explosives to firearm suppressors (silencers).

"Malice in Wonderland." Following the war, the government returned the club's 400 acres to pristine condition, a process that required replacing some very large divots.

61. CLOSING ACT FOR THE OSS

MAP 4 ➤ **Rock Creek Park Skating Rink:** area near present-day John F. Kennedy Center for the Performing Arts

Columnists and Washington wits enjoyed quipping about the OSS as a bastion of America's elite, where notable names such as Vanderbilt, Astor, Morgan, and Mellon were employed alongside Wall Street bankers and lawyers. Columnists Drew Pearson and Austine Cassini joked that the organization's abbreviation stood for "Oh, So Social." In her *Washington Times-Herald* society column "These Charming People," Cassini humorously derided the OSS recruits: "If you should by chance wander in the labyrinth of the OSS you'd behold ex–polo players, millionaires, Russian princes, society gambol boys, scientists and dilettante detectives . . . and the girls! The prettiest, best-born, snappiest girls who used to graduate from debutantedom to boredom now bend their blonde and brunette locks, or their colorful hats, over work in the OSS."

However, there was pragmatism behind the organization's blue-blooded personnel roster. At a time when international travel was largely limited to the well-to-do, the "upper crust" became a valuable source of firsthand knowledge of the European landscape, trusted commercial contacts, and foreign-language skills.

What columnists also missed was that Donovan's clandestine army was actually recruited from all strata of society. Recent immigrants and first-generation Americans, Hollywood actors, athletes, chefs, mechanics, bartenders, and bohemian artists all became part of the service. John Weitz, later a renowned fashion designer, was a German immigrant recruited into the OSS while in his early twenties. Others included the actor and author Sterling Hayden, professional wrestler Joseph "Jumping Joe" Savoldi, and Rene Dussaq, a Hollywood stuntman known as "the Human Fly." Dussaq returned to movies after the war, suitably appearing in the 1946 film *O.S.S.* as a French artillery officer. True to his espionage background, he is uncredited in the role.

On September 28, 1945, two days before official termination, OSS members gathered at the Rock Creek Park Drive Skating Rink, located near the current site of the Kennedy Center. "We have come to the end of an unusual experiment," Donovan said, addressing the assembled crowd. "This experiment was to determine whether a group of Americans constituting a cross-section of racial origins, of abilities, temperaments and talents, could risk an encounter with the long-established and well-trained enemy organizations. How well that experiment has succeeded is measured by your accomplishments and by the recognition of your achievements."

62. THE EMBASSY BURGLARS

MAP 3 ➤ Old Spanish embassy: 2801 16th Street NW (now a Spanish arts and culture gallery)

In a comedy of errors, an OSS surreptitious-entry operation attempting to steal codes from Spain's wartime embassy on 16th Street NW was thwarted by the FBI.

As World War II progressed, intelligence regarding Spain's plans and intentions became increasingly important to the United States and Great Britain. If Spain allowed Hitler to use Spanish Morocco as a staging area, the Allies' OPERATION TORCH strategy for the invasion of North Africa would be threatened. Breaking the Spanish military and diplomatic codes could provide critical intelligence, but the codes changed frequently.

The task to steal operational codes fell to Donald Downes, an OSS officer. Surprisingly, breaking into Spain's embassy, then located at 2801 16th Street NW, proved easy enough. Three successful covert entries were followed by a fourth. It was during the fourth break-in that things took an unexpected turn for the absurd. As the team exited the embassy grounds, they were surrounded by squad cars, sirens wailing. Downes and his men were arrested by the FBI. Efforts to explain just what they were doing at the embassy were ignored. Taken to the local jail, Downes called his boss, William Donovan. Donovan's reaction after the men were freed, as described by Curt Gentry in *J. Edgar Hoover: The Man and the Secrets*, was to protest directly to President Roosevelt that "the Abwehr [German military intelligence] gets better treatment from the FBI than we do."

As it turned out, the OSS had inadvertently intruded onto the FBI's clandestine turf. The bureau had already infiltrated the Spanish embassy. Nevertheless, the incident enraged Donovan. "When the FBI infiltrated us and pulled that stunt at the Spanish embassy, I thought that's a game two can play," Donovan later said. "I've had our men inside the Bureau for months."

Ralph Bunche

This Jackson Street NE residence was home to Ralph Bunche for much of his time in Washington.

63. NOBEL LAUREATE, DIPLOMAT, SPY

MAP 1 ➤ **Ralph Bunche residence: 1510 Jackson Street NE (private residence)**

Ralph Bunche is best known as a diplomat, Nobel laureate, and scholar. Less well known is that the African American political scientist began his career in government service with the Coordinator of Information (COI). Born in poverty, Bunche lost both his parents while still a child but excelled in academics. Entering the University of California at Los Angeles on an athletic scholarship that paid only tuition, he supported himself working as a janitor and installing carpeting, eventually earning a master's degree at Harvard. Following his distinguished academic achievements, Bunche taught political science at Howard University and served on President Roosevelt's Federal Council of Negro Affairs (known informally as the "Black Cabinet"), advising the president on minority affairs during the Great Depression.

With America's entrance into World War II, Bunche was an early recruit as an analyst into the COI and then the OSS in 1941. Three years later, he transferred to the State Department, becoming its first African American desk officer. He later served as undersecretary-general of the United Nations (UN) and then received the Nobel Peace Prize in 1950. Active in the civil rights movement, Bunche participated in the March on Washington in 1963. He retired from public service in 1971 and died that year at the age of 68.

Although Bunche lived at several addresses in the Washington area, his residence at 1510 Jackson Street NE is the best known. The home was designed by Hilyard Robinson, a fellow Howard University professor and modernist architect.

64. P.O. BOX 1142

MAP 8 ➤ **Fort Hunt Park:** George Washington Memorial Parkway, Fairfax County, Virginia

The idyllic 150 acres of Fort Hunt Park along the Potomac once served as a strategic artillery emplacement guarding the river approach to Washington. The scenic waterfront expanse of land, originally a portion of George Washington's Mount Vernon estate, was part of the National Park Service before the War Department appropriated the site in 1939. Situated less than 20 miles from downtown Washington, the park became a listening post for the Signal Intelligence Service (SIS) to intercept foreign diplomatic radio traffic. Following the US entrance into the war in 1941, the SIS moved to Vint Hill Farms, east of Warrenton, Virginia.

The Fort Hunt site, known only as P.O. Box 1142, was put under the control of the army and navy and operated as Military Intelligence Service-Y (MIS-Y) and Military Intelligence Service-X (MIS-X). Under the MIS-Y program, nearly 4,000 German POWs captured in Europe were secretly flown to the United States and ferried to the location in blacked-out buses under tight security.

Among those Germans who passed through the facility were prominent rocket scientist Werner von Braun and high-ranking intelligence officer Reinhard Gehlen, who had been tasked by the Third Reich to spy on the Russians. While von Braun would eventually play a role in America's space program, Gehlen was returned to Europe to operate a spy network targeting the Soviets for US intelligence and the West German government.

The MIS-X program, also known as the Escape Factory, worked with private contractors to create escape-and-evasion tools for American prisoners of war (POWs). Devices created by MIS-X included crude radios hidden in baseballs and mess kits, compasses and maps concealed in pens, and saws and other cutting tools secreted in smoking pipes. The disguised and concealed devices

The World War II "Escape Factory" at Fort Hunt, just south of Alexandria, Virginia, produced escape-and-evasion devices for American POWs, such as tiny compasses concealed inside penny-sized uniform buttons.

were then shipped to American POWs in European camps in "care packages."

Today a small granite monument at the base of a flagpole in the park commemorates the site of P.O. Box 1142.

65. HARVESTING THE AIRWAVES

MAP 11 ➤ Vint Hill: 4263 Aiken Drive, Warrenton, Virginia

Located approximately 50 miles outside Washington in Virginia's pastoral horse country, the Vint Hill Farms Station was once a top secret government cryptographic school and signals-intercept site. Its large antenna arrays collected radio signals for analysis and decryption. From the beginning of World War II until decommissioning and sale in the 1990s, activities of the Vint Hill installation remained closely guarded secrets. Today Vint Hill is a mixed residential and business community where the town square's Covert Café offers a nod to its espionage past.

Vint Hill Farms Station, once a top secret signals-intercept facility, has only a few of its original structures remaining.

The Vint Hill Covert Café recalls the community's clandestine history.

American-born Amy Elizabeth Thorpe, the wife of a British diplomat, used her sexual wiles to acquire intelligence for the British and American intelligence services.

66. FOR LOVE AND WAR

MAP 5 ➤ Amy Elizabeth Thorpe residence: 3327 O Street NW (private residence)

Amy Elizabeth Thorpe was a Washington debutante with an adventurous streak. While still a teenager, she married Arthur Pack, a British diplomat nearly twice her age. Following a series of diplomatic postings around the world that gave her a taste for espionage, she was recruited by William Stephenson as an operative for the BSC in the United States. Thorpe made no apologies for using sex as a tool of her

The Vichy French embassy, now the embassy of the Republic of Macedonia, was a priority intelligence target for the United States during World War II.

A Georgetown home on O Street NW served as the address for some of Amy Thorpe's seductions.

official duties. "Life is but a stage on which to play," she wrote in her diary. "One's role is to pretend, and always to hide one's true feelings."

Under journalistic cover, Thorpe (code name CYNTHIA) first lived in a house at 3327 O Street NW in Georgetown, then moved to the ***Wardman Park Hotel (now the Marriott Wardman Park Hotel), 2600 Woodley Road NW***. From the Wardman Park, she launched her honey-trap operations against German, Italian, and Vichy French diplomats.

Who Was "the Georgia Cracker"?

Colorful tales of embassy break-ins during World War II by the OSS and BSC are often accompanied by a cryptic reference to "the Georgia Cracker." Amy Elizabeth Thorpe, the American-born British spy, relied on the mysterious safecracker to assist her in clandestine operations. Reference to someone fitting the description was also made by OSS officer and writer Donald Downes.

In his book *The Scarlet Thread*, Downes detailed the recruitment of a convicted safecracker in New York City named G. B. Cohen. "I told him I was from the government, that for the war effort it was necessary to open a certain safe in Washington," Downes wrote. "Would he do it and how much did he want to be paid?"

According to Downes, the answer was unequivocal, which he wrote in colorful phonetic style. "Paid!" he screamed. "Paid. You've come into my place to insult me. Don't I have two nephews in the army? Ain't I an American as much as you? Aren't you ashamed? Pay me? You can't even tank me. Even a ticket to Vashington you can't buy me, or a Coca-Cola."

Was G. B. Cohen, the patriotic felon who refused payment for his espionage efforts, the Georgia Cracker and Thorpe accomplice? Maybe. After 1945, like most OSS recruits, the Georgia Cracker returned to civilian life, blending into the postwar society, and leaving little trace of his clandestine activities.

Perhaps her most valuable operation came after she began working for the OSS, which maintained a close relationship with the BSC. Thorpe enticed Vichy press attaché Charles Brousse into an affair and gained access to the code room of the ***Vichy French embassy, 2129 Wyoming Avenue NW*** (now the embassy of the Republic of Macedonia). Playing the roles of clandestine lovers, with Thorpe clad only in high heels and a necklace to throw off a suspicious guard, the pair let in an OSS safecracker known as "the Georgia Cracker," who opened the safe, transported code books for photographing, and then returned them to the safe, leaving no trace of the entry. "It would be difficult to over-emphasize the importance of her work," noted William Stephenson in *The Secret History of British Intelligence in the Americas, 1940–1945*. "Not only did she secure *en clair* copies of nearly all the telegrams despatched from and received by the Vichy Embassy, but she was also instrumental in obtaining both the French and Italian naval ciphers."

Following the war, Thorpe married Brousse and settled in France. Her thoughts about her spy work were captured in Mary S. Lovell's book *Cast No Shadow*. Asked if she was ashamed of her methods, Thorpe replied, "Ashamed? Not in the least. My superiors told me that the results of my work saved thousands of British and American lives. . . . Wars are not won by respectable methods."

■ 67. THE CHEF'S SECRETS

MAP 3 ➤ Julia Child residence: Gralyn Hotel, 1745 N Street NW (site under redevelopment)

The Washington residences of former OSS officer and world-famous chef Julia Child included the Gralyn Hotel (currently vacant) on N Street NW.

Julia Child was a spy before she became America's favorite foodie. When World War II erupted, the future acclaimed chef, then Julia McWilliams, sought to join the armed services but was turned away because she was too tall. However, the OSS welcomed the smart, energetic, six-foot-two Californian. McWilliams moved to Washington, became a researcher in the Secret Intelligence (SI) division reporting directly to OSS chief William Donovan, and lived in the ***Brighton Hotel, 2123 California Street NW***. She was later posted to Ceylon (today Sri Lanka) and then China. In 1946, she married an OSS officer, Paul Cushing Child, and the couple lived in Georgetown at ***2706 Olive Street NW***, then in an apartment at the Gralyn Hotel, 1745 N Street NW. Child returned to Washington in

Julia Child's Bathtub Brew

Julia Child's first recipe never was adopted by Le Cordon Bleu. During her time in the OSS, she experimented with a shark repellent for the US Navy. The first batches, which were mixed in a bathtub, included a recipe of black dye and copper acetate in water-soluble wax. Called "Shark Chaser," the mixture was issued to sailors and pilots in 1944. Its efficacy, although questionable, represented a pioneering effort into antishark research.

2001, at least in spirit, when she donated the kitchen from her Cambridge, Massachusetts, home (the set for her cooking show in the 1990s) to the Smithsonian Institution's National Museum of American History.

Inga Arvad's stylish apartment on 16th Street NW was bugged by the FBI in an investigation to determine if she was a German spy.

■ 68. REPORTER, LOVER, AND SPY RUMORS

MAP 3 ➤ **Inga Arvad residence: 1600 16th Street NW (private residence)**

Danish beauty queen and journalist Inga Arvad attracted famous and dubious company. She met with Nazi leaders in the 1930s, interviewed Hitler twice or more. In one profile she wrote, "You immediately like him. He seems lonely. The eyes, showing a kind heart, stare right at you. They sparkle with force." The Führer invited Arvad to accompany him to the 1936 Summer Olympics in Berlin, and she was a guest at Hermann Göring's wedding.

In Washington, Arvad worked at *The Washington Times-Herald*, then located at 1307 H Street NW, writing about Washington society figures. By 1941, she was having an affair with a young ensign assigned to the Office of Naval Intelligence, John F. Kennedy. The FBI suspected she was a German spy, so her apartment at 1600 16th Street NW was bugged and her telephone calls were monitored.

Kennedy was transferred out of Washington to avoid scandal, but Arvad continued to see him for weekend trysts at his new post in Charleston, South Carolina. Despite some talk of marriage, the romance eventually fizzled. As it turned out, she was also carrying on romantic liaisons with a former Danish flame, as well as with financier and presidential adviser Bernard Baruch. The FBI found no hard evidence of spying, but, by the summer of 1942, with rumors of espionage swirling around her, Arvad moved to California and eventually married cowboy actor Tim McCoy. She died in 1973.

69. ESPIONAGE MERRY-GO-ROUND

MAP 5 ➤ **Drew Pearson residence:** 2820 Dumbarton Street NW (private residence)

Drew Pearson, whose column appeared in more than 600 newspapers, lived and worked at this Dumbarton Street home.

Andrew Russell "Drew" Pearson, who lived at 2820 Dumbarton Street NW, was once one of Washington's most feared and revered journalists. Fired from his job at *The Baltimore Sun* for anonymously coauthoring a muckraking book, *The Washington Merry-Go-Round* (1931), with Robert S. Allen, Pearson launched a syndicated column by the same name. At its height, the column ran in more than 600 newspapers across the country, giving Pearson the power to make and break political careers. The staunch New Dealer was not, however, above criticizing the Roosevelt administration. He also regularly replayed material provided by the BSC and its head, William Stephenson. Pearson once called the OSS "one of the fanciest groups of dilettante diplomats, Wall Street bankers, and amateur detectives ever seen in Washington." However, the journalist himself became a target for espionage through his assistant, David Karr, a onetime reporter for the communist newspaper the *Daily Worker*. Karr had been recruited by Soviet intelligence and regularly fed his handlers information that Pearson gathered from his government sources.

70. A SPY IN SEARCH OF A COUNTRY

MAP 12 ➤ **Maurice Halperin residence: 9956 Georgia Avenue, Silver Spring, Maryland** (private residence)

Former Soviet spy Maurice Halperin, who lived in this apartment building in Silver Spring, Maryland, eventually concluded that communism was more appealing in theory than practice.

Maurice Halperin lived much of his life as a disillusioned exile. An early recruit to the OSS, he headed the organization's Latin American division while secretly spying for Soviet intelligence. Code-named ZAYATZ (HARE), he relayed information to Elizabeth Bentley's spy network.

Residing at 9956 Georgia Avenue, Silver Spring, Maryland, the scholarly Halperin was committed to the communist ideology. Following the war, he took a position in the State Department. Named by Bentley in her debriefings with the FBI, he fell under scrutiny, left government for a teaching position at Boston University, and eventually fled the country in 1954 as the authorities began closing in. Halperin first lived in Mexico, then moved to the Soviet Union in 1958. Within four years, he had become disenchanted with the Soviet regime and relocated to Cuba in 1962. There he found life under Castro also unappealing. In 1967, Halperin moved to Vancouver, Canada, where he became an outspoken critic of socialism. He died in 1995.

After World War II, Alexandria's Torpedo Factory was converted to a storage facility for government documents and German intelligence records. Today it is an arts center.

71. THE TORPEDO FACTORY

MAP 8 ➤ 105 North Union Street, Alexandria, Virginia

Built just after World War I, the US Naval Torpedo Station in Alexandria, Virginia, hummed with round-the-clock activity during World War II. The factory's submarine-borne Mark XIV torpedo and the aircraft-deployed Mark XIII were vital to the war effort. After 1945, the three-story plant was decommissioned and became a government repository for the Smithsonian Institution and congressional papers, along with German documents captured at the end of the war. Although the German material was neglected for years, intelligence historians eventually discovered new incriminating evidence against Third Reich officers such as Adolf Eichmann, who had previously minimized their role in intelligence operations or war crimes.

After its purchase by the city of Alexandria in 1969, the complex was renovated for commercial use. Today, the Torpedo Factory Art Center is a world-class arts hub, featuring studios and galleries, along with instructional and special events facilities.

72. DECODING CRYPTOGRAPHIC HISTORY

MAP 9 ➤ **Arlington Hall:** 4000 Arlington Boulevard (Route 50 and South Glebe Road, Arlington, Virginia)

By 1942, the US Army's Signal Intelligence Service (SIS)—a predecessor to the National Security Agency—had outgrown its quarters in the Munitions

After breaking Japan's wartime PURPLE code, the SIS created a machine to automate the deciphering process.

During World War II, the Signal Intelligence Service (SIS) was headquartered at the former Arlington Hall Junior College for Women in Arlington, Virginia.

Building on the Washington Mall near the Lincoln Memorial. There cryptographers proved their strategic value by cracking the Japanese army's code under a project code-named PURPLE and produced an intelligence product known as MAGIC.

Following Pearl Harbor, and in need of room for its expanding staff, the SIS identified Arlington Hall Junior College for Women in Arlington, Virginia, as the ideal location. Just off Route 50, Arlington Hall was only four miles from Washington, with a 100-acre campus that offered both security and the potential to expand with temporary buildings. In June 1942, the War Department took possession of the school, paying $650,000 for the property.

Barracks and other assorted buildings were rapidly constructed to accommodate an eventual 10,000-person wartime workforce of which only 10 percent was uniformed military. The majority were young women with an aptitude for math, who slept in dormitories "on campus." At Arlington Hall, code breakers continued to decrypt the Japanese messages and reverse-engineered the Japanese cipher machine called 97-shiki O-bun Injiki (Alphabetical Typewriter-97).

A parallel effort in 1943 targeted, examined, and exploited Soviet codes under a project code-named BRIDE, which later became known as VENONA. Fearing Stalin would negotiate a separate peace with Hitler, breaking the Soviet codes was given high priority. A breakthrough came when a female code breaker and former schoolteacher named Gene Grabeel began sorting through the coded messages and identified five different cryptographic systems. Another occurred when the Soviet intelligence apparatus mistakenly published duplicate sets of onetime pads used to encipher and decipher messages. The pads' numbers, which were no longer random, could be analyzed for patterns and were exploited by linguist and cryptologist Meredith Gardner.

With the end of World War II, the original purpose of breaking Soviet codes vanished, but what they revealed was no less significant or troubling.

Before and throughout the war, the Soviets were waging an aggressive espionage offensive against the United States. The decryptions yielded counterintelligence gold, identifying and verifying some of the most damaging spies in US history, including Whittaker Chambers, Alger Hiss, and Julius and Ethel Rosenberg. So secret were the VENONA decryptions that the program's existence was withheld from the public for decades.

Arlington Hall continued to host a variety of military and intelligence components until 1993. It has since been home for the State Department's Foreign Service Institute, with its historic buildings and grounds again housing an educational institution.

■ 73. THEY LEFT NO TRACE BEHIND

MAP 2 ➤ **Saboteurs' trial site:** Robert F. Kennedy Department of Justice Building, 950 Pennsylvania Avenue NW

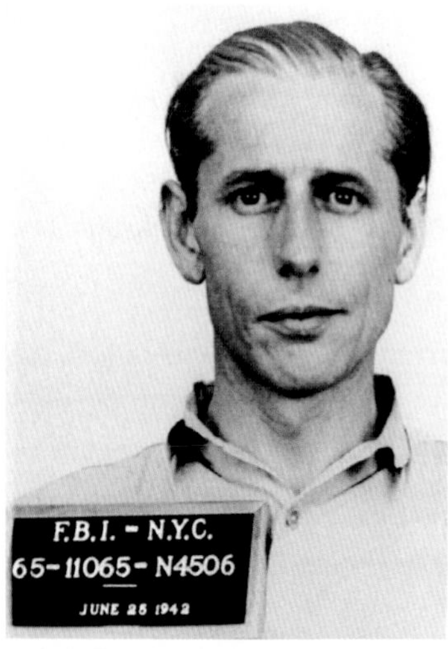

German saboteur George Dasch

On June 13, 1942, German U-boats infiltrated four men ashore at Amagansett, Long Island, New York, while a similar team landed at Ponte Vedra Beach near Jacksonville, Florida. Their mission for German military intelligence, code-named OPERATION PASTORIUS, was to bring mayhem and destruction to the United States by targeting factories and infrastructure critical to the war effort. The operation went awry almost immediately when one of the Long Island saboteurs, George Dasch, surrendered to the FBI. Within two weeks all the saboteurs were arrested.

The eight OPERATION PASTORIUS saboteurs were found guilty during their trial. Six were executed, and two received lengthy prison sentences.

World War II German saboteurs were tried in the fifth-floor Assembly Room 1 in what is now the Robert F. Kennedy Department of Justice Building.

Once in custody, all eight were tried before a military court in Assembly Room 1, on the fifth floor of what is now the Robert F. Kennedy Building, the main building of the ***Department of Justice, between 9th and 10th Streets and Pennsylvania and Constitution Avenues NW***. Found guilty, six were executed on August 8, 1942, at the District of Columbia Jail, 200 19th Street SE (torn down in 1978).

Unmarked graves for the saboteurs at the Blue Plains Potters Field cemetery in the Anacostia section of Washington were surrounded by a high wire fence dividing their graves from those of paupers. No names were placed on the wooden stakes marking the grave sites. Only numbers designated the dead: 276, Richard Quirimc; 277, Heinrich Harm Heink; 278, Herbert Hans Haupt; 279, Edward John Karling; 280, Hermann Otto Neubauer; and 281, Werner Thiel. The markers have since vanished, and the Blue Plains Cemetery, near the present-day Blue Plains Advanced Wastewater Treatment Plant, was closed in 1967.

Two saboteurs were not executed. Dasch and Ernest Burger received long prison sentences but were released in 1948 and deported to the American occupation zone of Germany. Burger died in 1975, Dasch in 1992.

■ 74. WASHINGTON'S "SECOND-BEST ADDRESS"

MAP 2 ➤ **Mayflower Hotel:** 1127 Connecticut Avenue NW

The elegant Mayflower Hotel has been a frequent site of intelligence operations during its prestigious history.

Most Washingtonians simply call it "the Mayflower." There FDR practiced his first inaugural speech with the historic phrase "the only thing we have to fear is fear itself." President Harry Truman is said to have called the 1925 structure "the second-best address" in Washington.

However, the luxury hotel retains an espionage as well as political history. German saboteur George Dasch briefly stayed in room 351 at the Mayflower in 1942 before surrendering to the FBI and disclosing the sabotage plans of Germany's OPERATION PASTORIUS.

The Mayflower's lobby became a demonstration site in the mid-1960s for an act of tradecraft called a "brush pass." Two CIA observers watched as a pair of agency officers made a rapid, virtually undetectable handoff of documents near a phone bank. Pleased with what they saw (or didn't see), the observers approved the advanced brush pass technique for use in denied area operations behind the Iron Curtain.

In the spring of 1985, CIA officer Aldrich Ames, using the cover name Rick Wells, was scheduled to meet with an officer of the Soviet intelligence service

Komitet Gosudarstvennoy Bezopasnosti (KGB), Sergey Chuvakhin, in the Mayflower's Town and Country Lounge (closed in 2011). When the Soviet intelligence officer failed to appear, Ames downed more drinks, left the bar, and walked a few blocks to the Soviet embassy to volunteer as a spy.

More recently, in October 2009, Stewart Nozette, who had been employed by the Department of Energy and the National Aeronautics and Space Administration (NASA), was arrested in a suite at the Mayflower during an FBI sting operation in which the scientist believed he was selling secrets to Mossad, the Israeli intelligence service.

Lauchlin Currie

While serving as economic adviser to President Roosevelt and spying for the Soviets, Currie lived in this townhouse on P Street NW.

75. STALIN'S MAN IN THE WHITE HOUSE

MAP 5 ➤ Lauchlin Currie residence: 3132 P Street NW (private residence)

Canadian born, Harvard-educated economist Lauchlin Currie became a US citizen in 1934. Sometime before joining President Roosevelt's White House economic team in 1939, he began working with Soviet intelligence. Among the most damaging secrets he provided Stalin's regime were diplomatic strategies in negotiating a postwar Europe and progress on the top secret VENONA code-breaking project.

Currie, who lived at 3132 P Street NW in Georgetown, left the White House in 1945 following FDR's death and eventually headed up World Bank programs in Colombia. When interviewed by the FBI in 1947, he denied working for the Soviets, though did offer that he knew some spies. A year later, Elizabeth Bentley, a Soviet spy turned government witness, testified that Currie was a Soviet agent. Currie was still working in Colombia in 1954 when the United States refused to renew his passport. He remained there as an adviser to that government, eventually becoming a Colombian citizen. Despite the evidence, Currie denied his role as a Soviet spy until his death in late 1993 at the age of 91. Declassified VENONA intercepts later confirmed his espionage role and revealed his code names as PAGE and VIM.

76. THE SPY WHO GOT AWAY

MAP 7 ➤ Nathan Silvermaster residence: 5515 30th Street NW (private residence)

Nathan Silvermaster conducted espionage from his home during the 1930s and 1940s.

Nathan Gregory Silvermaster (code names PAL and ROBERT) might have forever remained a footnote in history were it not for the covert communications intercept operation code-named VENONA and subsequent release of those decrypted messages nearly half a century later. When Soviet agent turned informer Elizabeth Bentley accused Silvermaster of espionage in 1945, she could offer little evidence to substantiate her claim that the federal government was penetrated by extensive Soviet espionage networks. The conspiracies she described to the FBI not only included stealing secrets, but also aiding careers to push spies into ever-higher government positions.

Silvermaster held a number of high-ranking positions in the government as an economist, including posts in the Department of Agriculture and the Department

Spy Soap Opera

At times, Soviet spy rings in the United States took on all the elements of a soap opera or reality television show. Rivalries, complaints, and gossip freely circulated. Harry Dexter White (code name LAWYER) was accused of "putting on airs," while Silvermaster was labeled a "petty tyrant." Bed-hopping was also common. Elizabeth Bentley (code names UMNITSA, or "CLEVER GIRL") was sleeping with her Soviet handler, Jacob Golos, when he dramatically died of a heart attack in her New York apartment on November 27, 1943. Helen Silvermaster (code name DORA), with consent of her husband, Nathan, began a long-term affair with William Ludwig Ullmann (code names POLO and PILOT). Living in the Silvermaster home, Ullman was a Treasury Department economist and the document photographer for the spy ring.

"Surely these unhealthy relations between them cannot help but influence their behavior and work with us negatively," their shocked Soviet handler complained to Moscow. Surprisingly, the Ullmann and Silvermaster trio outlived the spy ring. The three moved to New Jersey where they became successful seaside real estate developers.

of the Treasury. Living at 5515 30th Street NW, Silvermaster, according to Bentley, oversaw a spy ring that supposedly penetrated the White House and the OSS.

With his covert cohorts, Silvermaster appeared before the House Un-American Activities Committee to vehemently deny the charges. Since the government could offer no hard evidence of espionage without revealing the top secret VENONA program, the ring escaped justice. After leaving US government service, Silvermaster founded a successful New Jersey real estate development company. He died in 1964 at age 65 in Loveladies, Long Beach Island, New Jersey.

Victor Perlo, who ran a Soviet spy ring that infiltrated both the OSS and the State Department during World War II, lived in an unassuming suburban home.

77. SOVIET RAIDER

MAP 7 ➤ **Victor Perlo residence:** 4517 Brandywine Street NW (private residence)

A Washington-based Soviet-directed spy ring known as the Perlo Group operated in parallel to the Silvermaster spy ring during World War II. Headed by Victor Perlo, an economist in the War Production Board who lived at 4517 Brandywine Street NW, the network of spies infiltrated the OSS and the State Department. Perlo's network was said to have been assembled in late 1941 or early 1942 by Jacob Golos (aka Yakov Naumovich Reizen), a Soviet intelligence officer, with help from his American assistant and lover, Elizabeth Bentley.

After Golos's death in 1943, Bentley volunteered to become a confidential informant for the FBI and identified Perlo as a spy in 1945. Repeatedly called before congressional committees, Perlo offered contentious, but not incriminating, testimony. "The dragging of my name through the mud is part of a big Roman circus," he said at one point while denying any espionage activities. Similar to the case of the Silvermaster group, concrete proof of Perlo's culpability did not emerge until the release of the VENONA decryptions in the 1990s, which identified him by the code name RAIDER.

Perlo worked briefly on the failed 1948 presidential campaign of Henry Wallace, then faded from view. As an economist of the Communist Party USA and member of its board, he wrote several books, lectured, and taught. He died in 1999.

78. THE ALL-AMERICAN GIRL TRAITOR

MAP 5 ➤ **Georgetown Pharmacy:** 1344 Wisconsin Avenue NW (now a 7-Eleven)

Elizabeth Bentley seemed like an all-American girl. After graduating from Vassar College in 1930, she attended graduate school at Columbia University, went to Europe on a fellowship, and in Italy became enamored of radical politics. Fascism first caught Bentley's fancy before she took a liking to communism after returning to the United States.

After volunteering to spy on fascists in New York City, Bentley came to the attention of Soviet intelligence officer Jacob Golos, code name ZVUK (SOUND). Golos was an agent for the NKVD (organizational forerunner to the KGB) who ran spy networks that penetrated deep into the Roosevelt administration. He also played a supporting role in the assassination of Leon Trotsky in Mexico City in 1940. Recruited and later romanced by the older man, Bentley was assigned the code name UMNITSA (CLEVER GIRL).

Elizabeth Bentley

Elizabeth Bentley wore a flower on her hat and carried a copy of *Life* magazine as recognition signals when she met Anatoly Gorsky, head of Soviet espionage in the United States, at the Georgetown Pharmacy.

At first her roles were as a courier and something of a spy "girl Friday." Bentley traveled from New York City to ***Washington's Union Station, 50 Massachusetts Avenue NE***, every two weeks to meet with agents and collect classified materials, including undeveloped rolls of film from Nathan Silvermaster obtained through a network of Soviet spies in Washington.

Bentley often dined at ***Silvermaster's home, 5515 30th Street NW***, or met him in Georgetown's ***Martin's Tavern, 1264 Wisconsin Avenue NW***. A Washington landmark, Martin's Tavern is where a young congressman, John F. Kennedy, proposed marriage in 1953 to the "Inquiring Camera Girl" of *The Washington Times-Herald*, Jacqueline Lee Bouvier.

At the Georgetown Pharmacy, then located at 1344 Wisconsin Avenue NW, Bentley met Anatoly Gorsky (alias Gromov), chief of NKVD operations in the United States, who operated under the cover of first secretary in the Soviet embassy. She described Gorsky, who was flabby beneath his expensive clothing, as conveying a persona that sent "shivers running up and down your spine."

When Golos died in 1943 in Bentley's New York City apartment, Moscow grew alarmed. Golos had run his networks with alarmingly lax security. Members knew each other, even socialized together. A single arrest or loss of nerve by one jeopardized the entire operation. As a result, Bentley found herself engaged in a battle for control with a new handler, Itzhak Akhmerov (code names MER and ALBERT), and Moscow headquarters. Because she was not a Soviet citizen, she could not be as easily controlled.

Faced with increasing pressure, Bentley began drinking heavily and acting erratically. In fear of arrest and her Soviet superiors, she contacted the FBI in November 1945 and exposed more than 100 Soviet agents and communists, dozens of whom were employed in federal agencies.

Bentley briefly worked as a double agent for the FBI under the code name GREGORY until exposed by a press leak. She subsequently appeared before the House Un-American Activities Committee in 1948 but could offer little evidence to back up her sensational accusations. The press dubbed Bentley the "Red Spy Queen" in describing her underground life, which included shopping for Christmas gifts ranging from liquor to lingerie for members of the spy ring.

Bentley testified before Congress multiple times and made numerous high-profile court appearances. After writing a memoir, *Out of Bondage*, she managed to scratch out a living by teaching and giving lectures on the evils of communism. When Bentley died in 1963 from cancer, the brief obituaries that appeared relegated her to a Cold War footnote.

Elizabeth Bentley and other spies conducted clandestine business at the landmark Martin's Tavern in Georgetown.

79. COCKTAILS FOR SPIES

MAP 5 ➤ Martin's Tavern: 1264 Wisconsin Avenue NW

Martin's Tavern, a historic Georgetown bar and restaurant, boasts a colorful espionage history. Favored by spies Elizabeth Bentley and Nathan Silvermaster in the 1940s and rumored to still attract 21st century intelligence officers, Martin's has acknowledged its secretive history by offering a signature Spytini cocktail:

- 3 ounces vodka (Martin's uses Stolichnaya)
- 1 splash scotch (Martin's uses 25-year-old Macallan)
- 1 teaspoon fresh lemon juice
- 1/2 teaspoon buckwheat honey
- 1 dash bitters

Put a glass in the freezer. Fill a shaker with ice. Add to it bitters, lemon juice, honey, and vodka. Shake vigorously. Take the glass from the freezer, put in the scotch, and swirl. Strain the shaker's contents into the frosted glass, garnish with a lemon twist, and serve immediately. (Courtesy of Billy Martin Jr., owner of Martin's Tavern.)

Vespers

Ian Fleming introduced the Vesper Martini through James Bond in his 1953 book *Casino Royale*. Named after the beautiful MI6 agent Vesper Lynd, it is also the first instance in which Bond's martini is shaken, not stirred.

The origins of the Vesper—Latin for evening but also referencing a sunset prayer service in some churches—supposedly derives from an incident that occurred while Fleming was living in Jamaica. According to his friend Ivar Bryce, Fleming knocked on the door of a mansion near Goldeneye, his own island home. A butler showed the new neighbor in and announced him to the elderly residents of the stately home, a "colonel" and his wife. A short time later, the butler reappeared with cocktails, announcing, "Vespers are served."

The tale may or may not be true, but within the CIA late Friday afternoon informal conversations and cocktails are still affectionately referred to as Vespers. How to make the Vesper:

- Three measures Gordon's gin
- One measure vodka
- Half measure Kina Lillet (substitute Lillet Blonde or Cocchi Americano)

Shake (don't stir) until ice-cold. Serve in a chilled champagne coupe with a large thin slice of lemon peel.

80. INDISCRETIONS OF MR. STRAIGHT

MAP 8 ➤ **Michael Whitney Straight residence:** Green Spring Gardens, 4603 Green Spring Road, Alexandria, Virginia

Michael Whitney Straight was born into an American family of privilege. Mainly raised and educated in England, he unwisely fell in with a group of spies in the 1930s that would become known as the Cambridge spy ring. "In the course of a week I had moved out of the noisy, crowded world of Cambridge into a world of shadows and echoes," Straight later wrote in his autobiography, *After Long Silence*.

Michael Whitney Straight's home in Alexandria, Virginia, reflected his privileged background.

Returning to Washington in 1937, he went to work as a volunteer for the State Department while spying for the Soviets under the code name NIGEL. His first residence was a townhouse, ***1718 H Street NW***, shared with housemates who included columnist Joseph Alsop and the State Department's chief of protocol, George Summerlin. Straight married in 1939 and moved to Prince Street in Alexandria, Virginia.

"[Straight] is a typical American, a man of wide-ranging enterprise, who thinks he can do everything himself."

—Memo from Michael Whitney Straight's handler to Moscow Center

She Married a Communist

Michael Whitney Straight played matchmaker for his sister, Beatrice, by introducing her to Louis Dolivet. A passionate antifascist during the war, Dolivet was a Romanian by birth whose true name was Ludovic Brecher—and an NKVD agent by profession. The couple married in 1942 and divorced in 1949. Straight later claimed he did not know of Dolivet's work for the NKVD, though he did invest $250,000 in a Soviet propaganda publication called *Free World* run by Dolivet. Beatrice Straight, a noted stage actress, appeared in several films, including *Poltergeist*, *The Nun's Story*, and *Endless Love*. She won an Academy Award as best supporting actress for her role in the film *Network*. Dolivet eventually settled in France and became a successful film producer.

For the next few years, he shuttled between positions in Washington and his family's magazine, the *New Republic*, before joining the Army Air Corps and piloting B-17s during World War II. At that point, Straight wrote, he ended his espionage activities. After the war he became publisher of the *New Republic*.

By his own account, along with documents acquired from the KGB archives following the end of the Cold War, he did not prove particularly useful as a spy. However, to his discredit, even following his break from the Soviets, Straight continued to conceal the identities of members of the still-active Cambridge spy ring.

In 1963, following his nomination for chairman of the National Endowment for the Arts, Straight was prompted to approach the FBI and finally confess his espionage activities rather than undergo a security check. It was only then he revealed

Get Out!

Michael Whitney Straight did not betray the two members of the Cambridge spy ring he knew until decades after he abandoned his personal espionage activities. However, he did claim to warn one of its core members, Guy Burgess. According to Straight, a chance meeting with Burgess on the street in Washington in March 1951 led to a threat. In Straight's version of the story, he ordered Burgess out of the British government in a month's time or he would turn him in. The story, which has been contested by Straight critics, may contain a grain of truth. Burgess did leave the country not long after the purported encounter with his former comrade, although more likely on orders from fellow Soviet spy Harold "Kim" Philby.

the identities of Anthony Blunt and Guy Burgess as members of the ring. In 1970, Straight and his wife, Belinda, donated Green Spring Gardens, a park and 18th century manor house, at 4603 Green Spring Road, Alexandria, Virginia, to Fairfax County. In 1983, he made his espionage activities public in his autobiography. Straight died on January 4, 2004, at age 87.

81. SPYING ON WALTER LIPPMANN

MAP 4 ➤ **Mary Price residence:** 2038 I Street NW (private residence)

Through the mid-20th century, Walter Lippmann became one of the most influential power brokers in Washington. As syndicated columnist, author, cofounder of the *New Republic*, adviser to President Wilson, and Pulitzer Prize winner, Lippmann wielded enormous influence at the highest levels of government. Working from his home, first at ***1527 35th Street NW*** (the former residence of Alexander Graham Bell) and then at ***3525 Woodley Road NW***, Lippmann churned out his *New York Herald Tribune* columns and a stream of books. The use of stereotype to denote cliché commonalities and accompanying prejudice is attributed to Lippmann, an amateur philosopher and social scientist. The onetime intelligence analyst supported President Wilson's preparations for the World War I peace conference, became an early proponent of the United States entering World War II, and had close contacts with British intelligence. His brother-in-law was British intelligence officer Ivar Bryce.

Walter Lippmann

Mary Price's modest apartment on I Street NW was used as a safe house for Soviet agents while she worked as Walter Lippmann's assistant.

Lippmann's influence and contacts did not escape the notice of the NKVD. His assistant, Mary Price, code-named DIR and ARENA by the NKVD, was recruited by her sister, Mildred, a communist, prior to working for the famed scribe. Price sent the NKVD reports on Lippmann's contacts along with scraps of intelligence she managed to pick up by searching his office. Price's spy work also included acting as a cutout or intermediary between the Soviet officers and some of their agents in the US government. Her third-floor apartment at 2038 I Street NW functioned as a rendezvous point and safe house for Soviet agents such as Duncan Lee, an assistant to OSS chief William Donovan. Elizabeth Bentley, the New York City–based spy, would also stay at the Price residence during her regular trips to Washington.

Eventually Bentley's testimony before the House Un-American Activities Committee identified Price as a Soviet agent. Never arrested, Price ran unsuccessfully for governor in North Carolina before drifting from a series of liberal causes and jobs that included stints at the Czechoslovakian embassy and the National Council of Churches. She died in California in 1980.

■ 82. THE TRUE BELIEVER'S CRUSADER

MAP 7 ➤ **I. F. Stone residence:** 4420 29th Street NW (private residence)

Journalist I. F. Stone remains a controversial figure to this day. Rumors circulated for decades about his close association with, and possible spying for, the Soviets. His writing, which appeared in some of the nation's largest newspapers and magazines, solidified his reputation in progressive politics despite whispers of disloyalty. In his newsletter *I. F. Stone's Weekly*, written at his home at 4420 29th Street NW, Stone criticized Democratic and Republican politicians with equal vigor.

Not long after Stone's death in 1989, suspicions about him spying for the Soviets were confirmed. The VENONA decryptions, along with

Journalist I. F. Stone, who became disillusioned with communism in his later years, lived in this classic house.

files released following the fall of the Soviet Union, erased any remaining doubt that Stone worked for Soviet intelligence at one point. Code-named BLIN (PANCAKE), he acted as "talent spotter" as well as courier for the Soviets in the 1930s. Just how long that relationship was maintained is in dispute, although it seems unlikely his espionage activities extended beyond the 1950s. Following a disillusioning visit to the Soviet Union in 1956, Stone wrote, "Whatever the consequences, I have to say what I really feel after seeing the Soviet Union and carefully studying the statements of its leading officials. This is not a good society and it is not led by honest men."

83. THE SPY BATTED .243

MAP 3 ➤ **Griffith Stadium (demolished):** between Georgia Avenue, Fifth Street, W Street, and Florida Avenue NW (now site of the Howard University Hospital)

Moe Berg

Born in New York City in 1902, Morris "Moe" Berg studied at Princeton, then Columbia Law School, and, briefly, at the Sorbonne in Paris. Some said he spoke eight languages; others put the number at more than a dozen. After graduating from college in 1923, Berg spent 15 seasons in professional baseball as a shortstop, catcher, and coach, including a stint with the Washington Senators from 1932 to 1934 at ***Griffith Stadium, W Street and Florida Avenue NW.*** The well-traveled Berg also played for the Brooklyn Robins (renamed the Dodgers), the Chicago White Sox, the Cleveland Indians, and a series of minor league teams that included the Toledo Mud Hens. His major-league performance produced a .243 lifetime batting average with six career home runs. In Washington, Berg lived at the ***Wardman Park Hotel, 2660 Woodley Road NW***, and the ***Mayflower Hotel, 1127 Connecticut Avenue NW***.

Exactly when Berg began spying is open to debate, though it may have been as early as 1934. While playing an exhibition series in Japan, he feigned illness during one game, donned traditional Japanese clothing, and went to a hospital roof where he filmed the Tokyo skyline with a Bell & Howell 16mm camera, ostensibly for Movietone News.

In 1943, Berg joined the OSS and worked behind enemy lines assessing partisan forces in Yugoslavia, then infiltrated German-occupied Norway. However, his most noteworthy OSS assignment was attending a lecture by German physicist Werner Heisenberg in Switzerland in late 1944 to assess the state of Germany's nuclear weapons effort. If Berg judged the program near completion, he was to shoot Heisenberg on the spot. The gun stayed in his pocket. Although Berg did not join the CIA when it was formed in 1947, he retained a strong interest in intelligence and was involved briefly with the agency from 1952 to 1954.

Berg maintained a lifelong love of baseball, though it seems he may have been a better spy than ballplayer. "He can speak seven languages, but he can't hit in any of them," one former teammate quipped. Berg took his less-than-stellar performance on the field in stride, reflecting, "Maybe I'm not in the Cooperstown Baseball Hall of Fame like so many of my baseball buddies, but I'm happy I had the chance to play pro ball and am especially proud of my contributions to my country."

OSS security badge belonging to John "Ivar" Bryce.

■ 84. IVAR BRYCE, BUNNY PHILLIPS, AND TRUTH SERUM

MAP 5 ➤ Ivar Bryce residence, Volta Place NW (house number unknown)

John Felix Charles "Ivar" Bryce, classmate of Ian Fleming at Eton College, was a proper English gentleman. His great-grandfather founded W. R. Grace & Co., and he was distantly related to European royalty. The British statesman Lord Mountbatten reportedly quipped about Bryce, "It's terrible the advantages he's had to overcome." Brought into British intelligence by Fleming, Bryce was stationed as early as 1941 in New York producing propaganda for the BSC and then posted to Washington to work with the OSS.

Bryce rented a house on Volta Place NW in Georgetown with his cousin, Col. A. M. "Bunny" Phillips. The pair became a memorable duo. In one incident, Bunny and Ivar received a package from London containing what was proposed to be a truth serum. The encrypted instructions ordered one or the other to take a dose to test its efficacy. Bunny lost a coin toss, and Ivar injected him with the unknown substance. Almost instantly Bunny became violently ill, and Ivar spent an uneasy night standing watch. The next morning his stricken cousin awoke with only a severe headache. Described in Jennet Conant's *The Irregulars* as "tall, dark, and handsome to the point of absurdity," Bryce reputedly had many romantic liaisons, which seemed to obscure his intelligence work.

Following the war, Bryce helped Fleming create James Bond. He is acknowledged in the dedication of *Diamonds Are Forever* as "J. F. C. B." Bryce is also referenced in *Live and Let Die*, as well as *Dr. No*. Bond's CIA contact in multiple books, Felix Leiter, borrows one of Bryce's names, along with one of another friend, Tommy Leiter, the scion of the Marshall Field's department store fortune.

85. THE WRITE STUFF

MAP 5 ➤ Roald Dahl residence: 1610 34th Street NW (private residence)

Before writing the children's classics *Charlie and the Chocolate Factory*, *James and the Giant Peach*, and *Fantastic Mr. Fox*, Roald Dahl was a World War II pilot and, later, a spy. He flew in Greece, Syria, and North Africa, then briefly worked as an entry-level diplomat before joining British intelligence. Posted to the United States as an assistant air attaché in 1942, Dahl reported to senior British intelligence officer William Stephenson and the BSC.

Dahl cut a dashing figure through Washington in his Royal Air Force (RAF) uniform and acquired a reputation for an irreverent sense of humor, a fondness for practical jokes, and an eye for the ladies. He also acted as an agent of influence while hobnobbing with Washington's political elite and writing tales of RAF heroism for magazines such as the *Saturday Evening Post* and *Collier's*. British intelligence reportedly dispatched Dahl to romance conservative congresswoman Clare Boothe Luce and soften her views toward Great Britain. The influential Luce, 13 years Dahl's senior, was married at the time to Henry Luce, the founder of the widely read magazines *Time* and *Life*. Dahl's mission, according to some historians, was a success.

Roald Dahl, pictured here, lived in this house while serving as a British intelligence officer in Washington. He later became a popular children's book author.

Dahl's Washington addresses included the ***Willard Hotel, 1401 Pennsylvania Avenue NW***, and ***1610 34th Street NW***. As a frequent guest of Texas newspaper tycoon and power broker Charles Edward Marsh, who lived at ***2136 R Street NW***, Dahl gained access to politicians, journalists, financiers, and cabinet members. Marsh's opulent home was an ideal showcase for Dahl's natural charm and storytelling talents to shine.

The Ad Man Spy

Legendary British-born Madison Avenue advertising executive David Ogilvy served in the BSC, Sir William Stephenson's World War II spy organization in Washington. At first he moonlighted by providing the British spies polling data from his employer, George Gallup, and secret Office of War Information polls. He eventually joined the BSC full-time, rooming with another British agent, the future novelist Roald Dahl.

David Ogilvy

Working under diplomatic cover at the embassy, Ogilvy was first assigned the task of economic sabotage of Axis-friendly businesses in South America but soon applied his talents to intelligence. Using the methods learned from the Gallup organization, Ogilvy conducted secret polls to judge the opinion of Americans toward Great Britain. These were instrumental in creating propaganda to counter isolationist rhetoric, much of which was directed from Germany. Following the war, Ogilvy founded the famed ad agency under his name that launched such memorable campaigns as "The Man in the Hathaway Shirt" and "Only Dove Is One-Quarter Moisturizing Cream."

Misapplied Code Name

The best-selling *A Man Called Intrepid* made the Canadian-born British spymaster William Stephenson a household name. But was Stephenson really code-named INTREPID? In fact, Intrepid was the telegraphic address for the BSC in New York City and not Stephenson's official code name. In one instance, Stephenson, using the alias "Mr. Williams," met an agent in Washington who did not immediately recognize him and was confronted with a question about the BSC chief. "Mr. Williams" slyly replied, "Oh, the Chief . . . terrible chap."

86. HISS VS. CHAMBERS: RUMORS, SPIES, AND PUMPKINS

MAP 5 ➤ **Alger Hiss residence:** 3415 Volta Place NW (private residence)

Alger Hiss

Alger Hiss possessed the perfect résumé for success at the highest levels of the federal government. He earned degrees from Johns Hopkins and Harvard Law. As protégé of professor and future Supreme Court justice Felix Frankfurter, he

Alger Hiss lived in a small brick house at 3415 Volta Place NW that later became the home of Sen. Prescott S. Bush, father of President George H. W. Bush.

Whittaker Chambers passed documents to Soviet spy Harry Dexter White at the Uptown Theatre, today the AMC Lowes Uptown 1.

Did Kim Philby Slip Up?

Soviet double agent Harold "Kim" Philby was meticulous in maintaining his cover in British intelligence. However, even the best of spies can make mistakes. In his 1968 memoir *My Silent War*, Philby recalled, "It was the era of McCarthy in full evil blast. It was also the era of Hiss, Coplon, Fuchs, Gold, Greenglass and the brave Rosenbergs—not to mention others who are still nameless." Naming Alger Hiss, who was still passionately proclaiming his innocence, among a list of confirmed Soviet spies may have been an unlikely slip-up for an accomplished spy.

secured a clerkship with Supreme Court associate justice Oliver Wendell Holmes Jr. For a brief time, Hiss also practiced law in New York and Boston before joining the Agricultural Adjustment Administration in 1933. He then held positions as counsel to a Senate committee and as special assistant to the solicitor general, and in 1936 he moved to the State Department.

Throughout his fast-tracked career in Washington, Hiss lived in an assortment of fashionable residences, first at ***3411 Q Street NW*** and then others, including ***2905 P Street NW***, ***1245 30th Street NW***, and ***3415 Volta Place NW***,

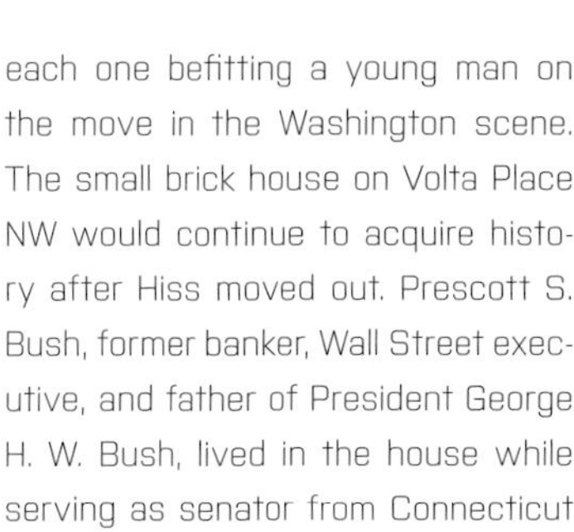

each one befitting a young man on the move in the Washington scene. The small brick house on Volta Place NW would continue to acquire history after Hiss moved out. Prescott S. Bush, former banker, Wall Street executive, and father of President George H. W. Bush, lived in the house while serving as senator from Connecticut from 1952 through 1963.

But the brilliant lawyer and rising star in the State Department was a Soviet spy. Hiss's early penchant for leftist politics in college somehow evolved into full-blown espionage. He photographed classified documents from work, which were passed to couriers for delivery to Soviet officials.

Whittaker Chambers Meets Bambi

Before Whittaker Chambers's name was linked to espionage and Alger Hiss, he gained some measure of fame for his 1928 translation of the beloved classic *Bambi: A Life in the Woods*, originally published in German by prolific Austrian author Felix Salten in 1923. Chambers's Simon & Schuster edition captured the hearts of Americans and was turned into the 1942 Walt Disney animated feature film.

By the late 1930s, with some members of the Communist Party USA becoming disillusioned with Stalin, fellow spy Whittaker Chambers turned on the Soviets. A journalist by profession, Chambers would meet his Soviet contacts near the ***Uptown Theatre (sometimes referred to as the Ordway and now AMC Loews Uptown 1), 3426 Connecticut Avenue NW***. Repulsed by Stalin's purges, he broke contact with Soviet military intelligence but kept incriminating documents as an insurance policy against likely reprisals by the Soviets and their American sympathizers. When Chambers first told officials about Hiss's involvement in Soviet infiltration of the US government, the revelations had little impact because the FBI was more focused on Nazi Germany.

More allegations emerged following the war when Soviet defector Igor Gouzenko offered additional information regarding major spy rings in America. By then Hiss had not only accompanied FDR to the historic Yalta Conference, but was also named acting secretary-general of the UN founding conference in San Francisco. However, when the still-unsubstantiated rumors forced his resignation from government, Hiss, with the assistance of loyal power-broker friends, including future secretary of state John Foster Dulles, became head of the Carnegie Endowment for International Peace.

In hearings of the House Un-American Activities Committee (HUAC), Hiss was again accused by Chambers of spying for the Soviets. Forced out of his position at the Carnegie Endowment, Hiss fought back, vehemently denying involvement in Soviet espionage and suing Chambers for libel. In response, Chambers produced documents in Hiss's handwriting and microfilm that Chambers had hidden in a pumpkin at his farm north of Baltimore, ***446 East Saw Mill***

Road, Westminster, Maryland. This evidence against Hiss became known as the Pumpkin Papers. The dramatic HUAC hearings rocketed a young California congressman, Richard Nixon, to overnight fame.

Hiss was charged with perjury and tried in 1949 (the statute of limitations for espionage had expired). The first proceedings ended in a hung jury, though a second trial found him guilty of two counts of perjury. Sentenced to five years in prison in 1950, Hiss was released in 1954 and continued to adamantly maintain his innocence. It was a fight he would continue to his death in 1996. Outliving most of his accusers, including Chambers (who died in 1961), Hiss appeared to be fighting a war of attrition. The perceived excesses of the HUAC investigations and Hiss's unwavering claims of innocence persuaded his friends and political supporters that he was innocent. For decades, judgments about his guilt or innocence were hotly debated.

The question was definitively settled in 1995 and 1996 with the declassification of the VENONA decryptions, which identified Hiss as a Soviet agent assigned the code name ALES. The government had possessed this proof of his guilt for decades but did not use the evidence in order to protect the fact it had broken Soviet codes.

■ 87. THE TROUBLED COLONEL LEE

MAP 5 ➤ Duncan Lee residence: 1522 31st Street NW (private residence)

Duncan Lee

Suspicions of Soviet penetration of the OSS were confirmed with the release of the VENONA decryptions in the 1990s. Among the named Soviet agents who penetrated the OSS was Lt. Col. Duncan Lee (code name KOCH). Of all the traitors in the OSS ranks, Lee stood out since his betrayal was personal as well as professional. OSS chief William Donovan had hand-picked Lee for the wartime intelligence organization from his white-shoe Wall Street law firm, Donovan, Leisure, Newton & Lombard.

Lee came with a sterling background for intelligence. He was born in China to a missionary and later moved with his family as a teen to ***Chatham Hall, 800 Chatham Hall Circle, Chatham, Virginia***, an exclusive all-girls finishing school where his father was pastor. A brilliant college student, Lee attended Yale University and then Oxford University as a Rhodes Scholar before returning to Yale for law school.

According to FBI informant Elizabeth Bentley (FBI code name GREGORY), Lee was recruited by the Soviets as early as 1941. Both wily and nervous in his dealings with the Soviets, he refused to pilfer or photograph documents, eschewed writing reports, and insisted on oral debriefings with his handlers. Bentley called Lee "the weakest of the weak sisters."

OSS officer and Soviet spy Duncan Lee lived in this home on 31st Street NW.

Lee lived at several Washington addresses, including ***1820 Clydesdale Place NW*** and ***3014 Dent Place***, fourth floor, apartment 18, before settling into 1522 31st Street NW with his wife, Ishbel. At some point, Lee began an affair with Mary Price, who served as a cutout for passing his information to the Soviets. Eventually Lee, plagued by fear, pleaded with his Soviet handlers to cease operations. During one meeting, according to a Soviet dispatch, Lee's hands trembled so much he could not hold a cup of coffee. His fears were well founded. Bentley had identified him when she switched sides.

Called before the House Un-American Activities Committee in 1948, Lee managed to evade prosecution and admission of guilt. He left government employment to become chief in-house counsel to the insurance company American International Group. Lee died in 1988, a few years prior to the public confirmation of his spying with the release of the VENONA decryptions.

60f
MAGYAR POSTA
KGB

5

SPIES NOT GUNS IN THE EARLY COLD WAR

(1946–1961)

Stalin's Soviet Union, a US ally during World War II, emerged in the late 1940s as the strategic adversary of Western democracies. The KGB labeled America "the Main Adversary." In a contest for international influence, an ideological struggle between democracy and Soviet communism confronted European and third-world nations trying to build free economies and democratic political institutions.

New words entered the American vocabulary to describe this conflict. Winston Churchill observed that "an iron curtain has descended across the Continent" in a 1946 speech at Westminster College in Fulton, Missouri. British novelist and essayist Eric Blair, writing under the pseudonym George Orwell, and American journalist Walter Lippmann both described the new international tension as a "cold war."

The National Security Act of 1947 formalized the US peacetime intelligence rolewith the creation of the CIA. Washington, home to the nation's military, policy, and intelligence agencies along with scores of foreign embassies, became a hub for international intrigue and espionage.

The FBI's counterintelligence agents disrupted scores of Soviet espionage operations in Washington throughout the Cold War, but several spies escaped detection for years, inflicting serious damage to American security. Intelligence operations by other nations, both friends and adversaries made Washington spying an inclusive profession.

■ 88. DISHONORABLE STUDENT SPY

MAP 5 ➤ **Judith Coplon residence:** 2634 Tunlaw Road NW (private residence)

Following her arrest for espionage in 1949, Judith Coplon, "good girl turned bad," became a media sensation.

As a stand-out student at Brooklyn's James Madison High School and Manhattan's Barnard College, Judith Coplon seemed destined for success. She moved to Washington after college to take a job with the Department of Justice. Superiors lavished praise on her work. When Coplon was promoted to a P-3 civil service grade in 1948, Attorney General Tom Clark sent a personal note. "P-3 is really an accomplishment and I congratulate you on it," he wrote. "I did not know we had political analysts in the criminal division, but on checking I find you are in the Foreign Agents Registration Section. Keep up the good work." The attorney general never suspected the seemingly diligent civil servant was also a secret agent for Soviet intelligence.

When Coplon (code name SIMA) was arrested in 1949 in New York City with her lover, Soviet diplomat Valentin Alekseevich Gubitchev (code name CARP), her purse contained a crumpled top secret document prepared by the FBI that she was about to pass to Gubitchev. Because Gubitchev had diplomatic immunity, he was declared persona non grata, sent back to the Soviet Union, and summarily dismissed from the intelligence service.

Coplon, facing charges of espionage, captured the headlines. The complex case, which involved some 80 FBI agents, made Coplon a public sensation. The press called her handbag "Pandora's Purse" and reported lurid details of her romantic trysts with a work colleague at the ***Southern Hotel (since razed), 11 Light Street, Baltimore, Maryland***. If someone with Coplon's upbringing could be lured into communism, it could happen to anyone. Nothing in her past offered a clue as to why she would become a spy. She first lived in an apartment at 2634 Tunlaw Road NW and then at the ***McLean Gardens apartment***

Judith Coplon lived at this Tunlaw Road NW apartment complex while spying for the Soviets.

complex, 3685 38th Street NW. Her motivations were never explained, and she never admitted guilt. The incriminating notes, she asserted, were research for a novel she was writing to be called "Government Girl."

In two trials, Coplon was convicted of both espionage and conspiracy. However, on appeal, her convictions were set aside on December 5, 1950. The court ruled that the government, despite the FBI operating under the attorney general's guidelines, had failed to obtain a warrant for Coplon's arrest, had conducted an illegal wiretap, and had not shared with her attorney the evidence it presented at trial.

The judicial move stunned many Americans. The evidence of her guilt, including secret papers found in her purse, seemed persuasive, if not conclusive. Pro-Coplon advocates saw vindication of the rule of law over heavy-handed law enforcement tactics, while the other side condemned legal hairsplitting and technicalities that allowed the guilty to go free. "Perhaps, if you reflect, you will agree that it is not desirable to convict people, even though guilty, if to do so it is necessary to violate those rules on which the liberty of all of us depends," noted jurist Learned Hand wrote on December 28, 1950, in a letter about the case that is quoted in *Reason and Imagination: The Selected Correspondence of Learned Hand.*

With the decision to set aside Coplon's conviction, Congress, at J. Edgar Hoover's urging, amended and clarified the law to allow federal agents to make warrantless arrests in certain serious cases, including espionage and sabotage.

Coplon moved back to New York, married her defense attorney, Albert Socolov, settled in Brooklyn, had four children, and ran two restaurants. She died in 2011.

89. COLD WAR BEDLAM

MAP 2 ➤ **Les Trois Mousquetaires:** 820 Connecticut Avenue NW (building replaced by an office building and restaurant complex)

In October 1948, two Soviet pilots, Pyotr Pirogov and Anatoly Barsov, flew their Tu-2 bomber from the Ukraine to Linz, Austria. The defectors were then flown onward to Washington, where they landed in the harsh glare of the media spotlight. As they were given a VIP tour of department stores, factories, and colleges, it soon became clear to the public that Pirogov was the "fun Russian" and Barsov the "moody Russian."

The Tupolev Tu-2 (NATO name BAT) was a high-speed, twin-engine, daylight and front-line Soviet bomber of World War II vintage.

Barsov tired quickly of the attention and life in America. In an attempt to redefect, he was told that he would face no punishment if he brought Pirogov back with him. A lunch with his fellow pilot was arranged at Les Trois Mousquetaires (The Three Musketeers), a restaurant then located at ***820 Connecticut Avenue NW, between Farragut Square and Lafayette Square***.

A tense meeting unfolded between the two former friends. The restaurant was filled with representatives from both the United States and the Union of Soviet Socialist Republics (USSR) with orders to protect "their guy." According to one eyewitness, at some point Barsov tried to hit Pirogov, and all hell broke loose between the Soviets and Americans. "It was a bedlam," said Walter L. Pforzheimer, the first CIA legislative counsel, when he later described the incident in a November 17, 1985, *New York Times* article. "Everyone in the restaurant suddenly rose and started pushing and shoving to get to the man he was trying to protect."

In the end, the embarrassing affair was hushed up by both sides. Barsov returned to the USSR and was executed not long afterward. Pirogov remained in the United States, wrote a book, *Why I Escaped*, and lived in the Washington area until his death in February 1987.

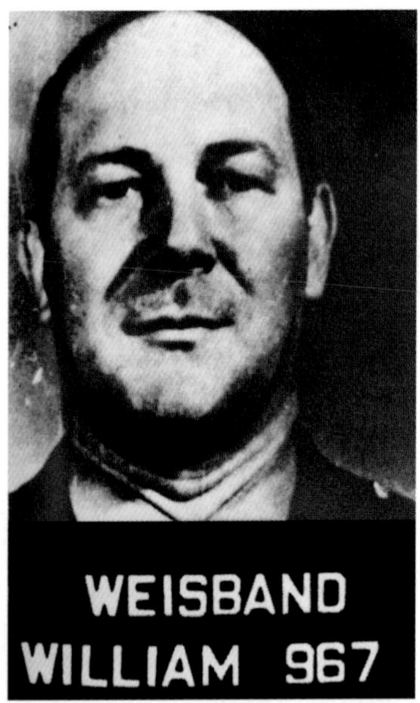

William Weisband

90. TRINKETS AND TREASON

MAP 8 ➤ **William Weisband grave: Presbyterian Cemetery, section 1, site 11, Hamilton Lane, Alexandria, Virginia**

William Weisband is one of the least known, but most damaging, of the Cold War spies. Although obscured by history, over his many years as an agent he betrayed some of America's most closely guarded communications secrets while operating under the code names ZHORA, LINK, and VASIN.

Weisband claimed to have been born in Alexandria, Egypt, in 1908, but his parents were probably residents of Odessa in the Ukraine, at the time of his birth. Likely recruited by Soviet intelligence in the 1930s, he served as a courier and sometime agent handler for several years.

Drafted into the US military during World War II, Weisband remained dormant until he was reactivated by the Soviets in 1948 while working at the Arlington Hall complex of the Armed Forces Security Agency (AFSA). Possessing a gregarious nature and knowledge of jewelry derived from his family's small chain of stores in New York City, Weisband roamed the secret facility selling jewelry as a credible sideline while eliciting secrets from secretaries and other personnel.

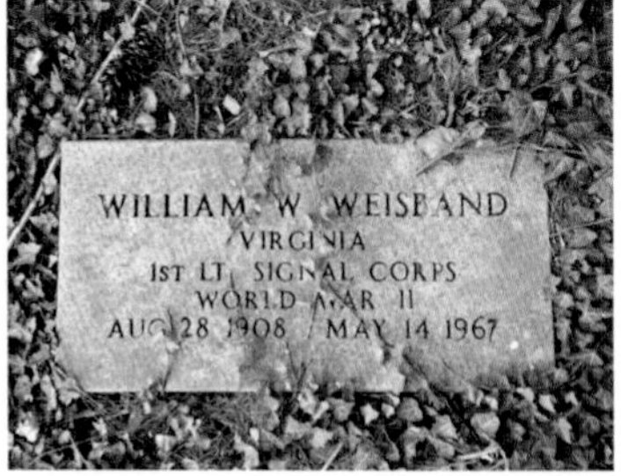

William Weisband's grave marker brazenly bears the name of one of the organizations he betrayed while spying for the Soviets.

Apparently Weisband—despite having no official contact with the secretive VENONA project team—and Kim Philby independently reported on the VENONA intercepts and the US code-breaking success. As a result, Soviet communication practices and codes were abruptly changed in 1948, slamming shut one of America's windows into Soviet espionage activities.

Alexander Vassiliev, a former Soviet intelligence officer, has revealed a 1949 KGB report, *File 43173*, that detailed Weisband's significant contribution: "We received from 'Zhora' [highly valuable documents] . . . on the efforts of Americans to decipher Soviet ciphers. . . . Our state security agencies implemented a set of defensive measures, which resulted in a significant decrease in the effectiveness of the efforts of the [US] decryption service."

Eventually identified by another agent, Weisband staunchly refused to cooperate with the FBI. He served only a single year in jail for contempt when he failed to appear before a grand jury. Weisband always maintained his innocence and dropped from public sight to become a door-to-door insurance salesman in Washington. Then, on Mother's Day, May 14, 1967, he suffered a fatal heart attack while driving on the George Washington Memorial Parkway in Virginia. His children, in the car at the time, managed to steer it to safety. Weisband is buried in the Presbyterian Cemetery on Hamilton Lane, Alexandria, Virginia.

91. COUNTERINTELLIGENCE ICON

MAP 7 ➤ J. Edgar Hoover residence: 4936 30th Place NW (private residence)

J. Edgar Hoover in the 1940s.

J. Edgar Hoover, director of the Federal Bureau of Investigation from 1935 until his death in 1972, was among the longest-serving law enforcement chiefs in American history. Hoover became head of the FBI's predecessor agency, the Bureau of Investigation in 1924. The name changed briefly to the

US Bureau of Investigation before becoming the FBI in 1935.

Hoover lived most of his adult life at 4936 30th Place NW, a pleasant tree-lined street. A Washington native and third-generation civil servant, Hoover was raised in a section of the city called Pipetown, at ***413 Seward Square SE***, today the site of the Capitol Hill United Methodist Church.

This house on 30th Place NW was J. Edgar Hoover's home for much of his life.

For more than 20 years, Hoover, along with principal associate and confidant Clyde Tolson, dined regularly at Harvey's, a well-known, and since closed, restaurant at ***1107 Connecticut Avenue NW***. Hoover also frequented the men-only Rib Room of the ***Mayflower Hotel, 1127 Connecticut Avenue***, for lunch. Among his favorite meals, according to historians, was cream of chicken soup, coffee, and Jell-O.

92. BRITISH DIPLOMAT, SOVIET MOLE

MAP 7 ➤ **Kim Philby residence:** 4100 Nebraska Avenue NW (private residence)

Harold "Kim" Philby, the senior British MI6 liaison officer with the CIA and FBI and a Soviet spy, lived in this stately brick home.

For several years beginning in 1949, one of the most damaging Soviet spies in history, Harold "Kim" Philby, served as the senior British liaison officer with the CIA and FBI. Holding the position of first secretary of the British embassy in Washington, Philby enjoyed nearly unrestricted access to the secrets and key personnel of America's intelligence community. Coincidently, for a time Philby lived at ***5228 Nebraska Avenue NW***, virtually across the street from John Boyd, then the FBI's director of security, whom he classified as "dreadful" and "childish." Eventually, citing a need for a larger home to accommodate a growing family, Philby moved to 4100 Nebraska Avenue NW.

Philby befriended CIA counterintelligence chief James Jesus Angleton. The pair dined regularly at the now closed ***Harvey's, 1107 Connecticut Avenue***, adjacent to the Mayflower Hotel. "Who gained the most from this complex game I cannot say. But I had one big advantage," Philby wrote in *My Silent War* after his defection to the Soviet Union. "I knew what Angleton was doing for the CIA, and he knew what I was doing for SIS. But the real nature of my interest was something he did not know."

With suspicion mounting in 1951 about fellow British diplomat and Soviet spy Donald Duart Maclean, Philby buried his espionage equipment in a wooded area off the George Washington Memorial Parkway, most likely in Great Falls, Virginia. The cache, supposedly encased in waterproof containers, included a camera, tripod, and other tools of the espionage trade. "I parked the car on a deserted stretch of road with the Potomac on the left and a wood on the right where the undergrowth was high and dense enough for concealment. I doubled back a couple of hundred yards through the bushes and got to work with the trowel," Philby wrote in his memoir, offering only vague clues as to the location.

93. JOLLY OLD GANG OF SPIES

MAP 3 ➤ **British embassy (now the ambassador's residence):** 3100 Massachusetts Avenue NW

The World War II British embassy is now the residence of the United Kingdom's ambassador.

At various times during the 1940s and 1950s, members of the Soviet-run Cambridge Five spy ring operated in Washington. Donald Maclean, Harold "Kim" Philby, and Guy Burgess all worked at the British embassy, 3100 Massachusetts Avenue NW, while another member of the group, Anthony Blunt, occasionally visited Washington to give art history lectures. However, Burgess, a British Foreign Office official, stood out.

Openly gay, a heavy drinker, and often ill-tempered, Burgess and his "eccentricities" were tolerated by the Foreign Office but made his

For Special Services

Ian Fleming, author of the original James Bond novels, wrote what is perhaps his most influential work at the British embassy, 3100 Massachusetts Avenue NW. With America on the verge of entering World War II, Lieutenant Commander Fleming, then assistant to Rear Adm. John Godfrey, prepared a detailed memorandum to William Donovan on the structure and function of an intelligence organization. According to Fleming's close friend John "Ivar" Bryce, the 70-page memo was drafted during the summer of 1941 under armed guard.

Fleming would later claim to have created the blueprint for the OSS and the CIA, with some justification. Donovan used some of the ideas presented by Fleming but discarded others. In appreciation, he presented Fleming with a memento of their work together—a .38-caliber Colt Police Positive revolver inscribed "For Special Services." A similar handgun makes an appearance in Fleming's Bond novel *Casino Royale*.

Cabbage: Boiled, Not Steamed

The KGB tried to compete with the global popularity of James Bond in the 1960s by hiring Bulgarian author Andrei Gulyashki to create a KGB equivalent of Bond. The Soviet Bond, Avakoum Zakhov, a true proletariat hero, preferred simple meals of cabbage and noodles compared to Bond's gourmet feasts and precisely prepared martinis. Unsurprisingly, Gulyashki's book, *Avakoum Zakhov vs. 07*, was not a success when translated into English.

Washington assignment rocky. In *My Silent War*, Philby recounted a message received from Burgess stating, "I have a shock for you. I have been posted to Washington." Philby, the disciplined master spy, sought to curtail future shocks by allowing Burgess to stay in the basement of his Nebraska Avenue residence. "It had occurred to me that he was much less likely to make himself conspicuous in my household than in a bachelor flat where every evening would find him footloose," Philby wrote.

At a dinner party in Philby's home one evening, Burgess came close to creating an international scandal. Guests at the cocktail-fueled social event included high-ranking intelligence officers from the CIA, the FBI, and the British embassy. After Burgess boasted of his skill as a caricaturist, the wife of CIA officer William Harvey implored him to draw her. Harvey, who led the effort to construct the famed eavesdropping tunnel between East and West Berlin, was also known as a heavy drinker and possessed a macho streak. When Burgess displayed the sketch of Harvey's wife in an obscene pose with her dress hiked above her waist, the reaction was predictable. The outraged Harvey swung at Burgess and missed. An international kerfuffle was avoided when James Angleton, head of CIA counterintelligence, intervened to defuse the situation.

In another series of incidents during a single afternoon, traffic patrolmen stopped Burgess three times for erratic driving. During each stop Burgess, while claiming diplomatic immunity, berated the officers with such abuse that the governor of Virginia lodged a complaint with the State Department.

However, Burgess's outrageous antics may have been purposeful. Philby later claimed the loutish behavior was part of a clandestine plot to get Burgess sent back to England to warn Maclean of an ongoing investigation. "It was just the sort of project in which Burgess delighted, and he brought it off in the simplest possible way," Philby noted. Burgess had an established reputation of bad behavior, leaving a trail of peccadilloes from London's Dean Street private Gargoyle Club to his earlier diplomatic postings in Tangiers and Dublin. If it was a planned operation, it worked. Burgess was recalled to London not long afterward.

■ 94. BRITISH DIPLOMAT, SOVIET SPY

MAP 5 ➤ **Donald Maclean residence:** 2710 35th Place NW (private residence)

Donald Duart Maclean, a member of the Cambridge Five spy ring, lived in this home at 2710 35th Place NW.

Donald Duart Maclean, a British diplomat posted in Washington from 1944 to 1948, was one of the few foreigners who knew America's atomic secrets. Maclean worked as first secretary at the ***British embassy, 3100 Massachusetts Avenue NW***, where he had access to sensitive communication between the two nations. Later he served as secretary of the Combined Policy Committee on Atomic Development. From his Washington residence at 2710 35th Place NW, Maclean delivered secrets to Soviet handlers during trips to New York City to visit his American-born wife.

Maclean was secretly recruited while still a university student as part the Soviet-directed Cambridge Five spy ring, which also included Harold "Kim" Philby, Guy Burgess, John Cairncross, and Anthony Blunt. Only after returning to England did Maclean come to the attention of the British security services, his spying having been revealed, in part, by the VENONA communications intercept program. He defected to Moscow in May 1951 prior to being questioned by investigators. There he worked in the Soviet government under the alias Mark Petrovich Frazer and was briefly joined by his wife and three children. He died at the age of 69 in 1983.

■ 95. NO SUCH AGENCY

MAP 13 ➤ **National Security Agency:** 4409 Llewellyn Avenue, Fort George G. Meade, Maryland

With initials once jokingly reputed to stand for "No Such Agency," the National Security Agency now has a website: www.nsa.gov.

For decades the National Security Agency at Fort Meade was the most secretive element of America's intelligence community. Employees joked that its initials stood for "No Such Agency" or "Never Say Anything." While the CIA acquired a reputation for daring clandestine operations during the Cold War, the NSA remained intentionally obscured in the background. Few outside government were even aware of its existence or mission.

Located on 650 acres within Fort Meade, the NSA is a city within a city that includes retail outlets, medical facilities, dining areas, banks, a library, and a barber shop. Its computing facilities were once said to be measured in acres. Closer to Baltimore than Washington, the 9-story headquarters building is one of the most tightly guarded pieces of real estate in the nation.

The NSA was created in 1952 by an authorization of President Harry Truman and merged elements of the US Army's Signal Intelligence Service (SIS) and the Armed Forces Security Agency (AFSA). Its founding document remains classified despite lawsuits for its public release, and the agency did not even appear by name in government manuals until 1957, when the *U.S. Government Manual* offered only a vague description: "The National Security Agency performs highly specialized technical and coordinating functions related to national security."

Defections by two NSA employees, Bernon Mitchell and William Martin, to the Soviet Union in 1960 brought the NSA to the attention of the American public for the first time. More recently, unauthorized releases of classified documents to the international media have created intense public debate, sensational claims, and controversy about the NSA's powerful, classified signals and electronic collection capabilities.

96. VENONA MYSTERY SOLVED!

MAP 13 ➤ **National Cryptologic Museum:** 8290 Colony Seven Road, Annapolis Junction, Maryland

The National Cryptologic Museum offers exhibits of cipher machines that were once among the nation's most closely guarded secrets.

The VENONA counterintelligence program initiated by the US Army Signal Intelligence Service (forerunner of the NSA) operated from 1943 to 1980. Among the most closely guarded secrets of the Cold War, VENONA ultimately enabled the United States to read thousands of encrypted messages from the Soviet Union's intelligence services.

How were the Soviet codes broken? History offers conflicting accounts as to the relative significance for American cryptanalysis of a codebook captured during World War II.

In 1944, members of the Finnish intelligence services, fleeing after an armistice was signed with the Soviet Union, loaded sensitive documents and equipment onto ships and sailed for Sweden. Code-named STELLA POLARIS by the Finns, this bold operation was intended to deny the Soviets a trove of intelligence. Later, some of the material was offered for sale, including a partially burned Soviet communications codebook the Finns had captured from a German battlefield. The OSS paid $63,000 for the document.

When Secretary of State Edward Stettinius heard about the secret purchase, he registered objections with the president about spying on allies, and the materials were ordered to be returned to the Soviets. Before complying, however, the OSS photographed 1,500 pages and developed a cover story that the book was obtained "by accident." Patrick K. O'Donnell recounted in *Operatives, Spies, and Saboteurs: The Unknown Story of the Men and Women of World War II's OSS* that an OSS officer who delivered the book to Soviet diplomat Andrei Gromyko at the ***Soviet embassy, 1125 16th Street NW***, reported, "He was cordial but had a look of disbelief on his face and seemed shocked that we actually had the codes."

NSA historians assert the VENONA breakthrough was the result of painstaking analytical efforts, not the codebook. However, the codebook assisted in creating an analytical understanding of how Soviet codes were organized and the kinds of vocabulary that might appear. The photographed codebook is on display at the NSA's National Cryptologic Museum, 8290 Colony Seven Road, Annapolis Junction, Maryland. The museum is open to the public, and admission is free.

■ 97. BEYOND UNDERSTANDING

MAP 13 ➤ **National Security Agency:** Buildings 2560 and 2561, Fort Meade, Maryland

US intelligence agencies, including the CIA, sponsored research programs into psychic phenomena beginning in the 1960s. Studies of extrasensory perception, once considered to have potential for identifying secret military facilities, focused on remote-viewing experiments under the code names SCANATE and STARGATE. A similar program at NSA, code-named GRILL FLAME, was conducted in buildings 2560 and 2561 at Fort Meade, Maryland. The research included military and civilian subjects believed to have natural psychic abilities, but, after more than two decades of testing, the weak correlations proved inconclusive and the programs were discontinued in 1996. These studies of the paranormal inspired the 2004 book and 2009 film *The Men Who Stare at Goats*.

■ 98. CATCHING A CODE BREAKER

MAP 7 ➤ **Signal Intelligence Service headquarters:** 3801 Nebraska Avenue NW

The World War II Signal Intelligence Center is now the Department of Homeland Security, Nebraska Avenue Complex.

When arrested on October 9, 1954, at his home in Arlington, Virginia, Joseph Sidney Petersen Jr. was a pitiable character. The gangly, sickly, and myopic former physics teacher became the center of the first spy scandal at the two-year-old National Security Agency (NSA), then based at the Naval Security Station, 3801 Nebraska Avenue NW.

Petersen had completed a US Army correspondence course in cryptanalysis and was hired by the NSA's forerunner, the army's SIS, during World War II. He stayed on after the war as an instructor, then began passing documents to a Dutch intelligence officer. Suspected of spying, he was fired from his $7,700-a-year job and arrested nine days later when the FBI agents found classified documents in his home.

The arrest not only caused friction between two allies, but also attracted unwanted media attention to the secretive NSA. The possibility of a trial, which could reveal more secrets in open court, only complicated the matter.

Under a plea bargain that saved the NSA from additional publicity, Petersen admitted guilt and received a seven-year sentence. He was paroled after four years, but authorities were fearful he would seek retribution against the government and had him surveilled briefly before he drifted into obscurity.

■ 99. DOUBLE TROUBLE FROM MITCHELL AND MARTIN

MAP 13 ➤ Bernon F. Mitchell residence: 1010 Eighth Street, Laurel, Maryland

Bernon F. Mitchell, a young NSA staffer who defected to the Soviet Union in 1960, lived in this modest home in Laurel, Maryland.

On June 25, 1960, two National Security Agency mathematicians, 31-year-old Bernon F. Mitchell and 29-year-old William Martin, boarded an Eastern Airlines flight at Washington National Airport (today Ronald Reagan Washington National Airport) for Mexico City. The two were officially approved for a three-week vacation, but as soon as they arrived, they sought political asylum at the Soviet embassy. When the KGB failed to persuade them to become "agents in place," they were put on a Cubana Airlines flight to Havana, then transported by freighter to the USSR. On August 11, Mitchell and Martin were granted political asylum by the Soviet government and each given a 500-ruble-a-month allowance.

Alarm bells sounded when the pair failed to return to work. A safety deposit key found at Mitchell's home in Laurel, Maryland, led investigators to box 174 at the State Bank of Laurel, which contained a note detailing reasons for their defection. The statement began by denouncing capitalism and the United States as evil, then oddly segued into praising Soviet women as more desirable mates than American women.

Given the low public profile maintained by NSA, the two would have been allowed to fade into obscurity behind the Iron Curtain if not for a Moscow press conference held on September 6. Hundreds of reporters packed the House of Journalists where the defectors were presented. During the staged event, the pair revealed details of classified operations, including secret collection programs against friendly nations.

The appearance of Martin and Mitchell in Moscow was not only an embarrassment to the US intelligence community—it also added to already deteriorating US-Soviet relations. Just four months earlier, Francis Gary Powers's U-2 reconnaissance aircraft was shot down while crossing the Soviet Union. A week later Cuba established formal diplomatic relations with the USSR, and that same month Soviet leader Nikita Khrushchev abruptly canceled a scheduled Paris summit with President Eisenhower. These dramatic developments were followed by the US ambassador to the UN, Henry Cabot Lodge Jr., revealing to the world that advanced KGB technology had been used to bug a carved wooden seal hanging in the US ambassador's office in Moscow.

Mitchell married Galina Vladimirovna Yakovleva, a professor at Leningrad Conservatory (today the N. A. Rimsky-Korsakov Saint Petersburg State Conservatory). Martin changed his name to Sokolovsky and married a woman whom he met on vacation at a Black Sea resort. Interviewed by Soviet radio, Mitchell, perhaps remembering his earlier note, described his wife as "a wonderful Soviet girl, an excellent housekeeper and I am very happy with her."

Mitchell and Martin were given employment at the Institute of Mathematics at Leningrad University (today Saint Petersburg State University). However, once out of the limelight, both proved troublesome for Soviet authorities. When they attempted to redefect to the United States, the KGB chief, Yuri Andropov, took a personal interest in their case. They were pointedly warned to stay away from the US embassy. The KGB told the defectors the US Supreme Court had sentenced them in absentia to twenty years in prison and showed them a bogus verdict as proof of the tale. Then a news story appeared in a Soviet newspaper reporting the arrest of two Americans carrying poison, which Martin and Mitchell were told was intended for them.

When requests to move to other countries—Australia, New Zealand, and Sweden—were denied, the pair began approaching random Americans, seeking help to escape. According to press reports, one approach was made to bandleader Benny Goodman during a concert tour of the Soviet Union. Martin appeared to be the most determined to flee the workers' paradise and was somewhat successful. Reportedly he died in the Hospital del Mar (today the Oasis of Hope Hospital) in Tijuana, Mexico, on January 17, 1987, within a few miles of the US border. A brief diplomatic cable indicates that his body was returned to his family for burial in the United States. Mitchell died in Russia in 2001.

■ 100. CHEERFUL MERCHANT OF DEATH

MAP 8 ➤ **Interarms warehouses:** 204 and 206 South Union Street, Alexandria, Virginia (now an office building)

The Interarms warehouses on South Union Street in Alexandria, Virginia, once held a cache of 700,000 small arms.

Samuel Cummings's love of weaponry began early. According to his own unverified account, he found an old Maxim machine gun in front of an American Legion Hall as a five-year-old and toted it home in his red wagon. From that somewhat peculiar start, he would become one of the largest arms dealers in the world.

Cummings, a weapons specialist during World War II, never saw combat. According to a 1988 *New York Times* article, he joined the fledgling CIA in 1950 before founding the International Armament Corporation in 1953. Opening an office at ***10 Prince Street, Alexandria, Virginia***, Cummings maintained warehouses nearby at 204 and 206 South Union Street, known as the Fowle Warehouses (now an office building), to store his weapons. At one point the company stockpiled more than 700,000 small arms—enough to outfit an army—just before the Gun Control Act of 1968 banned their importation.

In fact, Cummings outfitted several armies. His company, Interarms, became a major player in the international arms market. Along the way, Cummings cultivated the persona of a genial merchant of death, selling guns to nations, rebel groups, and guerrilla fighters. His retail operation at ***10 Prince Street*** did a brisk business under the name Potomac Arms, while two subsidiaries of Interarms, Ye Olde Hunter and Hunters Haven, also operated from the same address. As the "go-to guy" for weaponry, Cummings had a business strategy that dictated he not choose sides. He sold weapons to Cuban dictator Fulgencio Batista and his communist successor, Fidel Castro, as well as to South Africa's apartheid regime. Reportedly his weapons ended up on both sides of an attempted coup in Costa Rica. However, Cummings apparently did draw a line in refusing to supply arms to Muammar el-Qaddafi of Libya and Uganda's Idi Amin.

In the shadowy world of arms dealers, Cummings was uncharacteristically open, philosophical, and sanguine about his chosen profession. "The military market is based on human folly, not normal market precepts," he was quoted by *The Washington Post* in December 1986 as saying. "Human folly goes up and down, but it always exists. Its depths have never been plumbed." Cummings died in 1998 at the age of 71 in Monaco.

101. AMERICA'S LEGENDARY SPYMASTER

MAP 5 ➤ **Allen Dulles residence:** 2723 Q Street NW (private residence)

Allen Dulles's CIA credentials

Allen Welsh Dulles, the longest serving Director of Central Intelligence (1953–61), began his government career as a junior diplomat during World War I. After Pearl Harbor, he joined the OSS and served in Bern, Switzerland. Dulles returned to law practice and involved himself in Republican politics until appointed to head the CIA's overseas operations in 1951. A few months later he was promoted to deputy director, prior to President Eisenhower selecting him as DCI in February 1953.

Under Dulles's leadership, the CIA expanded as a global espionage organization. Ambitious collection systems, such as the U-2 spy aircraft and Corona satellite programs, ushered in a new era of technical intelligence collection. Dulles remained DCI following Kennedy's election but was forced to resign in November 1961 after the failed Bay of Pigs invasion of Cuba.

During the early 1950s, Dulles and his wife, Clover, lived in a home at ***3825 Wisconsin Avenue NW***. Built in 1827, it was once part of an expansive estate called "the Highlands" that included hundreds of acres of farmland. Today the structure is one of Washington's

DCI Allen Dulles, the CIA's longest-serving director (1953–61), lived in this home on Q Street NW.

Password Protected?

Early in his career, DCI Allen Dulles encountered what would become a 21st century problem of creating and recalling passwords. As a young OSS officer stationed in Bern, Switzerland, he needed an easily remembered combination for his briefcase lock. He set it to 23961, using the numbers of his home address of 239 East 61st Street in New York City. As it turned out, the code was not as secure as Dulles hoped. To the young spy's chagrin, his secretary, Mary Bancroft, quickly guessed the combination.

surviving 19th century homes and serves as the administrative building for the Sidwell Friends School. According to historians, the house once hosted political luminaries such as the Madisons and Thomas Jefferson. In the mid-1950s, during his tenure as Director of Central Intelligence, Dulles moved to 2723 Q Street NW.

The former DCI was called back into public service in November 1963 as a member of the President's Commission on the Assassination of President Kennedy (unofficially known as the Warren Commission). That year he authored, with retired CIA officer and novelist Howard Roman and the agency's first legislative counsel, Walter Pforzheimer, *The Craft of Intelligence*. More than 50 years after its publication, the book remains a classic of intelligence literature. Dulles died in 1969 and is buried in the Greenmount Cemetery in Baltimore, Maryland.

The historic Georgetown house was once the residence of OSS veteran and CIA officer Frank Wisner, an advocate of aggressive covert action to combat Soviet influence.

102. WISNER'S MIGHTY WURLITZER

MAP 5 ➤ Frank G. Wisner residence:
3327 P Street NW (private residence)

As a member of the OSS, Frank Gardiner Wisner served in Africa, Turkey, Romania, and France. Following the war, he briefly returned to a Wall Street law practice before joining the CIA's Office of Policy Coordination (OPC). Wisner, who was alarmed by aggressive post–World War II Soviet expansion, found a home in the OPC's mission of clandestine psychological and economic warfare against the Soviets. When the OPC was merged with the Office of Special Operations (OSO) in 1952 to form the Plans Directorate, with responsibilities for all CIA clandestine collection and paramilitary operations, Wisner's career continued to prosper.

Wisner, who lived at 3327 P Street NW, favored the aggressive actions of the wartime OSS, likening traditional intelligence gathering and analysis to "a bunch of old washerwomen, exchanging gossip while they rinse through the dirty linen." This colorful description, recounted in *The Old Boys* by Burton Hersh, hinted at the OPC's dashing panache, but Wisner and his staff were not universally admired. FBI director J. Edgar Hoover dubbed them "Wisner's gang of weirdos."

Under Wisner, CIA's covert-action operations attempted to counter Soviet propaganda with pro-American voices through covert funding of international student organizations, foreign labor unions, friendly journalists, and supportive publications. He called these operations "the Mighty Wurlitzer," after the well-known large theater organ, implying that he could play a tune heard around the world.

These propaganda campaigns involved a diverse and often surprising collection of personalities. In the late 1950s, the not-yet-famous Gloria Steinem was part of an organization that disrupted communist rallies abroad. "In my experience the agency was completely different from its image: it was liberal, nonviolent and honorable," she told *The Washington Post* in 1967 after her participation was revealed.

Wisner left the agency in 1961 and died of a self-inflicted gunshot in 1965. His wife, Polly, arranged for a memorial sprinkler system bearing his name in the Bishop's Garden, Pilgrim Road, of the ***Washington National Cathedral, 3101 Wisconsin Avenue NW***. Wisner is buried in Arlington National Cemetery.

103. FOILING A BLACKMAIL PLOT

MAP 5 ➤ Joseph Alsop residence: 2720 Dumbarton Street NW (private residence)

Joseph Alsop was one of Washington's more conservative journalistic pundits for nearly five decades. Some neighbors considered his distinctive, modern cinderblock home at 2720 Dumbarton Street NW "scandalous" for the upscale and historic Georgetown neighborhood. However, a larger potential scandal awaited him in 1957. Traveling to the Soviet Union on a reporting assignment, Alsop was given a VIP tour of factories, schools, and art communities. During a party with a group of bohemians, Alsop, a closeted gay man, was seduced by one of the party's male guests. The next day Alsop was confronted with explicit photographs of the tryst. Homosexuality, his hosts grimly explained, was a serious offense in the Soviet Union. He could be arrested, criminally charged, and made the object of international scandal. However, if he cooperated after returning to the United States, the matter would not only be forgotten—he would also be well compensated.

The architecture of journalist Joseph Alsop's home stood in sharp contrast to many of its Georgetown neighbors.

Alsop flatly refused, then contacted the US ambassador, who arranged for his swift departure. Arriving home, Alsop reported the incident to the CIA and the FBI. True to their word, the KGB circulated the photographs in an attempt to out the columnist. At a time in history when mere allegations of homosexuality could destroy a career, none of Washington's power brokers—friends or foes—revealed Alsop's secret life. Later, when the KGB again threatened blackmail, future DCI Richard Helms stepped in. Word was quietly passed to a KGB officer in Washington that unless the blackmail attempts stopped, the CIA would respond in kind. The threats immediately ceased.

■ 104. ANYTHING, ANYWHERE, ANYTIME, PROFESSIONALLY

MAP 2 ➤ **Air America headquarters:** World Center Building, 918 16th Street NW

During the Vietnam conflict, Air America's aircraft, such as this Pilatus Porter parked at a hangar in Thailand, operated throughout Southeast Asia.

The World Center Building was the site of one of Air America's headquarters locations in Washington.

Air America, a CIA proprietary company, cloaked both its operational and corporate activities in secrecy. Formed in the early 1950s as Civil Air Transport (CAT), it was reorganized in 1959 as Air America. The company, led by former US Army Air Corps and Pan American Airways pilot George Arntzen Doole Jr., operated for the next two decades from several Washington locations, including the World Center Building, 918 16th Street NW; 808 17th Street NW; 815 Connecticut Avenue NW; and 1725 K Street NW.

With an estimated 20,000 employees and 200 aircraft, Air America ranked among the world's largest airlines. Its diverse fleet included modern commercial jets, World War II–introduced transports such as C-46s, C-47s, C-119s, and Lockheed Constellations, various single-propeller aircraft, and Bell, Hughes, and Sikorsky helicopters.

Over time, CAT and Air America spun off subsidiaries or established interconnections with Civil Air Transport, Southern Air Transport, Air Asia, and other aviation firms. "We're all one family," Doole told an interviewer. "You can't tell one from the other.

We tie them together with contracts and don't even keep separate books except for tax purposes." At times even CIA management apparently struggled to untangle the interwoven corporate holdings. Reportedly when then Deputy Director Richard Helms requested an accounting of the company's planes, it took three months to compile the list due to the constant movement of aircraft among companies and changing of tail numbers as new owners acquired the equipment.

George Doole headed Air America, a CIA proprietary company and once among the world's largest airlines.

Air America pilots were legendary for flying hazardous missions in Southeast Asia and elsewhere in the world. They landed on remote, poorly constructed jungle airfields, dropped supplies while under enemy fire, and were given to swashbuckling understatement. Being shot at was called "sporty," harrowing situations were "fascinating," and particularly dangerous missions were deemed "absolutely fascinating." Doole obliquely acknowledged the risks in an April 5, 1970, interview with *The New York Times*, asserting, "Our work is more demanding of the pilot and he gets more fun out of the irregular jobs in remote places. Besides, one of the dreariest jobs in the world today is flying a 707 across the Atlantic."

A secretive man, Doole lived quietly in the stately ***Westchester Apartments complex, 4000 Cathedral Avenue NW***. Even his friends and neighbors may not have guessed he ran one of the largest clandestine operations of the Vietnam War, although Air America's unacknowledged link to the CIA was hardly secret. A 1966 *New York Times* headline proclaimed, "Air America, Inc., Believed An Arm of the C.I.A. In Asia." To which Doole drily responded, "If someone out there is behind all this, we don't know about it."

Air America's most public flight, as part of OPERATION FREQUENT WIND and seen around the world, was among its last. Dutch photographer Hubert van Es captured the image of an Air America UH-1 Huey helicopter on the roof of the Saigon apartment house of the CIA's deputy chief of station as personnel were evacuated on April 29, 1975. The CIA proprietary shut down shortly thereafter, although several of its interconnecting companies survived as independent commercial operations.

■ 105. POISONS AND PARANOIA

MAP 14 ➤ **Fort Detrick:** 810 Schreider Street, Frederick, Maryland

Soviet disinformation campaigns in the 1980s claimed that research at Fort Detrick was responsible for bioengineering the AIDS virus.

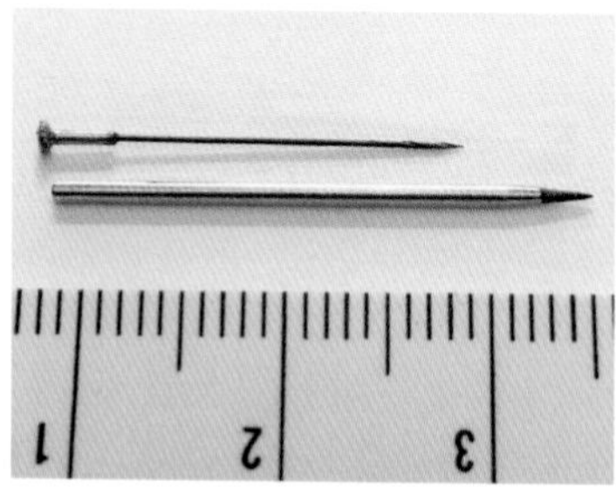

U-2 pilot Francis Gary Powers carried a "suicide needle" that would have caused his death within seconds.

In a lodge near Oakland, Maryland, CIA-sponsored LSD experiments were conducted with several government scientists.

Fort Detrick, location of the US Army's Medical Command at 810 Schreider Street, Frederick, Maryland, was the center for America's biological weapons program from 1943 until 1969. Some of Fort Detrick's projects were run jointly with the CIA. One of those, code-named MKNAOMI, involved development of a lethal shellfish toxin. U-2 pilot Francis Gary Powers carried a concealed needle impregnated with the toxin as a possible last-resort option to avoid capture and torture. The facility has also been identified in false conspiracy theories as playing a role in bioengineering the AIDS virus. That particularly malicious falsehood was spread by Soviet disinformation operatives in the 1980s in developing countries.

A dark episode in the CIA's relationship with Fort Detrick occurred in November 1953 near ***Deep Creek Lake, on Route 219 outside of Oakland, Maryland***. As part of a classified research program (code name MKULTRA) to assess the effects of mind-altering substances, Fort Detrick microbiologist Dr. Frank Olson, along with other government scientists, unwittingly received a dose of lysergic acid diethylamide (LSD) and experienced a "bad trip." The reaction persisted, and a few days later, during a CIA-arranged visit to New York City to see a psychiatrist, Olson committed suicide by jumping from a 10th-floor hotel window. The episode remained secret until the mid-1970s when MKULTRA projects came to national attention through a US Senate investigation led by presidential aspirant Sen. Frank Church.

106. COVERT EXPERIMENTS ON CAMPUS

MAP 5 ➤ **Gorman Building:** Georgetown University, 3800 Reservoir Road NW

During the 1950s, the CIA secretly provided some of the funds for the construction of Georgetown University's Gorman Building.

Some MKULTRA research was also conducted at Georgetown University Hospital in the 1950s and early 1960s by Dr. Charles Freeman Geschickter, unbeknownst to the university administration. The CIA also covertly funneled money through the Geschickter Medical Research Foundation, which partially funded the late 1950s construction of the university's Gorman Building, 3800 Reservoir Road NW. The CIA hoped Geschickter would use the new building's lab facilities for MKULTRA research experiments, but, in his 1977 testimony before the US Senate, Geschickter denied that the Gorman Building was used in MKULTRA.

107. "A DELIGHTFUL COUNTRY IN WHICH TO CARRY OUT ESPIONAGE"

MAP 3 ➤ **Pawel Monat residence:** Twenty-Four Hundred Hotel, 2400 16th Street NW (today the Envoy Apartments)

Polish intelligence officer Pawel Monat lived at the Twenty-Four Hundred Hotel on 16th Street NW after arriving in the United States in 1959.

Polish intelligence officer Pawel Monat was sent to the United States under military attaché cover in 1955. First residing at the fashionable Twenty-Four Hundred Hotel (today the Envoy Apartments) across from Meridian Hill Park, he then moved his family to an eight-story luxury building at ***2828 Connecticut Avenue NW*** (now the Connecticut Park Apartments). Following a series of intelligence successes in Washington and New York City, he was reposted to Warsaw in 1958 and promoted to head of intelligence for Polish military attachés around the world.

Then, in 1959, Monat defected to the West by walking into the US embassy in Vienna. His public statements describing Iron Curtain intelligence were revealing. Testifying before a Senate committee, he detailed the close, if somewhat unequal, relationship between Soviet and Polish intelligence services. His 1962 book, *Spy in the U.S.*, outlined to an even wider audience the ease of spying in a free country. "America is a delightful country in which to carry out espionage," Monat wrote. "I was able to find one American after another who seemed impelled—after a drink or two—to tell me things he might never have told his wife." Monat granted interviews to leading publications and even appeared on the popular television game show *To Tell the Truth*. The celebrity judges were unable to identify the real spy.

■ 108. THE GOVERNMENT'S DOOMSDAY RETREAT

MAP 11 ➤ 19844 Blue Ridge Mountain Road (Route 601, Berryville, Virginia)

During the Cold War, when nuclear conflict seemed a very real possibility, the government made contingency plans by creating a Continuity of Government (COG) facility. Located 17 miles west of Leesburg, Virginia, the government bunker was buried deep inside a mountain. Originally the site was used by the National Weather Bureau to launch weather balloons, then became part of the Bureau of Mines in 1936. In the 1950s, the bureau began digging to create a system of elaborate tunnels for an underground complex. The project was code-named OPERATION HIGH POINT.

When completed by the Army Corps of Engineers in 1958, the COG complex included office space, a hospital, a crematorium, dining and recreation areas, radio and television studios, sleeping quarters, reservoirs of drinking and cooling water, and an emergency power plant. The facility could reportedly accommodate several thousand people. The entrance was protected by a 34-ton, five-foot-thick, blastproof door that was said to require 15 minutes to open or close. Public attention to the site came in December 1, 1974, when *The Washington Post* reported the crash of TWA flight 514 near the facility.

Today the facility is part of the Federal Emergency Management Agency, designated the Mount Weather Emergency Assistance Center, FEMA. Located a few miles off Route 7 at 19844 Blue Ridge Mountain Road, Berryville, Virginia, the FEMA center is not open to the public.

■ 109. SPY AT THE Y

MAP 2 ➤ YMCA: 1736 G Street NW (now a redeveloped office building)

In 1959, US Army sergeant Joseph Edward "Joe" Cassidy began playing volleyball on Thursday evenings at the downtown YMCA, 1736 G Street NW. There Cassidy met a short, stocky Russian, also a regular at the games. A casual friendship was formed around informal dinners and drinking. Eventually the Russian, Boris Polikarpov, a Soviet military intelligence officer in the Glavnoye Razvedyvatel'noye Upravleniye (GRU), the Soviet foreign military intelligence service, asked the young sergeant for help—"a favor"—in obtaining some information on peaceful nuclear-power technology.

The sergeant, who was stationed at an army nuclear-power field office at ***9500 Pohick Road, Fort Belvoir, Virginia***, was happy to oblige. Polikarpov followed up with requests for increasingly sensitive material. When Cassidy continued to comply, he was given basic training in tradecraft and issued a sophisticated rollover camera that worked as a document scanner. The operation gained momentum, with numerous clandestine meetings in the ***Rose Hill Plaza shopping center at Franconia Road and Rose Hill Road in Alexandria***, at area restaurants, and in a local bowling alley.

Unknown to the Soviets, their well-placed and obliging spy was actually a double agent for the FBI. Code-named WALLFLOWER, Cassidy was part of OPERATION SHOCKER. He had been successfully dangled in the path of a known Soviet intelligence officer who took the bait. What began as a friendly game of volleyball at the local Y became one of the longest-running Cold War operations of its kind. For more than 15 years, Cassidy provided sanitized intelligence to a succession of six Soviet handlers, allowing the FBI to identify 10 Soviet spies, gain insight into Soviet operational tradecraft, and acquire Soviet spy gear.

In September 1980, Joe Cassidy was presented with a certificate of appreciation at FBI headquarters in a secret ceremony. The certificate signed by FBI Director William H. Webster read simply: "The Federal Bureau of Investigation expresses its appreciation to Sergeant Major Joseph Edward Cassidy for service in the public interest."

110. WORKING-CLASS HERO

MAP 3 ➤ **Czechoslovakian embassy (now the Cameroonian embassy):** Christian Hauge House, 2349 Massachusetts Avenue NW

In 1961, a Czechoslovakian intelligence officer stationed at his country's embassy in Washington, initiated contact with Frank John Mrkva, a US State Department courier of Czech background. Mrkva promptly reported the approach to the FBI, which urged him to maintain the contact. What followed was a classic recruitment operation of friendly wining and dining, leading to small favors for seemingly harmless information.

Playing the role of a double agent, Mrkva logged 37 meetings over five years with the First Department of

In the mid-1960s, FBI counterintelligence agents, posing as trash collectors, drove a garbage truck into the courtyard of the Czechoslovakian embassy to retrieve a cipher machine.

Regularly Scheduled Pickup

One of the more daring intelligence operations of the Cold War may have included the most unlikely of covers. According to the unconfirmed story, during the mid-1960s the FBI borrowed a garbage truck from a local service, disguised agents as a trash collection crew, and drove through the gates into the courtyard of the Czechoslovakian embassy, then located in the Christian Hauge House, 2349 Massachusetts Avenue NW. A cooperating Czechoslovakian official, waiting by an open window, handed the agents a cipher machine along with a large quantity of files. The FBI agents then made a hasty departure, forgetting to load the garbage. Subsequent surveillance of the embassy, according to one source, showed the Czechoslovakian deputy chief of security making his way to the Soviet embassy, perhaps to use its cipher machine to transmit news of the theft.

the Czechoslovakian intelligence service Státní Bezpečnost. Then came a request from the Czechs to plant a listening device in a bookcase in the office of Raymond Lisle, director of the Office of Eastern European Affairs at the State Department.

The bug was installed for Mrkva by FBI technicians but allowed to transmit only briefly before being disabled. Mrkva made excuses to his handler, telling him the device was probably malfunctioning because he had dropped it. The episode ended when Mrkva was revealed as a double agent during a high-profile FBI news conference in 1966 where the listening device was prominently displayed. In a July 22, 1966, *Life* magazine story, Mrkva explained the operation to his 10-year-old son, "There were some men who were trying to tear up the country and wanted your father to help. Well, your father's just not built that way. We caught them real good. God damn good."

■ 111. THE SAFE HOUSE MANSION

MAP 13 ➤ Ashford Farm: Talbot County, Maryland

Set on the Chesapeake Bay's Eastern Shore near Royal Oak, Maryland, Ashford Farm was a safe house for high-ranking defectors during the Cold War. The 8,688-square-foot mansion built in the late 1920s featured eight bedrooms on two floors set on 62 acres overlooking the shoreline where the Choptank River meets the bay. The CIA bought the estate for $65,000 in 1951. KGB majors Anatoliy Golitsyn and Peter Deriabin were debriefed at the Tudor-style mansion, as were other

The CIA's Ashford Farm safe house acquired unwanted media attention when it was identified as the temporary residence of U-2 pilot Francis Gary Powers following his return to the United States from captivity.

The Mad Russian of Ashford Farm

Defectors staying at CIA's Ashford Farm in Maryland would likely meet Russian-speaking Pete Sivess, who managed the estate for many years. As a youngster, Sivess, the son of Russian émigrés, learned the language and the American pastime—baseball. His skills carried him to the major leagues where a nickname, "The Mad Russian," stuck. "The Mad Russian is a combination of Babe Ruth and Carl Hubbell when it comes to ability," Baltimore Orioles business manager Johnny Ogden asserted in a widely quoted 1937 interview. "But he's as eccentric as he is talented. He has the long hair of a monk, the ascetic features of a Gandhi, and the arms of an ape." Sivess pitched for the Philadelphia Phillies from 1936 until 1938 and served in Naval Intelligence during World War II before joining the CIA.

Pete Sivess

Francis Gary Powers in the Ashford Farm safe house. A reporter familiar with the house's history identified Powers's secret location by recognizing the unique style of the hinges on the door in the background.

Soviet, Polish, Bulgarian, or Chinese defectors. However, Ashford's most notable guest may have been Francis Gary Powers, the U-2 pilot shot down over the Soviet Union on May 1, 1960, and exchanged for imprisoned Soviet spy Col. Rudolph Abel in 1962.

The Powers incident blew the CIA hideaway's cover. Upon arriving back in the United States, Powers was taken to the rural location for debriefing. The press, eager for any information about Powers, followed every clue as to his whereabouts. A sharp-eyed stringer for the Associated Press and resident of the Easton area, Mary Swaine, recognized the distinctive curtains and L-shaped door hinge of the Ashford Farm house in a photo the government released of Powers. The CIA continued to occupy the property for another decade before the government finally sold it in 1981 after it had been unused for several years.

■ 112. AN OFFICER BUT NO GENTLEMAN

MAP 8 ➤ **William Henry Whalen arrest site:** 5903 Dewey Drive, Alexandria, Virginia (private residence)

Arrested at his home, Lt. Col. William Henry Whalen, USA (Ret.), was the highest-ranking American officer ever recruited by Soviet intelligence.

William Henry Whalen met his Soviet handler at the Telegraph Road Shopping Center in Alexandria.

William Henry Whalen's arrest at his home at 5903 Dewey Drive, Alexandria, Virginia, on July 12, 1966, earned him the unwelcome distinction as the highest-ranking American military officer ever recruited as a spy by Soviet intelligence. For the GRU, Whalen was a prize with exceptional access to secrets. The disgraced officer had been assigned to the Army Intelligence Branch and held a staff position supporting the Joint Chiefs of Staff. According to the indictment, he passed classified information to the Soviet Union on nuclear weaponry, European military strategy, missiles, and the Strategic Air Command.

After actively spying from 1959 through 1961, Whalen experienced a heart condition that forced his retirement with the rank of lieutenant colonel in 1961. He temporarily terminated contact with his Soviet handlers in 1963, but the FBI continued its investigation. Eventually the FBI confirmed that clandestine meetings were continuing at locations such as the ***Telegraph Road Shopping Center at 5741 Telegraph Road in Alexandria***. Whalen was arrested and pled guilty to lesser crimes of promoting the interests of a foreign government and removing classified information from its place of safekeeping. In December 1967, at age 51, he was sentenced to 15 years in prison. He died in prison from his heart condition a few years later.

■ 113. CAUGHT IN THE CROSSFIRE

MAP 12 ➤ **Tom Braden residence:** 101 East Melrose Street, Chevy Chase, Maryland (private residence)

Journalist Tom Braden was an early recruit to the OSS and later a CIA operative. The host of the political cable-television show *Crossfire* is perhaps best remembered for his 1975 book *Eight Is Enough* and its subsequent television series. The television show, staring Dick Van Patten, detailed the adventures of raising eight children in a suburban home, reflecting Braden's family life at 101 East Melrose Street, Chevy Chase, Maryland, as well as in California.

During the 1950s, Braden was at the center of one of the CIA's most unusual operations. Post–World War II modern artists were under attack in communist countries for art deemed "decadent" and "elitist." Braden saw an opportunity to counter the Soviets. From operations run by the CIA's International Organizations Division, secret subsidies for Western arts included a European tour of the Boston Symphony Orchestra, exhibitions of abstract expressionists, including Jackson Pollock, and displays at the Museum of Modern Art in New York City.

Not everyone supported or appreciated the effort. Michigan congressman George Dondero hated the paintings. "Art which does not glorify our beautiful country in plain, simple terms that everyone can understand breeds dissatisfaction," he told Emily Genauer, an art critic for the *New York World-Telegram* in 1949. "It is therefore opposed to our government, and those who create and promote it are our enemies." In a speech before Congress on March 17, 1952, Dondero railed that modern art was a conspiracy orchestrated by Moscow to spread communism.

Tom Braden, former CIA officer, national columnist, and inspiration for the television series *Eight Is Enough*, needed a large home to accommodate his family.

Meanwhile, some of America's most influential artists, such as Alexander Calder, Willem de Kooning, Robert Motherwell, and Jackson Pollock, began denouncing communism.

Years later, former DCI James Woolsey offered a strong defense of the operation. "If you compare socialist realist art—the muscled worker in the Soviet Union pressing forward into the future—to Jackson Pollock's art, you have to ask yourself, 'Which society is freer?'" Woolsey told a *Playboy* reporter in 2013. "Pollock has three-dimensional canvases, really interesting patterns and—wow!—all these colors. Then you look at the socialist realist art, and it's crap—propaganda crap."

Although a strong supporter of the CIA, Braden fell afoul of the agency's leadership in May 1967 when the *Saturday Evening Post* published his article "I'm Glad the CIA Is Immoral." It contained information that angered former DCI Allen Dulles and ended a long friendship between the two.

114. THE SPY WHO FLED INTO THE COLD

MAP 8 ➤ **Philip Agee residence:** 3360 Gunston Road, Alexandria, Virginia (private residence)

Philip Agee in the Netherlands, 1977.

A tracking beacon was hidden in Philip Agee's typewriter case to track his movements. An arrow indicates tracking concealed batteries used to power the device.

Philip Agee once lived in the Parkfairfax apartment complex on Gunston Road, Alexandria, Virginia.

Philip Agee joined the CIA in 1957 and began what seemed like a promising career. With his first wife, he lived in the Parkfairfax apartment complex at 3360 Gunston Road, Alexandria, the same complex Richard Nixon once called home and referenced in his televised "Checkers Speech." Agee later moved to a house on Cherry Hill Lane in Washington, just south of M Street NW and the Chesapeake and Ohio Canal.

In his multiple postings in Latin America, Agee acquired a mixed reputation. Some considered him a potential star in the CIA, while others questioned his competence as a case officer. Reportedly, he was given to bouts of drinking, sloppy paperwork, and lechery. Agee abruptly left the agency in 1969 and lived in Mexico with his communist fiancée, whom he never married. Bitter with the CIA, he contemplated writing an expose of the agency's operations in South America. Agee contacted the Cubans for help, received assistance, and then went to Paris to write the book. By then, the agency knew of his intentions. Although out of reach of the American judicial system, Agee was surveilled, and his portable typewriter case, provided by a CIA agent, was bugged with a tracking beacon.

Over a four-year period Agee wrote *Inside the Company: CIA Diary*. More memoir than diary, the book, published in England in 1975, offered a poisonous view of the inner workings of the agency. With a photograph of the bugged typewriter case splashed across its cover, *Inside the Company* became an instant best seller. Initially banned, it appeared in American bookstores six months later.

Particularly damaging was Agee's naming of US government officials he claimed were CIA officers in Latin America and Washington. "I have decided to name all the names and organizations connected with CIA operations and to reconstruct as accurately as possible the events in which I participated," he wrote. "I have decided to seek ways of getting useful information on the CIA to revolutionary organizations that could use it to defend themselves better."

Agee's stated goal was to neutralize CIA field operations by blowing the cover of as many officers as possible. Not surprisingly, names from his book appeared in the local press of foreign countries. As deportation proceedings began in England, Agee remained in the spotlight. He went to the Netherlands, then bounced from one country to another, eventually landing in Hamburg, West Germany, before finally settling in Cuba. He began publishing a magazine, *CounterSpy*, and followed up with a newsletter called *Covert Action Information Bulletin*. Both listed the names and local addresses of alleged agency personnel at locations throughout the world.

Agee obsessively campaigned against the agency for years, writing more books as well as newsletters and sometimes returning to the United States to lecture on college campuses. Although he asserted that his decision to expose CIA officers was a moral one, KGB documents uncovered following the fall of the Soviet Union tell a contradictory story. Agee apparently first approached Soviet intelligence in Mexico in 1973 with reams of information. Rebuffed by the Soviets as "too good to be true," he was recruited by the Cubans a short time later, who shared his reporting with their KGB counterparts.

"As I sat in my office in Moscow reading reports about the growing list of revelations coming from Agee, I cursed our officers for turning away such a prize," former KGB major general Oleg Kalugin later wrote. Taking a better-late-than-never approach, the KGB began feeding the disgruntled Agee information for publication in *Covert Action Information Bulletin*. In all, Agee identified by name hundreds of US government officials, many falsely, as intelligence officers before dying in 2008 at the age of 72 in Cuba.

115. INTEL FOR THE WARFIGHTERS

MAP 6 ➤ **Defense Intelligence Agency: Joint Base Anacostia-Bolling, 20 MacDill Boulevard SE**

The Defense Intelligence Agency (DIA) was created on October 1, 1961, during President John F. Kennedy's first year in office, with a mission to

Headquarters of the Defense Intelligence Agency, Joint Base Anacostia-Bolling, Washington, DC.

integrate the separate uniformed services' intelligence activities into a single organization. Success came quickly. The following year, the DIA's collection and analysis played a critical role in identifying Soviet ballistic missile facilities in Cuba.

Expansion of the DIA's responsibilities followed when it assumed management of the Defense Attaché System in 1965. Through subsequent years, the agency's mission expanded to include counterterrorism, counterinsurgency, counterproliferation, and counternarcotics, as well as assessment of foreign military space and cyber capabilities.

Today's DIA is a global intelligence agency, with approximately 16,500 civilian and military personnel who provide all-source analysis, human intelligence, counterintelligence, and measurement and signature intelligence (MASINT) as the hub of America's defense intelligence wheel. In addition to preparing strategic estimates for policymakers and Department of Defense leaders, the DIA provides as a "combat support agency" tactical and operational intelligence to field commanders throughout the world. The DIA has supported US military operations with analysis and collection in every conflict since its founding, from Vietnam to Afghanistan and Iraq.

■ 116. COUPE DE VILLE DEATH OF A SUSPECTED SPY

MAP 9 ➤ Jack Dunlap grave: Arlington National Cemetery, section 43, site 976

US Army sergeant Jack Dunlap was assigned to drive for the NSA's chief of staff, Maj Gen. Garrison Cloverdale, before a promotion to clerk-messenger. Although earning only a $100-a-week salary, Dunlap owned by 1960 a 30-foot cabin cruiser purchased for $3,400 cash. More acquisitions followed, including

Although his home in Glen Burnie, Maryland, suited Jack Dunlap's modest salary, he turned to espionage to finance a craving for flashy cars and fast boats.

a Jaguar, two late-model Cadillacs, a state-of-the-art hydroplane, and memberships in yacht clubs.

Dunlap presented credible explanations for his high-flying lifestyle, and few suspected the decorated Korean War hero and father of five was a spy. He continued living in a modest home at ***1 Gilmore Street, Glen Burnie, Maryland***, while receiving an estimated $30,000 to $40,000 from his Soviet handlers.

This crime scene photograph surfaced shortly after Jack Dunlap committed suicide.

After leaving the army in March 1963, Dunlap applied to stay on at the NSA, presumably to continue spying, but reportedly failed the mandatory polygraph test for civilian employees. An investigation was opened, and Dunlap was transferred to duties that precluded access to sensitive material. Perhaps sensing his espionage had been detected, he twice attempted suicide and failed. A third effort, in which he drove his white 1962 Cadillac Coupe de Ville to an isolated spot near Marley Creek in Maryland and attached a rubber tube to the exhaust, proved successful.

A petition from Dunlap's wife that the former US Army sergeant be buried in Arlington National Cemetery was granted, and he was interred with full military honors on July 25, 1963, in plot number 976, section 43. Although the NSA employee was under investigation at the time of his death, Dunlap had never been charged with espionage. Confirmation of his spying did not come until shortly after his burial when Dunlap's widow handed the FBI a stack of classified documents she found in the attic. Given the substantial evidence indicating his guilt, many consider his grave at Arlington an uncorrected error. The identity of his Soviet handler and the scope of Dunlap's betrayal remain mysteries.

■ 117. SOVIET SPY NEST

MAP 2 ➤ **Pullman House:** 1125 16th Street NW

Built in 1910 by the wife of industrialist George Pullman for her daughter and son-in-law, the Pullman House, 1125 16th Street NW, possesses a complicated history. Grand enough to accommodate the daughter of the man who invented the Pullman railroad sleeping car and her congressman husband, Frank Lowden (R-IL), the oddly designed house

The fourth floor of the Pullman House, previously the Soviet embassy, afforded only cramped office space for KGB officers.

Just Walk Right In

Some of the Soviet Union's most effective Cold War spies were Americans who were not enticed into treason by blackmail or devotion to communist ideology. More typically, unadorned greed or disgruntlement motivated them to betray their country. Their treason often began with self-initiated contact with a Soviet embassy, mission, or trade office. Called "walk-ins" by American intelligence officials, the Soviets labeled these volunteers "well-wishers" (*dobrozhelatel*) or "someone who takes initiative" (*initsiativnik*).

Several walk-ins are well known. Aldrich Ames, John Walker, and Ronald Pelton became spies by personally going to the Soviet embassy. Among the lesser-known Cold War walk-ins was Brian Slavens, a US Marine Corps private who deserted his post in the early 1980s and volunteered to the Soviets. Christopher M. Cooke, a US Air Force second lieutenant, turned over classified Titan II missile intelligence to the KGB after making his offer at the 16th Street embassy. CIA officer Edward Lee Howard also contemplated volunteering to the GRU in Washington before defecting.

For the Soviets, as with all other intelligence services, walk-ins presented a security dilemma. Was the volunteer a provocation sent by US counterintelligence, an emotionally unbalanced crank, or an unexpected intelligence treasure? The KGB was wary because, for every possible true traitor, there could have been a hundred CIA or FBI dangles.

was never occupied by the couple. Health problems prevented the politician from running for another term in 1911, and Pullman sold the property in 1913. The mansion changed hands again a few months later, this time going to the czarist Russian government.

Additions were made to the structure, but after the Russian Revolution of 1917, the house remained in a state of legal limbo until the United States officially recognized the Soviet Union in 1933. It then served as the Soviet embassy and headquarters for the USSR's espionage operations in Washington. During the Cold War, the fenced and gated mansion was the initial contact point for several of America's most notorious spies, including Aldrich Ames, John Walker, and Ronald Pelton.

According to former KGB officer Yuri B. Shvets, those assigned to the embassy's *rezidentura* (intelligence office) worked in cramped quarters behind a locked door. Thirty officers were crammed into a dimly lighted, windowless, 860-square-foot fourth-floor room divided into tiny cubicles by thin

"I'm a naval officer. I'd like to make some money and I'll give you some genuine stuff in return." —John Walker volunteering to spy

The Embassy Listens

The old USSR embassy on 16th Street featured a large antenna array on its roof. Part of a major signals intelligence (SIGINT) operation code-named POCHIN, the antennas allowed the Soviets to intercept radio transmissions from the Pentagon, the State Department, Andrews Air Force Base, the White House, and even the FBI. In his book *Spymaster: My Thirty-Two Years in Intelligence and Espionage against the West*, KGB major general Oleg Kalugin described one intercept in which the Soviets listened to Secretary of State Henry Kissinger ask his fiancée, Nancy Maginnes, about a recent speech. "How did I look? You thought I sounded well?" Kissinger inquired. Though the conversation was of little intelligence value, Yuri Andropov, then chairman of the KGB, proudly presented the transcript to the Politburo in Moscow as proof of his organization's clandestine access to communications used by America's leadership.

security-enhanced partitions designed by the KGB. The USSR built a new embassy compound at ***2650 Wisconsin Avenue NW*** that was completed in 1985. Today the Pullman House is the Russian ambassador's residence.

118. THE SPY WHO SOUGHT VENGEANCE

MAP 2 ➤ **Mintkenbaugh-KGB meeting site:** Washington Monument, 15th Street NW and Constitution Avenue

Army sergeant Robert Lee Johnson Sr. became embittered when denied a promotion while stationed in Berlin. Using his prostitute girlfriend Hedy as an intermediary, he approached the Soviets looking to defect but was persuaded to become a spy for the USSR.

James Allen Mintkenbaugh was an accomplice of fellow army sergeant turned spy Robert Lee Johnson Sr.

From 1953 through the early 1960s, Johnson stole secrets—first from the Berlin Command G-2 (military intelligence), then from the Armed Forces Courier Transfer Station at Orly Airport outside Paris. Later he provided his handlers a sample of fuel for the new Nike Hercules missiles from a base in Palos Verdes, California. During his spying years, Johnson married Hedy, recruited an accomplice, army sergeant James Mintkenbaugh, and weathered a

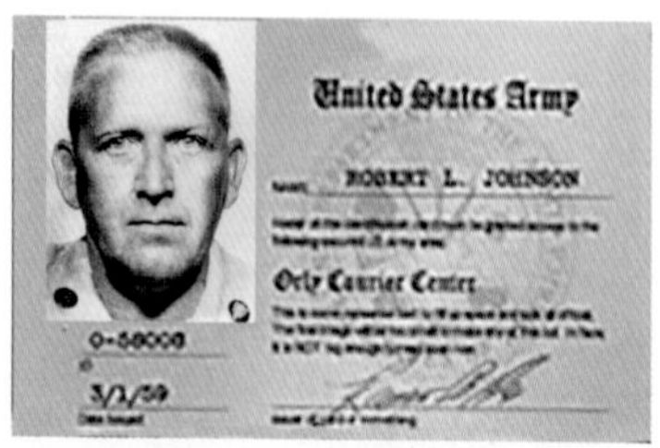

Robert Lee Johnson Sr.'s official courier identification card, which gave the spy access to the largest repository of classified US military documents in Europe.

series of chaotic episodes of heavy drinking, gambling, and erratic behavior. The Johnson family environment became so toxic that the son was placed in foster care.

Mintkenbaugh fared somewhat better. After leaving the military, he settled in Arlington, Virginia, and worked in real estate but continued to spy. At a clandestine meeting in 1960 at the Washington Monument, he was tasked with collecting birth certificates in Canada to be used by Soviet illegals to establish false identities, reporting on government employees looking for housing, and charting the route of an oil pipeline that ran from Texas to Pennsylvania.

Meanwhile, with Johnson assigned to the Pentagon, Hedy's emotional state rapidly deteriorated. In and out of psychiatric facilities, she was given to fits of rage, paranoia, and depression. Then, in October 1964, Johnson went AWOL. He withdrew $2,200 in savings from the Old Dominion Bank in Arlington and embarked on a cross-country drinking spree. At the request of the army, the FBI became involved and interviewed his wife. From a disturbed Hedy, they managed to obtain some information about Johnson's espionage and eventually tracked him to Reno, Nevada, where he was arrested as a deserter. Under questioning, he confessed. Mintkenbaugh, whom he implicated, was arrested.

Both Johnson and Mintkenbaugh received 25-year sentences. On May 18, 1972, Johnson's 22-year-old son, Robert Lee Johnson Jr., visited his father at the federal penitentiary in Lewisburg, Pennsylvania. As the elder Johnson extended a hand in greeting, Robert Jr. pulled a knife and stabbed his father in the chest. When the police questioned him about a motive for the murder, Robert Jr. would only say that "it was a personal matter."

■ 119. A DOUBLE-AGENT SCIENTIST

MAP 13 ➤ **John Huminik Jr. residence:** 5906 John Adams Drive, Camp Springs, Maryland (private residence)

For five years, John Huminik Jr. was an FBI double agent. Beginning in 1961, the scientist-engineer was aggressively courted by the Soviets with gifts of vodka, an expensive Seiko watch, and a bottle of "Midnight in Moscow"—perfume for his wife. Lucrative trade deals were dangled in front of him. The scientist, who specialized in metallurgy, would have been a prize for the Cold War Soviets, who sought Western technology and expertise. However, Huminik became uneasy with his new friends and reported the contact to the FBI. A double-agent operation emerged.

John Huminik Jr. enjoyed a quiet life in this Camp Springs, Maryland, home before becoming a double agent for the FBI. He met his Soviet handlers at places such as the Hospitality House Motor Inn in Arlington, Virginia (today the Hampton Inn & Suites Ronald Reagan Washington National Airport).

For Huminik, who lived modestly at 5906 John Adams Drive, Camp Springs, Maryland, life became a succession of clandestine meetings throughout Washington and the surrounding area. One of his first meetings with Soviet handler Valentin Revin occurred at one location of the now defunct ***Hot Shoppes eatery chain, 3128 14th Street NW***. In his 1967 testimony before the House Un-American Activities Committee (HUAC), Huminik recalled that Revin told his new asset, "We take care of our friends and we also take care of our enemies." Other meeting sites were at the Purple Tree Lounge in the ***Manger Hamilton Hotel (now the Hamilton Crowne Plaza), 1001 14th Street NW***, the long-gone ***Jefferson Movie Theater, 2936 Annandale Road, Falls Church, Virginia***, and the ***Hospitality House Motor Inn, 2000 Jefferson Davis Highway, Arlington, Virginia***.

Huminik's meetings with the Soviets were inevitably followed by equally secretive rendezvous with the FBI at strikingly similar locations, such as the Hot Shoppes in the Shirlington Shopping Center, Arlington, Virginia. At the direction of the FBI, Huminik gave sanitized technical information to his Soviets handlers and wrote reports about their meetings.

The operation ended in 1966 when Revin and other Soviets were rounded up and ordered out of the country. The publicity surrounding the arrests revealed a new side to Soviet espionage. Spies were not only looking for military and political secrets, but also insight into advanced American technology from the private sector. "My personal lesson indicates to me that there is danger to the small businessman, the scientist, and the engineer," Huminik testified before Congress in 1968. "The Soviets want technology more than anything else, and it is their plan to get it from technical people."

120. "ROMANTIC CAUCUSES"

MAP 1 ➤ Quorum Club at Carroll Arms Hotel: 301 First Street NW (now demolished)

The bar at the now defunct Carroll Arms Hotel, 301 First Street NW, was a favorite watering hole for congressmen and senators. Lawmakers joked it was an "ice

The Man Who Knew Everything

Often called the "101st senator," Robert "Bobby" Baker, as the secretary of the Senate, operated out of room F-80 near the Capitol rotunda. An unofficial power broker, Baker was known as a fixer and a dispenser of advice on everything from voting to shopping. According to a story in *U.S. News & World Report*, "the young man knew who drank, who was missing and who was sleeping with whom." Perhaps one reason he was so well informed was that he kept a luxury townhouse at 308 N Street SW and a room at his Carousel Motel in Ocean City, Maryland, for use by politicians. Baker fell from grace when a lawsuit by a competitor involving one of his side businesses, a vending machine company, uncovered potentially illegal practices. Lawmakers feigned an appropriate level of shock at such scandalous shenanigans, and the suddenly politically toxic Baker resigned from the Senate staff in 1963.

The Quorum Club in the Carroll Arms Hotel (now razed) was used as a honey-trap site by suspected East German spy Ellen Rometsch.

cube's throw from the Capitol." In fact, it was about a hundred yards from the Russell Senate Office Building. Upstairs, the second floor housed an even more exclusive venue, the Quorum Club. With its door marked by a large Q, the club was the brainchild of Robert "Bobby" Baker, a Senate page who rose to become secretary of the Senate and worked closely with Lyndon Johnson when he was Senate majority leader.

The Quorum Club's 200 members were entertained in the three-room suite by piano and cocktails, along with a retinue of beautiful hostesses. A side door allowed lawmakers to slip in and out unnoticed. With a nod and a wink, the press labeled the bipartisan goings on at the club as "romantic caucuses."

One hostess, Ellen Rometsch, was particularly popular. The attractive wife of a West German military aide assigned to Washington, Rometsch attracted the attention of President John F. Kennedy. Although rumors swirled about the relationship and suggestions that Rometsch might be an East German spy seemed persuasive, an FBI investigation turned up no conclusive evidence. However, to head off a scandal after a press leak, presumably from FBI Director J. Edgar Hoover, Rometsch was flown back to Germany on a US Air Force transport plane at the behest of the State Department.

■ 121. FBI'S WASHINGTON METROPOLITAN FIELD OFFICE

MAP 2 ➤ 1100 Pennsylvania Avenue NW (Old Post Office Pavilion)

The centrally located Old Post Office Building, today the Trump International Hotel, housed the FBI's Washington Metropolitan Field Office (WFO) for much of the Cold War. Built in 1899 at 1100 Pennsylvania Avenue NW, the building has a Romanesque Revival design that has both offended and delighted architectural critics. *The New York Times* once called it "a cross between a cathedral and a cotton mill."

Hundreds of FBI special agents once worked from the fourth and fifth floors of the Old Post Office Building.

Beginning in 1951, problems with the structure were recognized, and the government debated for years whether to renovate or condemn the building, located only two blocks from the Department of Justice headquarters. The need became urgent on October 10, 1956, when hundreds of federal employees—including those of WFO on the fourth and fifth floors—were stunned by a tremendous bang. A thousand pounds of clockwork in the building's tower had crashed down onto the ninth floor. No employees were seriously harmed, but it was clear something needed to be done.

The Hotel Harrington was a favorite for visiting FBI agents and potential recruits.

The WFO remained in the building until 1977, with the nearby ***Hotel Harrington, 436 11th Street NW***, providing inexpensive lodging for special agents or potential recruits. It then relocated to the ***Harkins Building at Buzzards Point, 1900 Half Street SW***. Twenty years later, the WFO moved to its current location, a modern, freestanding facility at ***601 Fourth Street NW***.

The FBI's Washington Metropolitan Field Office on Fourth Street NW is one of several Washington-area buildings occupied by the FBI.

THE COLD WAR HEATS UP

(1962–1991)

The shadow skirmishes of espionage grew in intensity as the Cold War progressed. At the CIA and within the KGB, a new generation of college-educated, internationally-minded intelligence officers began replacing the World War II veterans of armed combat. This first generation of Cold Warriors, who came of age in the years of covert conflict, began adapting first-of-their-kind technologies to clandestine operations.

On the unseen battlefield of the Cold War, the United States stood as the primary obstacle to Soviet expansionist strategy, while the Americans were determined to make Nikita Khruschev's impassioned proclamation "we will bury you" a hollow threat.

America's technological advances that put "eyes in the skies" with the U-2 spy plane and CORONA satellites were imitated by Soviet systems such as the ZENIT satellite. As remarkable as these technologies were, none displaced the value of traditional spies who worked at the centers of power. Each side would eventually demonstrate they could recruit and securely run agents on the opposition's home territory.

Espionage flourished in Washington. For the Soviets, the age of the ideological spy during the 1930s and 1940s may have passed, but the KGB understood that money often provided an equally strong motivation for treason. Simple greed lured some of the most damaging spies in America's history into the KGB and GRU nets, including the CIA's Aldrich Ames, the FBI's Robert Hanssen, the NSA's Ronald Pelton, and the US Navy's John Walker.

New tradecraft techniques based in skill and technology enabled the CIA to handle its spies in Moscow despite the pervasive Soviet counterintelligence presence. Advanced electronics provided the foundation for miniaturized, high-capacity communication and surveillance devices. At least temporarily, technology proved a substantial advantage for the spies over the spy catchers.

Known as "the year of the spy," 1985 produced numerous highly publicized espionage cases involving US, Soviet, Chinese, and even services from third-world nations. The headlines generated by arrests, trials, diplomatic expulsions, and formal denials provided the public a rare glimpse of the clandestine war being waged from Washington to Moscow to Beijing. That the Cold War would end within five years seemed unimaginable.

The CIA's headquarters in McLean, Virginia, has expanded since the Original Headquarters Building (foreground) was dedicated in 1962.

■ 122. HEADQUARTERS FOR AMERICA'S SPIES

MAP 10 ➤ CIA headquarters: Route 123 near the George Washington Parkway, McLean, Virginia

The CIA's headquarters, obscured by a thick tree line between Route 123 and the George Washington Parkway, sits seven miles northwest of the nation's capital in McLean, Virginia. Built on the estate of Thomas Lee—a member of the family that includes the Revolutionary War's Henry "Light-Horse Harry" Lee and the Confederacy's Robert E. Lee—the 258-acre campus was originally part of a 3,000-acre parcel. Personally scouted by DCI Allen Dulles in the mid-1950s, the site afforded requisite seclusion for an intelligence headquarters yet was only a 15-minute drive from downtown Washington.

For Dulles, a new headquarters in what was then rural Virginia offered the chance to consolidate the hodgepodge of quarters the agency then occupied. In addition to being housed in the CIA's headquarters at ***2430 E Street NW,*** personnel were scattered in dozens of buildings around the city, including several temporary wartime structures along the National Mall called "tempos." Logistically there was little centralized about the Central Intelligence Agency.

Part of the site Dulles selected was already owned by the federal government, while additional acreage from private owners would be acquired later. What Dulles could not have known was that the site he chose would offer decades of misinformation to lovers of espionage movies and fiction. "Langley, Virginia," often said to be the location of the CIA, does not officially exist. The town of Langley, once composed of a few stores and a post office, was absorbed into neighboring McLean in the early 1900s. Still, the name stubbornly persisted for the general area and ultimately became synonymous with the CIA.

With the location chosen, the government contracted with the New York architectural firm Harrison & Abramovitz. The two primary architects were acclaimed for their individual work. Wallace Harrison designed Rockefeller Center, where the OSS and its British counterpart, the BSC, had New York headquarters during World War II, while Max Abramovitz had done extensive work for the Pentagon during and after World War II.

Construction of the seven-story headquarters and associated infrastructure was not without controversy. Signage identifying the work site as the future location of the CIA, which Attorney General Robert F. Kennedy passed every day on his

Located in the CIA's Original Headquarters Building, a Wall of Honor pays solemn tribute to CIA officers and contractors who died in the line of duty. Each engraved star represents a life lost.

Visitors to the CIA's Original Headquarters Building are greeted by an imposing seal in the marble lobby.

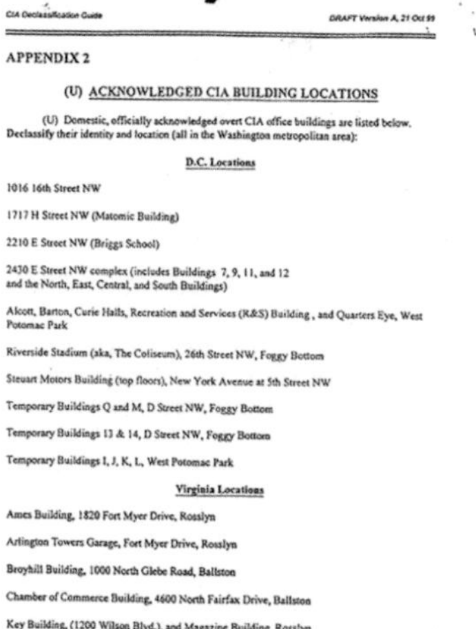

SECRET

CIA Declassification Guide DRAFT Version A, 21 Oct 99

APPENDIX 2

(U) ACKNOWLEDGED CIA BUILDING LOCATIONS

(U) Domestic, officially acknowledged overt CIA office buildings are listed below. Declassify their identity and location (all in the Washington metropolitan area):

D.C. Locations

1016 16th Street NW

1717 H Street NW (Matomic Building)

2210 E Street NW (Briggs School)

2430 E Street NW complex (includes Buildings 7, 9, 11, and 12 and the North, East, Central, and South Buildings)

Alcott, Barton, Curie Halls, Recreation and Services (R&S) Building , and Quarters Eye, West Potomac Park

Riverside Stadium (aka, The Coliseum), 26th Street NW, Foggy Bottom

Steuart Motors Building (top floors), New York Avenue at 5th Street NW

Temporary Buildings Q and M, D Street NW, Foggy Bottom

Temporary Buildings 13 & 14, D Street NW, Foggy Bottom

Temporary Buildings I, J, K, L, West Potomac Park

Virginia Locations

Ames Building, 1820 Fort Myer Drive, Rosslyn

Arlington Towers Garage, Fort Myer Drive, Rosslyn

Broyhill Building, 1000 North Glebe Road, Ballston

Chamber of Commerce Building, 4600 North Fairfax Drive, Ballston

Key Building, (1200 Wilson Blvd.), and Magazine Building, Rosslyn

CIA Headquarters Building complex

SECRET

70

(b)(1)
(S)

In recent years the CIA has declassified the addresses of several previously unacknowledged buildings in the Washington metro area.

The Intelligence Authorization Act for Fiscal Year 1999 named the CIA's headquarters compound the George Bush Center for Intelligence in honor of the only US president who also served as Director of Central Intelligence.

How to Answer the Phone

When answering telephone calls to the new CIA headquarters in April 1961, operators were instructed to say, "Central Intelligence Agency." However, the plain-language greeting generated controversy. The telephonic protocol did not live up to the public's idea of how a spy agency should present itself. So, within a few weeks, operators returned to the more shadowy greeting of repeating the number: "Executive 3-6115."

Where Is the CIA?

In the decades following its creation in 1947, the CIA has rented, leased, owned, or otherwise occupied all or parts of hundreds of office buildings and houses in Washington and its surrounding suburbs. Only a few locations were overt facilities during their lifetime, with the true tenant rarely acknowledged until the buildings were abandoned or destroyed.

drive to Washington from his home in McLean, became an annoyance. A secret spy agency, he felt, should remain secret. DCI Allen Dulles, who preferred an "open door" policy to the spy agency, resisted. "Too much secrecy can be self-defeating, just as too much talking can be dangerous," Dulles later wrote in *The Craft of Intelligence*, justifying his evasion of the attorney general's requests. The contractors, he argued, would get lost without the signs. The signs stayed up. The attorney general pushed back, imploring his brother, the president, to intervene, and the signs came down—for 10 years. During James R. Schlesinger's short tenure as DCI in 1973, a sign announcing the exit for the CIA was erected on the George Washington Memorial Parkway. Today, drivers along Route 123 as well as the parkway are clearly pointed to the George H. W. Bush Center for Intelligence.

The Original Headquarters Building totaled approximately 1.4 million square feet of space, with construction costs officially budgeted at $46 million. On November 3, 1959, President Eisenhower, assisted by DCI Dulles, laid the cornerstone along with a sealed time capsule containing historical artifacts before an audience of 5,000. A bit of trickery was required. Since neither the president nor the DCI was an experienced mason, the stone was laid with ceremonial cement composed of water, sand, and sugar. Following the ceremony, when asked by reporters what was in the time capsule, Dulles puckishly replied, "It's a secret."

A year later, the cornerstone was permanently installed by professionals, and, in September 1961, with only the northern half of the structure completed, personnel began to move in. On November 28, 1961, President Kennedy presided over the formal dedication of the new facility.

Dulles never worked in the building. Although he personally designed the DCI's seventh-floor office suite, the failed Bay of Pigs operation in April 1961 ended his career as America's top spy. During the official dedication ceremony for the building, Dulles was presented with the National Security Medal, and the next day John McCone was sworn in as Director of Central Intelligence. Twenty years later, President Ronald Reagan and DCI William Casey broke ground for an adjacent structure, known as the New Headquarters Building, which was occupied in 1988. Casey, who died in 1987, never saw the completion of the building he conceived.

123. MEMORIAL FOR CIA OFFICERS

MAP 10 ➤ Entrance to the CIA compound: Route 123, McLean, Virginia

A memorial to CIA employees murdered by Mir Aimal Kansi stands outside the CIA headquarters at the northwestern quadrant of the intersection of Route 123 with the restricted-access road to the headquarters. The solemn tribute marks one of the most tragic episodes in the CIA's history.

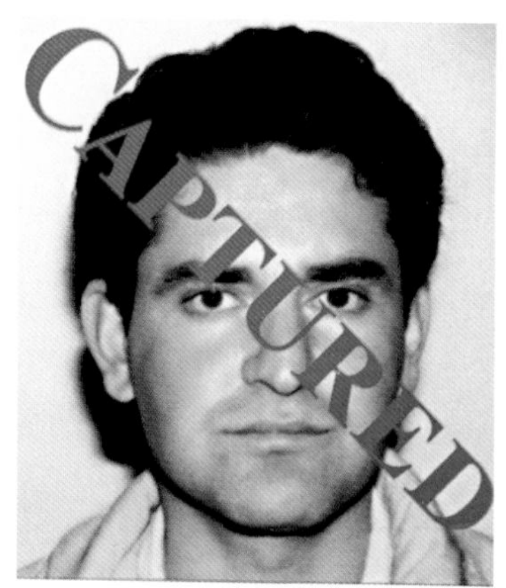

Mir Aimal Kansi

A public memorial just outside the CIA's headquarters compound pays tribute to CIA officers murdered by Mir Aimal Kansi on January 25, 1993.

On the morning of January 25, 1993, Kansi stopped his car near the intersection, got out, and began shooting as he walked alongside a line of vehicles waiting to turn onto the compound. Two CIA employees—Lansing Bennett, a medical doctor, and Frank Darling, a communications engineer—were killed. Three others were wounded in the attack.

Kansi quickly drove away from the scene and fled to South Asia, prompting a four-year international manhunt. Eventually he was lured out of hiding in Afghanistan, apprehended in the Punjab region of Pakistan, and returned to the United States for trial. Found guilty, Kansi was executed by lethal injection at the Virginia state penitentiary in Jarratt on November 14, 2002.

Near the site of the shooting, a simple memorial of a granite wall flanked by two benches facing each other was dedicated on May 24, 2002. The inscription reads:

> In Remembrance of Ultimate Dedication to Mission Shown by Officers of the Central Intelligence Agency Whose Lives Have Been Taken or Forever Changed by Events at Home and Abroad.
>
> Dedicato Par Aevum
> May 2002

Eloise Page, executive secretary to OSS director William Donovan, became the CIA's first female chief of station.

124. THE CIA'S IRON BUTTERFLY

MAP 4 ➤ Former offices of Intelligence Community staff: 1724 F Street NW

Eloise Randolph Page, a picture of early 20th century Southern propriety, was born in Richmond, Virginia, and graduated from Hollins College in Roanoke. Little in her genteel background, as a descendent of Thomas Jefferson's family, seemed likely preparation for success as an intelligence officer. Yet her illustrious four-decade career broke the glass ceiling for women working in US intelligence.

Page, once a secretary to William Donovan in the OSS, remembered him as "the most unreasonable man, with an Irish temper, but could charm the birds right off the trees." At the formation of the CIA in 1947, she was among the agency's first hires and worked with James Angleton, the controversial head of counterintelligence.

In a profession where women at the time were rarely promoted to senior ranks, Page made a steady climb through positions of increased responsibility, along the way earning the nickname "the Iron Butterfly" from Department of Defense colleagues. In one instance, when offered a job as chief of the Scientific Operations Branch, she insisted its name be changed before taking the job. "I'll be damned if I'll be the chief SOB," she was quoted as saying.

Often noted as the CIA's first female chief of station, Page is less well-known for twice turning down the position because the countries involved offered little challenge. She accepted assignment to a major post in 1979.

After returning to Washington, Page was appointed deputy director of the Intelligence Community, with headquarters then located at 1724 F Street NW. She retired in 1987 but remained active as an instructor for the Defense Information Systems Agency at Bolling Air Force Base.

In 1997, during the agency's 50th anniversary, Page was named one of 50 "CIA Trailblazers." She died in 2002 and is buried at the ***Old Chapel Cemetery, Millwood, Clarke County, Virginia***.

■ 125. THE CLANDESTINE MEETING THAT NEVER HAPPENED

MAP 8 ➤ CIA film-processing laboratory: Corner of Montgomery and North Columbus Streets, Alexandria, Virginia (redeveloped as an apartment building)

Oleg Penkovsky's passport

In 1962, the CIA made plans to meet one of its most valuable Cold War spies, Col. Oleg Penkovsky, an officer in the Soviet foreign military intelligence service GRU, at the Washington Monument. Code-named IRONBARK, HERO, and YOGA, Penkovsky, who provided critical intelligence to the Americans and British from 1960 to 1962, was at the time the highest-ranking Soviet officer to spy for the United States or the United Kingdom. Clandestine meetings were held in the United Kingdom and France when the spy was able to travel outside the USSR. While in Moscow, Penkovsky used a Minox camera to photograph classified documents and passed the rolls of film through brief encounters with Western officials and dead drops. A CIA technical component processed the invaluable images at a now redeveloped location on the northeastern corner of Montgomery and North Columbus Streets in Alexandria, Virginia.

During the early 1960s, Oleg Penkovsky used a Minox IIIs camera to secretly photograph classified Soviet military documents.

When Penkovsky scheduled a trip to the Seattle World's Fair for April 1962, the CIA created a plan to debrief him in Washington should his

In a commercial building in Alexandria (now redeveloped), CIA photo techs developed film provided by Oleg Penkovsky.

itinerary include a stop in the nation's capital. Mark Reibling, in *Wedge: From Pearl Harbor to 9/11; How the Secret War between the FBI and CIA Has Endangered National Security*, cited the CIA's precise instructions: "Go to the Washington Monument approaching it on foot from Constitution Avenue and Fifteenth Street. Walk around the monument. You will see one of your friends. If he is holding a newspaper do not contact him. If he is not holding a newspaper follow him to a waiting car."

Penkovsky would have been debriefed at a nearby safe house and potentially met with Attorney General Robert Kennedy. However, he never made the trip. Later that year, Penkovsky was arrested, tried, and found guilty of espionage. An announcement of his execution appeared on May 17, 1963.

126. A PERFECT SPY IN ALEXANDRIA

MAP 8 ➤ **Igor Orlov Gallery (now closed):** 1307 King Street, Alexandria, Virginia

Igor Orlov, a Soviet double agent, established the Orlov Galleries (now closed) in Old Town Alexandria.

In the chaotic days following World War II, the divided city of Berlin became a center for both US and Soviet intelligence operations. One spy working for the United States, Alexandr Grigoryevich Kopatsky (sometimes known as Franz Koischwitz), was a dapper Russian with a mysterious flower along with his blood type tattooed on his hand. Kopatsky managed a coterie of call girls who elicited information from their Soviet military patrons stationed in Berlin's Soviet sector.

This "international man of mystery" was married to Eleonore (sometimes spelled Eleanor), the daughter of a Nazi SS officer, yet kept his double life secret, even from her. The CIA eventually resettled the agent and his wife in the United States, giving him the name Igor Orlov. The couple first resided at a safe house in Maryland

and then for a short time lived at ***3301 O Street NW*** in Washington before moving to an apartment above Orlov Galleries, their art gallery and frame shop on South Pitt Street, in the Old Town section of Alexandria, Virginia.

Igor Orlov reportedly never told his wife, Eleonore, about his espionage activities. They lived a short time at 3301 O Street NW.

However, with the defection of Soviet major Anatoliy Mikhailovich Golitsyn in 1961, Orlov's life was suddenly cast in doubt. Golitsyn provided his debriefers details on a double agent who fit Orlov's description. If correct, then Orlov likely inflicted enormous damage to the West while working as a "double" in Germany following the war.

The FBI and CIA put the couple under intense scrutiny. Their home above the Alexandria shop was searched, but nothing was found. Physical surveillance also turned up nothing substantive, except a single visit to the Soviet embassy on 16th Street NW, which Orlov credibly explained away.

Nevertheless, Orlov later managed to enter the Soviet embassy undetected and arranged to redefect using a KGB-devised exfiltration plan. Orlov and his family would be picked up outside a bowling alley in the Arlandria section of Alexandria. When Eleonore refused, the plan was put on hold, and the couple eventually moved the gallery to 1307 King Street, also in Alexandria's Old Town, where the business prospered.

Orlov died in 1982 at the age of 60, but the mole hunt continued. Eleonore and her sons were questioned again, and she was given a lie detector test administered at the ***Morrison Hotel, 116 South Alfred Street, Alexandria***, which was inconclusive. Not until years after Orlov's death and the fall of the Soviet Union was the truth finally revealed by a KGB archivist, Vasili Mitrokhin, in his and Christopher Andrews's book *The Sword and the Shield.* Mitrokhin confirmed that Orlov first offered himself to Soviet intelligence in 1949 and was a KGB double agent with multiple code names, including ERWIN, HERBERT, and RICHARD.

■ 127. MORE SECRET THAN THE NSA

MAP 11 ➤ National Reconnaissance Office: 14675 Lee Road, Chantilly, Virginia

Formally established on August 25, 1960, the National Reconnaissance Office (NRO), currently located at 14675 Lee Road, Chantilly, Virginia, has both a reputation and history as the most secretive of America's secret spy organizations. "I can't acknowledge that we have a National Reconnaissance Office—if

The existence of the secretive National Reconnaissance Office was not officially confirmed until the early 1990s.

we do have one," former DCI Stansfield Turner told a reporter as late as 1985. The organization remained unacknowledged until 1992, when the government officially divulged its existence, more than three decades after it was established.

With the memory of the surprise Soviet atomic test on August 29, 1949, and uncertainty about the size and range of the USSR's strategic bomber fleet, the Eisenhower administration made an aggressive Cold War push for technical collection systems that could detect Soviet military capabilities. The NRO was formed to manage CIA and Department of Defense (DOD) programs that built first-of-their-kind overhead reconnaissance systems, such as U-2 spy planes and Corona satellites. Collectively the systems became known as America's "space sentinels" or "spies in the skies."

Today the NRO acknowledges capabilities in foreign instrumentation signals intelligence (FISINT), communications intelligence (COMINT), and electronic intelligence (ELINT). According to official statements, NRO imagery systems are capable of providing US military forces information for indications and warning, as well as intelligence for planning and conducting operations.

NRO satellites have also collected nonmilitary scientific and environmental data, including images of natural or man-made disasters. One of the first civilian uses of NRO images occurred in 1992 in the aftermath of Hurricane Andrew to assess damage. By 2005, the Federal Emergency Management Agency (FEMA) and the Army Corps of Engineers had ready access to NRO imagery of flooded areas and hazards in the Mississippi Delta after Hurricane Katrina struck the Gulf Coast.

■ 128. THE PEOPLE WHO LOOK AT PICTURES

MAP 2 ➤ **National Photographic Interpretation Center:** Steuart Motor Car Company Building, Fifth and K Streets NW, and Building 213 (now demolished), Washington Navy Yard, corner of First and M Streets SE

Arthur C. Lundahl

From the Steuart Motor Car Company Building, intelligence analysts evaluated U-2 photographs of Soviet missile sites under construction in Cuba in 1962.

Building 213, seen here undergoing demolition in 2014, was headquarters for the National Photographic Interpretation Center for nearly four decades.

Authorized by President Eisenhower on January 18, 1961, the National Photographic Interpretation Center (NPIC) expanded from a division within the CIA's Directorate of Intelligence into the now independent National Geospatial-Intelligence Agency. In 1962, the NPIC was housed in the unassuming Steuart Motor Car Company Building at Fifth and K Streets NW (today a parking lot). The staff, headed by CIA veteran Arthur C. Lundahl, was responsible for interpreting images from U-2 spy planes and the Corona satellite system.

NPIC officers occupied the top 4 floors of the 7-story building, while the Ford dealership took up the lower 3 levels, including a ground floor showroom. On those modest upper floors in 1962, photo interpreters studied images taken during U-2 flights over Cuba that revealed a construction pattern in San Cristóbal consistent with deployment sites for Soviet SS-4 medium-range missiles. The missiles, the CIA knew from a spy in the Soviet Union, had a 1,000-mile range and were capable of hitting Washington or New York. Those images and accompanying interpretations led to the Cuban Missile Crisis, solidifying the reputation of imagery analysis as a critical intelligence discipline.

However, the NPIC's facilities were far less impressive than its work. The neighborhood was dangerous, despite a police station across the street. Lundahl's recollections were detailed in a 1991 publication, *30 and Thriving: National Photographic Interpretation Center*. He recalled dirty streets where homeless men slept curbside. The interior was nearly as bad. Paint was peeling from the walls and ceiling, and the facility had no air conditioning. "I guess the best thing you could say is that we had wonderful security cover, because I'm sure nobody would ever believe that anything of importance to the United States could be taking place in this trashy neighborhood," Lundahl said. "But we were there, and that's where the Cuban photography arrived under the guard of a security detachment wielding machine guns."

Despite such wonderful security cover, the building and working conditions shocked senior visitors. After a visit by members of the President's Foreign Intelligence Advisory Board (PFIB), the board reported to President Kennedy, "Mr. President, you've got to get those people out of there. They're working under

They Never Close

The National Photographic Interpretation Center acquired one of the more memorable code names in US intelligence history. Its director, Arthur Lundahl, chose HTAUTOMAT, after the legendary chain of New York City automated eateries that operated 24 hours a day, seven days a week. "Why did we call it that?" Lundahl explained years later. "Well, I reasoned that as all the data flowed in, people would be coming in on weekends, holidays, and in the middle of the night—just like the Automats in New York City where people are eating turkey dinners at 3 a.m."

foxhole conditions." According to the NPIC's official history, Kennedy called DCI McCone, asking, "John, what are you doing about getting those people out of the Steuart Building?"

Better quarters were found in Building 213 of Washington's Navy Yard. The building, which previously stored steel blanks for guns, was renovated, and the NPIC moved in on January 1, 1963. "It seemed like a dream come true," Lundahl said. "Walking through the gates and seeing Building 213 in its white splendor, it almost looked like the Taj Mahal. Sure, everything wasn't perfect, but it looked like a palace to me. I was so delighted I couldn't get over it." Unofficially the 200,000-square-foot facility became known as the "Lundahl Hilton."

The traditional NIPC mission is now incorporated into the NGA, headquartered at ***7500 Geoint Drive, Springfield, Virginia***.

129. A War-Halting Lunch

MAP 2 ➤ **Occidental Grill:** 1475 Pennsylvania Avenue NW

One of the most dramatic clandestine meetings of the Cold War occurred at the Occidental Grill, 1475 Pennsylvania Avenue NW. On October 26th, 1962, with the Cuban Missile Crisis in danger of spinning out of control, ABC News reporter John Scali received an urgent phone call from Aleksandr Feklisov (also known as Aleksandr Fomin), a high-ranking KGB officer working undercover as a diplomat at the USSR's embassy. Although Scali had already eaten, he agreed to an immediate lunch at the Occidental. Sitting at a table on the left-hand side of the restaurant, Fomin offered an "unofficial plan" for

A plaque in the Willard Hotel's Occidental Grill marks the booth where ABC News correspondent John Scali met Soviet diplomat Aleksandr Feklisov during the Cuban Missile Crisis.

winding down the crisis. The Soviets would remove the missiles and not introduce new ones if the United States publicly promised not to invade Cuba.

Scali agreed to act as go-between for the back-channel diplomacy. "The rest of the meal was eaten in silence," Scali was quoted in his *New York Times* obituary of October 10, 1995. He added, "Incidentally Fomin got my crab cakes and I wound up with his pork chop, but he didn't notice it."

Scali continued in the role of courier between Soviet and American officials as the crisis was gradually unwound. Another meeting would take place in the coffee shop of the Statler Hilton (today the Capital Hilton), 1001 16th Street NW. The communications were delicate. Both Scali and the Kennedy administration well understood the potential for Soviet deception. A few days earlier, as the crisis developed, Soviet ambassador Anatoly Dobrynin had used back-channel diplomacy through Attorney General Robert F. Kennedy and White House aide Theodore Sorenson to falsely claim that no ground-to-ground missiles were being placed in Cuba.

Scali's involvement in the crisis remained secret for two years until revealed by other reporters, and some details remain in dispute. In a booth of the remodeled restaurant hangs a plaque commemorating the meeting.

Celebrating Success

How do you celebrate saving the world? With Chinese food. As the Cuban Missile Crisis wound down in 1962, two of its behind-the-scenes players, Aleksandr Feklisov and John Scali, met for a celebratory dinner at Yenching Palace, 3524 Connecticut Avenue (today a Walgreens), where the pair once conversed privately to help defuse the threat of nuclear war. The restaurant, which closed in 2007, would gain national attention in the 1970s when it hosted a news conference announcing the arrival of two giant pandas from China.

130. WHEN THE KGB RINGS THE DOORBELL

MAP 7 ➤ **Peter Karlow residence:** 5011 Klingle Street NW

A few days before Christmas in 1961, a Russian rang the doorbell of a CIA officer's house in Helsinki, Finland. Identifying himself as Anatoliy Klimov, a major in the KGB, the unexpected visitor said he wanted to defect. His true name was Anatoliy Mikhailovich Golitsyn.

Golitsyn's US debriefings began in a safe house in Great Falls, Virginia. Initially hailed as one of the greatest intelligence coups of the Cold War, the acquisition of Golitsyn's accounts of complex, far-reaching, KGB-orchestrated deception operations throughout the world sent shock waves through Western intelligence organizations. He identified dozens of putative KGB agents in France, England, and Canada.

At the CIA, Golitsyn's narratives, which initially seemed credible, kicked off one of the most extensive mole hunts in the agency's history. No officer with

Area of former residence of Peter Karlow, a CIA officer falsely accused of being a mole for the KGB.

Soviet contacts, past or current, seemed above suspicion. However, over time the defector's unsubstantiated, convoluted theories began to undercut his credibility with many senior CIA officers. These did not include James Angleton, head of the CIA's counterintelligence staff, who maintained a belief in Golitsyn's claims of penetrations at the highest levels of the agency and pursued a futile decade-long mole hunt.

Golitsyn's allegations of Soviet moles buried deep inside the CIA created paralysis in the agency's Soviet Russia Division, ended promising careers on scant evidence, and froze many operations. One victim was Serge "Peter" Karlow. Beginning his career in the OSS, Karlow, who lost a leg during World War II, rose through the ranks at the agency. Karlow's loyalty and commitment had not been otherwise questioned, yet Golitsyn's vague description of a mole with a Russian background code-named SASHA and a name beginning with the letter "K" was enough to cast suspicion on him.

A four-month FBI investigation, according to Karlow's autobiography, *Targeted by the CIA: An Intelligence Professional Speaks Out on the Scandal That Turned the CIA Upside Down*, included bugging his home at 5011 Klingle Street NW in a failed effort to produce any evidence of espionage. Yet the CIA officer remained under suspicion and was forced to resign. Determined to clear his name, Karlow eventually persuaded the agency to reopen his case in 1988. The new investigation found him innocent of the accusations. He received an official apology, a medal for his service, and nearly $500,000 in financial compensation in 1989. A second officer, wrongly tainted by Golitsyn's accusations, Richard Kovich, also received compensation for damage to his career and reputation.

■ 131. MON DIEU! THE FRENCH SPY TOO

MAP 12 ➤ **Philippe Thyraud residence:** 7009 Wilson Lane, Bethesda, Maryland (now site of Trinity Presbyterian Church)

Not only did Anatoliy Golitsyn's assertions of KGB penetration of US intelligence create turmoil in the CIA—he also unnerved the French intelligence service Service de Documentation Extérieure et de Contre-Espionnage (SDECE) with similar claims.

Philippe L. Thyraud de Vosjoli (code name LAMIA) arrived in Washington in 1951 with sterling credentials from his service in the French Resistance during

World War II. Living first at ***4512 Macomb Street NW***, then at 7009 Wilson Lane, Bethesda, Maryland, Vosjoli worked from a French diplomatic office at 2129 Wyoming Avenue NW. Assigned liaison responsibility with his American counterparts, Vosjoli was given access to Golitsyn (French code name MARTEL) and reported the debriefings to his superiors. Golitsyn spun tales of KGB penetrations of the French government that included some of President Charles de Gaulle's closest advisers.

The combination of a classified, hand-delivered letter from President Kennedy to de Gaulle, Vosjoli's report, and debriefing of Golitsyn by a French team eventually created a rift between France and America. The French suspected Golitsyn might be part of an elaborate CIA disinformation plot, with Vosjoli a willing accomplice. CIA counterintelligence officials, fearing Golitsyn's tale of French penetration was true, began treating the French warily. A rumor that Vosjoli had assisted the CIA's head of counterintelligence, James Angleton, with breaking into the French embassy increased the tensions.

Credible or not, Golitsyn's account fueled distrust between the two friendly nations. According to Vosjoli, French intelligence began to focus on allies, including America. Vosjoli claimed an intelligence officer was sent to Washington to gather military intelligence such as the deployment of missiles, as well as technological and scientific secrets. If Golitsyn's story was true, whatever information the French acquired would inevitably be given to the Soviets.

When Vosjoli received notification he would be relieved of his post in September 1963, he resigned with a bluntly worded letter he later made public. Fearing for his life, he fled to Mexico in a camper with his mistress. There, in a curious twist, the former French spy encountered American writer Leon Uris in the resort town of Acapulco. Uris, known for best sellers such as *Battle Cry* and *Exodus*, wrote a fictionalized account of Vosjoli's tale under the title *Topaz* (1967). The novel was turned into the 1969 film directed by Alfred Hitchcock.

■ 132. FOUND IN THE WHITE PAGES

MAP 7 ➤ **Richard Helms residence:** 3901 Fessenden Street NW (private residence)

One did not need to be a supersleuth to find America's top spymaster during the 1960s and early 1970s. Richard Helms, DCI from 1966 until 1973, made no secret of his 3901 Fessenden Street NW home. His name and address also

Richard Helms

Close-Shave Concealment

In 1939, the future head of the CIA, Richard Helms, married Julia Bretzman Shields, the daughter of Frank Shields, a professor at the Massachusetts Institute of Technology and the inventor of Barbasol shaving cream. Perhaps by coincidence, Barbasol's iconic and ubiquitous red, white, and blue can has been used as a concealment device for decades by real and amateur spies to hide secrets and valuables. However, no Barbasol concealment is more unique than the one deployed in the blockbuster movie *Jurassic Park* to smuggle dinosaur embryos.

While he was Director of Central Intelligence, Richard Helms's phone number and Fessenden Street NW address were listed in the Washington white pages.

appeared in the official records when he testified before Congress.

Helms, a career intelligence officer, worked briefly as a reporter for United Press before World War II and, notably, interviewed Adolf Hitler. Helms placed a high value on providing objective intelligence. "Objectivity puts me on familiar ground as an old wire service hand," he told the American Society of Newspaper Editors in 1971, "but it is even more important to an intelligence organization serving the policy maker. Without objectivity, there is no credibility, and an intelligence organization without credibility is of little use to those it serves." Recognizing the tension between secrecy and openness in a democratic society, Helms added, "The nation must to a degree take it on faith that we too are honorable men, devoted to her service." Helms died in 2002 at the age of 89.

133. THE POETRY OF SPY CATCHING

MAP 9 ➤ **James Jesus Angleton residence:** 4814 North 33rd Street, Arlington, Virginia (private residence)

In the Cold War's spy-vs.-spy game, few players were more controversial than the CIA's longtime counterintelligence chief, James Jesus Angleton. Known as a poet, a onetime friend of Ezra Pound, and an intellectual at Yale, he joined the OSS during World War II, then moved to the CIA at its founding in 1947. While serving more than 20 years as the agency's head of counterintelligence, he was well known for his love of orchids, fly fishing, and poetry. The phrase "wilderness of mirrors," a common characterization of counterintelligence often attributed to Angleton, was likely borrowed from the poem "Gerontion" by T. S. Eliot.

Called "Mother" or "the Gray Ghost" by journalists, Angleton built a career on identifying byzantine KGB plots, some of which seemed less and less credible as the Cold War progressed. Notably, Angleton did not suspect Soviet superspy Harold "Kim" Philby, despite their frequent meetings when Philby was MI6's official liaison in Washington in the 1950s. The high-ranking British intelligence officer and KGB agent later backhandedly taunted Angleton in his book *My Silent War*, written after his defection to the Soviet Union. Philby recalled how closely the two worked and their frequent dinners at Harvey's, a power-broker restaurant adjacent to the Mayflower Hotel. "He was one of the thinnest men I have ever met, and one of the biggest eaters," Philby wrote. "Lucky Jim!" Angleton's regular lunch at the now defunct ***La Niçoise, 1721 Wisconsin Avenue NW***, included martinis or I. W. Harper bourbon, and Virginia Slims cigarettes.

During the early 1970s, Angleton saw his reputation decline due to an obsession with KGB defector Anatoliy Golitsyn. The defector's intricate conspiracy theories led to a destructive, nonproductive hunt for moles in CIA. Eventually, Angleton was forced to retire in 1974. The spy hunter died in 1987 and is buried in Morris Hill Cemetery, Ada County, Idaho.

James Angleton, the CIA's top spy hunter for two decades, acquired multiple nicknames, such as Mother, the Gray Ghost, and Virginia Thin.

James Angleton's modest home belied the influence he exerted on the CIA's clandestine operations.

La Niçoise, the Wisconsin Avenue French bistro favored by James Angleton, is now the Casbah Café.

Air Force communications technician Herbert Boeckenhaupt met his Soviet handler in Langley Fork Park in McLean, Virginia.

134. DRIVEN TO TREASON

MAP 10 ➤ **Clandestine meeting site:** Langley Fork Park, 6250 Georgetown Pike, McLean, Virginia

Herbert Boeckenhaupt, a staff sergeant and communications technician with the US Air Force's 33rd Communications Squadron, spied for the USSR during the early 1960s. At the time of his arrest in 1966, Boeckenhaupt claimed to have begun spying in 1963 when he was approached by a Soviet who threatened his father, who was still living in West Germany. Although he

Blame It on Bond

James Bond's love of Aston Martin automobiles enthralled his fans. Even the princely Bentley, which Ian Fleming later wrote into the Bond books, couldn't compete with the sporty elegance of the Aston Martin in the minds of 007 enthusiasts. American spies also coveted fancy cars, which they could afford thanks to the clandestine cash from their Soviet masters.

CIA turncoat Aldrich Ames owned two Jaguars during his nine-year run as a traitor. When arrested, he was indelicately handcuffed leaning on the hood of his cherished maroon XJ6 less than two blocks from his house. NSA traitor Jack Dunlap similarly exhibited a fondness for Jaguars but also owned two late-model Cadillacs. With the authorities closing in, Dunlap committed suicide in his new 1962 Cadillac Coupe de Ville. Disgraced navy man and patriarch of a family spy ring John Walker drove a red MG convertible.

However, the young US Army communications technician Herbert Boeckenhaupt exhibited a particularly exotic automotive taste. Using his illicit Soviet pay, he bought a Studebaker Avanti, a high-performance luxury coupe built in Indiana. By contrast, Cdr. James Bond did not concern himself with the price of cars. His were all loaners from Her Majesty's Secret Service, which were usually destroyed.

Not all spies were car buffs. Jonathan Pollard, arrested in 1985 as a spy for Israel, drove a 1980 grungy green Mustang—not one of the classic models. What kind of car did Fleming himself drive? Although his writing often mirrored a personal penchant for exotic luxuries, Fleming's everyday automobile choice was more modest. "I can't be bothered with a car that needs tuning, or one that will give me a lot of trouble and expenditure," Fleming said in a 1964 *Playboy* interview, "So I've had a Thunderbird for six years, and it's done me very well."

later asserted his initial Soviet contact occurred at a Washington clothing store where he worked part-time, Boeckenhaupt could also have been contacted in 1962 while stationed in Morocco.

Serving in the Pentagon Communications Command Center, Boeckenhaupt met only a few times with his handler, Aleksey Malinin, alias "Robert," who lived at 6166 Leesburg Pike, Falls Church, Virginia. One of those meetings took place in a park off Route 193, likely in Langley Fork Park, 6250 Georgetown Pike, near the CIA in McLean, Virginia. The Soviets securely handled the young spy, whose primary means of covert communication was through dead-drop sites scattered around the Washington area. He also used pressure-sensitive paper called "carbons" to create secret writing messages sent to an address in England overseen by William Cecil Mulvane. Boeckenhaupt received sufficient funds to pay cash for an exotic Avanti sports car. After his arrest at March Air Force Base (today March Air Reserve Base) in Riverside County, California, the sports car spy was sentenced to 30 years of jail time. He claimed one reason for spying was the cost of maintenance on his expensive car.

■ 135. BUGGING CONGRESS

MAP 1 ➤ **Rayburn House Office Building:** Independence Avenue SW, between South Capitol and First Streets SW

Throughout the Cold War, the KGB attempted to bug sensitive areas of Capitol Hill and targeted members of Congress and staff for recruitment. In the 1960s, according to a former KGB officer, a covert listening device was placed in the hearing room of the House of Representatives Armed Services Committee, then located in suite 2120 of the Rayburn House Office Building, between South Capitol and First Streets SW. A KGB officer, posing as a reporter for the Soviet news organization TASS, secured the bug on the underside of a table, but the device was soon discovered and removed.

Rayburn House Office Building

Another attempt was made in 1973 when a listening device was planted in the House Foreign Affairs Committee room, also in the Rayburn House Office Building, in suite 2170. That device malfunctioned and fell from the underside of a chair.

■ 136. AMERICAN DACHAS FOR SOVIET SPIES

MAP 13 ➤ **Black Walnut Point Inn:** 4417 Black Walnut Point Road, Tilghman Island, Talbot County, Maryland

The Black Walnut Point Inn, once a country retreat for Soviet officials during the Cold War, is now a picturesque bed-and-breakfast.

From 1962 to 1972, Soviet diplomats and intelligence officers who wanted to get away from Washington headed to the southernmost tip of Tilghman Island, Maryland, named for Lt. Col. Tench Tilghman, an aide-de-camp to George Washington. There a heavily guarded 1840s house, featuring sophisticated antenna arrays, offered an idyllic retreat for the Soviet officials.

In 1972, the Soviets left Tilghman Island in favor of ***Pioneer Point Farm on Bulle Rock Drive, Centreville, Maryland***, which they purchased for $1.2 million. The 45 acres were once part of a 1,600-acre estate owned by DuPont and General Motors executive John Raskob, a primary developer behind New York's Empire State Building. The sale set off a Cold War controversy in the small community. *The New York Times* quoted an outraged letter to the county commissioners: "In the name of God and our God-given country, how could you sell property to the Soviet Union, our enemy?"

Littering Soviets

The Pioneer Point estate that served as a Cold War country retreat for Soviet officials also became a way station for disposing of spy trash. With budgets tight, Soviet intelligence officers in New York and Washington could not afford secure shipping of outdated, broken, or unused equipment back to Moscow. The waterfront luxury dacha provided a solution. Printers, teletype machines, and other equipment were smashed to bits and clandestinely hauled to the estate. From there, a pleasure boat owned by the Soviets made night cruises along the Corsica and Chester Rivers, where intelligence officers dumped the spy junk overboard. "Everyone assumed the boat was bought to appease the visiting generals—even the ambassador and the generals assumed this—because of all of the grumbling," one KGB defector later revealed to author Pete Earley in *Comrade J: The Untold Secrets of Russia's Master Spy after the End of the Cold War.* "That boat really was bought as a garbage truck for us."

The Soviets blunted local opposition with an aggressive charm offensive. The ambassador invited community leaders through the gates of a new, seven-foot-tall high-security fence for tea and cocktail parties. Boxes of caviar and bottles of vodka were sent to local officials at Christmas, while magazine features showed photos of an elegantly appointed mansion.

In an ironic twist of history, the Tilghman Island property later became a site for US national security meetings. Planning sessions for the first Gulf War were reportedly conducted in the sunroom. Now known as the Black Walnut Point Inn, 4417 Black Walnut Point Road, Tilghman Island, Maryland, the former Soviet dacha and American "war room" is an upscale bed-and-breakfast.

137. FBI HEADQUARTERS

MAP 2 ➤ **J. Edgar Hoover Building:** 935 Pennsylvania Avenue NW

The J. Edgar Hoover Building ranks as one of the least loved buildings in Washington among architecture critics. Disdain for the FBI's headquarters, 935 Pennsylvania Avenue NW, between Ninth and Tenth Streets, has little to do with the Bureau's mission or its first, long-serving, and sometimes controversial director, J. Edgar Hoover. "The swaggering bully of the neighborhood, the FBI headquarters is ungainly, ill-mannered, and seemingly looking for trouble," the American Institute of Architects proclaimed in its Washington guide.

The J. Edgar Hoover Building, with 2.4 million square feet of office space, occupies a city block but is too small to accommodate the FBI's Washington headquarters staff.

The Hoover Building was designed to accommodate the bureau after it outgrew its original home in the ***Robert F. Kennedy Department of Justice Building, 950 Pennsylvania Avenue NW***. Construction began in 1967 and was completed in 1974. The 2.4-million-square-foot structure occupies an entire city block. However, during the ensuing four decades, the FBI's mission expanded beyond traditional crime fighting and counterintelligence to include counterterrorism, investigations of economic espionage, and cyber security. In 2013, with the FBI working from dozens of annexes scattered throughout the Washington area, a Government Accounting Office report concluded the building was inadequate to meet the needs of the organization. Plans for a move to other quarters are under development.

David Truong residence.

Ronald Humphrey residence.

138. A SPY WHO LOVED TOO MUCH

MAP 4 ➤ **David Truong residence:**
2000 F Street NW

The Vietnam War–era espionage case of David Truong and Ronald Humphrey included enough melodrama to fill half a dozen paperback thrillers. Truong, a South Vietnamese national from a prominent family and a graduate student in the United States living at 2000 F Street NW, recruited Humphrey, then employed by the United States Information Agency, to spy on behalf of the North Vietnamese.

Humphrey had been stationed in South Vietnam in the late 1960s and was desperate to get his mistress and her children out of the country. Married and living at ***618 South Irving Street, Arlington, Virginia***, Humphrey reportedly owed his life to the mistress who had warned him against traveling a mined road. Using the mistress as leverage, Truong recruited Humphrey to provide classified diplomatic cables that eventually made their way to a courier, Yung Krall, the Vietnamese-American wife of a US naval officer in Europe and the daughter of North Vietnam's ambassador to the Soviet Union. Krall's role was to pass the intelligence to the North Vietnamese government.

Unknown to Truong, Krall (code name KEYSEAT) was a double agent working with both the CIA and the FBI to penetrate the North Vietnamese community in Paris. As the Truong-Humphrey case progressed, Krall became the subject of intense interagency conflict. Without her testimony in court, the FBI had a weak case against Truong and Humphrey. For its interests, the CIA vehemently objected to exposing a valued source producing important intelligence reporting on the North Vietnamese.

To build the case (code name MAGIC DRAGON) without Krall, the FBI surreptitiously opened Truong's mail and placed a bug in his Washington home. State-of-the-art video-surveillance technology was installed in Humphrey's office.

President Jimmy Carter authorized the investigation, but the arrest and trial of the pair set off a firestorm in the courts. The defendants' lawyers argued that the evidence acquired without a warrant was inadmissible and filed appeals. Eventually the court accepted admission of the phone taps and the mail-opening evidence under the exception in the law concerning foreign intelligence.

Both Truong and Humphrey denied they were spies. Truong insisted that he had shared the intelligence Humphrey provided with only a few academics and members of Congress in an attempt to normalize relations between the two countries. Humphrey's attorney painted him as a lovelorn romantic who only wanted to free his mistress. "My client's case is that of a man who loved too much and trusted too much," Humphrey's attorney pleaded during the trial.

The prosecution prevailed. Truong, then a graduate student at American University, and Humphrey were convicted in July 1978 of multiple counts involving espionage. Both received 15-year sentences but served only five years before release. In the wake of the trial, Congress passed and President Carter signed the Foreign Intelligence Surveillance Act (FISA), which created the Foreign Intelligence Surveillance Court. Massachusetts senator Edward M. Kennedy, a sponsor of FISA, said, "The recent prosecution against Humphrey and Truong points out the need for this legislation."

Truong died on June 26, 2014, in Malaysia.

139. WHEN FATHER DOESN'T KNOW BEST

MAP 12 ➤ **John Walker arrest site:** Ramada Inn (now Rockville Hotel & Suites), 1251 West Montgomery Avenue, Rockville, Maryland

In October 1967, US Navy warrant officer John Walker Jr. drove his red MG sports car with the top down from Atlantic Fleet Submarine Force headquarters in Norfolk, Virginia, to Washington. Once there "Smilin' Jack," as he was known, knocked on the door of the ***Soviet embassy, 1125 16th Street NW***, and asked to see "someone in security." Carrying documents to establish his access to sensitive information, he got straight to the point. "I'm a naval officer. I'd like to make some money and I'll give you some genuine stuff in return," Walker said. "I want to make arrangements for cooperation."

John "Smilin' Jack" Walker

John Walker demonstrates to the FBI how he used his Minox subminiature camera to photograph documents.

John Walker used his business as a private investigator to mask his spying.

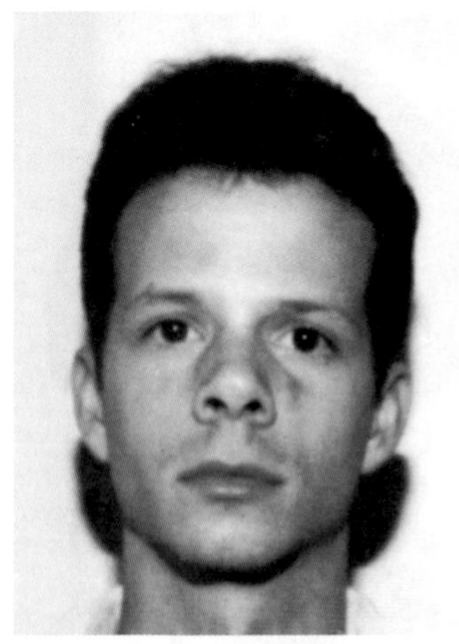

Michael Walker

The material was judged credible, and the new spy was smuggled off the compound with several thousand dollars and contact instructions for a meeting in two weeks' time at the now defunct Zayre department store in Falls Church, Virginia. During this second meeting, Walker received $5,000 in exchange for IBM cryptographic key cards that allowed the Soviets to read the code of the Atlantic Fleet's ciphers.

To ensure security of the operation, Walker would never again meet face to face with his KGB handlers in the United States. Dead drops were used there to exchange information, and a decade would pass before another personal meeting occurred—this one in suitably exotic Casablanca, Morocco. Thereafter regularly scheduled meetings occurred in Vienna, Austria.

During the ten years between the two meetings, Walker would become one of the most damaging spies in American history. His unprecedented compromise of intelligence about American cryptographic and antisubmarine warfare capabilities prompted Soviet KGB chief Yuri Andropov (later general secretary of the Communist Party of the Soviet Union) to refer to Walker as "Number One." Among the secrets he sold was the wiring pattern for the top secret KL-47 cryptographic machine, an essential piece of the puzzle that allowed the Soviets to construct their own version to decrypt American transmissions.

Walker eventually recruited his friend and fellow radioman Senior Chief Petty Officer Jerry Whitworth into the operation. Through Whitworth, the Soviets gained access to additional

Walker's Last Drop

John Walker did not realize he was under FBI surveillance in May 1985 as he drove from Norfolk, Virginia, to Rockville, Maryland, and checked into a Ramada Inn under the name Joe Johnson. That night, a soda can was placed by his Soviet handler at the base of a utility pole on Watts Branch Drive near its intersection with Circle and Ridge Drives to signal Walker to commence the dead drop. To acknowledge the signal and indicate he would make the drop, Walker left a 7-Up can at the base of a utility pole on Quince Orchard Road near DuFief Drive. Walker then placed his cache of documents in a paper bag beneath a layer of camouflaging household debris behind a utility pole near Partnership Road and Whites Ferry Road near Poolesville, Maryland.

Because the FBI surveillance team made an error in removing Walker's initial soft drink can for evidence, the Soviet handler did not see a signal the drop had been loaded and abruptly left the area. Consequently, Walker did not find his expected payment behind a tree at Old Bucklodge Lane and White Ground Road, near Boyds, Maryland. The FBI then retrieved the document-filled paper bag, leaving Walker with no money and no documents. A few hours later when the empty-handed Walker returned to the hotel, he was arrested in the hallway outside his seventh-floor room.

classified communication and cryptographic systems. Walker retired from the navy as a chief warrant officer in 1976 but in 1980 brought his brother Arthur, a lieutenant commander, into the ring. In 1984, Walker further expanded his network by recruiting his son, Michael, a yeoman aboard the carrier USS *Nimitz*, into the conspiracy. An attempt to recruit his daughter, Laura, then serving in the US Army, proved unsuccessful.

The intelligence that the Walker spy ring provided the Soviets likely would have seriously impaired American naval operations if full-scale war had broken out with the USSR. However, even absent that conflict, Walker's KGB handler

John Walker's spying abruptly ended in a hallway of the Ramada Inn, Rockville, Maryland, when he was arrested by FBI agents.

As exemplified by these detailed instructions, John Walker's KGB handlers were meticulous in planning operational meeting and drop sites.

later asserted that North Vietnam benefited from Walker's intelligence and used information provided from Moscow to compromise B-52 strikes and naval operations.

To make dead drops, Walker made regular trips from Norfolk, where he owned a home (and, after retirement, two investigative companies), to the Washington area. The Soviets guarded the operation closely and planned each dead drop meticulously. "My job was, first, go over every aspect of the drops to ensure they were foolproof," wrote Soviet intelligence officer Oleg Kalugin. "Walker was a huge catch, and we knew that if we fouled up and lost him it would not only be the end of one of the great spies of the cold war. It also would be the end of our careers. . . . We sweated over the sites and thankfully did not slip up."

For his part, Walker bragged about running a professional spy organization to his Soviet handlers. Norman Polmar and Thomas Allen's *The Spy Book: The Encyclopedia of Espionage* captures Walker's arrogance, expressed in a letter to his handlers: "No member of the organization or prospective member has any of the classic problems that plague so many in this business. We have no drug problems, alcoholic problems, homosexuality. All are psychologically well adjusted and mature."

These were hollow boasts. Behind the professional facade was a tangled soap opera of dysfunctional relationships and heavy drinking. At some point, Barbara, John Walker's ex-wife, had an affair with Arthur. In turn, John had an affair with Arthur's wife, Rita. Adding to the Walker family drama, Whitworth began to crack under the pressure. He intentionally ruined a roll of film in a clumsy attempt to get paid for the material twice. Then, either anxious to extricate himself or suffering remorse, he began an anonymous correspondence with the FBI field office in San Francisco using the name "Rus." The exchange

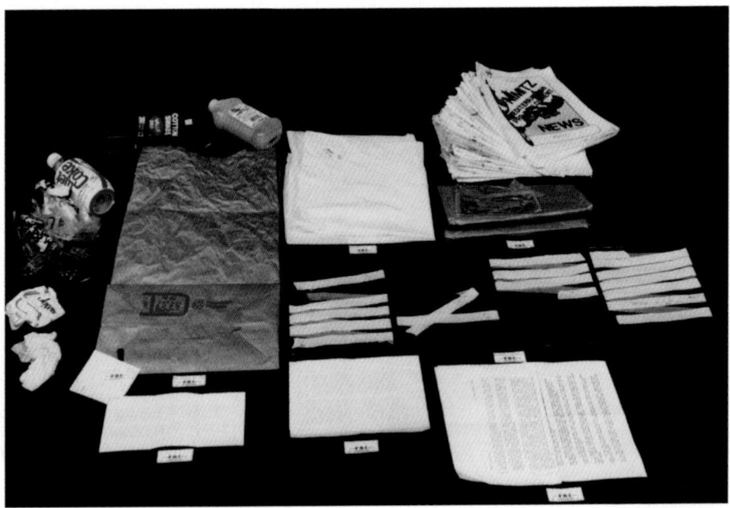

Contents of the package left by John Walker in his final dead drop to the KGB in May 1985.

went nowhere at the time, though it would later come back to haunt Whitworth.

Out of this increasingly chaotic situation, Barbara emerged as the weak link. A heavy drinker, she had known about John's espionage since the late 1960s and even accompanied him while servicing a dead drop. Feeling abandoned for younger women, embittered over years of abuse, and angry about missed alimony payments, but not knowing her son was involved in the conspiracy, she made a drunken, nearly incoherent call to the FBI in November 1984. Initially ignored as a crank, she was later interviewed by FBI agents and, although again intoxicated, managed to provide credible details about dead drops and her ex-husband's spying.

An investigation, code-named OPERATION WINDFLYER, was opened in late 1984. Working with the Naval Investigative Service, the FBI wiretapped suspected members of the spy ring. Surveillance was put in place, and, in May 1985, after leaving a cache of documents at a dead drop, Walker was arrested at the Ramada Inn (now the Rockville Hotel & Suites), 1251 West Montgomery Avenue, Rockville, Maryland.

Under questioning Walker seemed perversely proud of his treason. "I'll tell you this. If it was within my grasp, you can color it gone," he said during one interrogation. "Because it's gone." He quipped, "K-Mart has better security than the Navy."

All members of the ring were arrested and convicted. John and Arthur Walker received life sentences. Whitworth received a 365-year prison sentence, making him eligible for parole at the age of 107. Michael received a 25-year sentence but was released in 2000. Arthur died in prison in July 2014 and John a month later. Barbara was never charged in the case.

140. BLONDE AND BEAUTIFUL HONEY TRAP

MAP 5 ➤ **Jennifer Miles residence:** 2800 Wisconsin Avenue NW, apartment 107

Jennifer Miles exhibited an early taste for adventure. After growing up in South Africa, she toured the world on a tight budget, settled in Canada in the mid-1960s, and there, while recovering from an illness, fell in love with the Cuban Revolution. Tales of Ernesto "Che" Guevara and Fidel Castro prompted her to join pro-Cuban groups. She visited the tropical workers' paradise, met dignitaries, and worked in fields harvesting crops. Tall, blonde, and beautiful, Miles was given the code name MARY by the Cuban intelligence service and instructed to secure a diplomatic job in Washington. Working at a low-level

The beautiful, blonde Jennifer Miles used her residence for a perfect honey trap while spying for Cuban intelligence.

FBI surveillance photo of Miles leaving a New York City bar with Cuban intelligence officer Rogelio Rodriguez López.

position at the South African embassy and living in a small studio apartment at 2800 Wisconsin Avenue NW, Miles used her charm to meet and bed important men.

She was becoming a valuable asset for Cuban intelligence. Then, according to one report, a maintenance man in New York City discovered a secret communication she had left in a dead drop in the crevice of a wall next to an apartment house on 82nd Street in Jackson Heights, Queens. In another version of the story, Miles was seen meeting with Cuban handlers in New York City.

The FBI placed Miles under surveillance and then marveled at the number of male visitors she entertained. Once Miles began engaging White House staffers, the decision was made to terminate the operation, and she was arrested on October 4, 1970. At first refusing to cooperate, she eventually changed her mind and named her two Cuban handlers, UN diplomats, who left the United States five days later. Following Miles's deportation to South Africa, she publicly denied having been a Cuban spy but subsequently wrote a magazine story praising Cuba.

■ 141. RETIRED BUT NOT FORGOTTEN

MAP 12 ➤ **Patuxent River bridge dead-drop site:** Montgomery County–Howard County line, Maryland

As a 19-year-old soldier assigned to the National Security Agency in the mid-1960s, Robert Lipka became one of the youngest and most valuable KGB agents inside the American intelligence community. Mercenary in his motives, Lipka received between $500 and $1,000 for each package of intelligence delivered via dead drops at locations such as Washington's Rock Creek Park and a fishing spot just off Maryland Highway 108 where it crosses the Patuxent River at the Montgomery County–Howard County line. His Soviet handlers code-named the young clerk DAN

Robert Lipka

and later ROOK. "He gave us whatever he got his hands on, often having little idea what he was turning over," wrote former KGB major general Oleg Kalugin, who described a case that is almost certainly Lipka's in his memoir, *Spymaster: My Thirty-Two Years in Intelligence and Espionage against the West.*

Robert Lipka received money and instructions from his Soviet handlers in a dead drop near the Maryland Highway 180 bridge that crosses the Patuxent River at the Montgomery County–Howard County line.

What Lipka handed over, according to Kalugin, was indeed valuable. The documents included top secret reports to the White House, along with intelligence on US troop movements and NATO communications. Lipka's total profit for betraying his country was less than $30,000, and it was not until three decades later, in 1997, that he was finally brought to justice. Tipped off by a defector, Vasili Mitrokhin, and with the help of the spy's former wife, the FBI opened an investigation. Lipka, then living quietly as a schoolteacher and coin dealer in Millersvlle, Pennsylvania, was approached by an FBI agent posing as a Russian intelligence officer. He agreed to a meeting where he complained about being shortchanged by his previous Soviet handlers and then accepted additional money for his espionage decades earlier. Lipka was subsequently arrested at his residence on 17 Dublin Drive. The case ended with a plea bargain that included an 18-year prison sentence. "I feel like Rip Van Spy," he said when sentenced in September 1997. Lipka was released in 2006 and died in Meadeville, Pennsylvania, in 2013.

■ 142. TRACKING SPIES

MAP 2 ➤ FBI SPIDERWEB Surveillance System: Washington metropolitan area

The USSR packed its foreign diplomatic outposts with intelligence officers and other Soviet employees co-opted by the KGB. With so many spies to track, the FBI used technology to augment its limited number of counterintelligence agents. A system code-named SPIDERWEB tracked and analyzed the movements of Soviets throughout Washington. The system's primary component was a small transponder clandestinely installed above the glove compartment of USSR embassy vehicles. Wired into the vehicle's electrical circuit during routine servicing, the transponders worked in conjunction with a series of electronic "traps"

A secret FBI automotive-surveillance system code-named SPIDERWEB tracked the cars of suspected Soviet intelligence officers during the Cold War.

concealed along the Capital Beltway and other key roadways. The traps transmitted a constant low-power signal that would "excite" a vehicle's transponder as it passed. A signal identifying the vehicle and location would then be transmitted to an FBI monitoring post. The innovative system was one of the first applications of a technology that would eventually become the basis for "toll tag" systems used around the world.

SPIDERWEB was an effective tool until betrayed by FBI special agent Robert Hanssen to the Soviets in the late 1980s. Soviet spies then initiated countermeasures to defeat the system. Rather than removing all transponders, which would have revealed awareness of the system, the Soviets designated a single car as "operational" and guarded it fiercely to preclude installation of the transponder.

"The residency watched that car at all times. Never, under any circumstances, was it to be left unattended, lest the FBI should grasp the opportunity to plant a direction finder in it," wrote former KGB officer Yuri B. Shvets in his book *Washington Station*. "Each time it was slated to be driven to an important rendezvous, the operative car would be dismantled to its smallest components, inspected, sounded, and sniffed to make sure that it was clean, then reassembled. . . . In a word, that car was guarded much as a pathologically jealous husband guards his promiscuous wife, never letting it out of his sight. And it was worth it."

■ 143. FOLLOWING THE MONEY

MAP 8 ➤ David Henry Barnett pay phone: Exxon gas station, 7336 Little River Turnpike, Annandale, Virginia

Former CIA officer David Henry Barnett made clandestine calls to his Soviet handler from these pay phones in Annandale, Virginia.

David Henry Barnett was desperate for money. The former CIA officer had resigned his position in 1970 after serving several years as a case officer in Asia. Subsequent business ventures failed, and a job at a shrimp-processing plant in Indonesia did little to ease his money woes. By 1976, Barnett was $100,000 in debt and frantic. He approached the KGB in Jakarta, asking for $80,000. The usually tight-fisted Soviets at first balked at the sum but grudgingly relented when Barnett threatened suicide. It was money well spent for the Soviets. Barnett provided names of some 30 covert officers, along with information about CIA operations in Indonesia.

When Barnett returned to Washington, he continued to communicate with his Soviet handler, Igor Popov, then living in apartment 830, 1200 South Courthouse Road, Arlington, Virginia, using a series of pay phones, including those at an Exxon gas station at 7336 Little River Turnpike, Annandale, Virginia. Recognizing potential in his agent, Popov encouraged Barnett to apply for positions on the staffs of the Senate and House of Representatives intelligence committees. He refused, fearing he would not pass a mandatory polygraph examination but was rehired by the CIA under a contract where another polygraph test was not a prerequisite. Barnett then worked in that post for a little over a year.

Barnett's arrest came in 1980 along with attendant publicity. The CIA claimed Barnett was spotted meeting with his KGB handler in Europe. The story, while seemingly plausible, was not believed by Soviet counterintelligence. After launching an internal investigation, the KGB concluded Barnett's treason became known to the CIA through an American penetration of the GRU by double agent Col. Vladimir Piguzov, code-named GTJOGGER.

Put on trial in 1980, Barnett was sentenced to 18 years in prison. Paroled in 1990, he died in 1993. Piguzov was arrested and tried in Moscow in 1986, found guilty, and executed.

144. THE ART OF ESPIONAGE

MAP 7 ➤ Art Barn: Rock Creek Park, 2401 Tilden Street NW

Located in Rock Creek Park on Tilden Street, the Peirce Mill (also known as Pierce Mill) dates to the 1820s. Isaac Peirce built the water-powered gristmill, one of eight mills that once graced the banks of Rock Creek, to grind oats, wheat, rye, and corn for local farmers. Over 150 years later, the outbuilding that served as the carriage house hosted an electronic surveillance operation.

The rustic Art Barn in Rock Creek Park offered classes to aspiring artists while also serving as a secret listening post targeting nearby Iron Curtain embassies.

Rechristened as the Art Barn in 1971, the facility offered a showcase for local artists and free classes for children. It also provided an excellent site to eavesdrop on the nearby Hungarian and Czechoslovakian embassies. The concealed signals-collection equipment, hidden behind a false wall in an area that once served as a coop for homing pigeons, remained a secret until after the Cold War. However, those working in the Art Barn had their suspicions. "We always knew which guys were the CIA guys because they always wore sunglasses indoors, had real sharp creases in their pants, short haircuts and shiny shoes," a former director of the Art Barn said in a December 1, 1992, *Washington Post* article. CIA officers were amused by the assertion, since the agency's charter restricts it from such activity in the United States. Those mysterious, well-dressed men were most likely FBI agents.

145. RAKING THE MUCK

MAP 12 ➤ **Jack Anderson residence:** 7810 Kachina Lane, Bethesda, Maryland (private residence)

Writing from his home office in Bethesda, Maryland, columnist Jack Anderson compromised multiple CIA operations during the early decades of the Cold War.

Newspaper columnist Jack Anderson broke stories for decades that both embarrassed the CIA and jeopardized critical operations. The inheritor of Drew Pearson's muck-raking "Washington Merry-Go-Round" column, Anderson was syndicated in some 1,000 newspapers with an estimated readership of 40 million. His disclosures infuriated and frustrated both the FBI and the CIA. J. Edgar Hoover called him "lower than the regurgitated filth of vultures."

Sometimes it seemed Anderson was doing the KGB's job with his reporting, which created operational and security nightmares for the CIA. In 1971, he disclosed an active Moscow-based CIA operation code-named GAMMA GUPY that intercepted car-phone calls of high-ranking Soviet officials in their limos. The collection dried up almost immediately. Anderson columns revealed would-be Mafia-assisted assassination plots targeting Cuban dictator Fidel Castro and the ultrasensitive CIA effort to raise the Soviet submarine *K-129* using the USNS *Hughes Glomar Explorer*, operating under the cover story of a deep-sea magnesium-mining enterprise.

Anderson himself employed collection methods common to spies. His sources were often disaffected government employees. His staff sifted through the trash of public officials, including J. Edgar Hoover's, for information. While he abstained from alcohol, Anderson hired a hard-partying assistant, Opal Ginn, to make the rounds of Washington's cocktail party circuit for gossip and leads. Ginn, who was said to count lovers among her sources, reportedly once put on a cleaning lady's uniform to pilfer documents off a senator's desk.

"I don't like to hurt people, I really don't like it at all," Anderson was quoted in his 2005 Associated Press obituary, "but in order to get a red light [installed] at the intersection, you sometimes have to have an accident."

146. POLITICAL SURVEILLANCE

MAP 4 ➤ **The Watergate:** 2600 Virginia Avenue NW

The arrest of the five burglars breaking into the Democratic National Committee (DNC) headquarters at the Watergate complex, 2600 Virginia Avenue NW, on June 17, 1972, precipitated a national scandal. By the time it ended, President Richard Nixon had been forced to resign, and "Watergate"—or simply adding "gate" to a word—became Washington shorthand for scandal. With

A compromised break-in at the Watergate offices of the Democratic National Committee set in motion a chain of events that ended Richard Nixon's presidency.

Former FBI agent G. Gordon Liddy (pictured in 1964) served as general counsel of the finance operation for Nixon's Committee to Re-Elect the President. Along with E. Howard Hunt, he supervised the 1972 Watergate break-in that triggered events leading to President Nixon's resignation two years later.

Room 723 of the Howard Johnson Motor Lodge (now a George Washington University dormitory) on Virginia Avenue NW served as the Watergate burglars' listening post and operations center.

new revelations seemingly broadcast daily, the Watergate drama eventually encompassed scores of Washington insiders, including former spies, politicians, reporters, and law enforcement officers.

The break-in was run like a surreptitious-entry intelligence operation. The surreptitious-entry team established an operational base in a second-floor office of the Watergate building with the DNC target on the sixth floor. A command center (first in room 419, then in room 723) was established across the street at the ***Howard Johnson's Motor Lodge, 2601 Virginia Avenue NW***. An earlier entry into the same target had installed electronic bugs and phone taps. However, a second entry to reposition one of the bugs to transmit a better signal proved disastrous and ultimately doomed Nixon's presidency.

Two former CIA officers, James McCord and E. Howard Hunt, were supported by five Cuban Americans, one of whom was still on a small retainer by the agency. Hunt, who maintained contact with the agency through his job as a security consultant at the White House, would further draw the CIA into the scandal. His initial request for the loan of some unsophisticated spy gear was granted, although subsequent and more ambitious requisitions were denied.

DCI Richard Helms recalled in his autobiography telling Sen. J. William Fulbright, while Helms testified before the Senate Foreign Relations Committee, "It's as nutty an episode as I can recall. . . . We didn't have a damned thing to do with it." Seeking to distance the agency from the growing mess, he refused a White House request to secretly provide bail for the Watergate burglars and deflect a FBI investigation. Another request, to classify documents related to the burglary, was also refused. The White House, Helms later recalled, backed off from such requests, but, in Nixon's words, the agency was a collection of "Ivy League liberals."

For two *Washington Post* reporters, Bob Woodward and Carl Bernstein, their investigative reporting would also take on significant aspects of an intelligence operation. Working out of the paper's headquarters at ***1150 15th Street NW***, they developed anonymous sources and tracked down leads. To signal a clandestine meeting with his famed source "Deep Throat"—later revealed as the deputy associate director of the FBI, W. Mark Felt—Woodward placed a red flag in a flowerpot on the balcony of his studio apartment in the ***Webster House apartments, number 617, 1718 P Street NW***. So protective was Woodward of Felt that his identity was not known even to Bernstein until decades after the Watergate scandal and Felt's retirement from the bureau.

147. DEEP THROAT REVEALED

MAP 9 ➤ **Oakhill Office Building parking garage:** 1820 North Nash Street, Rosslyn, Arlington, Virginia

W. Mark Felt, eventually revealed as Deep Throat in the Watergate saga, played a high-stakes game with *The Washington Post*. An experienced FBI spy hunter during World War II and a protégé of J. Edgar Hoover, he was deputy associate director, third in command at the FBI, at the time of the Watergate break-in. He could hardly have expected that a friendship with Bob Woodward, the young naval officer he met outside the White House Situation Room delivering documents years earlier, would make history. As the Watergate drama played out, Felt acted in several roles. He fed information to Woodward in clandestine meetings in the parking garage of the Oakhill Office Building, 1820 North Nash Street, Rosslyn, Arlington, Virginia, blocked White House efforts to

Watergate scandal plaque at 1401 Wilson Boulevard, Rosslyn, Arlington, Virginia. The garage itself is nearby, at 1820 North Nash Street.

While investigating alleged wrongdoings of the Nixon White House, *Washington Post* reporter Bob Woodward met his clandestine FBI source in this Rosslyn garage.

Watergate-Gate

How the Watergate complex derived its name is unsettled. One author asserts the name comes from overlooking a gate that once regulated the flow of water from the Potomac River into the Tidal Basin. However, the *AIA Guide to the Architecture of Washington* contends the "curious name" references the nearby terraced Watergate Steps west of the Lincoln Memorial that lead down to the Potomac River. Built in the early 1930s, the graceful arc of steps was intended for grand, red-carpet entrances into Washington by visiting dignitaries. However, in subsequent years few dignitaries arrived by boat, and the steps were repurposed as an amphitheater seating up to 12,000, with performers often playing on a floating stage. That ended in the 1960s when noise from passenger jets landing and departing Washington National Airport (today the Ronald Reagan Washington National Airport) made such events impossible. Since then the steps have been used primarily for exercise-conscious joggers and stair runners.

quash the investigation, and launched seemingly genuine internal investigations to identify the "leaker."

Ironically, Felt would later find himself in hot water over "black bag" jobs. In 1972 and 1973, he approved nine surreptitious entries by the FBI into the homes of those associated with the violent left-wing organization Weather Underground. Unable to fully justify the actions, he was brought to trial in 1980, convicted of conspiracy, and fined $8,500. He was pardoned by President Reagan in 1981.

148. SCHOOL FOR SPIES

MAP 9 ➤ **Blue U:** 1000 North Glebe Road, Arlington, Virginia (demolished for redevelopment)

A multistory office building, that once stood at 1000 North Glebe Road, Arlington, Virginia, with its distinctive blue glass-and-steel exterior was affectionately called "the Blue Goose" by local residents. No signage identified the building's primary tenant, the CIA's recruiting and training office. During the 1960s and 1970s, CIA applicants were interviewed and tested there before they were shuttled to the main headquarters building a few miles away. One naive college graduate from the Midwest wrote to a

A distinctive office building (razed in 2015) at the corner of North Glebe Road and Fairfax Drive, Arlington, Virginia, was once a CIA recruitment and training facility.

friend, "I had my first interview with the CIA today. Their headquarters is in a curious looking blue building which is much smaller than I expected. It must have gone okay, they invited me back tomorrow."

Newly hired employees attended lectures and received specialized training at the building, also nicknamed "Blue U." Twenty-four-person blue vans provided hourly shuttle service from Blue U to headquarters and other CIA buildings. The vans, manufactured by the Blue Bird Corporation, displayed no markings other than a small sign on the dashboard with the van's next destination, such as "HEADQUARTERS," "GLEBE ROAD," or "STATE." The Blue Birds only carried passengers who discreetly flashed a "never to be worn in public" identification badge—with its distinctive royal blue background —to the driver.

Purchased by Marymount University in 1992, the two-tone, concave-front building was demolished in the spring of 2015 despite opposition by some community leaders who argued for its preservation as an example of endangered mid-20th-century architecture.

■ 149. INTERNATIONAL MAN OF MISERY

MAP 4 ➤ **Edwin P. Wilson residence:** 1016 22nd Street NW

After leaving a 20-year CIA career in the early 1970s, Edwin P. Wilson started a far more lucrative second career doing contract work for the intelligence community. His specialty was setting up companies structured to support intelligence operations. Wilson's firm, ***Consultants International Inc., 1425 K Street NW***, served him well. He made an estimated $23 million fortune and spent lavishly, acquiring a townhouse at 1016 22nd Street NW, a 2,388-acre farm near Upperville, Virginia, and other properties around the world. He kept a mistress he nicknamed "Wonder Woman" and reportedly maintained a scattering of love nests, including one at the ***River House Apartments, 1600 South Joyce Street, Arlington, Virginia***.

International arms dealer Edwin P. Wilson lived in this classic Washington townhouse in Foggy Bottom.

Wilson wined and dined CIA officials, Pentagon generals, and congressmen. A skilled and enthusiastic raconteur who was known to mix fact, fable, and fiction, he once claimed to have killed Che Guevara. Trading heavily on his past association with the agency, he operated in the international shadows, selling arms and providing training to Libya at a time when Muammar el-Qaddafi's government was sponsoring terrorism and viewed as a serious threat to the United States.

Following a lengthy investigation, federal authorities filed conspiracy charges against Wilson in 1980 that included training Libyans in bomb making and an attempt to sell 20 tons of the explosive C-4 to the Libyan dictator. Wilson fled to Libya but was lured to the Dominican Republic in 1982, arrested, and extradited to the United States. At his trial, the defense asserted Wilson had been working for the CIA all along.

In what already seemed a plot from an espionage novel, the trial took another twist when Wilson was accused of soliciting a fellow prisoner to kill the prosecutors, six witnesses, and his ex-wife. Eventually convicted for both arms smuggling and plotting murders, he was given a 52-year sentence.

Then in 2004, after years of doggedly accumulating documents through the Freedom of Information Act, Wilson discovered that a CIA witness lied during the trial, raising a slim possibility of truth to his claim that he was working for the agency. Apparently information about some unofficial contact between Wilson and CIA officials had, his lawyers argued, been improperly withheld. Wilson's conviction was voided. He had spent 22 years in prison, including long stretches in solitary confinement. Following his release, Wilson moved to Seattle, Washington, where he lived until his death following heart-valve replacement surgery on September 10, 2012, at age 84.

■ 150. ANYTHING FOR A BUCK

MAP 10 ➤ **Frank Terpil residence:** 1102 Chain Bridge Road, McLean, Virginia (private residence)

After six years with the CIA, Frank Terpil resigned in 1971, leaving questions of ethical conduct unanswered, to join Edwin Wilson in the shadowy arms-dealing business. From his residence at 1102 Chain Bridge Road, McLean, Virginia, Terpil formed his company as ***Inter-Technology, with an office at 1618 K Street NW***.

The pair's unsavory deals included the sale of sophisticated military hardware, weapons, and explosives to Libyan dictator Muammar el-Qaddafi. Their arms business thrived until undercover agents posing as Latin American revolutionaries obtained Terpil's agreement to sell 10,000 submachine guns and 10 million rounds of ammunition in an illegal conspiracy. While awaiting trial in 1980, Terpil fled the United States, eventually settling in Cuba. Nevertheless, the

Shadowy arms dealer Frank Terpil lived on Chain Bridge Road in McLean, Virginia, before fleeing to Cuba.

case proceeded, and he was convicted by a New York State court and sentenced to 53 years in prison. In 1981, a Federal grand jury indicted the absent Terpil for selling arms, ammunition, and torture devices to the Ugandan government of Idi Amin. In the years since, Terpil maintained residence in Cuba, out of reach of US authorities, where he reportedly died on March 1, 2016.

151. DCI IN THE SPOTLIGHT

MAP 5 ➤ William E. Colby residence: 3028 Dent Place NW (private residence)

William Colby's home would have been a refuge from the daily media circus of congressional investigations that engulfed the agency during his tenure as DCI.

An OSS officer during World War II and an early recruit to the CIA, William E. Colby served as Director of Central Intelligence (DCI) from September 1973 to January 1976. His tenure occurred during a tumultuous period in agency history. Press leaks shortly after he took the top spot revealed a long-abandoned counterintelligence program code-named MHCHAOS that included mail-opening operations in the United States. The controversy led to three investigations: a presidential blue-ribbon panel headed by Vice President Nelson Rockefeller, a Senate select committee led by presidential aspirant Sen. Frank Church, and the House of Representatives Select Committee on Intelligence Operations.

In response to congressional demands, Colby provided substantial amounts of classified material to the investigators. In his autobiography, *A Look over My Shoulder: A Life in the Central Intelligence Agency*, former DCI Richard Helms recounted that at one point Vice President Rockefeller voiced alarm, asking, "Bill, do you really have to present all this material to us? We realize that there are secrets you fellows need to keep and so nobody is going to take it amiss if you feel that there are some questions you can't answer quite as fully as you seem to feel you have to." The hearings generated sensational headlines, fueled unfounded conspiracy theories, and spurred wild accusations of agency misconduct.

Colby was replaced as DCI by George Bush in 1976 and retired. He lived at 3028 Dent Place NW in Georgetown until his death in 1996 while canoeing near Cobb Island, Maryland, and his weekend home on the Chesapeake Bay. He is buried in Arlington National Cemetery.

152. SCANDAL, COMMITTEES, AND THE FAMILY JEWELS

MAP 1 ➤ Church Committee hearings: Dirksen Senate Office Building, rooms S407 and G308, Constitution Avenue NE between First and Second Streets NE

On December 22, 1974, *The New York Times* splashed the headline "Huge C.I.A. Operation Reported in U.S. Against Antiwar Forces, Other Dissidents In Nixon Years." The story, by Seymour Hersh, alleged that the CIA carried out dozens of secret, illegal activities in the United States. A political firestorm followed that put the agency under intense scrutiny from the media, public, and elected officials.

From offices in the Dirksen Senate Office Building, Sen. Frank Church's special committee investigated alleged wrongdoing by the CIA and the FBI.

The controversy began two years earlier when reporting about the Watergate break-in and subsequent attempted cover-up seemed to implicate the CIA. Responding to allegations of agency involvement, DCI James Schlesinger ordered an agency-wide compilation of any past and present activities that might fall outside the CIA charter. William Colby, who replaced Schlesinger as DCI in mid-1973, became custodian of a 693-page report that covered a quarter century of intelligence operations, including some that were questionable or exceeding the charter. Internally, the document became known as "the Family Jewels," and portions were leaked to Hersh.

Within two weeks of Hersh's story, President Gerald Ford issued *Executive Order 11828* and impaneled a blue-ribbon commission headed by Vice President Nelson Rockefeller to investigate the allegations. The bipartisan commission, representing the government and the private sector, included former California governor and future president Ronald Reagan. The Senate, acting independently in January, established the Select Committee to Study Governmental Operations with Respect to Intelligence Activities, under the chairmanship of Sen. Frank Church. On February 19, the House of Representatives jumped into the fray and

The Family Jewels

The term "Family Jewels" used in the 1970s to describe sensitive intelligence information was not original. Former DCI Allen Dulles may have been the first to apply the term when, as an OSS officer in Bern, Switzerland, he operated under the code name AGENT 110. For Dulles, Family Jewels were details of sensitive operations contained in a personal notebook and the first thing to be destroyed in the event of trouble.

the media limelight with its separate Select Committee on Intelligence Operations, led by Rep. Otis Pike.

Of the three investigative bodies, the Senate's "Church Committee" captured most of the headlines. As the investigation began, Senator Church set an aggressive tone, asserting that "the agency may have been behaving like a rogue elephant on a rampage." The committee staff of more than 150 worked in room G308 of the Dirksen Senate Office Building, formerly an auditorium converted to office space for the previous Watergate committee hearings. The majority of the hearings themselves took place in room S407, a secure room used by the Joint Atomic Energy Committee.

It was a spectacle. The public revelations involved more than two decades of alleged illegal operations and dirty tricks by the US government, ranging from the potentially criminal to the bizarre. The CIA had conducted mail-opening operations, experimented on unwitting human subjects with drugs, including LSD, and plotted to assassinate foreign leaders. The FBI had bugged the hotel room of Martin Luther King Jr. The NSA had monitored international cable traffic. During one seemingly made-for-TV moment of testimony, DCI Colby held aloft a James Bond–ish dart gun. The scene provided a dramatic photo op of a futuristic looking weapon that was neither developed nor ever deployed by the CIA. Calls for disbanding the CIA were frequent. "I do fear the result could be a farce or a tragedy, or both," Colby said at the time.

Results of two years of investigations led to Congress having substantially greater insight into and authority over intelligence activities and, despite the initial sensationalism surrounding the hearing, dispelled for most the notion that the CIA was a "rogue elephant," as some initially asserted. Rather, America's secret agencies had acted, with a handful of exceptions, in response to presidential direction from both Democratic and Republican administrations, consistent with law and the National Security Act of 1947.

Nevertheless, permanent oversight committees were established in both houses of Congress—the Senate Select Committee on Intelligence and the House Permanent Select Committee on Intelligence. The committees, which conduct much of their work in secret, are located in the ***Hart Senate Office Building, room 211***, and the ***Capitol Visitors Center, room HVC-304***, respectively.

■ 153. EMBITTERED TRAITOR

MAP 12 ➤ **Edwin G. Moore II residence:** 4800 Fort Sumner Drive, Bethesda, Maryland (private residence)

On December 21, 1976, Vitaly Yurchenko, a KGB security officer working at the official Soviet residence, ***3875 Tunlaw Road NW***, alerted the Washington Metropolitan Police Department to a suspicious package someone had thrown inside the security fence. The bulky manila envelope wrapped in

From his home, Edwin G. Moore could observe the area across the street where a package was tossed from a moving vehicle in an FBI sting operation.

The FBI followed Moore's clandestine instructions and made a drop of money at this specific spot just yards away from the former CIA officer's Bethesda, Maryland, home.

plastic could have been a bomb but when opened by US authorities was discovered to contain a collection of classified CIA documents.

According to a February 1977 *Washington Post* article, the package contained the CIA's phone directory, office locations of employees, information on regulations, and a map pinpointing agency buildings, safe houses, and training facilities, along with information as to which employees were the best recruitment targets. A rambling typewritten note addressed "For Resident Eyes Only" read, in part, "I am offering your organization penetration inside [CIA] Headquarters . . . for a certain fee." The price was $3,000 to be paid immediately and $197,000 later on. Instructions for the initial payment, in specific denominations, directed the cash to be tossed from a gray Dodge van between a fire hydrant and telephone pole on Fort Sumner Drive, Bethesda, Maryland. A map, along with photographs of the telephone pole and fire hydrant, were helpfully included.

On December 22, the FBI followed the instructions and nabbed Edwin G. Moore II, a CIA officer who had left the agency three years earlier. The spot where the money was tossed was conveniently located directly across from Moore's home. Moore, who had pretended to rake leaves in his front yard, made five trips to it before finally picking up the package. A subsequent search of his house uncovered a large cache of classified documents.

Moore was no master spy. The 56-year-old father of five had a history of emotional and financial problems. Previously diagnosed as suffering from a paranoid-like state, he was once let go from the CIA after a conviction on arson charges but was rehired when the conviction was overturned. Before being caught as a spy, he sent an anonymous letter to then DCI William Colby that was nearly incoherent in its bitterness: "REMEMBER THIS . . . MY FAMILY HAS BEEN UNABLE TO HAVE THE FINER THINGS OF THE AMERICAN DREAM BECAUSE I CAN NOT ARN [*sic*] A DECENT SALARY. . . . Gosh, it seems strange to be a CIA defector."

Moore's trial brought the CIA into the unwanted spotlight. Initially pleading not guilty by reason of insanity, Moore later spun a story of how he believed he was working for the agency on a top secret mission at the behest of a mysterious contact known only as "Joe." A psychiatrist found Moore competent to stand trial, and he was sentenced to 15 years in prison, though he was granted parole in 1979.

154. SEXPIONAGE IN THE NATION'S CAPITAL

MAP 4 ➤ The Exchange Saloon: 1719 G Street NW

The Exchange Saloon was once a venue for Washington's swingers, including the husband-and-wife spy team of Karl and Hana Koecher.

As members of 1970s-era Capitol Couples, a Washington wife-swapping club, Karl and Hana Koecher frequented the Exchange Saloon, 1719 G Street NW, less than two blocks from the White House. Members of the free-wheeling, free-love group reportedly included CIA and military officers, journalists, and at least one US senator. Although presenting themselves as dedicated anticommunists loyal to their adopted country, the Koechers were *illegals* (foreign intelligence officers living undercover without diplomatic immunity) working under direction of the Státní Bezpečnost (StB), the Czechoslovakian intelligence service.

Karl secured work as a contract translator for the CIA and provided information to his Czechoslovakian handlers, who passed it along to Soviet intelligence. The Koechers' spying likely led to the compromise and death of at least one major American spy in Moscow, Alexander Ogorodnik, codenamed TRIGON.

Karl and Hana Koecher lived in Falls Church, Virginia, while spying on behalf of the Czechoslovakian intelligence service.

The Koechers lived at an apartment complex at ***3100 Manchester Street, Falls Church, Virginia***, until apprehended in New York City by the FBI in 1984 as they were about to flee the United States. They were later swapped for Soviet dissident Anatoly Scharansky in 1986 and now reside in the Czech Republic. The Exchange Saloon exists today as a sports bar.

155. CAR BOMB AT THE CENTER OF THE CITY

MAP 3 ➤ **Sheridan Circle NW**

On September 21, 1976, a powerful bomb exploded in Orlando Letelier's car as it rounded Sheridan Circle NW. The explosion killed the former diplomat and economist who once served in Chile's socialist government under deposed president Salvador Allende. Letelier's American assistant, Ronni Moffitt, also died in the blast, while her husband, Michael Moffitt, was injured. An outspoken opponent of Gen. Augusto Pinochet's current government, Letelier had established a high public profile through writing and speeches denouncing the regime.

A small plaque near Sheridan Circle marks the location where a car bomb killed Orlando Letelier, an outspoken critic of Chile's Gen. Augusto Pinochet, and Letelier's colleague Ronni Moffitt.

Suspicion for the bombing immediately fell on Chile's intelligence service, the Dirección de Inteligencia Nacional (DINA). An FBI investigation led to the arrests and international prosecutions of American Michael Townley, five anti-Castro Cubans, former DINA head Gen. Manuel Contreras, and DINA officer Brig. Pedro Espinoza. A small monument on Sheridan Circle NW commemorates Letelier and Moffitt.

156. THE WIFE DEFECTS

MAP 9 ➤ **Yelena Mitrokhina residence:** Chatham Apartments, 4501 Arlington Boulevard, Arlington, Virginia

The first Cold War defector from the Soviet embassy in Washington was a woman, Yelena Mitrokhina, wife of the first secretary, Lev Mitrokhina. The couple lived comfortably at the Chatham apartment complex at 4501 Arlington Boulevard, Arlington, Virginia, in the mid-1970s. Seeing the opportunities in America, she contacted the FBI through an unlikely intermediary, an employee at her local Oldsmobile dealership.

Yelena Mitrokhina, the wife of a Soviet diplomat and resident of the Chatham Apartments in Arlington, Virginia, sought help from employees at the local Oldsmobile dealership when she decided to defect.

Yelena met with the FBI at the ***Holiday Inn, 1900 North Fort Myer Drive, Rosslyn, Arlington, Virginia***, to plan her defection. She agreed that an attempt would be made to bring along her husband. However, when presented with the plan, he balked, refusing to follow his wife and two children.

Yelena was given a new name, Alexandra Costa, and with university degrees in sociology and Scandinavian languages, she envisioned a professional future for herself in America. However, problems arose when her resettlement officer unwisely suggested she attend secretarial school. "I was hysterical," Costa told a *Washington Post* reporter years later. "I thought, 'Jesus Christ, I've risked my life to learn typing!'"

The FBI intervened. Mitrokhina was admitted to the University of Pennsylvania, where she finished a two-year computer science program in 18 months. Afterward, the ambitious defector operated several successful businesses, including the ***Russian Gourmet, 1396 Chain Bridge Road, McLean, Virginia*** (since closed). In 1986, she published an autobiography, *Stepping Down from the Star: A Soviet Defector's Story,* and two years later married Stanislav Levchenko, a former KGB major who defected in Japan in 1979.

■ 157. *ILLEGAL* TURNED FBI SOURCE

MAP 9 ➤ Rudolph Herrmann residence: Arlington Towers (now River Place West), 1111 Arlington Boulevard, Rosslyn, Arlington, Virginia

Ludek Zemenek, a Czechoslovakian spy operating under deep cover who decided to cooperate with the FBI, once lived in the Arlington Towers (today River Place West).

Ludek Zemenek, a Czechoslovakian national, was a Soviet *illegal*, a spy living in alias under deep cover, virtually invisible to American authorities. Trained and outfitted with a false identity by the KGB, Zemenek became Canadian citizen Rudolph Albert Herrmann before immigrating to the United States in 1968. His profession as a freelance photographer and filmmaker in New York's Westchester County suburb of Hartsdale provided a cover that gave him the workplace flexibility and mobility to support Soviet spy networks throughout the United States. At one point he buried containers of instructions for later pickup near Chicago. In another operation, he sent an anonymous letter to NASA warning of damage to an Apollo 8 rocket in an unsuccessful ploy to delay or scrub the 1968 launch that sent three astronauts in orbit around the moon.

However, Herrmann's greatest long-term investment for the KGB was likely his son, Peter. In appearance an all-American kid, Peter was brought into the spy game while still in his teens and accompanied his father on operational trips. For the youngster, it was on-the-job training. The goal was for Peter to enter a prestigious college and become a US government employee.

Rudolph Herrmann and his son were living at Arlington Towers (now River Place West), 1111 Arlington Boulevard, Rosslyn, Arlington, Virginia, when Peter began attending Georgetown University. When the FBI became aware of Rudolph's true identity in 1977, he was confronted and agreed to cooperate. He then revealed names of Soviet operatives and reported on KGB tradecraft. Newspapers reported the family was given a new identity and relocated to an undisclosed location where Rudolph Herrmann / Ludek Zemenek made a living as a home builder and remodeler.

By 1986, Rudolph Herrmann had enough of America and wanted to return to his home country. He packed up the family's belongings and shipped eighteen pieces of luggage to Prague. However, Czechoslovakian officials, claiming the father's true name was Valousek, denied the application for repatriation, stripped him of Czechoslovakian citizenship, and confiscated his bank accounts. The luggage was returned, except for Peter's American comic book collection. "The bureaucrats can't face me," the elder Herrmann explained in a November 2, 1986, *Los Angeles Times* article. "That's it."

158. BELIEVE THEM OR NOT

MAP 3 ➤ Russian Trade Representation office: 2001 Connecticut Avenue NW

Department store magnate Alvin M. Lothrop built the 40-room beaux arts mansion in 1909 that now serves as the home for the Russian Trade Representation. Located at 2001 Connecticut Avenue NW, the landmark building was purchased by the USSR in 1975 and became home to Cold War spies working under business and trade representative covers. The mansion briefly came into the public spotlight in 1987 when the Soviet government accused US intelligence of bugging the premises. Displaying very clever concealments for the alleged listening devices, some of which looked like hairbrushes and pencils, Soviet officials expressed customary boilerplate outrage, asserting bugs had been implanted in window frames, heating systems, television antennas, walls, doors, and roof beams. Brushing aside the matter, President Reagan told reporters at Purdue University on April 9, 1987, "If you want to believe them, go ahead."

The historic Lothrop Mansion housed the Soviet Trade Representation. Soviet officials complained that spy gear had been secretly installed throughout the building.

159. THE DOUBLE LIFE OF A SPECIAL AGENT

MAP 10 ➤ **Robert Hanssen residence:** 9414 Talisman Drive, Vienna, Virginia (private residence)

Robert Hanssen

Spies lead double lives filled with deception and betrayal, but Robert Hanssen's espionage and double life surprised even those who thought they knew him well. Outwardly a serious-minded career FBI special agent for counterintelligence, a family man, a father of six, and a regular church attendee, he had a straight-laced demeanor that often seemed over the top, even for the traditionally conservative FBI.

Hanssen's secret life included disturbing sexual activities, explicit sexual postings on Internet bulletin boards, romps with a DC stripper overseas, and spying for the Soviet GRU and KGB, as well as the Russian foreign intelligence service Sluzhba Vneshney Razvedki (SVR). Over more than two decades, Hanssen accepted in excess of $600,000 in cash and diamonds from his spymasters.

Robert Hanssen's double life as a spy belied his quiet suburban home life on Talisman Drive in Vienna, Virginia.

Hanssen's espionage began in the fall of 1979 when he walked into the New York office of the Soviet trade organization Amerikanskoe Torgovlye (AMTORG), a known front company for Soviet military intelligence. After contacting a GRU officer there whom he had previously surveilled as part of his FBI duties, Hanssen sold secrets for $20,000. He later claimed financial pressure and the cost of living in the upscale Westchester suburb of Scarsdale drove him to betray his country. When his wife, Bonnie, stumbled onto his treason, he sought counseling from a priest and

Robert Hanssen marked the Foxstone Park entrance sign with a piece of white adhesive tape to indicate to his Russian handler that the dead drop, code-named ELLIS, was filled.

promised to stop spying. By 1985, that promise was broken.

After a second posting to New York City in the mid-1980s, Hanssen returned to bureau headquarters in Washington and moved his family into a house at 9414 Talisman Drive, Vienna, Virginia. Among his FBI colleagues at headquarters, Hanssen's somber manner seemed consistent with his techie-geek interests. Little did they suspect that he was a regular at a local strip club, the now defunct ***Joanna's 1819 Club, 1819 M Street NW***. At Joanna's, Hanssen met Priscilla Sue Galey (stage name Traci Starr) in 1990. Playing the sugar daddy with his ill-gotten income, he lavished gifts, cash, a credit card, and a preowned Mercedes on the stripper. Galey accompanied Hanssen on one of his official business trips to Hong Kong, and he gave her a special tour of the FBI training facility in Quantico, Virginia.

The ending of Hanssen's double life as a spy began in 2000. Aware of a well-placed penetration of American intelligence, the FBI's investigation first focused on CIA officer Brian Kelley, a onetime neighbor of Hanssen's who fit parts of the profile of the suspected mole. However, when a Russian source came forward to sell an audiotape of the suspected mole, known to him only as Ramon Garcia or simply "B," the attention quickly shifted away from Kelley. The voice on the tape was promptly recognized as that of Robert Philip Hanssen. The FBI agent's involvement was confirmed when the Russian source provided a plastic trash bag used at one of the dead drops with Hanssen's thumbprint on it.

The underside of a footbridge in Foxstone Park served as dead-drop site ELLIS—where Hanssen left his final package for Russian intelligence in February 2001.

The arrow indicates dead-drop site LEWIS in Long Branch Nature Center where the SVR left a package of money for Hanssen that he never had the opportunity to retrieve.

Robert Hanssen's first dead-drop site, code-named PARK and PRIME, was located under a wooden footbridge in Nottoway Park.

The FBI purchased a house across the street from Hanssen's home to use as an observation post.

The Careful Traitor

Robert Hanssen was not only one of the most damaging spies in US history but one of the most active. Over more than two decades of spying, he used dozens of signal and dead-drop sites for clandestine communication with his handlers. Preferring local parks, he chose operational sites that encompassed much of the Washington metropolitan area, with a few, such as Foxstone Park and Nottaway Park, only a short distance from his home. Some of those locations were the following:

Emergency signal site: Q Street and Connecticut Avenue

Signal site ELLIS: Signpost at entrance to Foxstone Park, Fairfax County, Virginia

Signal site PARK: Nottaway Park, pedestrian-crossing signpost just west of the main Nottaway Park entrance on Old Courthouse Road

Dead-drop site GRACE: Rock Creek Park

Dead-drop site LEWIS: Amphitheater, Long Branch Nature Center, Arlington, Virginia

Dead-drop site CHARLIE: Eakin Community Park, Fairfax County, Virginia

Dead-drop site DORIS: Canterbury Park, Springfield, Virginia

Dead-drop site PRIME: Wooden footbridge located just west of the entrance to Nottaway Park, Vienna, Virginia

Dead-drop site LINDA: Roundtree Park, Falls Church, Virginia

Dead-drop site AN: Ellanor C. Lawrence Park, Chantilly, Virginia

Dead-drop site FLO: under a footbridge in Lewinsville Park, near the intersection of Warner Avenue and Westbury Road, McLean, Virginia

To build its case, the FBI purchased a house at 9419 Talisman Drive, across the street from Hanssen's residence, for an observation post. Hanssen made his last dead drop on February 18, 2001, in the 14-acre Foxstone Park near his home. The site, code-named ELLIS by Hanssen and his Russian handlers, was located under a weathered wooden footbridge along the main pathway inside the park. Late that afternoon, Hanssen was under surveillance as he left a piece of white adhesive tape on Foxstone's entrance sign as a signal before entering the park. After filling the drop, he retraced his route and exited the park. As he approached his car, a five-man team of his fellow special agents arrested him. "So this is how it ends," Hanssen was reported to have said while seated, handcuffed in the back of the vehicle.

Hanssen pled guilty but never fully cooperated with authorities attempting to compile a damage assessment. He received life in prison without the possibility of parole and is confined at the United States Penitentiary, Florence, Colorado, in the Administrative Maximum Facility, popularly known as "Supermax."

160. UNBREAKABLE DEFECTOR

MAP 11 ➤ **Invicta Networks:** 13873 Park Center Road, suite 400, Herndon, Virginia

Vicktor Sheymov, a KGB defector, headquartered his consulting firm, Invicta Networks Inc., in this office building.

At age 33, Vicktor Ivanovich Sheymov (code name UTOPIA) was the youngest major in the KGB. A brilliant engineer and programmer, he played a critical role in Soviet code and communications security. Then in 1980, Sheymov, along with his wife and daughter, suddenly vanished from Moscow. With CIA assistance, the family resettled in the United States under assumed names. According to a June 2000 article in *The New York Times*, Sheymov assisted the NSA in attempts to breach code systems he previously defended.

"The KGB is a most sophisticated, deviously intelligent organization, and far more dangerous than the brutal thugs often presented to the public." —Vicktor Sheymov, *Tower of Secrets*

Sheymov also founded a computer security company, Invicta Networks Inc., once located at 13873 Park Center Road, Suite 400, Herndon, Virginia, and subsequently filed a lawsuit against the US government in a dispute over the amount of money promised in exchange for his defection. Represented by former DCI and Invicta board member R. James Woolsey, Sheymov eventually agreed to a confidential settlement with the agency.

An ironic twist occurred in Sheymov's life through his friendship with FBI special agent Robert Hanssen. Among the most notorious spies in American history, Hanssen thought of himself as a techie. He socialized with Sheymov and brought Invicta's patented security software to the FBI's attention. Only weeks before his arrest and with an eye toward his planned retirement, the disloyal FBI agent asked Sheymov for a job.

161. SPY FOR CASH

MAP 9 ➤ **Pizza Castle Restaurant:** 1523 North Danville Street, Arlington, Virginia (now the Good Food Company)

Ronald Pelton was deep in debt and in the process of declaring bankruptcy when he quit his job at the National Security Agency. The decision

Ronald Pelton

could possibly solve two problems: Working in the private sector might provide more money, and he could avoid potential security questions from the NSA about his financial dilemma. However, within a few weeks the former intelligence officer and the father of four became desperate for cash. He called the ***Soviet embassy, 1125 16th Street NW***, in January 1980 and identified himself as an American who would be there in two minutes. True to his word, he soon brazenly walked through the embassy's front door, presented sensitive documents to establish his bona fides, and offered other information stored in his remarkable memory from 14 years on the NSA payroll. Pelton's offer to spy was immediately accepted by the Soviets.

Instructed to shave his beard before departing, Pelton was also provided clothing that disguised him as a workman. Then he was quietly ushered out a side entrance accompanied by a phalanx of embassy employees, put into a van, and taken to the Soviet residential compound. After several hours he was transferred to a car, driven around Washington, and dropped off near one of the area's crowded shopping centers.

Former NSA employee turned spy Pelton was a frequent guest at his girlfriend's P Street NW home.

Using the alias Mr. Long, Pelton made regular dead drops for the next five years, receiving calls from his handlers at 8:00 p.m. on the last Saturday of each month at a public phone at the Pizza Castle Restaurant, 1523 North Danville Street, Arlington, Virginia. Other operational calls were made to a pay phone at the ***Huong Binh Bakery and Deli, 6781 Wilson Boulevard, Falls Church, Virginia***. Additional debriefings were scheduled overseas in Vienna.

The full extent of what Pelton sold to the Soviets has never been completely established or revealed. It is known that he disclosed at least five major operations, one of them a sophisticated deep-sea wiretapping operation code-named IVY BELLS. In this operation, a strong inductive coil placed around an underwater military communications cable in the Sea of Okhotsk recorded data that flowed through the cable. Reportedly, the system's "pod" could record weeks of communications traffic before a submarine operation—either a robot or divers—changed out the tapes. "IVY BELLS was a major success and Washington—which had spent hundreds of millions of dollars on the operation—was in the process of developing it further," recalled KGB officer Victor Cherkashin, author of *Spy Handler: Memoir of a KGB Officer; The True Story of the Man Who Recruited Robert Hanssen and Aldrich Ames*. "Pelton shut down the whole project for $35,000."

As Pelton's espionage career progressed, his personal life deteriorated. Separating from his wife and children, he began drinking heavily and took a job selling boats at ***Safford Marina, 4601 Annapolis Road, Bladensburg, Maryland***. Living on one of the boats in the marina, he regularly spent the night with his girlfriend, a former beauty queen named Ann Barry, at her apartment, ***1525 P Street NW***.

Pelton began injecting Dilaudid (hydromorphone), a powerful opioid. His spy work suffered. In one instance his car ran out of gas on the way to a scheduled phone call. In another episode, Pelton missed a planned meeting in Vienna, Austria, when his Soviet contact failed to recognize him because he had lost so much weight.

In August 1985, unknown to Pelton, KGB officer Vitaly Yurchenko defected in Rome and was secretly transported to the United States. He told the Americans he had been posted at the Soviet embassy in Washington when an NSA employee, whose name he did not know, walked in. The few details Yurchenko remembered, such as the spy's red hair and knowledge of classified information on NSA operations, were useful for investigators, who had a recording of an earlier, but unidentified, phone call to the Soviet embassy. When it was played for some NSA officers, a colleague recognized Pelton's voice.

Certain they had their man, but with scant evidence, the FBI planted bugs at the boatyard, Barry's apartment, and Pelton's car. Little more was learned from the bugs and surveillance operation other than Pelton liked to receive haircuts from his topless girlfriend as he sat at a kitchen window. However, when interviewed by two veteran FBI agents in room 409 of the ***Annapolis Hilton Hotel (today the Annapolis Marriott Waterfront), 80 Compromise Street***, Pelton confessed to spying possibly because he falsely believed the FBI wanted to use him as a double agent. Found guilty by a jury in June 1986, he received three consecutive life sentences. Pelton, at age 74, was released to home confinement in November 2015.

Ronald Pelton received calls from his handlers at a pay phone near what was then the Pizza Castle Restaurant in Arlington, Virginia.

Glenn Michael Souther used Dunn Loring Park as a dead-drop site while he spied for the Soviet Union.

■ 162. FROM TREASON TO SUICIDE

MAP 10 ➤ **Dunn Loring Park:** 2540 Gallows Road, Vienna, Virginia

In one sense, Glenn Michael Souther got away with spying for the Soviet Union. He was likely recruited by the KGB between 1979 and 1982 while stationed at headquarters of the US Navy's Sixth Fleet in Italy. Honorably discharged in 1982, he enrolled at Old Dominion University and joined the Naval Reserve. Stationed in Norfolk, Virginia, Souther had access to classified satellite imagery, which he gave to the Soviets using dead drops in Dunn Loring Park, 2540 Gallows Road, Vienna, Virginia.

Shortly after graduating from Old Dominion in 1986, Souther vanished. Two years later he resurfaced in the Soviet Union. As a minor celebrity behind the Iron Curtain, he gave television and print interviews critical of America and thanked the Soviet Union for granting him asylum. Investigators who reviewed the case discovered a report filed seven years earlier that included espionage accusations by his ex-wife. However, since she appeared intoxicated when speaking to officials, the information was discounted.

Then, in 1989, the 32-year-old Souther apparently committed suicide. The Soviet military paper *Krasnaya Zvezda* (Red Star) reported the death of "Yevgenyevich Orlov" with Souther's American name in parentheses. "For a long time he performed important special assignments and made a major contribution to insuring the security of the Soviet Union," the obituary read. The full extent of the damage Souther caused to national security remains unclear to this day. He is buried near British spy Kim Philby in the Kuntsevo Cemetery in Moscow. Also interred in the Russian cemetary are American spies Morris and Lona Cohen, who were involved in the Rosenberg atomic spy ring, and of Ramón Mercader, the assassin of Leon Trotsky.

■ 163. A DEFECTION THAT SHOCKED THE WORLD

MAP 3 ➤ **Iron Gate Inn:** 1734 N Street NW

When Soviet ambassador Arkady Shevchenko defected to the United States in April 1978, the news stunned the international diplomatic community. As undersecretary-general of the UN, Shevchenko became

Arkady Shevchenko's Washington, DC residence

the highest-ranking Soviet diplomatic defector of the Cold War. He had secretly worked with US intelligence for three years prior to his defection.

Soviet defector Arkady Shevchenko, former Under-Secretary-General of the United Nations, attracted unwelcome media attention when he was caught dining with a call girl at the Iron Gate Inn.

Shevchenko's debriefings were conducted at a Ramada Inn in Rockville, Maryland. Not long afterward, the former UN official became an unwilling celebrity at the center of a scandal. A call girl, Judy Chavez, arranged to meet Shevchenko at the Iron Gate Inn restaurant, 1734 N Street NW, and then alerted the media to the tryst. Reporters pounced on the story with gusto, while Chavez capitalized on her brief celebrity status with a book in 1979, *The Defector's Mistress: The Judy Chavez Story*.

For the disillusioned Soviet diplomat, the unwanted publicity was only part of the price to be paid for switching sides. Immediately after Shevchenko defected, Soviet authorities whisked his wife, Lina, and teenage daughter back to Moscow, eliminating any hope of reuniting. Just weeks later, Lina died under mysterious circumstances. The Soviet government ruled it suicide.

Shevchenko eventually married court reporter Elaine Jackson, and the couple lived at ***4941 Tilden Street NW***. He again entered the spotlight in 1985 with publication of his book *Breaking with Moscow*. "I had everything in the Soviet Union but my personal freedom," he told *People* magazine, "but it was a golden cage because I was under permanent surveillance. . . . When I came to the United States, I found that much of what I had heard about the free world was lies." Shevchenko died in 1998 at age 67.

■ 164. AMERICAN LIFE 101

MAP 2 ➤ **Jamestown Foundation: American Association of University Women Building, 1111 16th Street NW**

Headquartered on 16th Street NW, the Jamestown Foundation was established in 1984 to create public awareness of the personal stories of Soviet defectors.

Defectors from the Soviet Union often faced a difficult time adjusting to American culture. Even those who spent years in the United States under official or nonofficial cover were ill prepared for daily life without the security of government employment or a familiar career. Once debriefings ended, the defector faced a new, unfamiliar world, sometimes without family and always without previous friends. Early in its history, the CIA recognized that the challenge of a new language, the responsibility of being on one's own, and the loss of a prestigious position could combine to produce self-destructive behavior.

The CIA provided defectors a range of professional, educational, and counseling services to ease the transition into American society. Seemingly simple matters, such as refraining from asking how much a person earned when first meeting them (a socially acceptable practice in the Soviet Union) or proper casual and business attire, needed to be learned and sometimes unlearned.

"Former Soviets have some bad habits," defector Arkady Shevchenko, a diplomat who defected to the United States in 1978, told *People* magazine in 1985. "They are used to speaking rudely when they want something. Early in my time in the U.S., I might have walked into a store and been very impolite to a salesperson." To relieve anxieties in adjusting to the Western culture, the defector families with no experience in making choices among multiple shelves of similar products or American pricing practices were accompanied by a guide to shopping malls and supermarkets.

Despite the substantial assistance provided, resettlement was always difficult. "My life is here now," said Shevchenko, "but my affection for my motherland will always be with me."

In 1984, attorney William W. Geimer established an organization for defector assistance, the Jamestown Foundation. This private foundation sought to bring public attention to the stories and experiences of Soviet defectors beyond the CIA's unpublicized programs. Through the Jamestown Foundation, those who escaped to the West were assisted in publishing their memoirs and securing prominent lecture appearances. After the collapse of the USSR, the Jamestown Foundation, 1111 16th Street NW, expanded into becoming a research-and-analysis organization focusing on Eurasia. The organization produces analytical publications for scholars and the foreign policy community on issues relating to the post-Soviet region, China, and terrorism.

165. SCANDAL AT THE HAY-ADAMS

MAP 2 ➤ Hay-Adams Hotel: 800 Sixteenth Street NW

The upscale Hay-Adams Hotel was the site of Lt. Col. Oliver North's fundraising efforts that led to the Iran-Contra scandal in the 1980s. Using the hotel's bar and restaurant for privacy away from the White House, North raised more than $2 million from private donors during four meetings. The clandestine

The bar and restaurant of the Hay-Adams Hotel was used during the 1980s by Lt. Col. Oliver North for meetings to raise funds to support the Contras in Nicaragua.

operation, run from the White House, was exposed in 1986, with a congressional investigation and hearings following in 1987. North was indicted and convicted of obstructing Congress and unlawfully destroying official documents but cleared of all charges on appeal. CIA director William Casey was among those caught up in the investigation, but his death in May 1987 precluded any legal action against him.

166. AMERICA'S MOST DESTRUCTIVE SPY

MAP 9 ➤ Aldrich Hazen Ames residence: 2512 North Randolph Street, Arlington, Virginia (private residence)

One of the spies most damaging to CIA operations was not misguided, naive, or blackmailed. Aldrich Hazen Ames volunteered to betray his country for the most banal of reasons—money. A second-generation CIA officer, Ames attended McLean High School in McLean, Virginia, in the 1950s and worked a series of summer jobs at the agency. After dropping out of the University of Chicago, he returned to the agency while completing his education at George Washington University.

Aldrich Ames

Assigned to New York City in the 1970s, Ames participated in several major cases, including the defection of UN diplomat Arkady Shevchenko, the highest-ranking Soviet official to defect to the West, as well as Soviet weapons expert Sergei Fedorenko (code name PYRRHIC). However, even in these early years of success, Ames evidenced warning signs of instability, such as a tendency toward excessive drinking. On one occasion his driver's license was suspended after he was caught driving while intoxicated. In another inexcusable lapse, he left a briefcase filled with classified documents on the subway. The briefcase, according to one source, contained clandestine

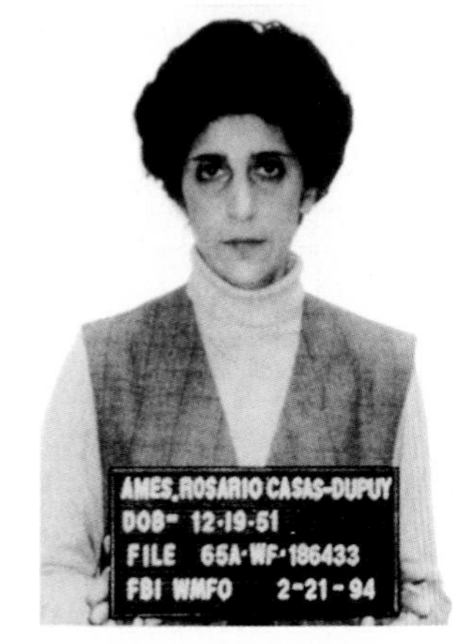

María del Rosario Casas Ames, known as Rosario Ames

Aldrich Ames's spying ended on February 21, 1994, near his home in Arlington, Virginia, when FBI agents handcuffed the CIA officer against his prized Jaguar.

Aldrich Ames's Arlington, Virginia, home was purchased for $540,000 in cash, then another $99,000 was spent on renovations.

Tasteless Extravagance

With the arrest of Aldrich and Rosario Ames, the government confiscated the ill-gotten goods from the couple's treasonous spending spree. The estimated value was more than $100,000 for a gaudy collection of personal items that included Rolex and Cartier watches along with Gucci purses. The jewelry included 16 pearl necklaces; 17 pairs of diamond earrings; 12 gold and jeweled bracelets; chokers; pendants; a silver pillbox with "Rosario" engraved on it; seven long gold chains; 14 rings in emerald, sapphire, diamond, and pearl; a tricolor gold wedding band; and an 18-karat-gold fountain pen. Displayed at Atlanta's Cobb Galleria Centre in 1994, the "spy bling" garnered both attention and ridicule. One auction associate quipped to the *Chicago Tribune*, "A lot of this stuff is a sabotage on good taste."

photographs of Soviet officials taken by Fedorenko.

While he was stationed in Mexico City, Ames's drinking began spiraling out of control. As his first marriage headed toward divorce, Ames met his future second wife, María del Rosario Casas Dupuy, a Colombian national and paid CIA asset. Returning to headquarters, Ames was assigned to the Soviet–Eastern European Division, which was responsible for targeting Soviet officials. Ames and his new wife, unable to indulge their pricey tastes on his annual salary of about $60,000, accumulated $40,000 in debt.

On April 16, 1985, after his KGB handler, Sergey Chuvakhin, failed to make a sanctioned meeting with Ames at the Town & Country Lounge (since closed) in the ***Mayflower Hotel, 1127 Connecticut Avenue NW***, Ames walked the short distance to the Soviet embassy on 16th Street NW.

Ames had been using an alias, Rick Wells, when contacting the Soviets, but his true identity was quickly established. For the Soviets, he must have seemed almost too good to be true. As an officer in the CIA's Soviet Counterintelligence Division, Ames was at the heart of American efforts against the Soviets. The usually tightfisted Russians paid him $50,000, with assurances much more would follow.

Aldrich Ames met with his KGB contact, Sergey Chuvakhin, for lunch at Chadwicks (now Mr. Smith's of Georgetown), 3205 K Street NW.

Two months later, Ames's third meeting with Chuvakhin was over lunch at ***Chadwicks (now Mr. Smith's of Georgetown), 3205 K Street NW***. The spy handed over a shopping bag of documents containing the names of Soviet agents working for the CIA and the FBI. Afterward he communicated exclusively through signal sites and dead drops around Washington. As the operation progressed, the money flowed in, and Ames was assigned code names: KOLOKOL (BELL), CRONIN, and LYUDMILA.

As a trained case officer, Ames knew the importance of tradecraft. For the first year of his espionage, his job permitted authorized contacts with Soviet diplomats to assess them for recruitment. His responsibilities also provided an ideal cover for handing over documents and receiving money. When the authorized meetings with Soviets ended, Ames used a series of signal sites and dead drops to communicate with his handlers. Spread throughout Washington and

The FBI Meets the "Prince of Darkness"

As the net tightened around Aldrich Ames in the summer of 1993, the suspected spy was invited to a pretext meeting at FBI headquarters. After Ames parked in the FBI's underground garage and went into the building, FBI technicians installed a tracking beacon in his Jaguar XJ6. However, problems arose almost immediately. The Jaguar, like many British Leyland cars at the time, had a Lucas electrical wiring system that was complex and noted for consistent unreliability. Car owners joked that the company had invented the three-position light switch—dim, flicker, and off—and that Lucas held a patent on short circuits. As a result, Lucas acquired the nickname "Prince of Darkness." Thereafter, whenever Ames took the car to a local dealership for routine service, FBI agents held their collective breath, worried a mechanic would find the beacon. Fortunately, the device went unnoticed amid the Lucas wiring.

A dead-drop site code-named PIPE, used by Aldrich Ames, along a horse path in Wheaton Regional Park, Wheaton, Maryland, could accommodate up to $100,000 in cash.

its suburbs, the sites included mailboxes, utility poles, and other common landscape features. Depending on how a signal was placed, an otherwise inconspicuous chalk mark could indicate danger, that a dead drop was loaded, or the drop had been cleared of its contents.

Signal sites are checked regularly and typically located in areas a spy or the handler passes during a normal day. Each signal site is linked to a specific dead-drop site. For instance, an *X* chalk mark at signal site *A* may tell the spy a dead drop has been placed at site *C*. In this way spies can convey an operational message with only a single mark and without the risk of a personal meeting. Some signal and drop sites Ames used are:

Signal site SMILE: Mailbox on the corner of 37th and R Streets NW

Signal site HILL: Guardrail on Massachusetts Avenue at Whitehaven Street NW

Signal site GROUND: At the base of a pedestrian bridge in Rock Creek Park near Beach Drive

Signal site JOY: Electric utility box at Reservoir Road and 35th Street NW

Signal site ROSE: Mailbox at the intersection of Garfield Terrace NW and Garfield Street

Signal site NORTH: Telephone pole at the intersection of Military Road and North 36th Street, Arlington, Virginia

Dead drop BRIDGE: Pedestrian bridge near Massachusetts Avenue and Little Falls Parkway, Bethesda, Maryland

Dead drop PIPE: Drain pipe in Wheaton Regional Park, Wheaton, Maryland

Aldrich Ames brought his wife, Rosario Ames, into the operation during dinner at Germaine's, a popular pan-Asian eatery, then located at ***2400 Wisconsin Avenue NW***. As an enthusiastic coconspirator, she pushed him for increasing production and more money. In one instance, the couple made a short detour to check a signal site on the way home from parents' night at their son's school.

After Ames returned from a posting in Rome, he and Rosario bought a new house at 2512 North Randolph Street, Arlington, Virginia, paid $540,000 in cash, and spent another $99,000 in renovations. Aldrich Ames added a new Jaguar XJ6, expensive clothing, jewelry, and a Rolex watch to his lifestyle. Any money left over was hidden in multiple safe-deposit boxes, bank accounts, and overseas accounts. Questions by agency coworkers about apparent lavish spending were deflected by a succession of lies that attributed the couple's wealth to the largess of Rosario's family in Colombia.

I AM READY TO MEET
AT B ON 1 OCT.
I CANNOT READ
NORTH 13 - 19 SEPT.
IF YOU WILL
MEET AT B ON 1 OCT.
PLS SIGNAL NORTH 4
OF 20 SEPT TO CONFI
NO MESSAGE AT PIPE.
IF YOU CANNOT MEE
1 OCT, SIGNAL NORTH AFTER
27 SEPT WITH MESSAGE AT
PIPE.

The FBI's discovery of pieces of this torn-up note in Aldrich Ames's garbage can during a "trash cover" operation provided evidence he was a Russian agent.

While the Ameses spent with abandon, one after another of the betrayed spies was arrested, tried, found guilty, and executed. Among them was GRU Lt. General Dimitri Polyakov, a military intelligence officer who had retired from his position and from spying several years earlier.

With the compromise of agent after agent during the late 1980s, alarm bells rang at CIA and FBI headquarters. A team of agency analysts narrowed the list of suspects to Aldrich Ames, who was then transferred to the CIA's Counternarcotics Center (CNC) in 1992. As the investigation continued, the FBI launched OPERATION NIGHTMOVER, designed to catch him in an espionage act. The couple's financial records were scrutinized, and a tracking beacon was placed in the Jaguar. A video-surveillance camera, code-named THE EYE, was installed on a utility pole across the street from his home, and the family's garbage was collected by FBI agents for analysis.

The end came on February 21, 1994, when Aldrich Ames was called to CIA headquarters to review materials in preparation for an overseas trip. The call was a ruse. As Ames left his residence, he turned right on North Randolph Street, then right again onto North Quebec Street. He never suspected he was driving into a trap. At the next stop sign, the car ahead of him stopped while a car in the left lane waited to turn left. As the car was blocked by these two FBI vehicles, two more units approached from behind with red lights flashing, leaving Ames no way out. Pulled from his car and bent over the hood of his beloved Jaguar, he was taken into custody. A few blocks away, Rosario Ames was arrested in their home.

Two months later, on April 28, the couple entered guilty pleas according to a deal that sentenced Aldrich Ames to life without parole in exchange for a shorter sentence for Rosario. He promised cooperation in assessing the damage done by his treason. In all, he betrayed more than 20 of America's spies, some active, others retired, and several were executed. "They died because this warped, murdering traitor wanted a bigger house and a Jaguar," said R. James Woolsey, the Director of Central Intelligence at the time of the Ameses' arrest.

■ 167. UNLUCKY IN LOVE

MAP 5 ➤ Au Pied de Cochon (now closed): 1335 Wisconsin Avenue NW

Vitaly Yurchenko (pictured in Moscow in 1997)

During dinner at the Au Pied de Cochon restaurant (now closed), Yurchenko walked away from his CIA handler and redefected to the USSR.

Senior KGB officer Col. Vitaly Yurchenko was the Soviet embassy's security officer in 1976 when would-be spy Edwin G. Moore II tossed a thick parcel of classified material over the embassy fence. Yurchenko, fearing a bomb or provocation, called local police.

Upon his return to Moscow, Yurchenko became chief of the Fifth Department of Directorate K (counterintelligence) in the First Chief Directorate and was eventually promoted to deputy chief of the First Department of the KGB's First Chief Directorate. Then, in August 1985, estranged from his wife and convinced he was dying of cancer, Yurchenko walked into the US embassy in Rome and defected. Within hours, he was aboard a special military flight to Andrews

KGB defector Vitaly Yurchenko was met and debriefed by US intelligence officers in an office building in Great Falls, Virginia.

Lured Back to Moscow

An "honor guard" of Soviet officials accompanied the redefector Vitaly Yurchenko on his return flight to Moscow on November 6, 1985. One member of the small contingent was Lt. Col. Valery Martynov, a KGB officer responsible for acquiring US scientific and technical intelligence. He was also a spy for the CIA and the FBI, code-named GTGENTILE and PIMENTA.

When the plane touched down in Moscow, Martynov vanished. Word trickled out that he had suffered an accident and was recuperating in a hospital outside Moscow. His wife, young son, and daughter were recalled from Washington to be at his bedside. But there had been no accident. Far from peaceful recuperation, Martynov, accused of espionage, was under interrogation at Moscow's Lefortovo Prison. Tried and found guilty, he was executed on May 28, 1987. The case baffled his American handlers; their tradecraft had been carried out by experienced professionals. Only years later did they learn that GTGENTILE had been betrayed by both CIA traitor Aldrich Ames and FBI turncoat Robert Hanssen.

Air Force Base in Maryland. There to meet the prize defector was Aldrich Ames, a CIA counterintelligence officer, who, unbeknownst to Yurchenko, had become a Soviet mole a few months earlier. According to author David Wise, the two men, each a traitor to his country, rode together to a safe house at ***2709 Shawn Leigh Drive in Vienna, Virginia***. Subsequent debriefings, author Ronald Kessler later related, occurred in an office complex at ***730 Walker Road, Great Falls, Virginia***.

Yurchenko revealed the existence of a Soviet spy at the NSA, eventually identified as Ronald Pelton, and proffered enough clues to place former CIA officer Edward Lee Howard under surveillance. He also provided detailed information on current KGB tradecraft but, to Ames's relief, had no knowledge of his treason.

Despite the offer of a million dollars and generous lifetime income, Yurchenko remained unsatisfied with his new life and considered the debriefing sessions that lasted up to eight hours a day a sign of disrespect. At night he pined for a married woman, Dr. Valentina Yereskovsky, with whom he once had an affair. Posted with her husband at the Soviet embassy in Ottawa, Canada, she had not maintained contact with Yurchenko.

A plaque formerly in Au Pied de Cochon identified the seat occupied by Yurchenko during his "last supper in the USA."

Thinking a reunion with a former flame would calm him, Yurchenko's handlers arranged for a secret visit to Canada where the Soviet defector appeared unannounced at his former lover's doorstep. It was a grand romantic gesture, but love did not triumph. Rebuffed, the lovelorn Yurchenko became increasingly morose. Only later was it learned that Ames not only arranged what must have been the painfully awkward reunion, but also alerted the KGB to the plan. As a result, Soviet officers were waiting at Yereskovsky's apartment to preclude any chance of a happy reunion between the two former lovers.

Growing increasingly despondent, in early November 1985 Yurchenko dined with a CIA security officer at Au Pied de Cochon, 1335 Wisconsin Avenue NW. Both men ordered the salmon fillet, then the Russian politely excused himself to go for a walk, leaving the security officer to pay the bill. When next heard from, Yurchenko was inside the Soviet embassy in Washington. At his "welcome home" press conference in Moscow, the former KGB colonel told the implausible, though publicly convenient, tale of being kidnapped and drugged by the CIA at the Vatican.

■ 168. DELIVERING CLASSIFIED TRASH

MAP 2 ➤ Acme Reporting Company: 1220 L Street NW

Randy Miles Jeffries, a messenger for Acme Reporting Company, located in this Northwest Washington building, attempted to peddle transcripts of secret intelligence briefings to FBI agents posing as Soviet officials.

In late 1985, an FBI surveillance team observed a man entering the Soviet Defense, Military, Air and Naval Attaché Office, then located at ***2552 Belmont Road NW***. The stranger, later identified as Randy Miles Jeffries, was a messenger for the Acme Reporting Company, 1220 L Street NW, a service used by Congress to transcribe classified hearings on sensitive military and intelligence issues.

Jeffries, living at ***143 Rhode Island Avenue NW***, had been at his $500-a-month job for only six weeks. The former FBI employee also had a history of drug problems. Suspicious of Jeffries's actions, FBI special agents posing as Russians arranged a meeting at a ***Holiday Inn, 14th Street and Massachusetts Avenue NW.*** During the meeting, Jeffries revealed he had passed documents to the Soviets that included transcripts of US military vulnerabilities, along with operating areas of the Trident submarine. He explained that he simply grabbed hundreds of pages slated for destruction and walked out of Acme's building with them under his coat. Following his arrest on December 20, 1985, Jeffries pled guilty to a single count of espionage and received a sentence of 3 to 9 years in prison.

169. THE THIRTY-YEAR MOLE

MAP 8 ➤ **Larry Wu-Tai Chin residence:** Watergate at Landmark, 205 Yoakum Parkway, building 2, apartment 1723, Alexandria, Virginia (private residence)

For three decades, Larry Wu-Tai Chin worked for the CIA. The Chinese-born translator and analyst was considered a loyal employee and awarded a medal on his retirement in January 1981 at age 63. Then a CIA source in China came forward with information that led the FBI to identify him as having been an active People's Republic of China (PRC) agent since 1952. Born in Beijing in 1922, Chin was assigned code number 2542 by the PRC's intelligence service.

Larry Wu-Tai Chin

After his arrest by the FBI in 1985, Chin (FBI code name EAGLE CLAW) claimed he was engaged in personal backdoor diplomacy to reconcile China and the United States. Regardless of motivation, Chin had profited handsomely from his efforts. He and his wife lived in an Alexandria, Virginia, condominium complex, Watergate at Landmark, 205 Yoakum Parkway, building 2, apartment 1723, and amassed numerous rental properties in the area. These included two row houses in an eastside neighborhood of Baltimore just above Patterson Park. He also had bank accounts in Hong Kong.

At his trial, which began on February 4, 1986, Chin admitted to providing information to the Chinese government over a period of 11 years in return for $180,000 in cash. However, by other estimates he received more than $1 million for his efforts over three decades. Chin was convicted on February 8 of 17 counts of espionage and tax violations. Four days later, he was found dead in his jail cell at the ***Prince William–Manassas Regional Adult Detention Center, 9320 Lee Avenue, Manassas, Virginia***. The life-long spy had tied a plastic trash bag over his head and secured it with laces from a pair of high-top sneakers. By committing suicide prior to sentencing, Chin exploited a seldom-used legal loophole that prevented government seizure of his ill-gotten wealth. Instead, his estate—money and property—was inherited by his wife.

The Watergate at Landmark apartment complex was home to CIA officer Larry Wu-Tai Chin, who spied for China for more than three decades.

■ 170. $40,000-A-GALLON MILK

MAP 9 ➤ **Vladimir Ismaylov residence:** Wildwood Towers, 1075 South Jefferson Street, Arlington, Virginia

Soviet air force colonel Vladimir M. Ismaylov lived at the Wildwood Towers apartment complex until being apprehended for espionage and expelled from the United States.

On June 19, 1986, FBI agents detained Col. Vladimir Ismaylov on an isolated stretch of Riverview Road, Fort Washington, Maryland, between Freedom Road and Battlement Lane. He was burying a milk carton containing $41,100 near a utility pole on the north side of Riverview Road for later retrieval by an agent he mistakenly believed would become a premier spy inside the US Air Force. At the time of his detention, Ismaylov, a GRU military intelligence officer, was the highest-ranking Soviet air force officer at the Soviet embassy in Washington.

FBI agents detained Colonel Ismaylov for spying at this dead-drop site in Fort Washington, Maryland. The electric company's metal tag number, 798329-2242, indicated the correct pole number for the drop.

Ismaylov was duped despite having spent a year validating and testing his prospective agent, a US Air Force officer. The officer, identified only as "Yogi" and who was working as a double agent for the FBI and the Air Force Office of Special Investigations, lured Ismaylov to several meetings. At one encounter at the ***Belle View Shopping Center in the 1600 block of Belle View Boulevard, Alexandria, Virginia***, Yogi handed over sanitized intelligence on the Reagan administration's Strategic Defense Initiative. In return, he received a 35 mm camera, ultrathin film with capacity of over 100 exposures per roll, and a rollover camera (the film version of a pocket scanner).

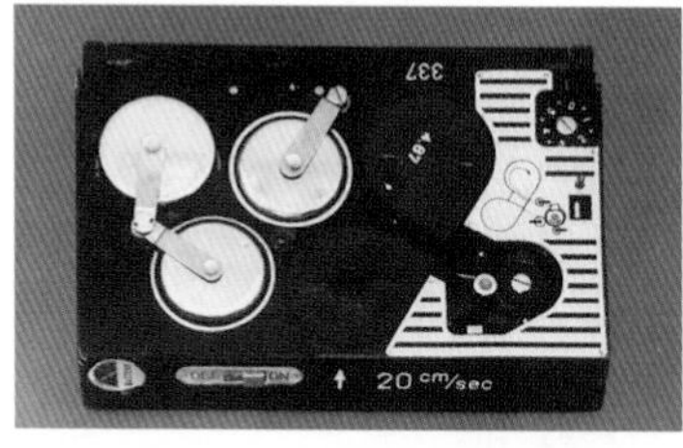

This GRU rollover camera and film were secreted in an empty milk carton at Ismaylov's dead-drop site.

Within 24 hours of his apprehension, Ismaylov was expelled from the United States, abruptly vacating his apartment at the Wildwood Towers complex, 1075 South Jefferson Street, Arlington, Virginia.

■ 171. FISHING FOR SPIES

MAP 12 ➤ **Old Angler's Inn:** 10801 MacArthur Boulevard, Potomac, Maryland

The Old Angler's Inn was the site of a failed recruitment effort aimed at KGB counterintelligence officer Victor Cherkashin.

The Old Angler's Inn, 10801 MacArthur Boulevard, Potomac, Maryland, is a gracious, family-owned restaurant that can trace its roots back to the 1860s. The venue, known locally for its bill of fare and discretion, was a favorite of British spy Harold "Kim" Philby and CIA counterintelligence chief James Angleton. It was also chosen as the venue for an FBI recruitment pitch to Victor Cherkashin, one of the most skilled KGB officers working in Washington during the latter stages of the Cold War.

A second-generation Soviet intelligence officer, Cherkashin headed the KGB's Line KR (counterintelligence) at the USSR's Washington embassy and ran two of the Soviet Union's most valuable spies—Aldrich Ames and Robert Hanssen. While Cherkashin firmly resisted the FBI's recruitment offer, his loyalty to the KGB and remarkable successes with Ames and Hanssen seemed to have counted for little among his superiors. On his return to Moscow, he was pushed aside and retired to a country home where he penned his memoirs. The former spy enjoyed a touch of fame as host to celebrity chef Anthony Bourdain for a segment of the television show *Anthony Bourdain: No Reservations*.

■ 172. ONE FOR THE HISTORY BOOKS

MAP 13 ➤ **National Maritime Intelligence Center:** 4600 Silver Hill Road, Suitland, Maryland

Samuel Loring Morison was an analyst with the Naval Intelligence Support Center (NISC), now the National Maritime Intelligence Center, Suitland, Maryland, and grandson of Rear Adm. Samuel Eliot Morison, one of America's foremost naval historians and two-time Pulitzer Prize recipient. The younger Morison also moonlighted as an editor for *Jane's Fighting Ships*, an annual reference book published by the British-based company Jane's Information Group. Eventually and predictably, a conflict between the two careers developed. At one point Morison used his NISC credentials to enter a shipyard and take photographs for *Jane's*. Then, classified material was found in a copy of a *Jane's* reference guide he had loaned to a friend.

These relatively small infractions were followed by a major security violation. In 1984, Morison lifted satellite images of a Soviet shipyard from a colleague's desk, removed the classified markings, and mailed them to Jane's. The photos of a nuclear-powered *Kiev*-class aircraft carrier under construction, revealing the classified imaging resolution of a US spy satellite, were published in the August 1984 edition of *Jane's Defence Weekly*. An investigation led back to Morison and a search of his apartment at ***1830 North Forest Court, Crofton, Maryland***, uncovered an alarming stockpile of classified documents. At his trial, Morison defended his actions by asserting the public should be aware of the new Soviet submarine construction.

With Morison's conviction on October 17, 1985, he became the first person successfully prosecuted under the *Espionage Act of 1917*. The grandson of the renowned historian entered the history books. Fighting the conviction to the doorstep of the Supreme Court, which refused to hear his appeal, Morison was later pardoned by President Bill Clinton in 2001 over CIA objections.

Morison reappeared in the news in 2014 when he was arrested for stealing and attempting to sell historic treasures contained in more than 30 boxes of material from the Navy Archives. The material, a portion of his grandfather's papers, included maps, illustrations, charts, photographs, and textural material. Pleading guilty in March 2015 to the charges, he received a sentence of two years' probation.

■ 173. FRIENDS SPYING ON FRIENDS

MAP 3 ➤ Jonathan Jay Pollard residence: Nelson Apartments, 304, 1733 20th Street NW (private residence)

Throughout his 30 years in prison, Jonathan Jay Pollard was a point of diplomatic tension between the US and Israeli governments, as well as a dubious cause célèbre for many ardent supporters of Israel. As a US Naval Intelligence analyst in the 1980s, Pollard approached the South African, Israeli, and other foreign governments to sell himself as a spy. His information proved valuable to Israeli intelligence, which gave Pollard a monthly $2,500 stipend, cash for expensive vacations, an engagement ring for his girlfriend, and other rewards. He eventually provided some 800 classified publications and more than 1,000 cables—enough documents to fill a space of 360 cubic feet.

Jonathan and Anne Pollard

Pollard first met his Mossad recruiter, Col. Avi Sella, in May 1984 at the ***Washington Hilton Coffee Shop, 1919 Connecticut Avenue NW***. A second meeting

Anne Pollard tried to dispose of a suitcase filled with incriminating classified documents in a dumpster behind her and her husband's apartment.

Israeli spy Jonathan Pollard breached the gates of the Israeli embassy by tailgating another car. Ordered out by Israeli security, Pollard was arrested once he exited the compound.

took place at the ***Dumbarton Oaks Research Library and Collection, 1703 32nd Street NW***, in July 1984. The 1801 Federal-style Georgetown mansion turned museum, featuring an exquisite art collection and expansive gardens, was an ideal location for a quiet talk between spy and handler. As the two men were seated at a picnic table in shaded woods, financial arrangements were negotiated, and Sella provided a wish list of documents.

Jonathan Pollard and his Israeli handler held some of their first meetings in the gardens of the Dumbarton Oaks Research Library.

During this time, Pollard, who was living at the Nelson Apartment Building, 1733 20th Street NW, apartment 304, was turned over to Yoseg Yagur, who worked under the cover of the Consul of Scientific Affairs in the Israeli Consulate in New York City. Given the code name HUNTING HORSE, Pollard was aggressive in his collection. Multiple times a week, he loaded his briefcase with documents and drove to ***Sam's Carwash, 3437 Branch Avenue, Temple Hills, Maryland***, where he transferred the documents to a suitcase before delivering them to the Israelis, who would copy and return them.

Pollard's spying career did not last long. A little more than a year after first contacting the Israelis, his wide-ranging computer searches for classified information were detected by a supervisor who notified the Naval Investigative Service (NIS) and the FBI. Soon aware that he was under investigation, Pollard and his new wife, Anne, tried to shake the surveillance team following them, then made a dash for the ***Israeli embassy, 3514 International Drive NW***. Tailgating a diplomat's car as it entered the embassy's security gate, the Pollards seemed to be home free. However, they were immediately ordered to "get out" and moments later were apprehended by NIS and FBI agents. Anne was initially allowed to go home but was arrested the next day when evidence against her was found. Pollard pled guilty to espionage and was sentenced to life in prison. Pollard's wife received a five-year sentence, and, after she was released after 37 months, the two divorced.

The diplomatic uproar over "friends spying on friends" created headlines in both countries. Israel denied Pollard was its spy until 1998 but then made him a citizen. Supporters advocated for decades for his release, but repeated official Israeli government requests for his relocation to Israel were denied by both Democratic and Republican administrations. On November 20, 2015, Pollard was released on parole.

■ 174. ON THE WRONG SIDE OF HISTORY

MAP 3 ➤ **South African embassy:** 3051 Massachusetts Avenue NW

Embassy of South Africa. While South Africa was governed by apartheid laws, spies both for and against the system operated in the United States.

Thomas Dolce, the first American convicted of spying for South Africa, lived at ***107 concove Way, Havre de Grace, Maryland***. Prosecutors claimed that Dolce, a civilian army weapons analyst at the Aberdeen Proving Ground, delivered more than 200 documents to the South African government from 1979 to 1983 in meetings in Washington and overseas, as well as through messenger and mail channels. At the time, the South African government was locked in a bitter fight over its apartheid policies, with the antiapartheid movement gaining substantial sympathy in the United States.

Arrested in October 1988 long after his last contact with the South Africans, he pled guilty to a single count of espionage and received the maximum punishment of 10 years imprisonment and $10,000 fine. In a statement read at his sentencing, Dolce admitted to passing documents to a succession of attachés from South Africa's Washington embassy, 3051 Massachusetts Avenue NW. The ideological spy received no payment for his espionage, asserting that the information he was supplying covertly for South Africa was what the United States should have been doing as official policy.

South Africa's apartheid system ended in 1991.

■ 175. IN SEARCH OF ADVENTURE

MAP 10 ➤ **Frank Nesbitt arrest site:** Tysons Corner Marriott, 8028 Leesburg Pike, Vienna, Virginia

Frank Arnold Nesbitt longed for adventure. In June 1989, the former US Marine and onetime courier at the Los Alamos National Laboratory abruptly quit his information technology job at a Memphis, Tennessee, law firm and left home. Family, friends, and coworkers were baffled by the sudden departure. Limited details of the case reported in *The Washington Post* in October 1989 included a description of a brief note Nesbitt attached to his weed trimmer. However, the cryptic note offered little insight to his disappearance: "I'm gone. Don't look for me."

Frank Nesbitt's brief work as a Soviet spy ended with his arrest at the Tysons Corner Marriott.

Nesbitt's odyssey took him first to Belize, then Guatemala, and, finally, Bolivia. There he happened to board a bus filled with Russian ballet dancers. The chance meeting led to an introduction to a Soviet official and then a trip to Moscow. He was given a tour of the city and debriefed on US communication systems but denied a request for Soviet citizenship. Handed $2,000, he was sent on his way with a promise of more cash if he could deliver additional intelligence.

Nesbitt returned to South America, where he told American officials his story and offered to become a double agent. Brought back to the United States, Nesbitt was questioned and then arrested at the Tysons Corner Marriott in October 1989. Nesbitt's lawyer claimed his client just "wanted to have some excitement in his life," but psychiatric evaluations revealed the would-be adventurer suffered from several personality disorders. He pled guilty to "passing secret information to the USSR" and was sentenced to 10 years in a psychiatric treatment facility at a federal prison.

■ 176. EAST GERMAN SPY HIVES

MAP 3 ➤ **East German embassy:** 1717 Massachusetts Avenue NW (now the John Hopkins University Bernstein Office Building)

The German Democratic Republic (East Germany) conducted espionage activities from its embassy at 1717 Massachusetts Avenue NW. Today the building is part of the Johns Hopkins University School of Advanced International Studies.

The German Democratic Republic (East Germany) chose 1717 Massachusetts Avenue NW for the site of its embassy. Although the Soviet intelligence services considered Washington its espionage domain, East Germany's Ministerium für Staatssicherheit (MfS, known as the Stasi) was also active. Its foreign intelligence arm, Hauptverwaltung Aufklärung (HVA), or General Reconnaissance

Administration, was headed by Markus Wolf, who earned the nickname "Man without a Face" for his penchant for secrecy.

The public record of HVA activities in Washington is surprisingly sparse. Wolf even claimed he did not consider spying inside the United States a priority. "It was easier to find out what we needed in West Berlin, rather than go to Fort Bliss," he said in a post–Cold War interview with *The Baltimore Sun* on August 5, 1997. "We knew a lot about American policy."

However, Wolf also suggested operating in America's capital city may have been difficult for the East Germans. "I knew from my own, mainly abortive attempts to run agents from our Washington embassy that they could hardly move out of the building without having an FBI man on their tail," he wrote in his autobiography, *Man without a Face*, "although years later I met Ivan Gromakov, who had served as KGB resident in Washington, and he maintained that FBI surveillance was easy to detect and never proved an obstacle for him in dealing with his sources." Wolf's clever doublespeak that simultaneously praised and denigrated FBI counterintelligence efforts revealed little.

Two East German spies are known to have been active in Washington during the Cold War. Konrad Grote (code name KOREN) and Hans-Joachim Zabel (code name FROEBEL) were embedded in the East German embassy from 1980 to 1985, although both seemed to deal in material from technical journals as opposed to political intelligence and running agents. Heinz-Joachim Switalla (code name SIEGEL), son of one of the Stasi's founding members, also served in Washington. Alfred Zehe, officially a US resident alien living in Mexico under the cover of a college professor, crossed the border to spy and spent time in Washington.

Arrested as part of a joint FBI and Naval Investigative Service (NSI) sting operation in Boston in 1983, Zehe pled guilty to espionage in 1985. He was eventually sent back to the East Germans in a spy swap.

All the Little Duckies

The scenes that followed the fall of the Berlin Wall in November 1989 were often surreal. Crowds rampaged through Stasi headquarters while revelers partied in the streets and atop the wall itself. Among the most unreal realities following the demise of the East German government was a shortwave radio broadcast on the Stasi frequency. On May 23, 1990, a seemingly drunken radio operator relayed the following message: "All my little duckies, swimming on the pond . . . heads deep in water, tails to the sky."

The traditional German nursery rhyme, broadcast around the globe, signaled that the Stasi was closing up shop.

177. DIPLOMAT, BUS DRIVER, SPY?

MAP 3 ➤ **Felix Bloch residence:** The St. Nicholas, 2230 California Street NW

Few espionage investigations received as much media attention as that of Felix Bloch. In 1989, the senior US diplomat met a man he knew as Pierre Bart in an expensive Parisian restaurant. The shoulder bag Bloch brought with him into the restaurant was discreetly carried out of the eatery by Bart, a KGB *illegal*, known to American intelligence as Reino Gikman. What neither realized was that officers of the French counterintelligence organization Direction de la Surveillance du Territoire were also present. Every bite of the pricey meal was filmed by surveillance cameras.

Not long after returning to the United States but before confronted by the FBI with this evidence, Bloch received a call from "Paul," a stranger who said he was calling on behalf of "Pierre." Paul advised that Pierre was sick and "cannot see you in the future." According to a James Risen article in *The New York Times*, Paul ended the conversation with a warning that "a contagious disease is suspected" and "I am worried about you. You have to take care of yourself." The call, made to Bloch at his residence at the St. Nicholas co-op, 2230 California Street NW, was monitored by US officials who immediately realized their operation was compromised and Bloch was now alerted.

When confronted with the evidence the next day and questioned by the FBI, Bloch was uncooperative.

Felix Bloch, a senior American diplomat accused of spying for the Soviet Union, lived at the St. Nicholas on California Street NW.

The Final Piece of the Puzzle

One aspect of the Felix Bloch case continued to puzzle investigators long after the suspected spy faded from view. Who leaked FBI information to Bloch's alleged KGB contact Pierre Bart / Reino Gikman? Suspicion pointed to an unidentified mole buried deep inside the US intelligence community and set off a decade-long search that yielded nothing. In 1999, FBI investigators focused attention on a CIA officer, Brian Kelley, whose career was subsequently ruined by the allegations. Despite Kelley passing multiple polygraph tests, his name was not cleared until 2001, after the arrest of FBI special agent Robert Hanssen—the spy who informed the KGB and triggered the call warning of a "contagious disease."

The dinner with Gikman/Bart was simply a discussion about stamps by two avid philatelists, he explained. Under suspicion, Bloch was placed on administrative leave from the State Department. After accusations of espionage were leaked to the press, the FBI placed Bloch under 24-hour car surveillance. The press, sensing an arrest might be imminent, formed a small caravan that followed directly behind the FBI cars. Representatives of the Soviet embassy trailed the press convoy for their own unstated reasons.

Additional details emerged in the press about unsavory aspects of Bloch's personal life, fueling speculation that the leaks and surveillance were intended to pressure the suspected spy. Bloch seemed unfazed. In one instance he hiked 22 miles around Washington in the August heat in an apparent attempt to make unpleasant and unproductive work for FBI surveillants. Analysis of Bloch's financial records and a grand jury inquiry yielded little. Finally, in 1990, the State Department officially dismissed Bloch by invoking a little-used regulation that authorizes termination in matters of national security.

Bloch moved to Chapel Hill, North Carolina, where he took a job as a bagger at a local supermarket and then became a bus driver. After being apprehended for shoplifting $21.74 of merchandise, including two pepperonis, pita bread, a can of Crystal Light, and two bottles of aspirin, from a local grocery store in 1994, Bloch received a 30-day suspended sentence, paid a $100 fine, and faded into obscurity.

178. COURTING THE ENEMY

MAP 8 ➤ COURTSHIP office: 6551 Loisdale Court, Springfield, Virginia

Responding to an intensified Cold War environment following the Soviet invasion of Afghanistan in 1979 and the US boycott of the 1980 Moscow Summer Olympics, the CIA and the FBI launched an aggressive joint counterintelligence program. Under the code name COURTSHIP, Soviet intelligence officers were targeted for recruitment in the United States, after which they would be handled by the CIA when they returned to Moscow. In his book *Inside the CIA*, author Ronald Kessler reported COURTSHIP was run from an office complex at 6551 Loisdale Court, Springfield, Virginia,

OPERATION COURTSHIP, a joint FBI-CIA program, was run from a suburban office complex in Springfield, Virginia.

One COURTSHIP recruit was Lt. Col. Valery Martynov, a Line X officer in the KGB's T Directorate (scientific and technical secrets). Another success was KGB major Sergei Motorin, an officer who focused on collection of political

Sergei Motorin

Valeri Martynov

intelligence. Martynov was code-named GTGENTILE by the CIA and PIMENTA by the FBI. Motorin was GTGAUZE and MEGAS, respectively.

Tragically for the new spies, the ranks of the CIA and FBI were penetrated by two of America's most damaging turncoats, FBI special agent Robert Hanssen and CIA officer Aldrich Ames. Hanssen, from his position as supervisor in the FBI's Soviet counterintelligence division, and Ames, from his assignment to the COURTSHIP program, learned Martynov and Motorin's identities and then independently betrayed the pair to the KGB. Motorin, who lived at ***12815 Bluhill Road, Silver Spring, Maryland***, returned to Moscow as part of his normal rotation in early 1985. He was subsequently arrested, tried, and then executed in February 1987. Martynov, a member of the 1985 "honor guard" accompanying KGB redefector Vitaly Yurchenko to Moscow, was detained, tried, and convicted of espionage. He was also executed in 1987.

■ 179. A TARGET WHO COULDN'T BE BOUGHT

MAP 9 ➤ Yuri Leonov residence: Wildwood Park Apartments, 5550 Columbia Pike, Arlington, Virginia

Even carefully orchestrated recruitment operations can turn out poorly. Beginning in 1981, Yuri Leonov, a Lt. Col. in Soviet military intelligence (the GRU), began a painstaking development of Armand B. Weiss, president of ***Associations International, suite 107, 6845 Elm Street, McLean, Virginia***. Leonov, operating under the cover of assistant military attaché at the

Office of Associations International in McLean, Virginia, where association president Armand B. Weiss was targeted for recruitment by Soviet military intelligence.

Yuri Leonov, a lieutenant colonel in Soviet military intelligence (the GRU), lived in the Wildwood Park Apartments in Arlington, Virginia.

Soviet embassy and living at the Wildwood Park Apartments, 5550 Columbia Pike, Arlington, Virginia, targeted Weiss as a potential source of classified technical data from the association's member organizations. Leonov met more than two dozen times with Weiss, developing a relationship to the point where he could confidently request classified data. Weiss reported the Soviet's recruitment pitch to the FBI and began acting under FBI instructions. He accepted money from Leonov and pretended to accede to his requests for the material.

The FBI detained Leonov as he walked out of the association's headquarters on August 18, 1983. The GRU officer was declared persona non grata and expelled from the country.

■ 180. NOT THE JOB HE WANTED

MAP 3 ➤ **William J. Casey residence:** 2501 Massachusetts Avenue NW (private residence)

William J. Casey, the Director of Central Intelligence (DCI) from 1981 to 1987, lived at 2501 Massachusetts Avenue NW during much of his time in Washington. Following his commissioning as a US Naval Reserve officer, Casey transferred to the OSS and served as head of the Special Intelligence Branch in the European Theater of Operations from 1944 to 1945. When the OSS was disbanded after World War II, Casey traded the world of espionage for law, Wall Street, and Republican politics. During the Nixon and Ford administrations, he served as chairman of the Securities and Exchange Commission, undersecretary of state for

DCI William J. Casey and his wife split their time between this Massachusetts Avenue NW residence and their New York City home.

economic affairs, and chairman of the Export-Import Bank. In 1976–77, Casey was a member of the President's Foreign Intelligence Advisory Board (PFIAB).

Casey became Ronald Reagan's presidential campaign chairman in 1980. Although disappointed at not being nominated for secretary of state following the election, Casey accepted the DCI position. At his Senate confirmation hearings, he described the CIA as a "sacred institution" and vowed to improve its performance.

The Year of the Spy

William Casey's fifth year as Director of Central Intelligence, 1985, is remembered as the year *Back to the Future* became a hit movie, Elmo made his debut on *Sesame Street*, and "the Year of the Spy." Espionage flourished in the early 1980s, and few could imagine the Cold War would be over by the end of the decade.

Casey's tenure as DCI saw a marked increase in covert action operations and often controversy. The most prominent operations involved support of anticommunist forces in Nicaragua, expanded military assistance to Afghan rebels fighting the Soviets, and secret arms-for-hostages agreements with Iran. However, Casey seemed unfazed by numerous battles with congressional committees and individual members, including Sen. Barry Goldwater, who called for the DCI's resignation. Quoted in 1984 by *Time* magazine, Casey dismissed Congress as "a bunch of meddlers."

Despite the controversies, the DCI never lost the confidence of President Reagan. Incapacitated by a brain tumor in December 1986, Casey resigned the next month and died in May 1987.

181. DEAD IN HIS DACHA

MAP 10 ➤ Edward Lee Howard residence: 9654 Scotch Haven Court, Vienna, Virginia (private residence)

After joining the CIA in 1980, Edward Lee Howard spent a year training for a covert assignment in the Soviet Union. Howard first lived at the Idylwood Towers, ***2300 Pimmitt Drive, Falls Church, Virginia***, then at ***9654 Scotch Haven Court, Vienna, Virginia***. He seemed to be an ideal candidate for the job and, along with his wife Mary, received additional training in a special course that taught tradecraft for operating securely behind the Iron

While training as a CIA case officer in 1981, Edward Lee Howard lived on Scotch Haven Court in Vienna, Virginia.

WANTED BY THE FBI

ESPIONAGE; INTERSTATE FLIGHT - PROBATION VIOLATION

EDWARD LEE HOWARD

FBI No. 720 744 CA2

Photograph taken 1983

Aliases: Patrick Brian, Patrick M. Brian, Patrick M. Bryan, Edward L. Houston, Roger H. Shannon

DESCRIPTION

Date of Birth:	October 27, 1951	Hair:	brown
Place of Birth:	Alamogordo, New Mexico	Eyes:	brown
Height:	5' 11"	Complexion:	medium
Weight:	165 to 180 pounds	Race:	white
Build:	medium	Nationality:	American
Occupations:	economic analyst, former U.S. Government employee		
Remarks:	knowledgeable in the use of firearms		
Scars and Marks:	2 inch scar over right eye, scar on upper lip		
Social Security Number Used:	457 92 0726		
NCIC:	D05407191911O8101419		
Fingerprint Classification:	4 0 1 R 00 19 / 5 17 U 00		

CRIMINAL RECORD

HOWARD HAS BEEN CONVICTED OF ASSAULT WITH A DEADLY WEAPON.

CAUTION

HOWARD SHOULD BE CONSIDERED ARMED AND DANGEROUS AND SHOULD BE APPROACHED WITH CAUTION INASMUCH AS HE HAS BEEN CONVICTED OF ASSAULT WITH A DEADLY WEAPON AND IS PRESENTLY ON SUPERVISED PROBATION.

A Federal warrant was issued on September 23, 1985, at Albuquerque, New Mexico, charging Howard with Espionage (Title 18, U.S. Code, Section 794 (c)). A Federal warrant was also issued on September 27, 1985, at Albuquerque, charging Howard with Unlawful Interstate Flight to Avoid Confinement – Probation Violation (Title 18, U.S. Code, Section 1073).

IF YOU HAVE ANY INFORMATION CONCERNING THIS PERSON, PLEASE CONTACT YOUR LOCAL FBI OFFICE. TELEPHONE NUMBERS AND ADDRESSES OF ALL FBI OFFICES LISTED ON BACK.

William H Webster
DIRECTOR
FEDERAL BUREAU OF INVESTIGATION
UNITED STATES DEPARTMENT OF JUSTICE
WASHINGTON, D. C. 20535
TELEPHONE: 202 324-3000

Entered NCIC
Wanted Flyer 524
October 4, 1985

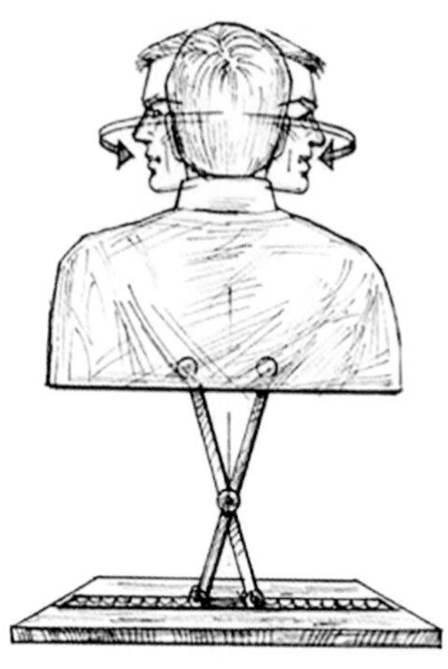

Edward Howard constructed a simple homemade jack-in-the-box, similar to the CIA's more sophisticated devices, to mislead an FBI surveillance team.

Commuter Tradecraft

The CIA designed a jack-in-the-box (JIB) in the 1970s for officers operating in the Soviet Union. When deployed, the JIB displayed a pop-up silhouette of a human head and torso in the passenger seat of a vehicle. As the officer exited the car, the spring-loaded JIB, which might be concealed in a duffel bag or briefcase, popped up, making it appear to trailing surveillance that a passenger was still in the seat. The CIA officer on the street was now "black" (without surveillance) and could safely meet with an agent.

Edward Lee Howard's use of a makeshift JIB to elude his FBI watchers may not have been his only unofficial use of such a device. One report intimated Howard used a JIB to drive in the multiple-occupancy lanes of Interstate 66 in Virginia. A few years later, another driver was pulled over using the JIB in a carpool lane. The incident caused a minor media stir when the driver identified himself as a CIA officer.

Curtain. There he learned about some of the CIA's most sensitive human and technical operations.

However, questions about Howard's suitability arose after the end of his training. During a routine polygraph test, he admitted to drug use, heavy drinking, petty theft, and cheating on training exercises. The indiscretions were sufficient to have the assignment canceled and Howard dismissed from the agency in 1983.

The couple moved to Santa Fe, New Mexico, where Howard acquired a mid-level job at the New Mexico State Legislature but continued drinking heavily.

He was arrested for a late-night barroom brawl that included gunfire, and he inexplicably made nearly incoherent telephone calls to the American embassy in Moscow asking for the chief of station. In another instance, Howard appeared unannounced at the home of a former agency colleague in Washington to voice bitterness about his dismissal. His erratic behavior culminated in a trip in late 1983 to Europe, where he met with representatives of Soviet intelligence. When implicated by KGB defector Vitaly Yurchenko in 1985 for having contacted the Soviets, Howard became the subject of an FBI investigation.

Once Howard realized he was under FBI surveillance, he planned an escape by applying the tools of his tradecraft training. During what seemed like a routine trip to dinner with his wife behind the wheel, he rolled out of the passenger seat as the car turned a corner. In his place a crude jack-in-the-box (JIB) device popped up to simulate the silhouette of a man in the passenger seat. Howard vanished into the night while Mary returned to the house and played a recording of his voice over the phone for the benefit of FBI phone taps.

The following year, on August 7, 1986, Howard, now a defector and code-named ROBERT by the KGB, surfaced in Moscow and was granted asylum. His alcoholism continued unabated, and on July 12, 2002, he was found dead in his dacha. The Russian press reported the 50-year-old died of a broken neck from a fall.

■ 182. FALLING FOR THE DANGLES

MAP 9 ➤ Training site: Key Bridge Marriott, 1401 Lee Highway, Arlington, Virginia

Soviet intelligence failed to detect a textbook counterintelligence operation in 1982. For the operation (code name JAGWIRE), FBI counterintelligence agent William P. O'Keefe recruited John L. Stine as a double agent. O'Keefe saw an opportunity to disrupt Soviet espionage in the United States by dangling Stine, as a forty-year-old security officer for a defense contractor, in front of the GRU.

The operation required Stine to play the role of a free-spending miscreant desperate enough for money to commit treason. After a training course at the Key Bridge Marriott, 1401 Lee Highway, Arlington, Virginia,

The FBI gave double agent John L. Stine a crash course in tradecraft in an eighth-floor suite of the Key Bridge Marriott.

Along a pathway behind a 7-Eleven store near the Twinbrook Shopping Center in Rockville, Maryland, the GRU selected a dead-drop site for Stine's use.

The GRU directed Stine to meet Vyacheslav Pavlov at this pay phone near the Giant grocery store (now a Korean grocery store called H-Mart) in the ***Heritage Shopping Center in Annandale, Virginia***.

Stine walked into the ***Soviet Military Office, 2552 Belmont Road NW***, on Thanksgiving Day. Offering a tale of woe about gambling debts and owing money to a bookmaker, he handed over a file of what appeared to be classified documents to GRU officer Vyacheslav Pavlov.

Persuaded that Stine was a genuine volunteer, Pavlov had the "walk-in" climb into the trunk of a car to avoid surveillance, then dropped him off at a secluded location on Connecticut Avenue. For several months, Stine communicated with the Soviets through dead drops in the Washington area, such as one at the base of the fourth supporting pole around a small utility building behind the 7-Eleven convenience store adjacent to the ***Twinbrook Shopping Center on Veirs Mill Road, Rockville, Maryland***. Stine's once-classified documents, which the FBI had sanitized, were accepted as genuine, and he began receiving GRU spy training.

On April 16, 1983, the FBI decided to end the operation. As a Soviet approached a dead-drop site in a hollow tree at ***Schaeffer and White Ground Roads in Boyds, Maryland***, FBI agents moved in. To their surprise, it was not Pavlov clearing the dead drop, but his superior—a more senior intelligence officer, Lt. Col. Yevgeniy Barmyantsev. Apprehended and declared persona non grata, Barmyantsev, along with Pavlov, was ordered out of the United States, and Stine retired from his brief, successful career as a spy catcher.

■ 183. CLOAK-AND-DAGGER IN THE VEGETABLE AISLE

MAP 5 ➤ **Safeway supermarket:** 1855 Wisconsin Avenue NW

This popular supermarket, nicknamed the "social Safeway" by Georgetown patrons, was chosen by the FBI as the site to cold-pitch KGB officer Dimitry Yakushkin with a generous financial offer to defect.

The Georgetown Safeway supermarket became the venue for an FBI recruitment pitch to KGB officer Dimitry Yakushkin in 1982. Posted to the Soviet embassy since 1975 under diplomatic cover, Yakushkin was scheduled to return to Moscow. FBI agents, thinking the Soviet official would miss the conveniences he had long enjoyed in America, followed him to the store. Then, as Yakushkin and his wife shopped separately, a special agent approached the middle-aged KGB officer in the produce aisle by the oranges. In *Spy*, author David Wise described a straightforward and uncomplicated FBI offer of $20 million to the Soviet to defect. "Young man," Yakushkin is said to have politely replied, "I appreciate the offer. Twenty years ago I might have been interested." The loyal Yakushkin returned to Moscow. He died in 1994 at age 71.

■ 184. CONGRESSIONAL STAFFER TURNS SPYBUSTER

MAP 1 ➤ **Hawk 'n' Dove restaurant:** 329 Pennsylvania Avenue SE

Soviet spy Aleksandr N. Mikheyev wined-and-dined congressional staffer Marc Zimmerman at the Hawk 'n' Dove restaurant before making an unsuccessful recruitment pitch.

Soviet spy Aleksandr Mikheyev earned a footnote in modern espionage history for a bungled recruitment. In 1983, Mikheyev approached Marc Zimmerman, an aide to Maine congresswoman Olympia Snowe. Taking the young staffer to lunch at the Hawk 'n' Dove, 329 Pennsylvania Avenue SE, the Soviet spy wasted little time before asking for a specific classified document. Zimmerman not only did not have access to the document but immediately reported the approach to Representative Snowe and the FBI. The FBI instructed the young aide to meet with Mikheyev again, this time wearing a clandestine recorder. When Mikheyev asked for the document a second time, sufficient cause was in hand to expel him from the United States. "Somebody's not doing their homework," Zimmerman later said in an interview. "It would be great if they were all that inept."

7

NEW THREATS AND OLD ADVERSARIES

(1992–2016)

The collapse of the Soviet Union ended the Cold War but did not diminish foreign spying on the United States. Hope for a more peaceful world at the beginning of the 1990s soon faded with the increasing number of deadly terrorist attacks. The fear of Soviet nuclear missiles was supplanted by the specter of a stateless, anonymous terrorist detonating a backpack-sized nuclear bomb in a major US city. The Russian spy agency Sluzhba Vneshney Razvedki (SVR) replaced the Soviet KGB but behaved with aggressiveness equal to its predecessor organization.

Digital technology opened a new clandestine battlefield, in cyberspace. Unidentified hacker spies could steal America's secrets without leaving their home countries. The clandestine world, historically symbolized by the cloak and dagger, became a cyber battleground of code and keyboards. The 21st century threat by state-sponsored hackers, malicious "lone wolf" operators, and transnational criminal organizations extended beyond government agencies and private defense contractors to the national infrastructure, the media, and international financial markets.

For foreign intelligence organizations, now armed with tools of digital technology and new "cyber agents," Washington's officials, companies, and institutions offered a target-rich environment.

■ 185. UNDERGROUND ESPIONAGE

MAP 5 ➤ Russian embassy (formerly Soviet embassy): 2650 Wisconsin Avenue NW

The Russian embassy on Wisconsin Avenue was purportedly the target of a counterintelligence tunneling operation.

The US government has neither confirmed nor denied press reports that in the late 1970s, the FBI and the NSA launched one of the Cold War's most aggressive and costly intelligence operations. The target was the new Soviet embassy under construction at 2650 Wisconsin Avenue NW in the Mount Alto section of Washington. Said to be code-named MONOPOLY, the alleged plan called for the construction of a clandestine tunnel under the city's streets and below the embassy for technical intelligence collection. The FBI reportedly bought several properties in the neighborhood from which to work. One house is said to have been the starting point and entrance for the tunnel, while the others supposedly served as observation posts. Quiet, specialized equipment allegedly dug the tunnel, though how the excavated dirt could have been spirited away from the subterranean construction site unnoticed remains a mystery. According to at least one unsubstantiated account, the lighted tunnel was large enough for a man to stand in.

The alleged operation was not trouble free. The tunnel was said to be prone to water leaks, and some of the sophisticated collection equipment did not work properly. As costs grew into the hundreds of millions of dollars, the FBI is reported to have suddenly canceled the project in the 1990s and sealed the tunnel.

If it existed, would MONOPOLY have eventually produced any valuable intelligence? The question is likely moot, as the Soviets may have learned about any such operation from their mole at the FBI, Robert Hanssen.

■ 186. COMMITTED AMATEURS

MAP 1 ➤ Theresa Squillacote and Kurt Stand residence: 3809 13th Street NE (private residence)

Retired spies Theresa Squillacote and Kurt Stand planned their ill-fated reactivation as spies from their 13th Street NE home.

In mid-January 1990, demonstrators stormed the headquarters of East Germany's Ministerium für Staatssicherheit (MfS), known as the Stasi, in East Berlin. Some protesters vented rage at the repressive secret police organization, while those who had been collaborators were desperate for an opportunity to destroy personally incriminating files in the voluminous Stasi records.

Some of the Stasi files were acquired by US intelligence and used for counterintelligence analysis and spy hunting. Among the discoveries was a pair of files, VX2207/73 and XV/2207/73, describing two trained and reliable agents code-named JUNIOR and RESI. Detective work led to Kurt Alan Stand and his wife, Theresa Squillacote, 3809 13th Street NE, along with a friend, James Michael Clark, 3705 South George Mason Drive, apartment ***2310-South, Falls Church, Virginia***.

Stand was recruited by his German immigrant father to spy for East Germany while still a teen and eventually brought both his wife and Clark into the ring. All three received training in a variety of tradecraft techniques, such as surveillance detection, the use of microdots, and radio operation. True believers, they described themselves as Marxists and received little compensation for their efforts.

Squillacote, a lawyer by profession, had access to classified material, while Clark was a civilian employee of the Department of Defense. Stand, though not employed by the government, was a regional representative for the International Union of Food, Agricultural, Hotel, Restaurant, Catering, Tobacco and Allied Workers' Associations.

The fall of the Soviet empire and the reunification of Germany must have initially terrified the three coconspirators. According to credible sources, Clark smashed his spy camera to bits and tossed the parts off the ***Theodore Roosevelt Bridge*** into the Potomac. Another spy camera, disassembled, was later found in the couple's home. However, an initial investigation revealed that even after German reunification, the trio maintained contact with Lothar Ziemer, their former East German handler.

Then in 1995, Squillacote obtained a post office box in Maryland under the alias Lisa Martin and attempted to contact Ronnie Kasrils, South Africa's deputy defense minister and a Communist Party official. Squillacote sent an introductory letter filled with revolutionary rhetoric offering their espionage services to Kasrils. The letter referred to "class enemies" and the "horrors" of the system of "bourgeois parliamentary democracy."

The FBI intercepted the letter, and by 1996 the three were under investigation. Listening devices planted in Clark's apartment revealed he was given to paranoid rants and fear of discovery. Next, the FBI devised a sting operation in which an FBI

As authorities closed in on James Michael Clark, the former East German spy destroyed his miniature spy camera and threw its pieces off the Theodore Roosevelt Bridge into the Potomac.

special agent, posing as Kasrils's representative, met with Squillacote in a New York hotel bar. Anxious to resume her espionage, Squillacote revealed code words and true names to establish her credibility.

"I'm coming with a history [of espionage work]," she told the undercover FBI agent. In all, she attended four meetings with the agent and handed over classified documents. Then, to improve her access to more sensitive information, Squillacote quit her Pentagon job and interviewed for a position at the White House, from which she hoped to move onto the National Security Council staff.

The FBI arrested the trio in 1997. A trial filled with motions and briefs ended in convictions. Squillacote received 21 years and 10 months, while her husband was given 17 years and 6 months. Clark, who testified against the couple, received a sentence of 12 years and 7 months.

187. STINGING ONE OF THEIR OWN

MAP 8 ➤ **Earl Pitts's storage site:** Public Storage, 7400 Alban Station Boulevard, unit A425, Springfield, Virginia

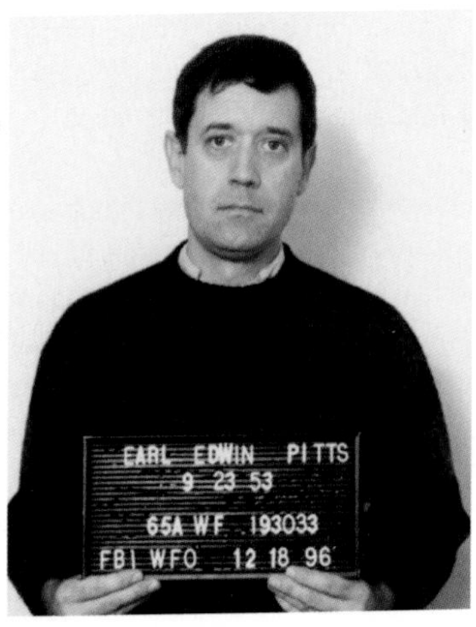

Earl Edwin Pitts

FBI special agent Pitts used a Public Storage unit in Springfield, Virginia, to hide incriminating documents.

Veteran FBI supervisory special agent Earl Edwin Pitts began spying for the Soviets in the 1980s. By the time he was taken into custody on December 18, 1996, the FBI had amassed nearly 6,000 pieces of evidence against him.

Originally assigned to Squad 19, the FBI surveillance team targeting KGB officers in New York City, Pitts betrayed his oath by volunteering to spy for the KGB for money. He first contacted the Soviets in 1987, meeting his handler in the Main Branch of the New York Public Library. The spying continued after his reassignment to Washington in 1989, with Pitts making numerous trips to New York City to hand over sensitive files to his Soviet contacts. In all, he collected some $200,000 for his efforts and seemed to have gotten away with treason.

Then in 1995, Pitts's Russian handler defected and offered to identify an FBI mole in exchange for permanent US residency. By using the former

KGB officer to gain Pitts's confidence, investigators arranged a meeting with a "new Russian contact" at the Chancellorsville Battlefield National Park Visitors Center, ***9001 Plank Road, Spotsylvania, Virginia***. An FBI special agent posing as a Russian intelligence officer enticed Pitts to resume his spying. During the sting operation, Pitts used a variety of locations for meetings as well as dead-drop sites and storage sites. These included the Ronald Reagan Washington National Airport parking lot; the Fas Mart convenience store, ***5022 Plank Road, Fredericksburg, Virginia***; and storage unit number A425 at Public Storage, 7400 Alban Station Boulevard, Springfield, Virginia. Pitts received $65,000 during the course of the sting, which he deposited in multiple bank and credit union accounts as well as safe-deposit boxes.

The old terminal at Ronald Reagan National Airport. As part of a sting operation, an FBI undercover agent paid Russian spy Pitts $20,000 when the two met in a vehicle parked at the airport.

A fire hydrant near the Burke Centre Shopping Center served as one of Pitts's signal sites during the FBI undercover operation.

Sufficient evidence was gathered during the FBI's 16-month investigation to arrest Pitts in December 1996. At first Pitts asserted innocence but, when confronted with the specifics of the case against him, accepted a plea bargain of 27 years in prison.

■ 188. SPYING FOR JOURNALISTS

MAP 3 ➤ **Dominic Ntube residence:** 1400 block, Columbia Road NW (exact address unknown)

In 1993, State Department secretary Geneva Jones traded a respected profession for prison. Jones held a top secret clearance in the Bureau of Politico-Military Affairs when she was arrested for passing classified information to her friend, freelance journalists Dominic Ntube of Cameroon and Fabian Makani of Kenya. FBI agents found thousands of classified cables and 39 CIA documents stamped SECRET in Ntube's apartment in the 1400 Block of Columbia Road NW. Some related to then current US military operations in Somalia and Iraq. Prosecutors claimed Jones smuggled the documents out of the State Department in rolled-up newspapers and her purse.

Following arrest at her State Department office, Jones pled guilty to 21 counts of theft and two counts relating to the unlawful communication of national defense information, in exchange for a 37-month prison sentence. In sentencing Jones in 1994, US District Judge Harold H. Greene lectured, "Somebody would have to be a complete moron not to know that when you work for the State Department you can't take documents out and give them to anybody."

■ 189. WELCOME HOME—YOU'RE UNDER ARREST

MAP 11 ➤ Dulles International Airport: 1 Saarinen Circle, Dulles, Virginia

Several spies have been arrested at the Washington Dulles International Airport since the facility's 1962 dedication.

Joseph Garfield Brown, a spy who had passed classified US Air Force documents to Philippine officials in the early 1990s, seemed immune from prosecution. The former airman lived in Manila teaching tae kwon do for the Philippine Department of Tourism. Positively identified by his accomplice, Virginia Jean Baynes, a CIA secretary, Brown was beyond the reach of American law enforcement as long as he remained in Manila. To lure him back to the United States, the CIA made Brown a bogus offer to teach martial arts to its staff. Jumping at the opportunity, Brown even paid his own airfare to the United States for an interview at CIA headquarters. However, once he stepped off the plane at Washington Dulles International Airport, FBI agents arrested him. Brown pled guilty and received a six-year prison sentence, while Baynes, who cooperated in the investigation, received 41 months jail time.

Another spy who received a surprise welcome at Dulles International Airport was Jean-Philippe Wispelaere, a former employee of Australia's Defence Intelligence Organisation. Wispelaere, hired in July 1998 as an entry-level analyst, began his spying when he walked into an unnamed embassy in Bangkok, Thailand, in January 1999, offering to sell secret documents. Since the documents focused on American intelligence, the FBI was alerted, and a sting operation launched. A few weeks later, the 28-year-old sold more than 700 classified documents out of a backpack to an undercover agent in Bangkok for $70,000 and mailed another 200 documents to a post office box in Virginia, which netted him an additional $50,000.

With evidence in hand, the FBI lured Wispelaere to Dulles International Airport, where he was arrested on May 17, 1999. *The Sidney Morning Herald* on July 6, 2012, reported that during his trial Wispelaere said that he thought of himself as "James Bond pulling the coup of the century" and exhibited enough bizarre behavior while incarcerated to warrant a psychiatric evaluation. In press interviews in Australia, his father bluntly called his son "an idiot," "a loon," and "a fool."

Facing a possible 25 years or more in prison, Wispelaere accepted a plea bargain for a 15-year sentence in exchange for cooperation. He served a decade in a US prison before being released under an international prisoner-transfer program in 2012 to Canada, the country of his birth.

190. RUM AND STOGIE DIPLOMACY

MAP 3 ➤ **Cuban Interests Section:** 2630 16th Street NW (the Cuban embassy as of 2015)

For more than five decades, the United States and Cuba had no formal diplomatic relations, although each country maintained an Interests Section through the Swiss embassy in the other's country. Interests Section representatives enabled minimum official functions, such as consular services. In Washington, the Cuban Interests Section operated from a grand, Italianate building at 2630 16th Street NW. Located in a section of the city know as Meridian Hill, the gated mansion had housed Cuba's embassy prior to the 1959 revolution. "The Cuban Embassy, which once had the appearance of an austerely beautiful museum, now looks lived in. It looks as if it had been lived in by a herd of buffalo," *The Washington Post* reported on April 22, 1959. Describing the scene of a reception to welcome Fidel Castro, the newspaper reported food thrown against walls and cigarettes extinguished on expensive rugs.

Although Cuba and the United States maintained no formal diplomatic relationship between 1960 and 2015, Cuba intelligence officers have worked from the "Cuban Interests Section" in an ornate mansion in the Meridian Hill neighborhood.

Senator Fidel Castro?

One of the enduring myths surrounding Fidel Castro is that he once tried out for the Washington Senators baseball team, though other versions include the New York Yankees and New York Giants. The folktale, repeatedly debunked by baseball historians, often includes details of a lucrative contract and signing bonus. In reality, the Cuban dictator simply was not good enough to compete professionally. However, one researcher found a mention of him pitching in an intramural game at the University of Havana—law school versus business school—in the 1940s.

The Cuban Interests Section also provided official cover for the country's intelligence officers. In 2000, two Cuban diplomats, Jose Imperatori and Luis Molina, became embroiled in a spy scandal involving an American immigration official, Mariano M. Faget. Then acting deputy director of the Immigration and Naturalization

Service (INS) in Miami, Faget was seen at multiple meetings with the Cubans. The FBI launched a sting operation that resulted in Faget passing classified information to what he thought was a Cuban national. Convicted of espionage, the senior INS official was given a five-year prison sentence.

In 2011, the Cubans opened the Hemingway Lounge & Bar (sometimes called Hemingway's) on the second floor of the 16th Street mansion. The bar, an invitation-only venue, featured tropical ceiling fans, a six-foot-long bronze replica of Hemingway's signature, and numerous photographs of the macho American author. Hemingway, who maintained a residence named Finca Vigía (meaning Lookout Estate) in Cuba, is remembered in the island nation, as well as in the United States, as a literary icon.

While the Cuban officials insist the bar is neither political nor a clandestine lair, others are not so sure. The comfortable social venue provides a private environment for Cuban intelligence officers to "chat up" reporters and invitees. Regardless of any espionage function, an evening at Hemingway's guarantees the opportunity to enjoy embargoed Cuban rum and forbidden Cohiba cigars. With restoration of formal diplomatic relations between the United States and Cuba in 2015, both the country's rum and the cigars are again legal.

■ 191. THE QUEEN OF CUBAN SPIES

MAP 7 ➤ **Ana Montes residence:** Cleveland Apartments, 3039 Macomb Street NW, apartment 20 (private residence)

Ana Belén Montes

At the time of her arrest, Ana Belén Montes generated little public attention outside the intelligence community. Taken into custody less than two weeks after the terrorist attacks of September 11, 2001 (9/11), Montes could not compete in the news cycle with the horrific events in New York, Virginia, and Pennsylvania. Yet Montes just may have been one of the most damaging spies in recent US history. A senior Defense Intelligence Agency (DIA) analyst at DIA headquarters, located on Chappie James Boulevard at Joint Base Anacostia-Bolling, Montes had access to classified human and technical intelligence reporting on Cuba. Called the "Queen of Cuba" by colleagues, the occupant of cubicle C6-146A was recognized as a no-nonsense professional who received numerous commendations and cash bonuses.

No hostile intelligence organization could hope for a more dedicated or better-placed spy. For 17 years Montes spied for Cuba's intelligence service. She traveled clandestinely to Cuba under a false passport and received guidance through covert communication systems. She accepted no payment for her efforts beyond modest expenses.

Ana Montes memorized entire classified documents at work and later created detailed reports for her Cuban handlers in her Macomb Street NW apartment.

Montes, the oldest child of a US Army physician, with a sister and brother employed by the FBI, seemed an improbable candidate for a Cuban spy. Exactly when she was recruited remains unclear, though likely the first contact was made in 1983 or 1984 when she attended the Johns Hopkins School of Advanced International Studies. What is known is that she disagreed with America's Latin American foreign policy pertaining to Nicaragua in the 1980s, and at some point Cuban operatives manipulated that opposition to recruit her to spy.

Ana Montes placed clandestine calls to her handlers from public pay phones using prepaid phone cards. The arrow indicates the location of one phone (now removed) she used.

Montes avoided copying or carrying classified documents out of the office. She memorized information, then typed reports at home, in apartment 20 (second floor) at the Cleveland Apartments, 3039 Macomb Street NW. She received ciphered communications from Cuban radio broadcasts of seemingly random numbers on a Sony model ICF-2010 shortwave radio, copying the groups of five-digit numbers for decryption on her laptop. She did not call her handlers from her home or work and instead made clandestine calls from an array of pay phones at gas stations, department stores, and the National Zoo. Both she and her handlers used prepaid phone cards to leave coded messages on pagers. Personal meetings with Cuban contacts were held at Starbucks coffee shops throughout Washington when needed.

Montes left few clues she was a spy. In the late 1990s, DIA and FBI counterintelligence agents were attempting to identify a suspected Cuban spy within the intelligence community. One vital clue was that the individual used a Toshiba laptop to communicate covertly with Cuban intelligence. Another clue was that the individual had visited Cuba at least once for tradecraft training. As investigators combed through financial records and other documents, a narrow list of suspects emerged, and the DIA identified Montes for closer

This straddling checkerboard, a cipher sheet for encryption and decryption found in Montes's apartment, became a key piece of evidence used to convict the Cuban spy.

examination.

A court-authorized search of her home discovered a Toshiba computer containing incriminating instructions for using Cuban decryption software in the slack space of the laptop's hard drive. Inexplicably, the usually meticulous Montes failed to follow instructions from Cuban intelligence to use data-erasure software to "wipe" her computer following receipt of each ciphered message. Since that was not done, her computer contained digital forensic evidence confirming she was a spy for Cuba.

Arrested on September 21, 2001, Montes was convicted and given a 25-year prison sentence. Showing no remorse, she remained defiant through sentencing and during incarceration.

192. VIEW FROM VERY HIGH GROUND

MAP 8 ➤ National Geospatial-Intelligence Agency: 7500 Geoint Drive, Springfield, Virginia

Aerial reconnaissance evolved from balloons and biplanes to space-based platforms in less than 100 years. Today the US classified view from space is delivered by the National Geospatial-Intelligence Agency (NGA). Imagery data—called "geospatial intelligence," or GEOINT—is analyzed and integrated by the NGA's cartographers and analysts to create a diverse set of visual and text intelligence products.

The NGA's immediate predecessor, the National Imagery and Mapping Agency (NIMA), was formed in 1996 when the CIA's National Photographic Interpretation Center (NPIC) merged with the Defense Mapping Agency. NIMA was renamed NGA in 2003, causing one spy wag to observe that management realized that without a three-letter abbreviation like CIA, NSA, or FBI, the organization could never be a major player in the US Intelligence Community.

The NGA, with its headquarters in Springfield, Virginia, is the principal source of classified geospatial intelligence (GEOINT) for virtually every type of intelligence consumer. Military planners and combat commanders use the imagery for strategic and tactical operations. Diplomats consult NGA data for negotiations. Independent scientists apply the organization's declassified imagery to climate change and geological research. First responders to natural disasters such as hurricanes and typhoons, as well as those responsible for security of international events such as the Olympic Games, have also applied NGA imagery to their needs.

193. RIGHT SIDE OF HISTORY, WRONG SIDE OF THE LAW

MAP 1 ➤ **African National Congress agent meeting site:** Union Station, 50 Massachusetts Avenue NE

State Department official Donald Lieber gave classified documents to a representative of the African National Congress at Washington's Union Station.

Donald Charles Lieber, who vehemently opposed South Africa's apartheid laws, was recruited to spy by the African National Congress (ANC) in 1986. Four years later, in 1990, from his position as a clerk/typist in the State Department's Public Affairs Office, Lieber began providing classified information to his ANC handler at meetings in Union Station, 50 Massachusetts Avenue NE; ***George Washington University's Marvin Center, 800 21st Street NW***; and other locations around Washington. Between 1990 and 1993, Lieber passed an estimated 175 to 300 documents to the ANC during at least 16 clandestine meetings. As an ideological spy, Lieber received little money from the ANC for his efforts.

Then, sometime in 1995, a former South African intelligence officer walked into the American embassy in Nairobi with information that implicated Lieber in espionage. When confronted by the FBI, Lieber admitted guilt and, in return, received a reduced sentence.

194. AN AWKWARD ARREST

MAP 3 ➤ **South Korean embassy:** 2320 Massachusetts Avenue NW

The South Korean embassy

In September 1996, federal agents arrested Robert (Chae-gon) Kim, a civilian computer specialist with the Office of Naval Intelligence (ONI), in the parking lot of the ***Fort Myer Officers' Club, 214 Jackson Avenue,***

Robert Kim, who lived in this home in Sterling, Virginia, had a short spy career—less than a year—before he was arrested at the Fort Myer Officers' Club.

Fort Myer, Virginia. The arrest made during a reception honoring a South Korean dignitary may have caused diplomatic angst, but there was little doubt about Kim's guilt. Kim had removed SECRET and TOP SECRET indicators from documents and mailed the material to Capt. Baek Dong-Il, a naval attaché in the South Korean embassy, ***2320 Massachusetts Avenue NW***. Surveillance also observed Kim playing golf at the Fort Meade golf course with the captain.

Kim, a 19-year veteran of the ONI, had been an American citizen since 1974 and led a comfortable suburban life at his 20765 Bank Way, Sterling, Virginia, residence. According to investigators, Kim surfed the ONI's computer system for documents during a short-lived career as a spy, which lasted from May through September 1996. Pleading guilty to one count of espionage, he was sentenced to nine years in prison. Kim served seven years before release and was hailed as a hero when he returned to South Korea.

Harold Nicholson

■ 195. A FAMILY TRADITION

MAP 8 ➤ **Harold Nicholson residence: 5764 Burke Towne Court, Burke, Virginia (private residence)**

CIA case officer Harold Nicholson received strong reviews from his superiors during his career at the agency. A *New York Times* article on June 6, 1997, quoted performance evaluations lauding the officer as having "no weaknesses" and saying that "his future is bright." Neither proved true. On November 16, 1996, he was arrested at Dulles International Airport while waiting to board a flight to Switzerland.

Sometime before his arrest, the spy had tripped on a routine polygraph question of whether or not he was concealing contact with foreign nationals. The ensuing investigation revealed

Nicholson's bank transactions included large deposits with no explanation of the income source. Covert video surveillance of his office showed him photographing sensitive documents beneath his desk using a CIA-issued camera. As the investigation intensified, officials learned he communicated with his Russian handlers through the mail, posting letters and postcards at a variety of mailboxes, including a mailbox at ***Gallows Road and Electric Avenue, Dunn Loring, Virginia***, and another at ***8283 Greensboro Drive, Tysons Corner, Virginia***. Whether sending letters or postcards, he used the same oversized commemorative stamps with a face value of $1.00 and a false return address of 2206 Pimmit Run, Falls Church, Virginia, with an incorrect 22041 zip code. His chatty, nonalerting messages were signed Nevil R. Strachey.

Evidence found on a laptop in Nicholson's home in Burke, Virginia, included classified and sensitive operational information.

Harold Nicholson used a series of local mailboxes for posting letters and postcards to his Russian contacts.

A search of Nicholson's home, 5764 Burke Towne Court, Burke, Virginia, uncovered a laptop with information on planned assignments of CIA officers to Moscow, biographical data on other agency officers, and extensive personal observations. The SVR paid Nicholson an estimated $300,000 for his betrayal.

With his guilt established, Nicholson played the role of a desperate family man before the court. "I reasoned that I was doing this for my children . . . for the long hours at work and for failing to keep my marriage together," he said, according to a 1997 *New York Times* article. Nicholson accepted a plea bargain that put him behind bars for 23 years, 7 months.

Nicholson's proclamations of concern for his three children were also lies. The senior Nicholson subsequently taught his son, Nathaniel, the fundamentals of intelligence tradecraft during visiting hours at the Federal Correctional Institution in Sheridan, Oregon. Beginning in 2006, Nathaniel began making trips out of the United States to meet with his father's former Russian handlers and eventually collected some $35,000.

When the FBI arrested Nathaniel in 2009, a search of his apartment turned up a birthday card and note from his father dated July 11, 2008. According to a *New York Times* report on January 29, 2009, the incarcerated spy wrote, "You have been brave enough to step into this new unseen world that is sometimes dangerous but always fascinating. God leads us on our greatest adventures. Keep looking through our new eyes. I understand you and me."

Nathaniel Nicholson was sentenced to five years' probation for conspiring with his father to maintain contact with Russian intelligence. Eight years were added to the elder Nicholson's sentence, making him the first person ever convicted twice for committing espionage against the United States.

■ 196. THE SPY WHO ALMOST GOT AWAY

MAP 11 ➤ **Arrest site:** Washington Dulles Airport Marriott Hotel, room 1431, 45020 Aviation Drive, Dulles, Virginia

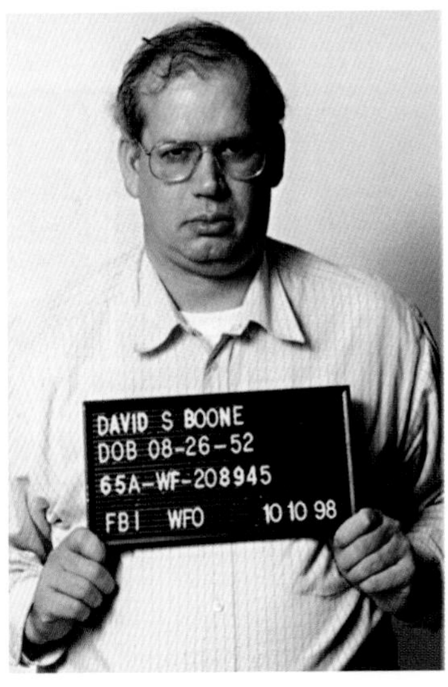

David Sheldon Boone

Facing a contentious divorce, David Sheldon Boone, a US Army signals analyst assigned to the NSA, ran up unsustainable debt in an effort to deny his wife settlement money. In 1988, with his modest army pay garnished and trying to live on $250 a month, Boone became desperate for quick cash. Realizing his top secret work as a senior cryptologic traffic analyst could be profitable, he walked into the ***Soviet embassy at 1125 16th Street NW***.

KGB officers welcomed the hard-luck case and paid $300 in cash for the material Boone provided to establish his bona fides. It must have seemed easy money for Boone, who continued to supply Soviet intelligence with a stream of classified documents. With the traitorous income a welcome supplement to his salary, he agreed to continue spying when reassigned to West Germany. However, upon retirement in 1991 and remarriage, Boone abruptly halted his espionage. Three years as an active spy had earned him more than $60,000 from the Soviet and Russian intelligence services.

For several years, it seemed as if Boone's activities had gone undetected. Then, in 1998, the FBI launched a sting operation. Boone was invited to a hotel near his home in Germany to meet an individual posing as a Russian official. During the meeting, Boone boasted of his previous exploits, insisted on $9,000 cash to be reactivated, and instructed no payments be deposited in a bank. A November 1998 *Baltimore Sun* article quoted Boone telling the undercover FBI agent, "It's called a paper trail. Don't leave something for anyone to track. It's called, it's called, uh, paranoia." In fact, the serial number of each bill he received was recorded by the FBI prior to the meeting.

Boone's confession to espionage was sufficient cause for arrest, but as long as he remained in Germany he was outside of the FBI's jurisdiction. Persuaded to return to the United States with the promise of more cash and work, the money-hungry spy arrived at Dulles International Airport on October 2, 1998, with plans to meet his contact the next day and return to Germany on October 4. He checked into room 1431 of the Washington Dulles Airport Marriott Hotel, 45020 Aviation Drive, Dulles, Virginia, where the FBI promptly arrested him. Prior to trial, Boone plea-bargained for a prison sentence of 24 years and four months.

Lured back into the US by an FBI undercover sting, Boone was arrested at the Washington Dulles Airport Marriott Hotel for spying for the USSR.

How Boone came to the attention of the FBI remains classified.

■ 197. BUGGING FOGGY BOTTOM

MAP 4 ➤ **Department of State:** Harry S. Truman Building, 2201 C Street NW

In the summer of 1999, an FBI surveillance team from the Special Surveillance Group (SSG), called "Gs," watched Stanislav Gusev, a 54-year-old Russian diplomat repeatedly loiter in the general area of the State Department's headquarters. Suspicions arose when Gusev's behavior followed a similar routine on each visit. He parked his car, fed coins into the parking meter, then walked around aimlessly before returning to the vehicle. Sometimes he would sit on a bench in ***Edward J. Kelly Park*** across the street from the Harry S. Truman Building, fiddling inside his shoulder bag. Rather than confronting the Russian prematurely, the FBI watched patiently as he sought parking spaces close to the building and continued surveillance of his movements.

Stanislav Borisovich Gusev

When alerted to Gusev's activities, the Truman Building was swept for bugs, and a device was eventually found in the chair rail that ran along the wall, approximately three feet above the floor, in a seventh-floor conference room.

Brand-Name Concealment

Stanislav Gusev was not the first Russian spy to use a Kleenex box as a concealment device. When atomic spy/courier Lona Cohen traveled from Albuquerque to New York City by train in August 1945, she hid stolen plans for the nuclear device in a box of the ubiquitous facial tissues. At one point during her journey, she eluded security by feigning forgetfulness and handing the invaluable secret nuclear documents to a conductor as she pretended to hunt through her purse for her ticket. The conductor helpfully returned the Kleenex box and its cache of nuclear secrets, and Cohen continued on her journey. "I felt it in my skin, the conductor would return the box of Kleenex and indeed later he handed it to me," she recalled.

An FBI surveillance team apprehended Russian technical officer Stanislav Gusev and incriminating eavesdropping equipment outside the State Department.

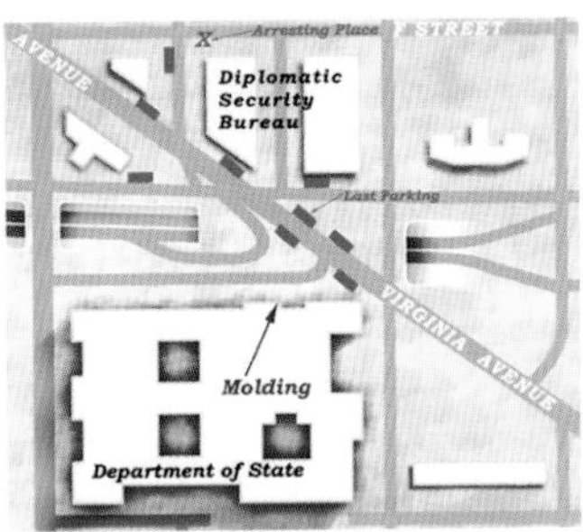

Drawing depicting parking locations used by Stanislav Gusev while conducting an audio operation against the State Department.

The Russian intelligence service bugged the State Department's headquarters in the 1990s. An arrow points to the area where an audio device was concealed in a chair rail running along the wall of a conference room.

Any bug would have been a cause for concern, but this device was particularly troubling because the seventh floor housed the State Department's most senior staff, including the secretary of state.

According to the FBI, the device had been "professionally introduced" into the room. Installation required someone to cut away a two-foot length of the molding to accommodate a perfectly matched section of wood that hosted the audio device. Investigators concluded that multiple visits to the conference room would have been needed to complete the operation. How long the bug was in place could not be determined.

Most technical details about the bug remain classified, but the transmitter used a frequency-skipping feature to avoid detection and a remote-activation capability powered by a long-life battery configuration. Captured conversations would likely have been transmitted to a recorder secreted in a Kleenex box in Gusev's car or a mobile receiver concealed in a shoulder bag he carried when out of the automobile.

Predictably, Russian officials denied the allegations, dismissing them as "implausible and nonsensical." Gusev was expelled from the United States for spying.

198. BETTER SPYING THROUGH TECHNOLOGY

MAP 9 ➤ **In-Q-Tel headquarters:** 2107 Wilson Boulevard, Arlington, Virginia

The CIA established a new form of government–private business partnership in 1999 with the creation of In-Q-Tel. The goal was to stimulate investment in advanced technologies that offered promise for the nation's intelligence organizations. The nonprofit company operates similar to a venture capital firm by identifying, evaluating, and making early investments in start-up companies. In-Q-Tel's portfolio includes diverse technologies ranging from imaging systems and power sources to big data analytics.

Formed in 1999, In-Q-Tel makes strategic investments in new private companies on behalf of the intelligence community.

In-Q-Tel's investments underwrite creation of capabilities or products that are both useful to the US Intelligence Community and commercially viable. An early investment in Keyhole Inc. (also the code name of an early reconnaissance satellite program) became a major financial success when Google acquired the firm. Keyhole's Earth Viewer system was renamed Google Earth, while other components of the original technology were integrated into Google Maps and Google Mobile.

Another success, Palantir, received a relatively modest initial $2 million from In-Q-Tel along with other private investments. Originally focused on financial fraud detection, the company, now approaching $1 billion in annual revenues, created intelligence augmentation software that integrates data, technology, and human experience for government and commercial applications.

199. THE SPY WHO COULDN'T SPELL

MAP 10 ➤ **Operational site:** Tysons-Pimmit Library, 7584 Leesburg Pike, Falls Church, Virginia

In August 2001, FBI agents apprehended Brian Patrick Regan on a shuttle bus at Washington Dulles International Airport. In one pocket Regan had

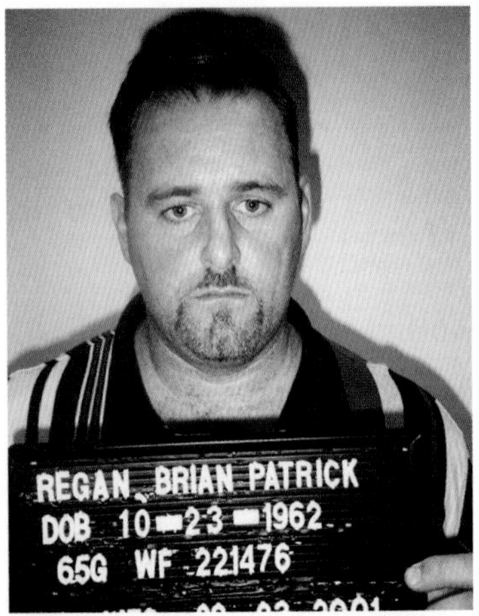

Brian Patrick Regan

Failed spy Regan chose public computers, such as those at the Tysons-Pimmit Library, Falls Church, Virginia, to send anonymous emails.

a ticket for Zurich. Hidden in the soles of his shoes were addresses of foreign embassies. He also carried a spiral notebook containing an unrecognizable code.

Regan had been under surveillance for months prior to his arrest. The retired US Air Force master sergeant was employed by TRW Inc. as a contractor at the ***National Reconnaissance Office (NRO), 14675 Lee Road, Chantilly, Virginia***. There he had access to classified information about the NRO's spy satellites.

An odd trail led to Regan, who was then living at ***13011 Minetta Lane, Bowie, Maryland***. From an overseas source, US intelligence acquired a letter from an unidentified sender offering to sell secrets to foreign governments. The letter offered few clues about its author, other than an unusually large number of spelling errors. Counterintelligence officials began looking for a spy who couldn't spell. Regan, who was dyslexic, became a suspect, in part through spelling errors he made at work.

Evidence against him mounted when the investigation revealed he was deeply in debt and given to surfing an intelligence database known as Intelink for information unrelated to his duties. As Regan's activities were surveilled, more evidence accumulated. He used computers at local libraries, such as the Tysons-Pimmit Library, 7584 Leesburg Pike, Falls Church, Virginia, and others in Prince George's County and Anne Arundel County, Maryland, as well as in Crofton, Virginia, to compile information on potential overseas contacts and anonymously send e-mails to arrange meetings abroad with the staff of the Iraqi and Chinese embassies.

The missing piece of the espionage puzzle was his code, a bewildering string of seemingly random words, such as *tricycle*, *glove*, and *rocket*, found in the three-by-five-inch notebook Regan carried with him to the airport. The words did not conform to any of the standard codes used by spies and resisted all known decryption techniques. A break in the case, code-named CAST ABOUT, came when one of the FBI agents noticed a similar code that referred to a brokerage account of Regan's. The words *hand, tree, hand, car* seemed to represent a four-digit PIN code. Could the hand-tree-hand-car code be based on a mnemonic device of visual clues? Entering five for a hand's five fingers, one for tree, and four for car's wheels, the FBI agent gained access to the account.

Brian Regan used a complex personal coding system to record the locations of his cached packages and buried the code key at the base of the Interstate 95 130A exit sign for Fredericksburg, Virginia.

Seemingly random words in the notebook, such as *tricycle* (three), when taken together represented the latitude and longitude coordinates of a foreign missile site that Regan wanted to use to establish his credibility abroad. Another code on an index card, when deciphered, revealed the names and coordinates of Swiss banks he wanted to use to receive money from the sale of the secret information. However, the most difficult code in a folder Regan also carried was written on four pages filled with three-digit numbers. The FBI later learned these specified the coordinates of caches Regan buried in ***Pocahontas State Park, 10301 State Park Road, Chesterfield, Virginia***, and ***Patapsco Valley State Park, 8020 Baltimore National Pike, Ellicott City, Maryland***. In all, Regan secreted in the two parks 19 caches of classified documents, some 20,000 pages of images on CD-ROMs, and video tape. The key to the code, secured in a blue plastic toothbrush holder, was buried near the ***Fredericksburg sign by exit 130A on Interstate 95 South***.

Regan's trial ended with a guilty verdict and a life sentence without the possibility of parole. He is incarcerated at the Lee Federal Prison, Pennington Gap, Virginia.

■ 200. LIES OF A FALSE MODERATE: AL-QAEDA'S US RECRUITER

MAP 10 ➤ Dar al-Hijrah Islamic Center: 3159 Row Street, Falls Church, Virginia

Anwar al-Awlaki (sometimes spelled Anwar Aulaqi) reportedly preached a message of peace at the Dar al-Hijrah Islamic Center, 3159 Row Street, Falls Church, Virginia, where he served as imam from January 2001 to April 2002. Living at ***3331 Kaywood Drive, Falls Church***, al-Awlaki had been

Anwar al-Awlaki

Anwar al-Awlaki presented himself as a moderate imam at the Dar al-Hijrah Islamic Center in Falls Church, Virginia, but had ties to the 9/11 terrorists.

born in New Mexico, attended college in Colorado, and held dual American and Yemeni citizenship.

The cleric's public pronouncements suggested a pious man seeking religious harmony. For many members of the press and official Washington, the well-spoken al-Awlaki was a youthful face of the moderate Muslim community. Following 9/11, he publicly condemned the attacks but portioned out blame on American foreign policy as well.

Secretly al-Awlaki led a different life. His Falls Church mosque was attended by at least two of the 9/11 hijackers, while his links to the terrorists responsible for the attacks may have begun as early as the late 1990s. Then, as an imam at a San Diego mosque, he met with 9/11 hijackers Nawaf al-Hazmi and Khalid al-Mihdhar. Al-Hazmi and another of the 9/11 hijackers, Hani Hanjour, attended the Virginia mosque just weeks prior to the attacks.

Exactly when al-Awlaki became radicalized is unclear. He may have been indoctrinated into the jihadist cause while in Yemen in the early 1990s as a teenager. After returning to the United States to attend college, he is reputed to have spent a summer undergoing training in Afghanistan. Returning to the United States, he dropped out of engineering school, became an imam, and likely recruited for al-Qaeda as well.

Even his devout pronouncements were proven to be a sham. FBI investigations revealed a slew of religious transgressions, including numerous assignations with $400-an-hour prostitutes at upscale Washington hotels. Among his illicit tryst locations were the Washington ***Melrose Georgetown, 2430 Pennsylvania Avenue NW; Lowe's Madison, 1177 15th Street NW***; the ***Monarch (today the Fairmont Washington, DC), 2401 M Street, NW***; and the ***Washington Suites (today the Avenue Suites), 2500 Pennsylvania Avenue NW***.

In 2002, al-Awlaki left the United States, dropped the mask of moderation, and began preaching violent jihad against the West. He became an effective online recruiter through e-mails, sermons, and uploaded videos. Nidal Malik Hasan, the Fort Hood mass murderer, exchanged e-mails with al-Awlaki before going on a rampage that killed 13 people and injured 30. Umar Farouk Abdulmutallab, the Nigerian terrorist dubbed the "underwear bomber," who attempted to blow up Northwest Airlines flight 253 on Christmas 2009, met with al-Awlaki prior to launching his failed attack. Another terrorist, Faisal Shahzad, reached out to al-Awlaki online prior to his unsuccessful car bombing attempt at Times Square in 2010.

On September 30, 2011, a US government–sanctioned missile strike killed al-Awlaki in Yemen along with another American citizen turned jihadist, Samir Khan, who ran al-Qaeda's English-language online magazine *Inspire*.

■ 201. WHERE TERRORISTS PLOTTED

MAP 13 ➤ **Valencia Motel:** 10131 Washington Boulevard (Route 1), Laurel, Maryland

The terrorist hijackers of September 11, 2001, temporarily lived in the suburban town of Laurel, Maryland. The community is known for the Laurel Park horse-racing track, the shopping center where segregationist presidential candidate George Wallace was shot in 1972, and the NSA in nearby Fort Meade. It was also once the home of future president Dwight D. Eisenhower, who has a Laurel middle school named after him.

Several of the 9/11 airplane hijackers stayed temporarily in the Valencia Motel in Laurel, Maryland.

Laurel made news following the 9/11 attacks. Five of the terrorists—Hani Hanjour, Khalid al-Mihdhar, Majed Moqed, Nawaf al-Hazmi, and Salem al-Hazmi—all stayed at the Valencia Motel, 10131 Washington Boulevard, for several days prior to boarding American Airlines Flight 77 at the Washington Dulles International Airport and crashing it into the Pentagon. According to the follow-up investigation, the hijackers occupied room 343 at the motel from August 23 to September 10, 2001.

While in Laurel, the hijackers moved easily around the community and frequented nearby stores, such as the Giant supermarket, Laurel Mall's food court, a Pizza Time restaurant, and Kinko's copy center. They exercised at a nearby gym, shopped at Safeway, and used the Internet at the Laurel Library.

Nawaf al-Hazmi joined United Airlines Flight 93 hijacker Ziad Jarrah for several nights at the nearby ***Pin-Del Motel, today a Days Inn & Suites, 9860 Washington Boulevard***, in early September. Jarrah was a member of the terrorist team aboard Flight 93 that crashed in a rural area of Shanksville, Pennsylvania, when passengers thwarted the hijacking.

On September 10, the hijackers moved to the ***Marriott Residence Inn, 315 Elden Street, Herndon, Virginia***, near Dulles airport, for their final staging area prior to the attack.

■ 202. A SPY IN THE WHITE HOUSE

MAP 2 ➤ **White House:** 1600 Pennsylvania Avenue

A spy worked for both Vice President Albert Gore and Vice President Richard Cheney. Leandro Aragoncillo, a US Marine serving as a staff assistant to the vice presidents' military advisers, passed top secret information related to US government interests in the Philippines through a contact in

New York City. He often simply walked out of his office with data on a floppy disk, although in at least one instance he faxed the information directly from the White House.

When he retired from the Marine Corps in 2004, Aragoncillo applied for work at the CIA, the NSA, and the FBI. Hired by the FBI as an analyst, he continued to spy from his posting at Fort Monmouth, New Jersey, until tripped up by a simple mistake. When his contact in New York City encountered immigration problems in 2005, Aragoncillo attempted to intervene with US Immigration and Customs Enforcement officials. The telephone call he made was so far out of the ordinary that it triggered alarm bells. A security audit of his computer activity led to a full-scale spy hunt that uncovered Aragoncillo's unauthorized searches from his office computer along with indebtedness of nearly $500,000.

Confronted with the evidence, Aragoncillo eventually confessed, putting him at the center of one of the few known spy cases originating in the White House. Under a plea-bargain agreement, he was sentenced to ten years in prison.

203. MYSTERIES OF THE INTERNATIONAL SPY MUSEUM

MAP 2 ➤ **Atlas Building:** 800 F Street NW

The International Spy Museum, 800 F Street NW, is the only public museum in the United States dedicated to espionage. Opened in 2002, it immediately became a must-see Washington attraction. More than 600,000 people visit each year, curious about the tools of espionage and personal stories of intelligence officers. The exhibits feature artifacts that were once among the most technically sophisticated and deadly devices of the world's intelligence services. From clandestine weaponry and disguises to concealment devices and spy cameras, the museum's exhibits reveal secret battles and silent wars that shaped world history. Visitors can also test their tradecraft skills through true-to-life interactive spy scenarios.

The Atlas Building, which housed the Fourth District headquarters of the Communist Party USA from 1941 to 1948, is now home to the International Spy Museum.

The Warder Building (later known as the Atlas Building), in which the International Spy Museum is located, has its own clandestine history. In addition to the Warder Building housing correspondence schools,

The current location of the International Spy Museum. After opening its doors in 2002, it became one of the favorite attractions in Washington, drawing over 600,000 visitors each year.

A proposed design for a new, larger building for the International Spy Museum, scheduled to open in 2018.

watchmakers, lawyers, and other small business tenants, its third-floor offices served as the Fourth District headquarters of the Communist Party USA (CPUSA) from 1941 through 1948. The CPUSA often acted as "talent spotter" for potential spies and support arm for Soviet intelligence. After the organization moved to new quarters, a large hammer and sickle was found painted on a false wall. Today the International Spy Museum prominently displays the door to the CPUSA district headquarters.

In 2015, the International Spy Museum announced plans to relocate to a new facility in 2018 that will offer larger exhibit areas, expanded technical intelligence displays, and numerous spy-versus-spy events.

■ 204. CAREER TAINTING ROMANCE

MAP 8 ➤ Potowmack Landing Restaurant (now Indigo Landing Restaurant): 1 Marina Drive, Alexandria, Virginia

Donald Keyser's distinguished diplomatic career came to an inglorious end when he began an affair with the much younger Isabelle Cheng (also known as Cheng Nian-Tzu) from Taiwan's National Security Bureau. According to the criminal complaint, Keyser and Cheng exchanged e-mails as early as 2002 and rendezvoused in Taiwan as well as the Washington area. Two covert meetings occurred in July and September

The Potowmack Landing Restaurant, now the Indigo Landing Restaurant, was a rendezvous site for US diplomat Donald Keyser and Taiwanese intelligence officer Isabelle Cheng.

At this outdoor dining setting, Keyser met Taiwanese intelligence officers. He was arrested as he departed the restaurant on September 15, 2004.

2004 at the Dangerfield Island waterfront restaurant Potowmack Landing (today Indigo Landing), 1 Marina Drive, Alexandria, Virginia. During the second meeting, an FBI surveillance team witnessed Keyser pass documents to two Taiwanese agents and arrested the three as they departed the restaurant.

Keyser, a senior official in the State Department's East Asia Bureau, was only days away from retirement.

FBI investigators discovered a small mountain of 3,559 pages of classified documents during a search of Keyser's home, along with a home computer and floppy disks containing classified data. Keyser negotiated a plea bargain to avoid espionage charges, although the deal was later rescinded when the disgraced diplomat became uncooperative. At the time of his plea bargain, Keyser admitted to an intimate relationship with Cheng and a secret trip to Taiwan to meet with her. However, he denied giving her any information not authorized for release to Taiwanese officials. Following a protracted legal battle, he was sentenced on January 23, 2007, to one year and a day in jail, three years of supervised release, and fined $25,000. Cheng, who was not charged, reportedly returned to Taiwan.

■ 205. DIPLOMACY ABOVE HIS PAY GRADE

MAP 9 ➤ Tivoli Restaurant (now closed): 1400 North Moore Street, Rosslyn, Arlington, Virginia

Lawrence Franklin, a Pentagon analyst, met with suspected Israeli agents and passed classified information at the now-closed Tivoli restaurant that was located on the second floor of this building in Rosslyn, Arlington, Virginia.

In June 2003, Lawrence Franklin, a Pentagon analyst working in the office of the secretary of defense for policy, lunched with two members of the American Israel Public Affairs Committee (AIPAC) at the Tivoli Restaurant, 1400 North Moore Street, Rosslyn, Arlington, Virginia. Franklin, an ideological neoconservative, and his AIPAC lunch companions, Steven J. Rosen and Keith Weissman, shared common concerns about Middle East policies. During the meeting, Franklin conveyed classified information to the AIPAC officials, who were unaware of an ongoing FBI investigation of AIPAC's connections to the Mossad, the Israeli intelligence service.

Afterward, Franklin's contacts with AIPAC were monitored, and a search of his West Virginia home turned up more than 80 classified documents.

When arrested in May 2005, Franklin pleaded not guilty to six counts of espionage. Tried and found guilty, he was sentenced to twelve and a half years in prison but was released in 2009. He had received no money for his espionage, apparently, and was motivated solely by ideological fervor.

206. THE MAYFLOWER STING

MAP 12 ➤ **Stewart Nozette residence:** 141 Grafton Street, Chevy Chase, Maryland (private residence)

Stewart Nozette, a scientist with top secret clearances and a reputation for brilliance, moved through significant assignments at the US Department of Energy's Lawrence Livermore National Laboratory, NASA, and the Defense Advanced Projects Research Agency (DARPA). Married to attorney Wendy McCollough, he lived at 141 Grafton Street, Chevy Chase, Maryland.

A hidden camera in a room at the Mayflower Hotel captured Stewart Nozette accepting a bribe from an FBI agent posing as a Mossad intelligence officer.

Stewart Nozette's scientific career and spying ended when the FBI discovered classified documents in a search of his residence.

After Nozette left government service to set up a nonprofit entity called Alliance for Competitive Technology, he did consulting work for Israel Aircraft Industries. However, when financial and tax problems mounted, he began hinting to colleagues that he might be open to espionage. The FBI set up a sting operation with an undercover agent posing as a Mossad (Israeli intelligence) operative. Meeting multiple times in a suite at the upscale ***Mayflower Hotel, 1127 Connecticut Avenue NW***, Nozette enthusiastically discussed his spy plans while relishing quality room-service meals. The September–October 2011 edition of *Bethesda Magazine* described Nozette as telling his bogus Mossad contact, "I knew this day would come. . . . I just had a feeling. . . . I knew you guys would show up . . . I thought I was working for you already."

Using a US post office box as a dead drop, Nozette answered technical questions regarding US satellites, early-warning systems, and defense or retaliation against large-scale attacks. With enough evidence in hand, the FBI arrested Nozette on October 19, 2009, at the Mayflower but not before the spy tried to hide $10,000 cash in the tank of the hotel room's toilet. Eventually accepting a plea bargain, Nozette received a 13-year sentence.

207. SEPTUAGENARIAN SPIES

MAP 7 ➤ **Kendall and Gwendolyn Myers residence:** The Westchester, 3900 Cathedral Avenue NW, apartment 610-A (private residence)

Walter Kendall Myers

Cuban spies Kendall and Gwendolyn Myers prized their teak-trimmed, 37-foot sailboat *Helene* and longingly spoke of their idea to "sail home" to Cuba.

When the FBI arrested Walter Kendall Myers on June 4, 2009, at the ***Capital Hilton, 1001 16th Street NW***, he seemed the most unlikely of spies. Known as Kendall, the stately six-foot-six, slightly stooped 72-year-old with a distinguished mustache looked every bit the highborn patrician. His great-grandfather was Alexander Graham Bell, inventor of the telephone, while his grandfather, Gilbert Grosvenor, served as editor of *National Geographic* magazine for more than half a century. Myers, who holds a PhD from Johns Hopkins, and his wife, Gwendolyn, had been Cuban spies for 30 years.

The couple was known among their friends and neighbors for their quiet lifestyle, a love of sailing their custom 37-foot, teak-trimmed sailboat *Helene*, and devotion to each other. They lived comfortably in the art deco apartment complex called the Westchester, 3900 Cathedral Avenue NW, apartment 610-A.

To their Cuban handlers, the pair was known as Agent 202 and Agent 123 (or E-634). In the couple's shared secret life, they received coded shortwave transmissions in both

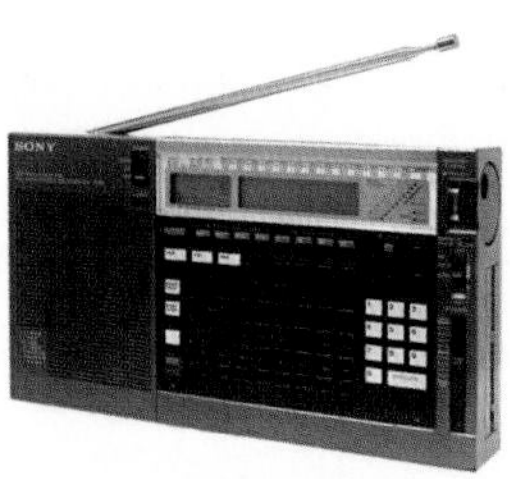

Kendall and Gwendolyn Myers received ciphered messages from Cuba using a commercially available Sony shortwave radio, model ICF-2010. Other Cuban spies used the same make and model radio.

Apartment 610-A at the Westchester Apartments on Cathedral Avenue NW was home to Cuban spies Walter Kendall Myers and Gwendolyn Myers.

Morse code and voice through number stations, which broadcast short strings of seemingly random numbers on open radio frequencies. Purloined documents would be delivered to Cuban contacts through brush passes or inconspicuously exchanging shopping carts in the ***Safeway supermarket, 1855 Wisconsin Avenue NW***, or the ***Whole Foods supermarket, 2323 Wisconsin Avenue NW***. They also traveled regularly overseas under false identities for personal meetings with Cuban intelligence.

Kendall Myers taught for decades part-time at the Johns Hopkins University's School of Advanced International Studies and worked in multiple mid-level contract positions in the State Department, including in the Bureau of Intelligence and Research, where he held a top secret clearance. The couple's value to the Cuban government was underscored by their secret personal meeting with Fidel Castro in 1995.

The investigation that led to the septuagenarian spies took three years. FBI monitoring of high-frequency transmissions by the Cuban Intelligence Service

Clandestine Radio Broadcasts

The shortwave radio of choice for Cuban spies was the Sony model ICF-2010. Used by both the Myerses and Ana Montes, the radio was compact, inexpensive, commercially available, and popular among shortwave enthusiasts. The Cuban codes, sometimes broadcast at 7887 kHz, were announced by a woman who would begin the transmission with "*Atención! Atención!*" A sequence of 150 groups of five-digit numbers followed.

Although the use of such "number stations" for one-way communication to spies is as old as broadcasting, the Cuban service provided Montes and the Myerses with a significant upgrade. Rather than hand-decrypting the numbers using a cipher pad, the spies were given a software program that performed the otherwise exacting deciphering work. They only needed to type the number sequences into their computers, and the preloaded program would generate a plain-text decryption.

Washington's Fashionable Spy Address

Kendall and Gwendolyn Myers were not the only spies to live in the Westchester. During the 1940s, Harry Dexter White, a leading economist for the Roosevelt and Truman administrations, resided at the fashionable Cathedral Avenue address. White held senior positions in the US Treasury and participated in the historic Bretton Woods Conference. Following the war, he was among the chief architects of the International Monetary Fund.

White, identified as a Soviet agent by former Soviet spies Elizabeth Bentley and Whittaker Chambers, was accused of passing economic intelligence to his Soviet handlers and acting as an agent of influence by crafting memos and policy papers that reflected or complemented the Soviet agenda. When called before the House Un-American Activities Committee (HUAC), White adamantly denied spying for the Soviet Union. His role in espionage remained in dispute for decades until the release of the VENONA decryptions confirmed his identity as a Soviet agent code-named JURIST.

collected tantalizing clues to overseas travel schedules, references to a medical procedure, and other seemingly minor personal details that narrowed the search. A sting operation was initiated whereby the couple met several times with an undercover agent posing as a Cuban contact, "Hector."

Ideology apparently motivated the couple to spy for Cuba. Money seemed incidental. The Myerses appeared to be true believers in Castro's Cuba, even as they spent a lifetime enjoying the traditional version of the American Dream along with many of the accompanying luxuries. "We wish to add at this time that we acted as we did for 30 years because of our ideals and beliefs," the pair said in a joint statement broadcast by CNN on July 26, 2010. Pleading guilty on November 20, 2009, Kendall Myers received a life sentence without possibility of parole. Gwendolyn was sentenced to 80 months in prison.

208. DOING IT FOR LOVE

MAP 8 ➤ **Holiday Inn:** 6401 Brandon Avenue, Springfield, Virginia

CIA employee Sharon M. Scranage confessed to FBI agents at this Holiday Inn that romance induced her to become a spy for Ghana.

Love can be a powerful motive for espionage. Sharon M. Scranage, a 22-year-old administrative secretary for the CIA, was a member of her church choir with a clean record until she fell in love with Ghanaian citizen Michael Agbotui Soussoudis. The two met while she was stationed in Africa, and, as romance blossomed, Soussoudis persuaded

Scranage to provide names of agency officers and assets. Soussoudis, a self-described consultant and cousin to Ghana's then leader Jerry J. Rawlings, gave the information to Kojo Tsikata, head of Ghanaian intelligence. When Scranage attempted to stop spying, Soussoudis threatened to end the relationship.

After failing a polygraph test, Scranage confessed when questioned by FBI agents at the Holiday Inn, 6401 Brandon Avenue, Springfield, Virginia. She received a five-year prison sentence that would later be reduced to two years. Soussoudis, who was also arrested, pled nolo contendere and was sentenced to 20 years. However, his sentence was suspended on the condition he leave the United States.

209. FRIENDLY NEIGHBORHOOD SPIES

MAP 9 ➤ **Michael Zottoli and Patricia Mills residence:** River House Apartments, 1400 South Joyce Street, apartment 904, Arlington, Virginia (private residence)

News of the FBI arrest of ten Russian spies in June 2010 sounded like an unwelcome echo of Cold War espionage. Initial denials by Russian authorities could have been recycled sound bites from a previous generation. However, American counterintelligence officials who conducted the investigation, given the FBI code name GHOST STORIES, recognized that aggressive Russian intelligence operations remained a dangerous 21st century threat.

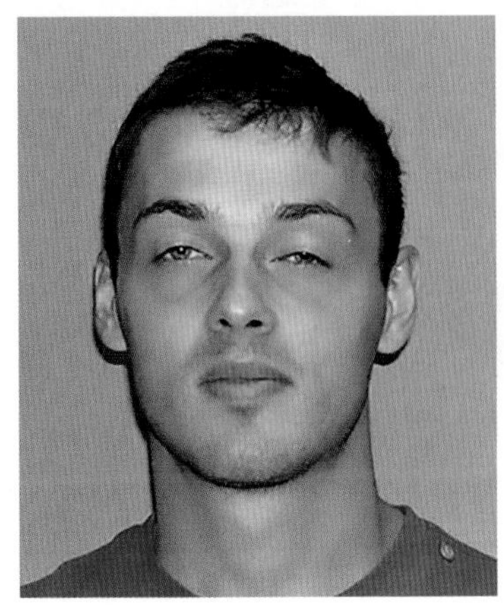

Mikhail Semenko

Three of the illegals lived in the Washington suburbs. Mikhail Kutsik (alias Michael Zottoli) and Nataliya Pereverzeva (alias Patricia Mills) lived at the River House Apartments, 1400 South Joyce Street, apartment 904, Arlington, Virginia. They had arrived by way of Seattle, attended the University of Washington, earned bachelor's degrees in business, and over several years meticulously constructed their covers. At the time of their arrest, both were in their mid-forties. Kutsik worked a number of jobs, including telecommunications company accountant, car salesman, and teleconference firm employee. Pereverzeva played the role of stay-at-home mother, caring for their two young children.

The third member of the Washington-based spy trio was Mikhail Semenko. He reportedly attended school at the Harbin Institute of Technology in China, then received a master's degree from Seton Hall University in New Jersey.

Youthful Russian spy Semenko lived in a modest apartment building in Arlington, Virginia, and established an active social media presence on Facebook and LinkedIn.

Russian illegal Semenko, unaware of concealed surveillance cameras, made a dead drop beneath this footbridge in Arlington's Lubber Run Park.

From a Ruby Tuesday restaurant (now closed) on Wisconsin Avenue, Russian spy Semenko transmitted covert messages wirelessly to a Russian diplomat parked in the McDonald's lot across the street.

Semenko spoke at least four languages fluently. After a series of jobs in New York City, including with the Conference Board, he began working for ***Travel All Russia, a travel agency at 2300 North Pershing Drive, suite 202, Arlington, Virginia***. His residence was nearby, ***1505 North Quinn Street, apartment 15N, Arlington***.

How the FBI learned of the spies remains classified, but some had been under surveillance for nearly a decade. Run by the SVR, the illegals used American aliases and led workaday lives that appeared routine, fooling even their closest contacts. Semenko maintained an active Facebook page with more than 300 friends. His LinkedIn profile described him as impressively multilingual, with native Russian, fluent English, Mandarin Chinese, and Spanish, plus intermediate skills in German and Portuguese. His stated interests were nonprofits, think tanks, public policy, advocacy, and educational institutions.

The Washington-based spies, like their seven compatriots living in other parts of the United States, used digital technology for covert communications back to Moscow. Semenko used an ad hoc wireless network to send and receive messages. When FBI agents surveilled him at a ***Ruby Tuesday restaurant, 4200 Wisconsin Avenue NW*** (now closed), they observed the Russian spy enter the crowded eatery, power-up a laptop computer, enable his wireless mode, then position his laptop to link to a computer in the car of his Russian

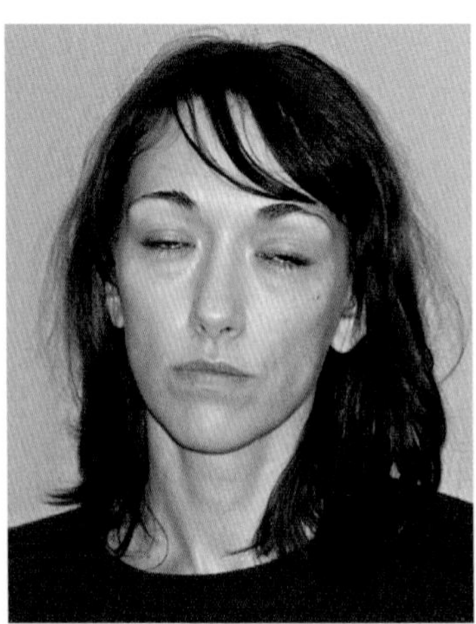

Nataliya Pereverzeva (alias Patricia Mills)

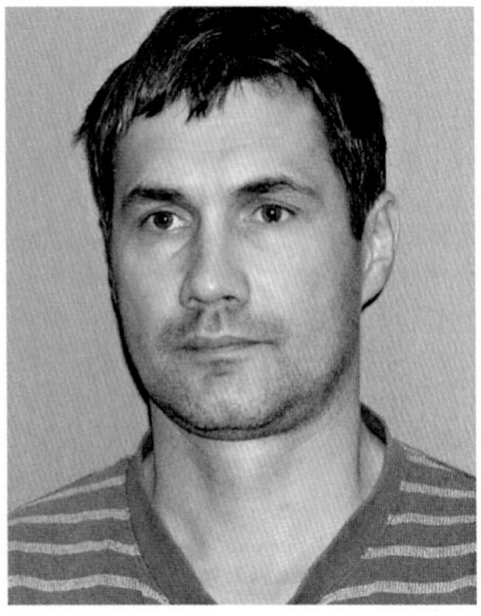

Mikhail Kutsik (alias Michael Zottoli)

contact parked at the McDonald's restaurant across the street. His tradecraft represented a cyber version of a well-executed car toss or brush pass.

When the FBI moved against Semenko, their first step was not arrest but to conduct an undercover operation to gather evidence for potential use in court. Posing as a Russian intelligence officer, an FBI agent arranged to meet Semenko, who operated in his true name, in late June 2010 near the intersection of ***10th and H Streets NW***. Taking seats on a bench in a nearby park, the FBI agent feigned to report on a problem with Semenko's communication from a few weeks earlier, while eliciting nonalerting information such as where and how long his training took. Finally he handed Semenko a newspaper with $5,000 folded into its pages and instructed him to make a dead drop the next day under a footbridge in ***Arlington's Lubber Run Park, North Columbus and Second Streets in Arlington***. Concealed cameras set up by the FBI recorded Semenko making the drop, and agents later recovered the money. The video was necessary evidence for the FBI to prove that he was in the United States as a spy.

Instructions from Moscow

The 10 illegal intelligence officers rolled up by the FBI in 2010 were well-trained and dedicated professionals, yet when exposed to the American lifestyle, some apparently required stern reminders of their primary mission. A communication from Moscow included in the FBI's criminal complaint of June 27, 2010, against Richard and Cynthia Murphy made clear the spies were not to forget their purpose: "You were sent to USA for long-term service trip. Your education, bank accounts, car, house etc.—all these serve one goal: fulfill your main mission, i.e. search and develop ties in policymaking circles in US and send intels [intelligence reports] to C [Center]."

Targeting Prada and Jimmy Choo

Russian-American diplomatic relations frayed in late 2013. Press reports based on newly released FBI documents revealed a sustained pattern of fraudulent behavior by Russian consulate embassy officers and their family members in the United States. The FBI charged 25 current and former Russian diplomats along with 24 of their spouses in New York and Washington with participating in a massive Medicaid scam. Some of the Russians were suspected intelligence officers.

Using traditional tradecraft, including falsification of salaries and citizenship, the diplomats systematically scammed the Medicaid system. They then used the estimated $1,500,000 in fraudulently received benefits for luxury shopping sprees that included vacations and designer shoes, jewelry, and clothing from Tiffany & Co., Jimmy Choo, Prada, Bloomingdale's, and Burberry.

Russian illegals Mikhail Kutsik and Nataliya Pereverzeva lived in the River House Apartments in Arlington, Virginia.

On June 27, 2010, Semenko, Kutsik/Zottoli, and Pereverzeva/Mills were arrested and jailed for several days before being deported to Russia in a swap for individuals held by Russian authorities.

The roll-up belied any notion that Russian spying in the United States ended with the fall of the Soviet Union. The case further dispelled any public misconceptions about a 21st century Russian spy's physical appearance. The stereotypical grim-faced Cold War KGB *apparatchiks* had been replaced by youthful, smiling neighbors, men and women with iPhones and Facebook friends.

■ 210. SECOND-GENERATION SPY?

MAP 4 ➤ **Tim Foley residence:** George Washington University's Lafayette Hall, 2100 I Street NW

Andrey Bezrukov (alias Donald Heathfield) and Elena Vavilova (alias Tracey Lee Ann Foley) were spies sent to Canada by the Soviet Union in the 1980s. They moved to the United States in 1999 and continued to spy for the SVR until arrested by the FBI in 2010 as part of OPERATION GHOST STORIES and deported to Russia. Their oldest son, Tim Foley, was enrolled at George Washington University in Washington. In 2012, *The Wall Street Journal*, citing unnamed US officials, reported he was being groomed as a second-generation spy. Foley denied this in a 2016 interview with *The Guardian*.

Had Foley become a Russian spy, he would have been a formidable threat. He spoke fluent English as well as German and French and was studying

Chinese. He had just finished his sophomore year at ***George Washington's Elliott School of International Affairs, 1957 E Street NW***, when his parents were arrested. Friends described Foley as a typical undergraduate. He lived at Marquis de Lafayette Hall, 2100 I Street NW, and *The Wall Street Journal* article said he not only knew about his parents' secret lives as spies, but had also agreed to be trained in clandestine operations. After returning to Russia with his family, young Foley attempted to gain re-entry into the United States. His requests were denied.

While a student at George Washington University, Tim Foley, the son of Russian *illegals* and a potential future spy himself, lived in Marquis de Lafayette Hall.

This family's clandestine life was reportedly the inspiration for the critically acclaimed fictional television show *The Americans.*

211. THE PRC COMES TO WASHINGTON

MAP 7 ➤ **Embassy of the People's Republic of China:** 3505 International Place NW

The embassy of the People's Republic of China (PRC), 3505 International Place NW, completed in 2008, was designed by award-winning Chinese American architect I. M. Pei. Among Pei's best-known buildings are the Rock and Roll Hall of Fame in Cleveland, Ohio; the National Gallery East Building, Washington, DC; and New York City's Jacob K. Javits Convention Center. For cost and security, the embassy's construction was done by Chinese workers flown in for the project.

Architecturally the new embassy was a welcome change from the previous facility, the former ***Windsor Park Hotel, 2300 Connecticut Avenue NW, and adjoining 2310, the St. Alban's Apartments***. Those connected structures provided offices for Chinese diplomats, some of whom were also intelligence officers, for more than three decades prior to completion of the new embassy.

However, not all spies have a connection to an embassy or diplomatic compound. While China and the United States have maintained friendly diplomacy for more than 30 years, repeated cyber-spying incidents in the 21st century have strained those relations. In the new battlefield of cyberspace, China has emerged as one of

Completed in 2008, the Chinese embassy was designed by internationally acclaimed architect I. M. Pei.

America's most aggressive threats. Computer networks of congressional offices, law firms, think tanks, embassies, federal agencies, and human rights groups have all been alleged targets of Chinese cyber espionage. Major news organizations such as *The Washington Post*, *The New York Times*, and *The Wall Street Journal* have suffered computer attacks by suspected China-based hackers.

The independent cybersecurity company Mandiant Corporation has traced some cyber attacks to a shadowy Chinese military component named PLA Unit 61398, operating from a 12-story building at 208 Datong Road in Shanghai. Chinese hackers are suspected of stealing plans for new US missile systems and a May 2013 *Washington Post* report detailed other potentially compromised advanced weapon programs, including those of the F/A-18 fighter jet, the V-22 Osprey, the Black Hawk helicopter, the US Navy's new Littoral Combat Ship, and the F-35 Joint Strike Fighter.

Beyond targeting US military and technological secrets, the scope of China's alleged cyberwarfare offensive suggests political as well as economic targets. In 2015, China was implicated in hacking into federal government personnel records, which included biographical and personal information on employees of the IC and the DOD.

212. FIRST SPY FROM CHINA

MAP 2 ➤ Tony Cheng's Mongolian Restaurant: 619 H Street NW

Hou Desheng, working under the cover of assistant military attaché, is remembered for the dubious honor of being the first People's Republic of China official expelled from the United States for spying after diplomatic relations were re-established between the United States and China in 1979.

Chinese assistant military attaché and spy Hou Desheng was apprehended at this Mongolian restaurant in 1987 for "activities incompatible with his diplomatic status."

Working out of the Chinese embassy, then located in the former ***Windsor Park Hotel, 2300 Connecticut Avenue NW***, Hou, along with a PRC consular official from Chicago, were told to leave the country in December 1987 for "activities incompatible with their diplomatic status." The matter was handled with quiet diplomatic propriety by both sides. "We asked them to leave, and they left, and we hope that's that," one anonymous US official was quoted as saying.

The actions were the culmination of a year-long investigation by the FBI.

Little information regarding the counterintelligence operation leaked following the spies' forced departure. However, according to one source, Hou was detained at Tony Cheng's Mongolian Restaurant, 619 H Street NW, in the Chinatown section of Washington. He is said to have accepted documents he believed came from the NSA but were really the product of an FBI sting. One report labeled the Chinese spy as bumbling, talkative, and given to grumbling about his $75-a-month salary.

■ 213. CHINA'S FALSE FLAG

MAP 8 ➤ **James Fondren Jr. arrest site:** 4136 Whispering Lane, Annandale, Virginia (private residence)

Gregg William Bergersen, a Pentagon weapon systems policy analyst in the Defense Security Cooperation Agency, began passing classified documents to Louisiana entrepreneur and spy handler Tai Shen Kuo in 2007. Bergersen, who lived at ***6226 Littlethorpe Lane, Alexandria, Virginia***, most likely believed Kuo was a representative of the American-friendly Taiwanese government. In fact, Kuo, who came from a prominent Taiwanese family, was spying for the PRC and running a "false flag" operation.

James Fondren Jr., a retired US Air Force lieutenant colonel, and Tai Shen Kuo were arrested at this Whispering Lane residence in Annandale, Virginia, for spying for the People's Republic of China.

Kuo, a naturalized US citizen, had business interests that included a furniture store in New Orleans. In addition to receiving cash payments from his contacts in China, his role in espionage would buy favor with Chinese officials and benefit the manufacturing side of his furniture business. From 2007 through 2008, Kuo paid Bergersen for classified documents with cash, trips to Las Vegas, and a promise of a lucrative job down the road.

Bergersen was not Kuo's first recruitment. Beginning in 2004, Kuo handled James Wilbur Fondren Jr., a retired US Air Force lieutenant colonel working as deputy director of the US Pacific Command's Washington liaison office. Fondren's espionage took the form of opinion papers that intentionally included classified information, which he sold to Kuo for between $350 and $800 apiece. Fondren, code-named FANG, knew his reports violated security standards. According to a May 13, 2009, Department of Justice press release, he told Kuo, "This is the report I didn't want you to talk about over the phone. . . . Let people find out I did that, it will cost me my job."

Kuo, Fondren, and Bergersen were arrested in February 2008. The FBI picked up Kuo and Fondren at Fondren's home, 4136 Whispering Lane, Annandale,

Virginia. The trio of traitors all received prison sentences: Kuo 188 months, Bergersen 57 months, and Fondren 36 months.

214. A PERFECT VIEW

MAP 9 ➤ **Pentagon Ridge Condominiums:** 1515 South Arlington Ridge Road, Arlington, Virginia

Once the residence of East German diplomats and spies, this 32-unit apartment building overlooks the Pentagon. An attempted purchase of the building by China's Xinhua News Agency in 2000 was blocked by Congress.

In 1974, the East German government constructed a 32-unit apartment building at 1515 South Arlington Ridge Road, Arlington, Virginia, to house the staff of its diplomatic mission. Perhaps not coincidentally, the building's upper floors offered clear views of a portion of the Pentagon's E-ring, where senior Defense Department officials have offices.

Following German reunification, the building was bought by a private developer. Then, in 2000, word leaked that China's *Xinhua News Agency* had purchased the seven-story building for a reported $4.6 million for office and living space. The prospect of the Chinese news organization, which had been accused of serving as an intelligence-gathering arm of the Chinese government, owning the building caused a diplomatic stir.

On June 27, 2000, *The Washington Times* reported that Louisiana congressman David Vitter characterized the structure as "an ideally suited spy tower, ideal to capture our military secrets," and Congress quickly enacted the *Chinese News Agency Divestiture Act of 2000*. As a result, the Chinese government eventually agreed to sell the building and not occupy it while the property was being marketed.

This Reston, Virginia, townhouse was headquarters to Sabern Instruments, which shipped prohibited technology to Iran.

215. SUPPLY CHAIN ESPIONAGE

MAP 11 ➤ **Sabern Instruments:** 2170 Greenkeepers Court, Reston, Virginia (private residence)

Vahid Hosseini ran a profitable export business from his residence at 2170 Greenkeepers Court, Reston, Virginia. Apparently it was a bit too profitable to be legal. Sabern Instruments' specialty was shipping

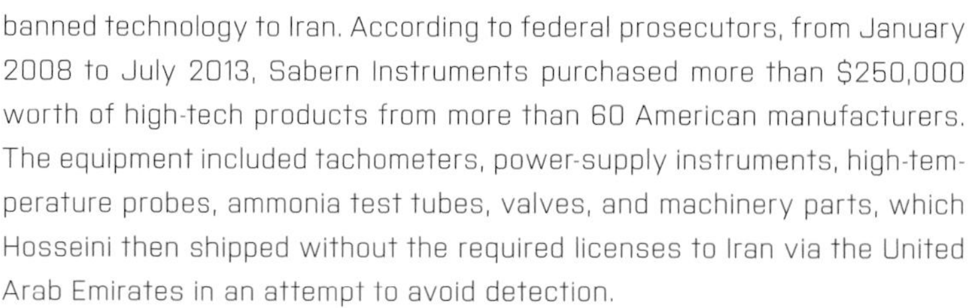

banned technology to Iran. According to federal prosecutors, from January 2008 to July 2013, Sabern Instruments purchased more than $250,000 worth of high-tech products from more than 60 American manufacturers. The equipment included tachometers, power-supply instruments, high-temperature probes, ammonia test tubes, valves, and machinery parts, which Hosseini then shipped without the required licenses to Iran via the United Arab Emirates in an attempt to avoid detection.

Confronted with the evidence, Hosseini pled guilty to conspiracy to violate the Iranian transactions and sanctions regulations under the *International Emergency Economic Powers Act*, along with a separate count of money laundering. In return for his guilty plea to the two felonies, Hosseini was sentenced to 30 months in prison.

■ 216. NO TIME LIKE JAIL TIME

MAP 8 ➤ **William G. Truesdale Adult Detention Center:** 2001 Mill Road, Alexandria, Virginia

The William G. Truesdale Adult Detention Center, 2001 Mill Road, Alexandria, Virginia, is named after a sheriff's deputy murdered in 1981 during an attempted escape from the original facility two miles away on the 500 block of Princess Street. Although the Mill Road site is primarily a city jail, it has also held several high-profile accused spies awaiting trial at the nearby Federal Court, including Aldrich Ames, Harold Nicholson, and Robert Hanssen. Also jailed there were 9/11 terrorist Zacarias Moussaoui and John Phillip Walker Lindh (aka Abu Sulayman al-Irlandi and known as "the American Taliban"). Judith Miller, a *New York Times* reporter, was also incarcerated at the Alexandria facility after refusing to cooperate with a grand jury investigating the disclosure of the identity of CIA officer Valerie Plame.

The William G. Truesdale Adult Detention Center in Alexandria has housed high-profile inmates, including 9/11 terrorist Zacarias Moussaoui.

■ 217. BIG-DATA TRAITOR

MAP 13 ➤ **Edward Snowden residence:** Woodland Village, Old Stockbridge Drive and Village Drive, Ellicott City, Maryland

The dollar cost to US national security from former National Security Agency contractor Edward Snowden's willful and reckless breach of sworn security obligations begins at tens of billions of dollars. The damage to national security is incalculable. Press reports estimate the number of

Edward Snowden lived in the Woodland Village community while working at the NSA.

classified documents downloaded from NSA computer networks in the tens of millions, along with thousands from the British and Australian intelligence services. A Pentagon report described Snowden's actions as the largest theft of classified documents in US history.

Press descriptions of the Snowden material revealed top secret electronic surveillance capabilities under NSA management, including collections of phone records, Internet traffic, and communications of foreign targets. Although the surveillance programs had been authorized by legislation and executive orders, the revelations strained diplomatic relations with friendly nations, alarmed American citizens over secret government intrusions into private communications, and may have jeopardized critical counterterrorism operations.

Whether Snowden is described as a conscience-driven whistleblower or unrepentant traitor, his background is unremarkable. He dropped out of high school, joined the US Army in May 2004, and was discharged five months later. Nevertheless, his computer skills landed him jobs first at the CIA, then the NSA and Dell, before he was hired by the government contractor Booz Allen Hamilton.

As a child, Snowden moved with his family to Crofton, Anne Arundel County, Maryland, where he attended Crofton Woods Elementary School, then Crofton Middle School. Dropping out of high school, he enrolled at ***Anne Arundel Community College, 101 College Parkway, Arnold, Maryland***, and eventually earned a GED. He lived in the Woodland Village subdivision of Ellicott City, Maryland, while working at the NSA before he secured a posting in Hawaii with Booz Allen Hamilton supporting an NSA program.

With a stolen cache of digital documents, Snowden flew to Hong Kong on May 20, 2013, where he leaked the material to reporters from *The Guardian* and *The Washington Post*. Hong Kong officials allowed Snowden to escape to Russia, where he was granted temporary asylum and then temporary residency. Although his relationship with the Russian or any other intelligence service remains murky, the programmed release of national secrets through the media continues to undermine American defenses against terrorists and foreign adversaries. "When you are talking about revealing the ways in which we track terrorists or the identities and locations of agents, I struggle to understand how you can apply hero whistle-blowing label to that kind of information," said FBI director James Comey in a widely quoted statement.

218. THE LITTLE SPY SHOP AROUND THE CORNER

MAP 4 ➤ **Bureau of Intelligence and Research:** Department of State, 2201 C Street NW

Among the least-known US Intelligence Community organizations is the highly respected State Department's Bureau of Intelligence and Research (known as INR). With a history that extends back to World War II's OSS, INR can lay claim to being America's oldest continuously operating all-source intelligence agency. When the OSS was abruptly disbanded and many components dismantled, its Research and Analysis Branch was transferred to the State Department.

Tiny by comparison to the CIA and DIA, INR has fewer than 400 employees and fields no spies. Rather, the bureau is home to expert analysts working with all-source information collected by other elements of the IC to support State Department officials, national policymakers, and other consumers of intelligence.

219. HUB OF THE INTEL WHEEL

MAP 10 ➤ **Office of the Director of National Intelligence:** 1500 Tysons Drive, McLean, Virginia

Established on December 17, 2004, the Office of the Director of National Intelligence (DNI) is a product of a bipartisan effort to strengthen the collaboration and effectiveness of America's 16 intelligence agencies. The DNI's creation followed a recommendation of the 9/11 Commission Report (officially *The Final Report of the National Commission on Terrorist Attacks upon the United States*) to address perceived

Thick vegetation obscures the headquarters of the Office of Director of National Intelligence in McLean, Virginia.

shortfalls in intelligence sharing prior to the 9/11 al-Qaeda terrorist attacks. In addition to creating the DNI, the *Intelligence Reform and Terrorism Prevention Act of 2004*, which passed through Congress with little opposition, established the National Counterterrorism Center along with the Privacy and Civil Liberties Oversight Board. President George W. Bush appointed then US ambassador to Iraq, John D. Negroponte, as the first director of National Intelligence.

■ 220. FINAL RESTING PLACE OF HEROES

MAP 9 ➤ **Arlington National Cemetery:** Memorial Drive, Arlington, Virginia

Arlington National Cemetery, once part of Gen. Robert E. Lee's expansive estate, was appropriated by the Union in 1864 as the final resting place for its war dead. Today more than 300,000 graves occupy grounds that cover over 600 acres. This place of honor includes many who also served their country's intelligence needs:

- William Francis Buckley: CIA station chief in Beirut, he was kidnapped in 1985 by Hezbollah militants and subsequently murdered. Section 59, grave 346.
- Brig. Gen. Marlborough Churchill: This distant relative of Winston Churchill took over as head of military intelligence from Ralph Van Deman in 1918. With the assistance of Herbert O. Yardley, Churchill instituted the jointly controlled State Department and War Department's Cipher Bureau. Section 11, grave 385.
- William Eagan Colby: An OSS veteran, he served as Director of Central Intelligence, 1973–76. Section 59, grave 655.
- Ernest L. Cuneo: Professional football player, newspaperman, lawyer, and confidant of New York City mayor Fiorello La Guardia, President Franklin Delano Roosevelt, and Ian Fleming, Cuneo served as liaison between British and US intelligence during World War II. Court 2, section S, column 18, niche 1.
- Maj. Gen. William J. "Wild Bill" Donovan: A World War I hero and Medal of Honor recipient, Donovan led America's World War II intelligence

organization, the OSS. Section 2, grave 4874-RH.

- Agnes Meyer Driscoll: Known as Madame X, she led the way for women in cryptography. Through two world wars and into the Cold War, she broke some of the world's most difficult codes. Section 35, grave 4808.
- William F. Friedman and Elizebeth S. Friedman: Husband-and-wife code-breaking team, instrumental in unlocking Japan's PURPLE code as World War II approached. Elizebeth is also credited with breaking the "Doll Code" of New York City–based Japanese spy Velvalee Dickinson. William, initially working under the wartime Signals Intelligence Service, became the first chief cryptologist of the NSA in 1952. Section 8, graves 6379 and 6379-A.
- Richard McGarrah Helms: An OSS veteran, he served as Director of Central Intelligence, 1966–73. Section 7, grave 8142-1.

United States v. Lee

Following the Civil War, Gen. Robert E. Lee's family attempted to regain ownership of the Arlington estate. After Lee's death, a lawsuit, filed in 1877 by George Washington Custis Lee, then a professor at Virginia Military Institute, was decided by the Supreme Court in the favor of the family, but the Lees never returned to the estate. In 1883, the property, then firmly established as a cemetery, was sold back to the government for $150,000.

Arlington National Cemetery is the burial site for many who served in US intelligence agencies.

- Adm. Roscoe H. Hillenkoetter: Director of Central Intelligence, 1947–50. Section 6, grave 5813-C-1.
- George G. Kisevalter: A CIA case officer who handled some of the most valuable Soviet spies of the Cold War, including GRU officers Lt. Col. Pyotr Popov and Col. Oleg Penkovsky. Section 60, grave 7292.
- Maj. Gen. Edward G. Lansdale: Served in both the OSS and CIA. He is best remembered as a counterinsurgency strategist. Section 8, grave 7022.
- James B. "Earthquake McGoon" McGovern Jr: A pilot for the CIA-operated Civilian Air Transport, which provided clandestine air support in Vietnam. When his Fairchild C-119 was hit by antiaircraft fire while air-dropping supplies to French troops in Dien Bien Phu in 1954, McGovern, his copilot, and two French paratroopers crashed in Laos. The crash site was discovered in 2002, and DNA matched McGovern's remains in 2006. Court 8, section M4, column 11, niche 6.
- Walter L. Pforzheimer: A member of the first generation of CIA officers, Pforzheimer began his intelligence career in the Army Air Corps and subsequently joined the Central Intelligence Group / CIA. Pforzheimer later served as the agency's first legislative counsel. Section 66, grave 7427.
- Francis Gary Powers: The U-2 pilot was shot down over the Soviet Union in 1960 and held as prisoner until exchanged for Soviet spy Rudolph Abel in 1962. Section 11, grave 685-2.
- Gen. Walter Bedell Smith: World War II aide to General Eisenhower and Director of Central Intelligence, 1950–53. Section 7, grave 8197-A.
- Johnny Michael Spann: A paramilitary officer with the CIA's Special Activities Division who was killed in Afghanistan in 2001. Section 34, grave 2359.
- Sarah E. Thompson: A Union spy, Thompson received credit for the successful ambush of Confederate general John Hunt Morgan and his men in Greenville, Tennessee. Section 1, grave 1261-WH.
- Gen. Lucian K. Truscott Jr.: He followed a distinguished military career in World War I and World War II with an assignment as the CIA's deputy director for coordination in 1957. Section 1, grave 827-B.
- Gen. Hoyt S. Vandenberg: Director of Central Intelligence, 1946–47. Section 30, grave 719.
- Richard S. Welch: CIA chief of station in Athens, who was murdered by a terrorist organization in 1975. Section 1, grave 1857.

APPENDIX A: SPY SITES MAPS

This appendix provides a breakdown of spy sites by areas or quadrant within the District of Columbia, by county or area in Virginia, and by county in Maryland. The numbers correspond to the entry's number in the text. A map of metro-accessible sites in Washington, DC, is on the inside back cover.

Readers should note that the locations depicted on the maps are approximate and may not represent the precise address of a site. If visiting or looking for a specific site, please refer to the text for the complete address.

Addresses cited in the book are accurate as of press time. The physical appearance of many sites may have changed since the location was last used for spy activity. Ownership, redevelopment, and business changes have and will continue to occur. Particularly for private residences, we urge readers to respect the privacy of occupants and owners.

MAP 1

DISTRICT OF COLUMBIA

➤ Capitol Hill, Northeast, and Southeast

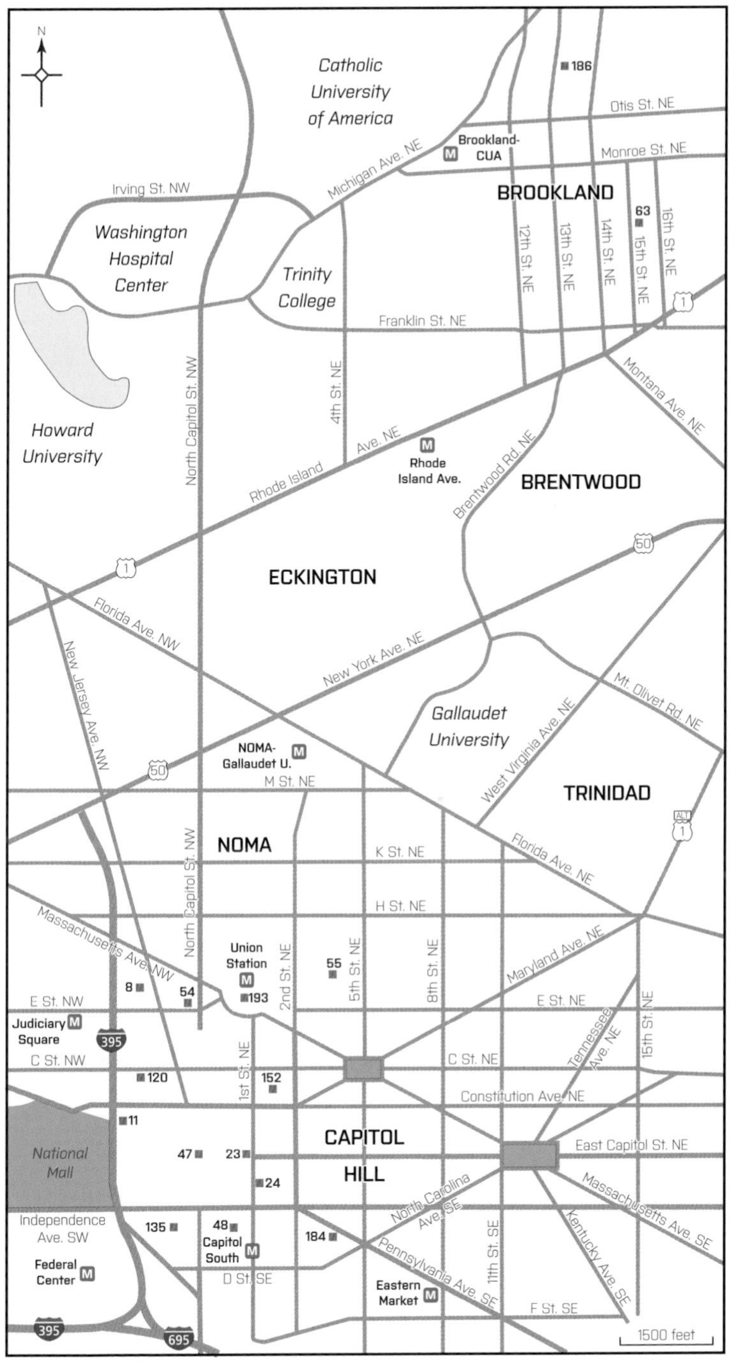

Catholic University of America
186
Otis St. NE
Brookland-CUA
Monroe St. NE
Michigan Ave. NE
Irving St. NW
BROOKLAND
63
Washington Hospital Center
Trinity College
12th St. NE
13th St. NE
14th St. NE
15th St. NE
16th St. NE
Franklin St. NE
Montana Ave. NE
Howard University
North Capitol St. NW
4th St. NE
Rhode Island Ave. NE
Rhode Island Ave.
Brentwood Rd. NE
BRENTWOOD
ECKINGTON
Florida Ave. NW
New Jersey Ave. NW
New York Ave. NE
Mt. Olivet Rd. NE
Gallaudet University
West Virginia Ave. NE
NOMA-Gallaudet U.
M St. NE
TRINIDAD
NOMA
K St. NE
Florida Ave. NE
H St. NE
Massachusetts Ave. NW
Union Station
2nd St. NE
55
5th St. NE
8th St. NE
Maryland Ave. NE
8
54
193
E St. NW
E St. NE
Tennessee Ave. NE
15th St. NE
Judiciary Square
395
C St. NW
1st St. NE
C St. NE
120
152
Constitution Ave. NE
11
CAPITOL HILL
National Mall
47
23
East Capitol St. NE
24
North Carolina Ave. SE
Massachusetts Ave. SE
Independence Ave. SW
135
48
Capitol South
184
11th St. SE
Kentucky Ave. SE
Pennsylvania Ave. SE
Federal Center
D St. SE
Eastern Market
F St. SE
395
695
1500 feet

MAP 2

DISTRICT OF COLUMBIA

➤ Downtown

104. Air America headquarters (p. 132)

109. YMCA (p. 136)

117. Pullman House, original embassy of the Soviet Union (p. 145)

118. Mintkenbaugh-KGB meeting site (p. 147)

121. FBI's former Metropolitan Field Office (p. 151)

128. Old National Photographic Interpretation Center, Steuart Motor Car Company Building (p. 162)

129. Occidental Grill (p. 164)

137. FBI headquarters (p. 173)

142. FBI SPIDERWEB surveillance system (p. 181)

164. Jamestown Foundation (p. 205)

165. Hay-Adams Hotel (p. 206)

168. Acme Reporting Company (p. 214)

203. International Spy Museum, Atlas Building (p. 254)

212. Tony Cheng's Mongolian Restaurant (p. 266)

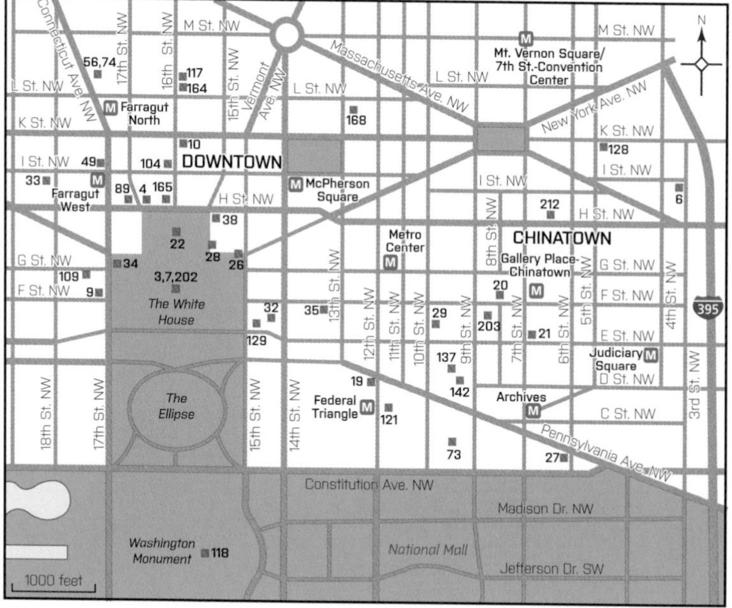

MAP 3

DISTRICT OF COLUMBIA

➤ Dupont Circle, Embassy Row, Logan Circle, Adams Morgan, and U Street Corridor

163. Iron Gate Inn (p. 204)

173. Jonathan Jay Pollard residence (p. 218)

174. South African embassy (p. 220)

176. East German embassy (p. 221)

177. Felix Bloch residence (p. 223)

180. William J. Casey residence (p. 226)

188. Dominic Ntube residence (p. 237)

190. Cuban Government Interests Section, now Cuban embassy (p. 239)

194. South Korean embassy (p. 243)

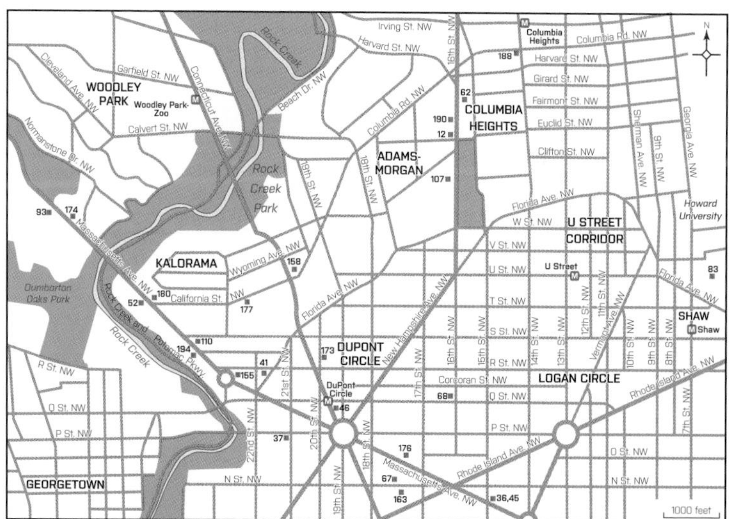

MAP 4

DISTRICT OF COLUMBIA

➤ Foggy Bottom and West End

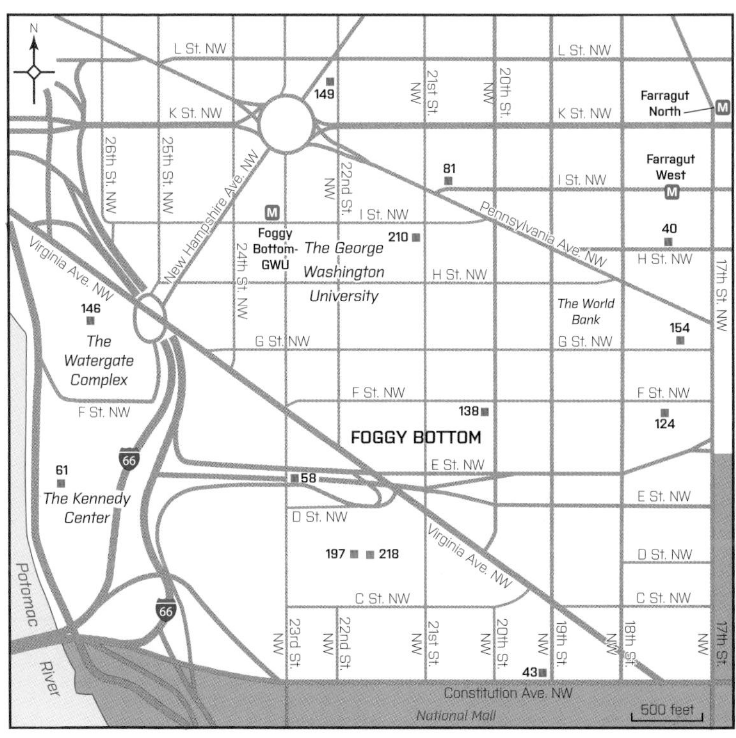

N
L St. NW
L St. NW
149
21st St. NW
20th St. NW
K St. NW
K St. NW
Farragut North
26th St. NW
25th St. NW
New Hampshire Ave. NW
22nd St. NW
81
I St. NW
Farragut West
I St. NW
Pennsylvania Ave. NW
Foggy Bottom-GWU
The George Washington University
210
40
H St. NW
24th St. NW
H St. NW
17th St. NW
Virginia Ave. NW
146
The Watergate Complex
The World Bank
154
G St. NW
G St. NW
F St. NW
F St. NW
F St. NW
138
124
FOGGY BOTTOM
66
61
The Kennedy Center
58
E St. NW
E St. NW
D St. NW
D St. NW
197
218
Virginia Ave. NW
C St. NW
C St. NW
Potomac River
66
23rd St. NW
22nd St. NW
21st St. NW
20th St. NW
19th St. NW
18th St. NW
17th St. NW
43
Constitution Ave. NW
National Mall
500 feet

MAP 5

DISTRICT OF COLUMBIA

➤ Georgetown, Burleith, and Glover Park

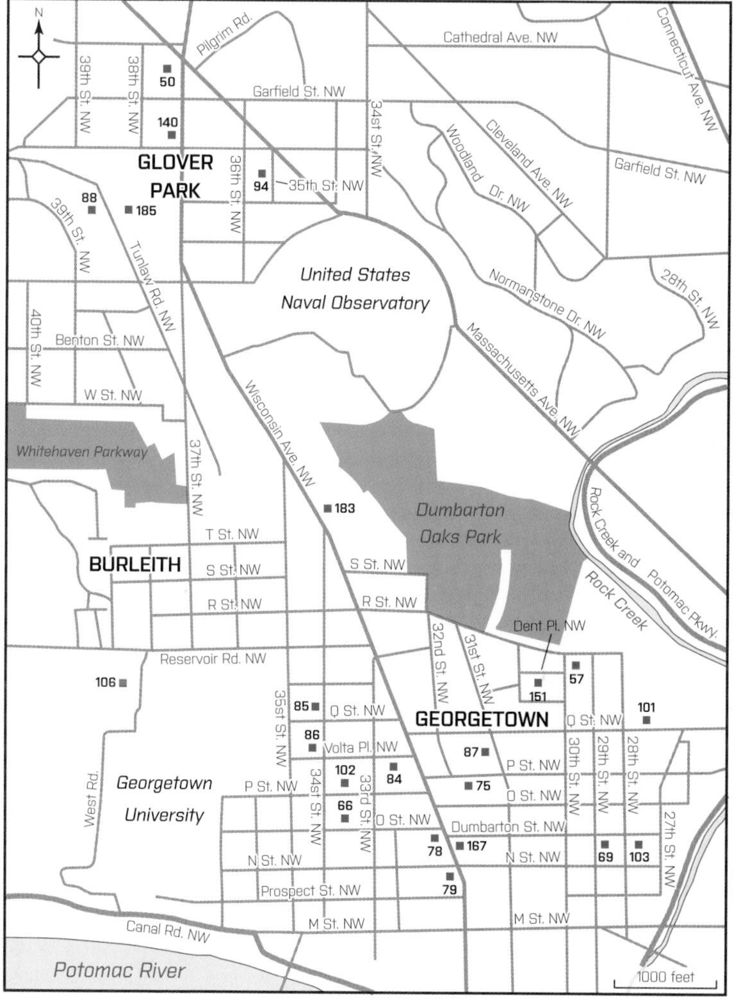

Cathedral Ave. NW
Connecticut Ave. NW
Pilgrim Rd.
39th St. NW
38th St. NW
50
Garfield St. NW
140
34th St. NW
Woodland Dr. NW
Cleveland Ave. NW
Garfield St. NW
GLOVER PARK
36th St. NW
94
35th St. NW
88
185
39th St. NW
Tunlaw Rd. NW
United States Naval Observatory
Normanstone Dr. NW
28th St. NW
40th St. NW
Benton St. NW
Massachusetts Ave. NW
W St. NW
Wisconsin Ave. NW
Whitehaven Parkway
37th St. NW
183
Dumbarton Oaks Park
Rock Creek and Potomac Pkwy.
T St. NW
BURLEITH
S St. NW
S St. NW
Rock Creek
R St. NW
R St. NW
Dent Pl. NW
32nd St. NW
31st St. NW
Reservoir Rd. NW
57
106
151
35st St. NW
85
Q St. NW
GEORGETOWN
Q St. NW
101
86
Volta Pl. NW
30th St. NW
29th St. NW
28th St. NW
87
P St. NW
102
84
Georgetown University
P St. NW
34st St. NW
33rd St. NW
75
O St. NW
West Rd.
66
O St. NW
Dumbarton St. NW
27th St. NW
78
167
N St. NW
N St. NW
69
103
79
Prospect St. NW
M St. NW
M St. NW
Canal Rd. NW
Potomac River
1000 feet

MAP 6

DISTRICT OF COLUMBIA

➤ Southwest

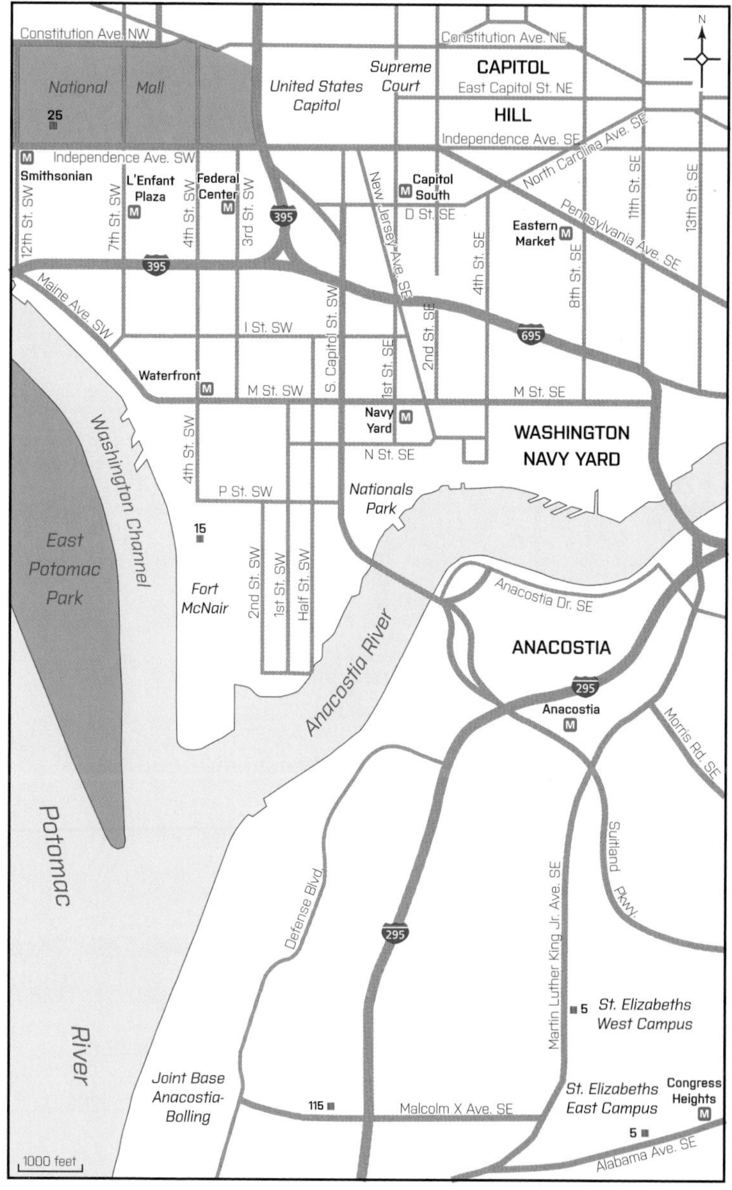
Constitution Ave. NW
Constitution Ave. NE
National Mall
25
Supreme Court
CAPITOL HILL
United States Capitol
East Capitol St. NE
Independence Ave. SE
Independence Ave. SW
North Carolina Ave. SE
Smithsonian
L'Enfant Plaza
Federal Center
Capitol South
D St. SE
Eastern Market
Pennsylvania Ave. SE
12th St. SW
7th St. SW
4th St. SW
3rd St. SW
New Jersey Ave. SE
4th St. SE
8th St. SE
11th St. SE
13th St. SE
395
Maine Ave. SW
I St. SW
S. Capitol St. SW
2nd St. SE
1st St. SE
695
Waterfront
M St. SW
M St. SE
Navy Yard
WASHINGTON NAVY YARD
N St. SE
Washington Channel
4th St. SW
P St. SW
Nationals Park
15
East Potomac Park
Fort McNair
2nd St. SW
1st St. SW
Half St. SW
Anacostia River
Anacostia Dr. SE
ANACOSTIA
295
Anacostia
Morris Rd. SE
Potomac River
Suitland Pkwy.
Defense Blvd
Martin Luther King Jr. Ave. SE
5
St. Elizabeths West Campus
Joint Base Anacostia-Bolling
115
Malcolm X Ave. SE
St. Elizabeths East Campus
Congress Heights
Alabama Ave. SE
1000 feet

MAP 7

DISTRICT OF COLUMBIA

Upper Northwest

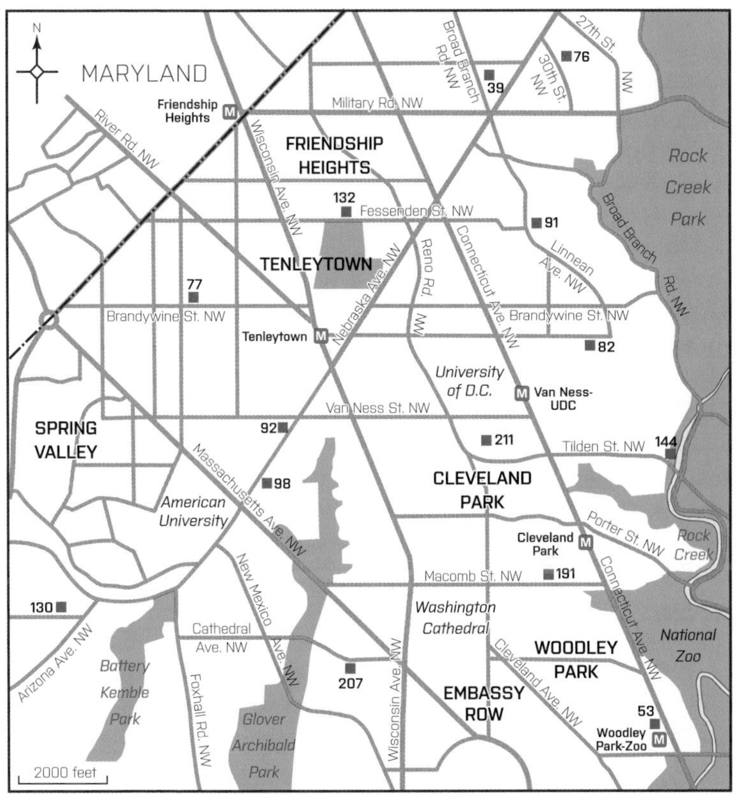
N
MARYLAND
Friendship Heights
River Rd. NW
Military Rd. NW
Broad Branch Rd. NW
39
76
30th St. NW
27th St. NW
FRIENDSHIP HEIGHTS
Wisconsin Ave. NW
132
Fessenden St. NW
91
Rock Creek Park
Broad Branch Rd. NW
Linnean Ave. NW
Reno Rd. NW
Connecticut Ave. NW
TENLEYTOWN
Nebraska Ave. NW
77
Brandywine St. NW
Tenleytown
82
University of D.C.
Van Ness-UDC
Van Ness St. NW
SPRING VALLEY
92
211
Tilden St. NW
144
Massachusetts Ave. NW
98
CLEVELAND PARK
American University
Porter St. NW
Cleveland Park
Rock Creek
New Mexico Ave. NW
Macomb St. NW
191
130
Washington Cathedral
Cathedral Ave. NW
National Zoo
Arizona Ave. NW
Battery Kemble Park
WOODLEY PARK
Cleveland Ave. NW
207
Wisconsin Ave. NW
EMBASSY ROW
Foxhall Rd. NW
Glover Archibald Park
53
Woodley Park-Zoo
2000 feet

MAP 8

VIRGINIA

➤ Alexandria, Annandale, Burke, Mount Vernon, and Springfield

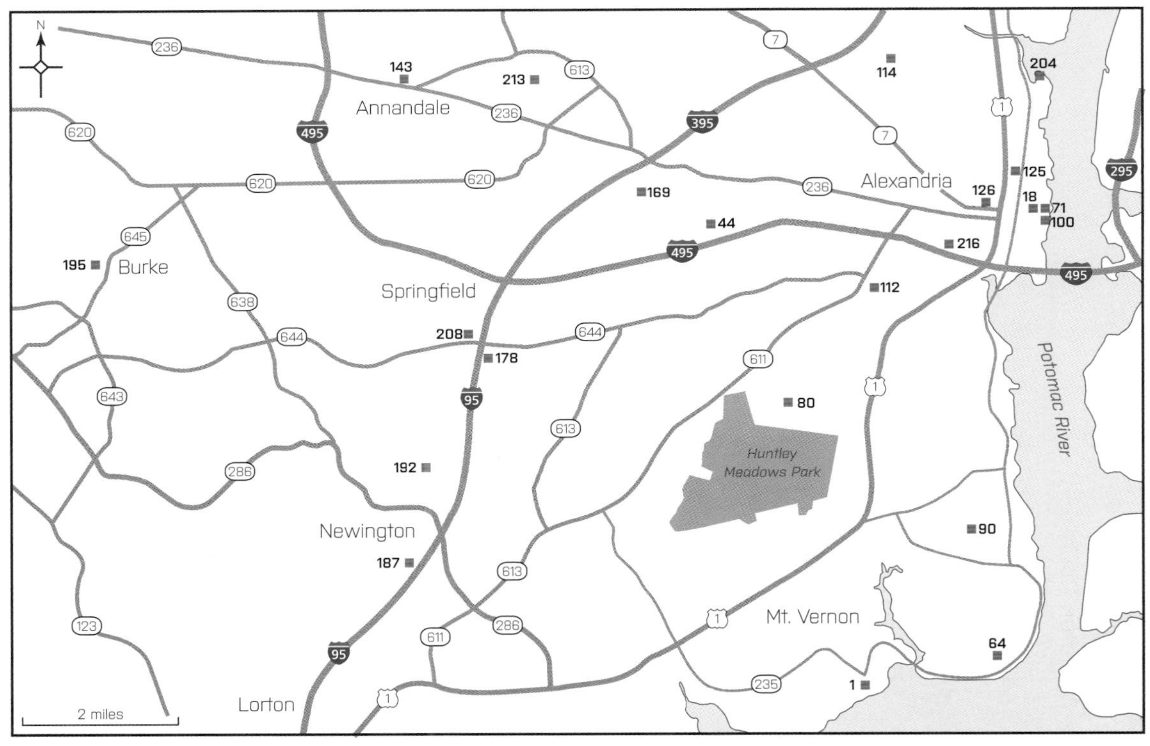

N
143
213
114
204
Annandale
Alexandria
125
126
18
71
100
169
44
216
195
Burke
Springfield
112
208
178
80
Potomac River
Huntley Meadows Park
192
Newington
187
90
Mt. Vernon
64
1
Lorton
2 miles

MAP 9

VIRGINIA

➤ Arlington County

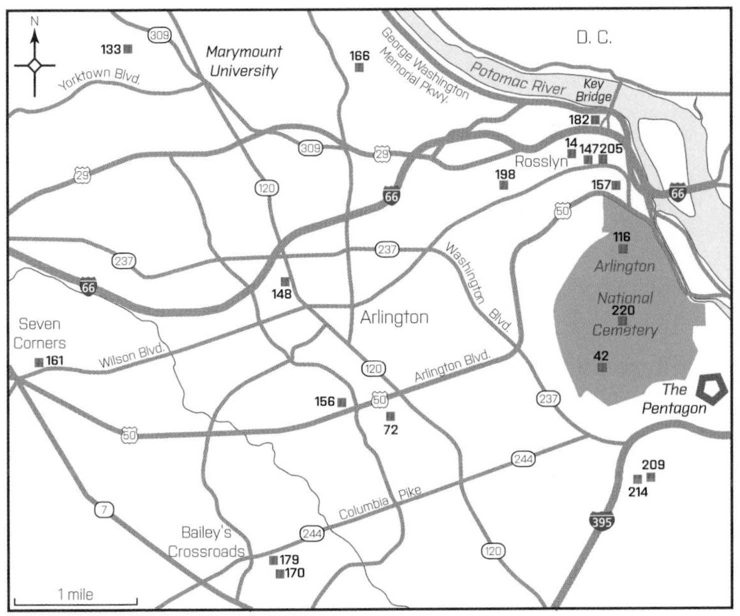
N
133
309
Marymount University
166
George Washington Memorial Pkwy.
Potomac River
D. C.
Key Bridge
Yorktown Blvd.
182
14
147
205
Rosslyn
309
29
29
198
120
157
66
66
50
116
Arlington
237
237
Washington Blvd.
National
220
Cemetery
66
148
Arlington
Seven Corners
161
Wilson Blvd.
120
Arlington Blvd.
42
156
50
237
The Pentagon
72
50
244
209
214
Columbia Pike
7
395
Bailey's Crossroads
244
120
179
170
1 mile

MAP 10

VIRGINIA

➤ Falls Church, McLean, and Vienna

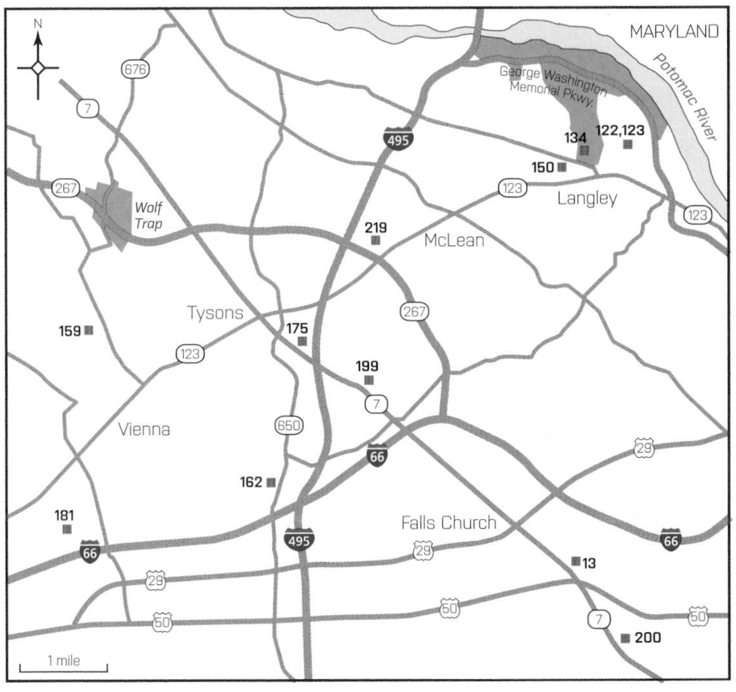
N
MARYLAND
Potomac River
George Washington Memorial Pkwy.
676
7
495
134
122,123
150
267
123
Langley
Wolf Trap
219
McLean
Tysons
267
159
175
123
199
7
Vienna
650
66
162
181
Falls Church
29
495
66
66
13
29
29
50
7
50
50
200
1 mile

MAP 11

VIRGINIA

➤ Herndon, Dulles, Reston, Chantilly, and Fairfax

➤ Other Virginia

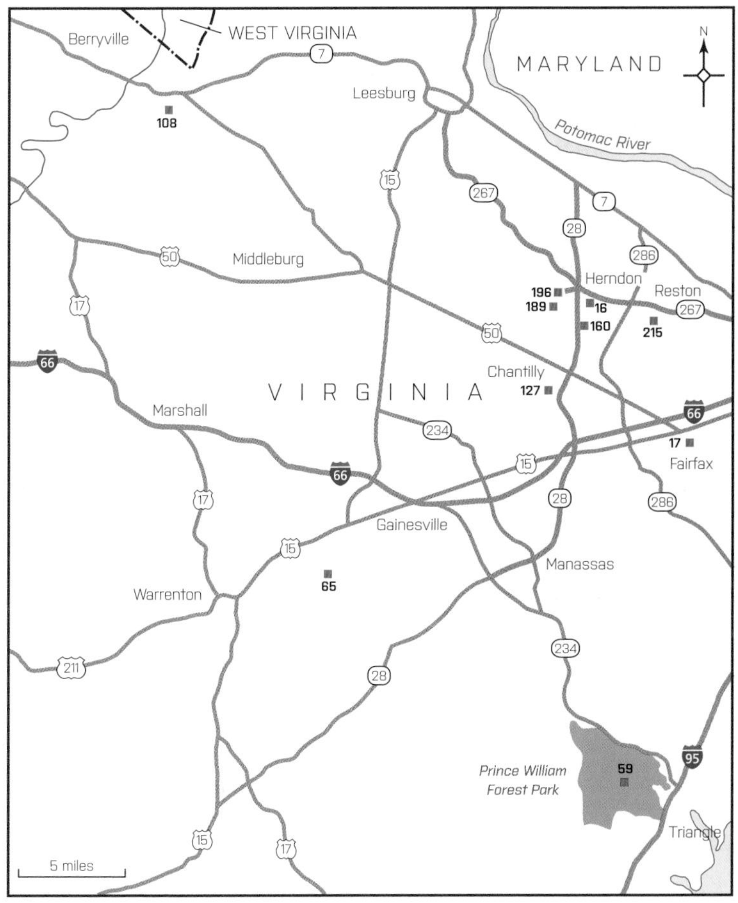
Berryville
WEST VIRGINIA
MARYLAND
N
Leesburg
Potomac River
108
Middleburg
Herndon
Reston
196
189
16
160
215
Chantilly
127
VIRGINIA
Marshall
17
Fairfax
Gainesville
Manassas
Warrenton
65
Prince William
Forest Park
59
Triangle
5 miles

MAP 12

MARYLAND

➤ Montgomery County

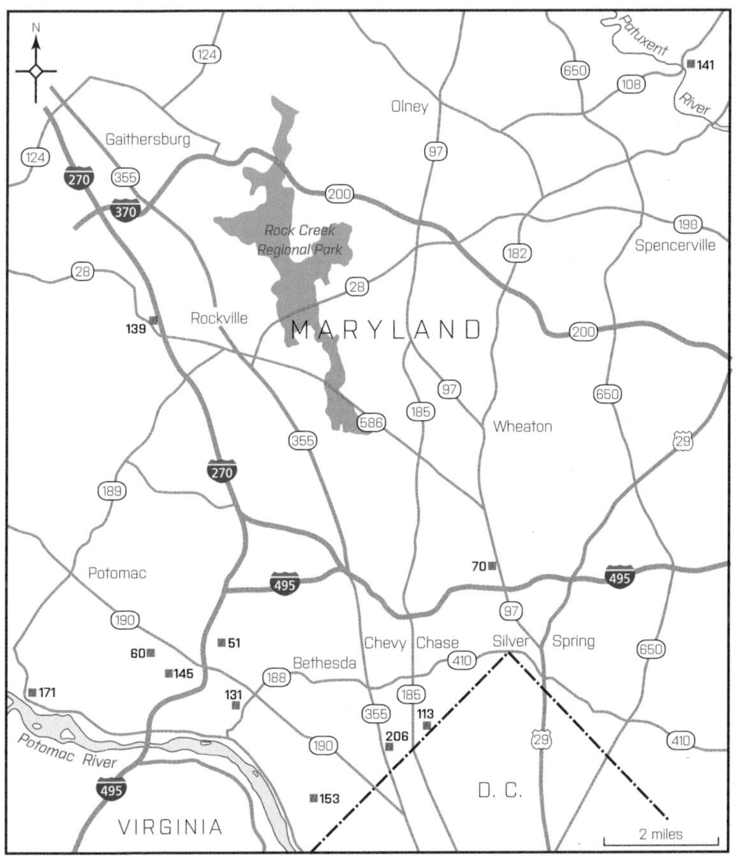
N
Patuxent River
141
124
650
108
Olney
Gaithersburg
97
124
270
355
200
370
Rock Creek Regional Park
198
Spencerville
182
28
28
139
Rockville
MARYLAND
200
97
650
185
586
Wheaton
355
29
270
189
70
Potomac
495
495
97
190
51
Chevy Chase
Silver Spring
60
650
145
Bethesda
410
188
171
131
185
355
113
206
410
Potomac River
190
29
495
153
D. C.
VIRGINIA
2 miles

MAP 13

MARYLAND

➤ Anne Arundel County

95 and **97.** National Security Agency (p. 123 and p. 125)

96. National Cryptologic Museum (p. 124)

➤ Howard County

217. Edward Snowden residence (p. 269)

➤ Prince George's County

2. Warburton Estate, Fort Washington Park (p. 3)

30. Surratt's Tavern (p. 41)

99. Bernon F. Mitchell residence (p. 126)

119. John Huminik Jr. residence (p. 148)

172. National Maritime Intelligence Center (p. 217)

201. Valencia Motel (p. 253)

➤ Talbot County

111. Ashford Farm (p. 138)

136. Black Walnut Point Inn (p. 172)

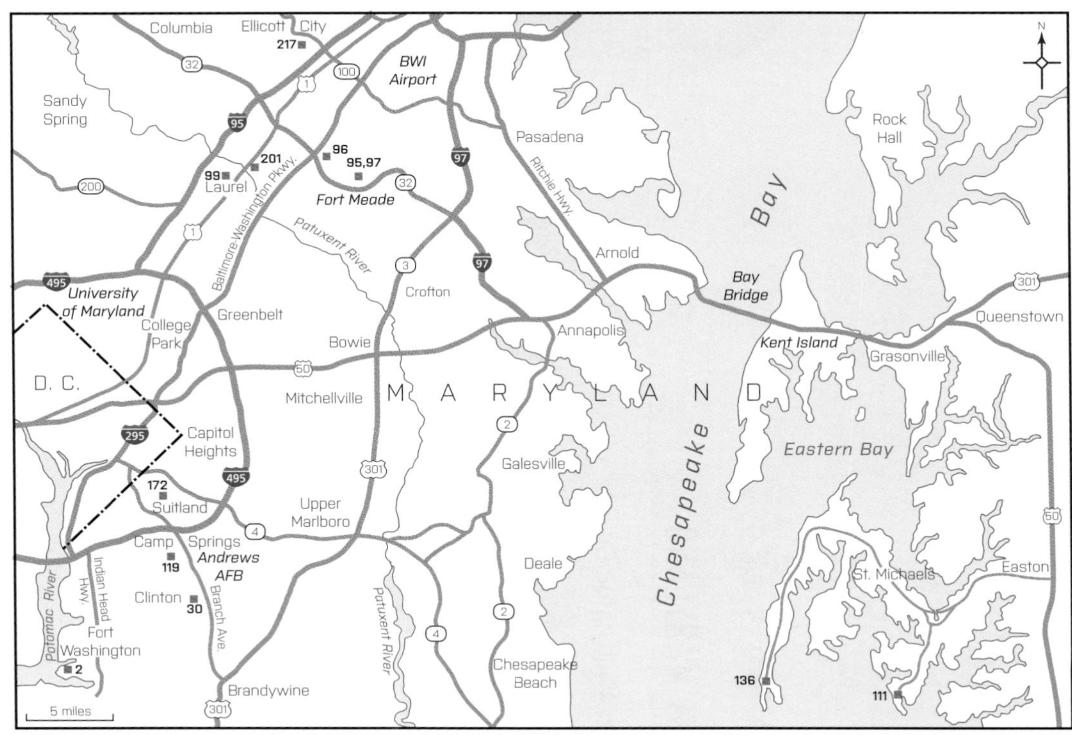
Columbia
Ellicott City
217
BWI Airport
N
Sandy Spring
Rock Hall
Pasadena
96
95,97
201
99
Laurel
Fort Meade
Baltimore-Washington Pkwy.
Ritchie Hwy.
Bay
Patuxent River
Arnold
Bay Bridge
University of Maryland
Crofton
Queenstown
College Park
Greenbelt
Bowie
Annapolis
Kent Island
Grasonville
D. C.
Mitchellville
M A R Y L A N D
Capitol Heights
Galesville
Eastern Bay
Chesapeake
172
Suitland
Upper Marlboro
Camp Springs
Andrews AFB
119
Deale
St. Michaels
Easton
Clinton
30
Branch Ave.
Indian Head Hwy.
Potomac River
Fort Washington
2
Patuxent River
Chesapeake Beach
136
111
Brandywine
5 miles
32
100
1
95
200
97
3
495
50
295
301
2
4

MAP 14

MARYLAND

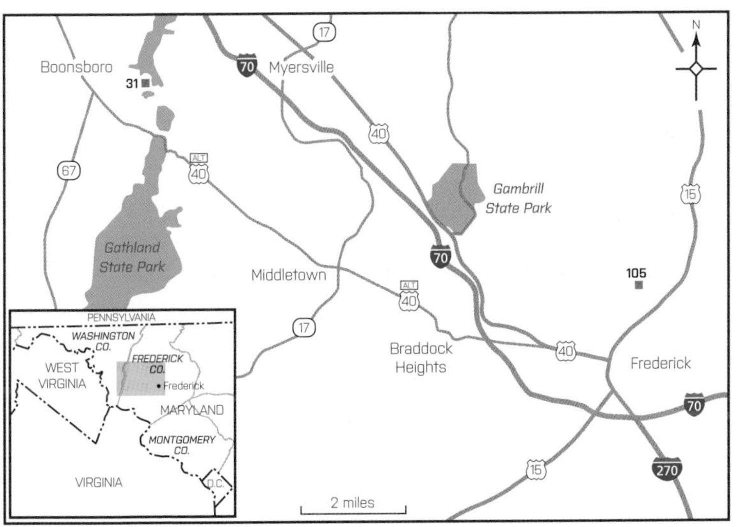
Boonsboro
31
Myersville
Gambrill
State Park
Gathland
State Park
Middletown
105
Braddock
Heights
Frederick
N
2 miles
PENNSYLVANIA
WASHINGTON
CO.
WEST
VIRGINIA
FREDERICK
CO.
Frederick
MARYLAND
MONTGOMERY
CO.
VIRGINIA
D.C.

APPENDIX B: THE US INTELLIGENCE COMMUNITY

Air Force Intelligence: The US Air Force Intelligence, Surveillance, and Reconnaissance Enterprise conducts intelligence, surveillance, and reconnaissance for combatant commanders.

Army Intelligence (G-2): Coordinates policy, planning, management, and oversight for intelligence disciplines in the US Army.

Central Intelligence Agency: Collects and analyzes national security intelligence and disseminates it to senior US policymakers.

Coast Guard Intelligence: Collects and reports maritime intelligence that supports Coast Guard missions.

Defense Intelligence Agency: Provides military intelligence to war fighters, defense policymakers, and force planners within the Department of Defense and the Intelligence Community.

Department of Energy: The Office of Intelligence and Counterintelligence protects the department's facilities against foreign intelligence efforts and cyber threats.

Department of Homeland Security: Manages intelligence for the homeland security enterprise.

Department of State: The Bureau of Intelligence and Research provides the secretary of state with analysis of global developments from all-source intelligence.

Department of the Treasury: The Office of Intelligence and Analysis analyzes foreign intelligence and counterintelligence related to the operations of the Department of the Treasury.

Drug Enforcement Administration: Enforces US laws and regulations regarding controlled substances.

Federal Bureau of Investigation: Responsible for counterintelligence within the United States.

Marine Corps Intelligence: Produces tactical and operational intelligence for battlefield support for US Marine Corps units.

National Geospatial-Intelligence Agency: Provides geospatial intelligence to civilian and military leaders.

National Reconnaissance Office: Designs, builds, and operates the nation's reconnaissance satellites.

National Security Agency: Coordinates, directs, and performs cryptologic collection to protect US information systems and collects foreign signals intelligence.

Navy Intelligence: Provides maritime intelligence to the US Navy, joint war-fighting forces, and other consumers in the Intelligence Community.

Office of the Director of National Intelligence: Established December 17, 2004, to streamline intelligence integration and foster collaboration among the 16 agencies of the Intelligence Community.

ILLUSTRATION CREDITS

All images and photographs are property of the authors, except as noted below (with page numbers):

Aaron Siirila, Wikipedia: Russian embassy (234).

Ad Meskens.jpg, Wikipedia: Torpedo Factory Art Center (92).

AgnosticPreachersKid, Wikipedia: Anchorage Building (65); Alban Towers (68); Twenty-Four Hundred Hotel (135); Czechoslovakian embassy (137); Pullman House (145); Old Post Office Building (151); Hay-Adams Hotel (206); Theodore Roosevelt Bridge (235).

Alexandria Sheriff's Office: William G. Truesdale Adult Detention Center (269).

Architect of the Capitol: Rayburn House Office Building (171); Dirksen Senate Office Building (191).

Black Walnut Point Inn: Black Walnut Point Inn (172).

Bob Adams, http://www.adamsguns.com: High Standard pistol (82).

Carlyle House Historic Park: Benjamin Franklin Stringfellow (26).

Central Intelligence Agency: William J. Donovan (76); headquarters for the OSS and then the CIA (77); CIA's E Street NW headquarters sign (78); Judith Coplon (116); Allen Dulles's CIA credentials (129); Francis Gary Powers (139);

CIA headquarters (tk; by Carol M. Highsmith); seal, CIA's Original Headquarters Building (154); Wall of Honor, CIA's Original Headquarters Building (155); Mir Aimal Kansi (157); Eloise Page (158); Arthur C. Lundahl (162); Richard Helms (167); James Angleton (169); Aldrich Ames (207).

Command History Office; US Army Intelligence and Security Command: Allan Pinkerton (12); Lafayette C. Baker (17); Lowe balloon (19); Confederate cipher device (23); Alexander Gardner's gallery (29); Ralph Van Deman (47); Herbert O. Yardley (49); Hooe Iron Building (50); Vint Hill Farms Station (87), William Weisband (118).

David Washington, DC, Wikipedia: Letelier-Moffitt plaque (195).

***A Death in Washington* by Gary Kern and the *New York Journal-American*:** Bellevue Hotel floor plan (72).

Defense Intelligence Agency: DIA seal (143); DIA headquarters (144).

Estate of Edith Wharton and the Watkins / Loomis Agency / Beinecke Rare Book and Manuscript Library, Yale University Library: Edith Wharton (49).

Fairfax County Park Authority: Langley Fork Park (170).

Federal Bureau of Investigation: George Dasch (94); Alger Hiss (109); James Allen Mintkenbaugh (147); John Walker (175); Michael Walker (176); Jennifer Miles (180); Robert Lipka (180); Rosario Ames (207); Aldrich Ames's arrest (208); Ames note (211); Larry Wu-Tai Chin (215); Sergei Motorin (225); Valeri Martynov (225); Ana Belén Montes (240); straddling checkerboard (242); David Sheldon Boone (246); Stanislav Gusev outside State Department (248); Brian Patrick Regan (250); Stewart Nozette (257).

Federal Communications Commission: German spy radio map (63); Radio Intelligence Division mobile detection unit (63).

Franklin D. Roosevelt Library and Museum: map of South America (75).

German Federal Archives: Hanfstaengl with Hitler and Göring (62).

Hawkeye58 at en.wikipedia: Surratt's Tavern (41).

H. Schlesinger: Barbasol can (168).

I, Aude, Wikipedia: J. Edgar Hoover Building (173).

International Spy Museum: current International Spy Museum (255); proposed International Spy Museum (255).

Jacqueline Dupree / JDLand.com: Steuart Motor Car Company Building (163); Building 213 (163);

Jason Quinn, Wikipedia: Union Station (243).

Jerry Thompson: Ashford Farm safe house (138).

Joe Ravi / CC-BY-SA 3.0: George Washington Masonic National Memorial (21).

Jüregen Matern, Wikimedia Commons: Wardman Park Hotel (71).

Keith Clark: Myers' sailboat (258).

Ketone16, Wikimedia Commons: Dar al-Hijrah Islamic Center (252).

KGB Archive: Oleg Penkovsky's passport (159).

KROKODYL, Wikipedia: Israeli embassy (219).

Library of Congress: Mount Vernon (2 [Carol M. Highsmith Archive]); White House (5); Daniel Webster (6); Daniel Webster's residence (7); White House (13); Signal Corps headquarters (14); signal tower atop the Winder Building (14); Winder Building (16); Rose O'Neal Greenhow and daughter (16); Secret Service headquarters (18); Carver Barracks (19); John Mosby (22); Mansion House Hotel (25); Lafayette Park (30); Belle Boyd (32); Carroll Prison (33); National Hotel (35); William H. Seward (36); William H. Seward house (37); gun that killed Lincoln (38); Mary Surratt's boardinghouse (39); Willard Hotel (43); Old Executive Office Building (47); Leland Harrison (47); German embassy (51); Johann Von Bernstorff (51); P Street NW tunnel (52); old Cosmos Club (53); A. Mitchell Palmer residence (56); Munitions Building (58); Samuel Dickstein (67); Cannon House Office Building (67); Japanese embassy (70); Ralph Bunche (85); Ralph Bunche residence (85); Amy Elizabeth Thorpe (87); OPERATION PASTORIUS trial (94); Lauchlin Currie (96); Elizabeth Bentley (99); Walter Lippmann (103); Roald Dahl (107 [Carl Van Vechten Photographs]); J. Edgar Hoover (119); Hotel Harrington (151); Atlas Building (254).

Matthew Bisanz, Wikimedia Commons: FBI's Washington Metropolitan Field Office (151).

Mr. and Mrs. Paul Cook: Oakland, Maryland, lodge (134); Jack Dunlap residence (144); Woodland Village (270).

Muhammad ud-Deen, Wikimedia Commons: Anwar al-Awlaki (251).

National Archives and Records Administration: Walt Whitman (19); Fairfax County Courthouse (24); Mary Walker (28; by Matthew Brady); Old Capitol

Prison (31); John Wilkes Booth (38); Arthur Vandenberg (71); Ruth Shipley (79); OSS small arms training (80); Duncan Lee (112); G. Gordon Liddy (185).

National Baseball Hall of Fame and Museum: Moe Berg (105); Pete Sivess (139).

National Counterintelligence Executive: Ronald Pelton (202); Jonathan and Anne Pollard (218). Harold Nicholson (244); Walter Kendall Myers (258).

National Cryptologic Museum: William and Elizabeth Friedman (58); SIGABA (59); Japanese PURPLE cipher machine (93); Arlington Hall (93); National Cryptologic Museum (124).

National Defense University: Washington Arsenal (21); Building 20 / Grant Hall (39 [courtesy of Scott Gower and Dachun Bao]); Lincoln assassination coconspirators' hanging (40).

National Geospatial-Intelligence Agency: seal of the National Geospatial-Intelligence Agency (242).

National Park Service: Ford's Theatre (39); Charles Alexander Sheldon (53).

National Security Agency: Agnes Meyer Driscoll (57).

Netherlands National Archives: Philip Agee (142; photograph by Bert Verhoef).

New York Public Library, Louis Waldman Papers: George Krivitsky's body (73).

Occidental Grill and Seafood / Mary Parker Photography: plaque, Occidental Grill (164).

Ogilvy & Mather: David Ogilvy (108).

Old Angler's Inn: Old Angler's Inn (217).

Safeway Inc.: Safeway supermarket (230).

San Diego Air and Space Museum: Laura Ingalls (63).

SimonP@ en.wikipedia: World War II British embassy (121).

simonpaul@en.wikipedia: South African embassy (220).

Slowking4, Wikipedia: Cuban Interests Section (239).

Shutterstock.com / chrisdorney: Josef Stalin Postage Stamp (115).

Tamiment Library and Robert F. Wagner Labor Archives: Philip Agee's typewriter case (142).

Tomf688, Wikipedia: St. Elizabeths (8).

United States Court of Federal Claims and the United States Court of Appeals: Howard T. Markey National Courts Building (37).

University of Michigan: Sarah Emma Edmonds (25).

University of Texas–Dallas, McDermott Library: Air America Pilatus Porter (132); George Doole (133).

US Marshals Service: Mikhail Semenko (261); Nataliya Pereverzeva (263); Mikhail Kutsik (263).

Wikipedia: First Bull Run marker (15); Smithsonian Institution Building (33); Assembly Room 1 (94); Tu-2 aircraft (117); National Security Agency (123); South Korean embassy (243).

ZeWrestler, Wikipedia: Washington Monument in Maryland (42).

INDEX

Page numbers in italics refer to photos and illustrations.

E

F

H

N

W

X

Y

Z

ABOUT THE AUTHORS

ROBERT WALLACE is a retired senior intelligence officer and the former director of the CIA's Office of Technical Service. He is coauthor of *Nine from the Ninth*, a collection of essays about experiences in the Vietnam War.

H. KEITH MELTON is owner of the world's largest private collection of espionage artifacts, an intelligence historian, and the author of several books, including *Ultimate Spy: Inside the Secret World of Espionage*. He and Mr. Wallace have coauthored four previous intelligence books: *Spycraft: The Secret History of CIA's Spytechs from Communism to al-Qaeda*; *The Official CIA Manual of Trickery and Deception*; *Spy Sites of Philadelphia: Two and a Half Centuries of Espionage in the City of Brotherly Love*; and *Spy Sites of New York City: Two Centuries of Espionage in Gotham*.

HENRY R. SCHLESINGER is a New York–based writer who has collaborated previously with the authors on *Spyycraft*, *Spy Sites of Philadelphia*, and *Spy Sites of New York City*.

MAKE A DAY OF IT: SPY SITES BY METRO

Arlington Cemetery
42, 116, 220. Arlington graves (pp. 57, 144, 272)
Archives
121. FBI's Metropolitan Field Office (p.151)
137. J. Edgar Hoover Building (p.173)
Capitol South
47. House of Representatives (p. 66)
48. Old House Office Building (p. 67)
135. Rayburn House Office (p. 171)
Dupont Circle
41. Alexander Mitchell Palmer residence (p. 55)
46. Restaurant Pierre (p. 64)
52. Japanese embassy (p. 70)
68. Inga Arvad residence (p. 90)
155. Sheridan Circle NW (p. 195)
163. Iron Gate Inn (p. 204)
194. South Korean embassy (p. 243)
Farragut North
56, 74. Mayflower Hotel (pp. 75, 95)
104. Air America Headquarters (p. 132)
164. Jamestown Foundation (p. 205)
Farragut West
9. War Department (p. 15)
33. Alibi Club (p. 46)
154. The Exchange Saloon (p. 194)
165. Hay-Adams Hotel (p. 206)
Federal Triangle
19. Kirkwood House Hotel (p. 26)
121. FBI's Metropolitan Field Office (p. 151)
Foggy Bottom
58. OSS and Original CIA headquarters (p. 77)
81. Mary Price residence (p. 103)
146. The Watergate (p. 184)
197. Harry S. Truman Building (p. 247)
210. Tim Foley residence (p. 264)
Gallery Place
29. Ford's Theatre (p. 37)
203. Spy Museum (p. 254)
212. Tony Cheng's Mongolian Restaurant (p. 266)
McPherson Square
3, 7, 202. White House (pp. 5, 13, 253)
22. Lafayette Square Park (p. 30)
26. US Treasury (p. 34)
28. Seward Residence Plaque (p. 36)
168. Acme Reporting Company (p. 214)
Metro Center
32. The Willard (p. 42)
129. Occidental Grill (p. 164)
Rosslyn
147. Oakhill Office Building (p. 186)
157. Rudolph Herrmann residence (p. 196)
182. Key Bridge Marriott (p. 229)
Smithsonian
25. Smithsonian Castle (p. 33)
118. Washington Monument (p. 147)
Union Station
54. Bellevue Hotel (p. 72)
55. Foreign Broadcast Monitoring Service headquarters (p. 73)
152. Dirksen Senate Office (p. 191)

Georgetown area sites accessible from various metro stations
57. William Donovan residence (p. 76)
66. Amy Elizabeth Thorpe residence (p. 87)
69. Drew Pearson residence (p. 91)
75. Lauchlin Currie residence (p. 96)
78. Georgetown Pharmacy (p. 98)
79. Martin's Tavern (p. 100)
85. Roald Dahl residence (p. 107)
86. Alger Hiss residence (p. 109)
87. Duncan Lee residence (p. 112)
101. Allen Dulles residence (p. 129)
102. Frank G. Wisner residence (p. 130)
103. Joseph Alsop residence (p. 131)

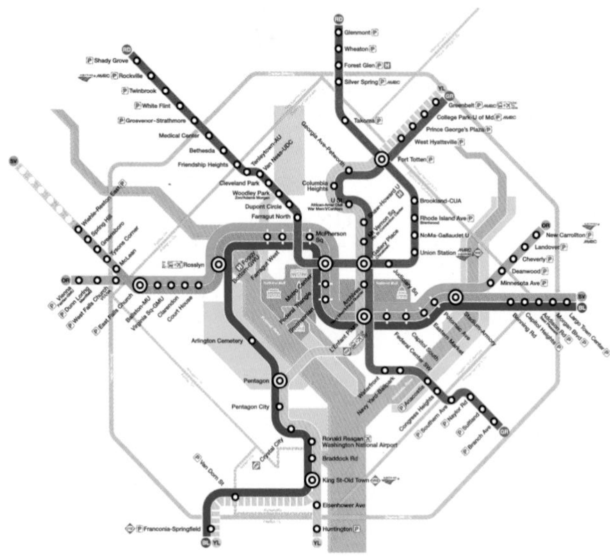

Sites may be accessible from more than one metro station. For a detailed map of the Washington, DC metro system, please visit www.wmata.com. Particularly for private residences, please respect the privacy of occupants. The site list is not comprehensive and site names may have changed.